The bearer
of the DNB in
since and has
the last days,
But since he
George Thiers,
that he claimed, he was ignored until one day, his mendacity
having come home to roost, he was arrested, and in the
course of search the document was discovered, sewn in ~~his~~ the
~~coat~~ lining

whole stor
panions
and Wilhe
nay. I
of Johann
Burgdorf's
that ~~Lou~~
the other n
Johanne
with his f
interrogated
in the Bu
at the e
caught h
I went
questionin

, the representatin
estioned long
oherently about
sketable knowledge.
ist called
re knowledge
two com-
Willi Johannmeier
Hanover in
nt the name
en General
tone believed
ed to someone

iving quietly
tained and
ad never been
n hospital
had
Dissatisfied,
'ts long
, the Bunker,

and that his first story had been untrue. But of
Hitler's will, he said, he knew nothing, nothing at all. He
had been ordered to escort two men, Lorenz & Zander, through
the Russian lines. He had understood them to be the bearers
of documents to Doenitz & Schoerner, but of what documents
it was not his business to know. He was simply a soldier

Hugh Trevor-Roper was perhaps the most brilliant historian of his generation. An expert in the history of both early modern Britain and Nazi Germany, he was Regius Professor of Modern History at Oxford University and latterly Master of Peterhouse, Cambridge. He received a life peerage in 1979. During the Second World War, Trevor-Roper served in the Secret Intelligence Service and this book contains his journals written during the war and in its immediate aftermath, including the period in Berlin during which he undertook detailed enquiries into the circumstances of Hitler's death under commission from the SIS. It was these investigations that formed the basis for one of his most best-known books: *The Last Days of Hitler*.

Richard Davenport-Hines is a Fellow of the Royal Historical Society and the Royal Society of Literature and a past winner of the Wolfson Prize for History. He is the author of many books, including *A Night at the Majestic* (2006) and *The Pursuit of Oblivion* (2001). He edited Hugh Trevor-Roper's *Letters from Oxford* (2006) and is a regular reviewer for the *Spectator, Sunday Telegraph, Sunday Times, Literary Review* and other publications.

HUGH TREVOR-ROPER
THE WARTIME JOURNALS

EDITED BY RICHARD DAVENPORT-HINES

I.B. TAURIS
LONDON · NEW YORK

Published and reprinted twice in 2012 by I.B.Tauris & Co Ltd
6 Salem Road, London W2 4BU
175 Fifth Avenue, New York NY 10010
www.ibtauris.com

Distributed in the United States and Canada Exclusively by Palgrave Macmillan
175 Fifth Avenue, New York NY 10010

ISBN: 978 1 84885 990 6

A full CIP record for this book is available from the British Library
A full CIP record is available from the Library of Congress

Library of Congress Catalog Card Number: available

Printed and bound by CPI Group (UK) Ltd, Croydon, CR0 4YY

MIX
Paper from
responsible sources
FSC® C013604
www.fsc.org

Contents

Editorial Acknowledgments   vii

Glossary of Names and Initials   ix

List of Illustrations   xi

Introduction   1

1940–41   24

1942   55

1943   126

1944   194

1945   211

1946   274

1947   285

Index   301

Editorial
Acknowledgments

My chief debt is to Professor Blair Worden, literary executor of Lord Dacre of Glanton, for entrusting the editing of these journals to me. His advice during the editorial process has been a model of delicacy, good sense and gaiety. Judith Curthoys, archivist of Christ Church, has been indispensable and forbearing during the preparation of this manuscript for publication. Discussions with Adam Sisman, during his research of his biography *Hugh Trevor-Roper*, informed my editorial work: his comments, and those of Alan Bell, on a draft of the editorial introduction were helpful. Simon Malloch of Nottingham University read the main text, encouraged me by his enthusiasm, caught several mistranscriptions, corrected a scattering of errors and made other discreet suggestions – for all of which patient kindness I am grateful. He introduced me to Professor Michael Reeve, of Pembroke College, Cambridge, who has generously identified, translated, glossed and indeed typed the quotations from classical Greek that pepper the text. Henry Hardy, of Wolfson College, Oxford, provided further help.

It seemed unnecessary to provide footnotes identifying people of the stature of Bach, Blake, Botticelli, Donne, El Greco, Handel, Homer, Shakespeare, Stendhal and Tennyson when editing the manuscript for publication. For the elucidation of material in the footnotes and editorial introduction I thank the Archivist of Charterhouse school, the late Lord Beaumont of Whitley, Lord Gladwyn, and Carraigh Thompson of Patmos.

For permission to quote from Trevor-Roper's correspondence with Charles Stuart, I am grateful to his children Susan Chater and William Stuart; and for permission to quote from the diary of the Marquess of Lincolnshire, I thank the Hon. Rupert Carington. The photograph of Stuart Hampshire is © The Isaiah Berlin Literary Trust 2009, and reproduced with the permission of the trustees.

The index of the text of *The Wartime Journals* was compiled by Trevor-Roper himself. For rendering Trevor-Roper's index cards into a manageable form, as for certain technical refinements and supplementary material, Christopher Phipps has been invaluable. Jenny Davenport's scrutiny of the proofs detected a dribble of irregularities.

It is wrong for an editor to foist a dedication on a book which has been written by someone else, and I do not think of doing so; but I wish to acknowledge the kindness and generosity shown to me by Simon Barrow and Charles Sebag-Montefiore during my work on this volume. They are both, however, so modest that they would doubtless disavow the extent of their goodness to me.

Le Meygris, Ailhon

Glossary of Names and Initials

B-W   John Barrington-Ward

Dickie   Richard Dawson

Dicksie   Richard Marshall

Gilbert   Gilbert Ryle

Logan   Logan Pearsall Smith

M.E.   Kenneth Morton Evans

List of Illustrations

1. Hugh Trevor-Roper *circa* 1940 (Estate of Lord Dacre of Glanton)

MENTORS

2. Gilbert Ryle (National Portrait Gallery, London)

3. Logan Pearsall Smith (National Portrait Gallery, London)

OXFORD DONS

4. H.W. Garrod (Warden & Fellows of Merton College, Oxford)

5. S.G. Owen (Christ Church, Oxford)

6. John Barrington-Ward (Christ Church, Oxford)

7. Michael Foster (Christ Church, Oxford)

OXFORD VIEWS

8. Mercury in Tom quad (Christ Church, Oxford)

9. Peckwater quad, at Christ Church (Christ Church, Oxford)

10. H.W. Garrod's rooms in Merton (Warden & Fellows of Merton College, Oxford)

ARKLEY COLLEAGUES

11. Charles Stuart (Christ Church, Oxford)

12. Stuart Hampshire with Isaiah Berlin (Isaiah Berlin Trust, Oxford)

LONDON FRIENDS

13. Frank Pakenham (National Portrait Gallery, London)

14. Rose Macaulay (National Portrait Gallery, London)

PLACES

15. Chillingham Castle, Northumberland (*Country Life*, London)

16. Bewshaugh (Northumberland Archives, Ashington)

17. The lake at Wotton, Buckinghamshire (*Country Life*, London)

18. 11 St Leonard's Terrace, Chelsea (Royal Borough of Kensington & Chelsea, London)

Introduction

Hugh Trevor-Roper was born in 1914 and died in 2003. He became a Student of Christ Church, Oxford in 1946; Regius Professor of Modern History at Oxford University in 1957; a life peer with the title of Dacre of Glanton in 1979; and Master of Peterhouse, Cambridge in 1980.[1]

The existence of Hugh Trevor-Roper's wartime journals was unknown to his family or confidants during his lifetime. Sixty years earlier, their discovery could have rendered him liable to prosecution. It was forbidden for secret service agents to keep diaries: the one exception was Guy Liddell, deputy director general of MI5, who with official cognisance kept an office diary which served as an informal record of news, meetings and rumours.[2] In defiance of the rules, until the end of 1940, Trevor-Roper kept a diary, which continued the record of his quotidian activities that he had spasmodically maintained in the late 1930s. It contained official secrets, and in July 1942, rattled by a night of German bombing, he destroyed it.

Earlier – perhaps late in 1941 but probably early in 1942 – he had begun to keep a separate notebook. This was never a record of daily doings, as the diaries had been, but a stylised effort written in emulation of the published

---

1 Adam Sisman's *Hugh Trevor-Roper* (2010) provides a full account of his life. Blair Worden has contributed an essay in *Biographical Memoirs of Fellows of the British Academy*, 6 (2008), 247–84. My introduction to Trevor-Roper's *Letters from Oxford* (2006), xiii–xxxix pictures him in 1945–1959.

2 Nigel West (ed.), *The Guy Liddell Diaries: MI5's Director of Counter-Espionage in World War II* (2005) contains several references to Trevor-Roper.

notebooks of Samuel Butler, author of the satire *Erewhon* (1872). The drab routine and departmental backbiting of Trevor-Roper's war work were so depleting to his mind that he felt impelled to begin a work of aesthetic and intellectual ambition. Even this self-consciously literary journal breached Secret Intelligence Service rules. Trevor-Roper was an Intelligence Officer engaged in confidential work. His departmental enemies would have used such contemptuous journal entries as 'The Secret Service' (March 1942) and 'S.I.S.' (May 1942), or the revelations in 'Eavesdrops' (March 1943) and 'Götterdämmerung' (July 1945), to have him court-martialled. Nevertheless, he confided his thoughts, contacts and plans in four slender notebooks with the initials OHMS (On His Majesty's Service) printed on their covers.

After Trevor-Roper's death, the notebooks were found secreted in his house near Oxford by his literary executor and the editor of this volume. They are written in Trevor-Roper's elegant, precise and legible script. As there are no corrections or revisions, it is likely that the longer, more elaborate journal entries were drafted on scrap paper before being entered in finished form in the OHMS notebooks. A few passages from his diaries of 1940–41 he preserved long enough to transcribe into his new *cahiers* (see pp. 91–93). He also incorporated extracts from a notebook of dream analysis which he had compiled in 1938 after reading Freud. It is impossible to establish the intervals or revisions between the first draft of new journal entries and their final neat transcription into an OHMS notebook. Internal evidence hints that in the first year or so of the journal Trevor-Roper waited longer before transferring his drafts into the notebook, that their chronological order is looser and that the definitive copies were sifted from a greater multitude of drafts. Although his methods of drafting and fair copying apparently became more direct and systematic after the autumn of 1942, it is doubtful if Trevor-Roper took a *cahier* with him to North Africa and Asia in 1944, or to Germany in 1945 and 1946.

The probability that he made preliminary versions, which he then worked to improve, is strengthened because Trevor-Roper's journals were influenced by the delicate volumes of maxims, reflections and whimsy that had been compiled over many years by the anglicised American man-of-letters Logan Pearsall Smith. These were collected in one pocket-sized book, *All Trivia* (1933), which Trevor-Roper took with him to the Life Guards training camp in Surrey in the summer of 1939, and read aloud there to other young officers – almost a year before being befriended by the author. It was Smith's compulsion to draft paragraphs or even a single sentence, and then to revise, polish and veneer: 'writing & re-writing, day after day, year after year, in the indefatigable pursuit of an unobtainable perfection', as he told Trevor-Roper.[3] Trevor-Roper imitated this method, although with more restraint than Smith.

Later, Trevor-Roper amused himself by compiling an index of the journals, which is reproduced (with some amendments) as the index of this published volume. Possibly he did this when he had free time but little to do; that is, a year after the journals close, when he was encased in plaster and confined in his college rooms after breaking his spine in a hunting accident in 1948. Trevor-Roper found pleasure in a well-made index, and was amused by the frivolous index which Samuel Butler had devised for his *Alps and Sanctuaries* (1881). His index to his journals had three purposes: a playful tribute to Butler's self-made prototype; a wry commentary on his own text; and a key to its contents.

These journals provide a privileged view of the Allied war effort against Nazi Germany. Trevor-Roper spent most of the war in England and saw little violence until he went to Germany after the collapse of the Third Reich. He had, however, an unusually fruitful war. In 1940, in an Ealing house where they were paying guests, he and another Oxford man broke the cipher code of the Abwehr, the German secret service – Trevor-Roper doing some of his best thinking while lying in a hot bath and calling out his deductions. During the war he became an expert in German plots against Hitler, and afterwards interrogated many of the Fuhrer's immediate circle, and retrieved his will from its hiding-place. To the OHMS notebooks he confided parts of his post-war research for his book, *The Last Days of Hitler*, which remained in print throughout his lifetime and has never been superseded.

Trevor-Roper's journals are as eloquent in their evocation of the wartime Home Front as the novels of Elizabeth Bowen, Anthony Powell and Evelyn Waugh. They provide an ironical, reflective, mischievous study of the comedy, sorrows and *ennui* of Whitehall officials, Chelsea literary coteries, Oxford dons, Midlands fox-hunting men, Secret Service operatives, Northumberland gentry and Irish raconteurs. They include transcripts of conversations between captured German generals in a bugged prison cell, and Trevor-Roper's account of being 'beaten up at midnight ... by a posse of four armed policemen' in the

---

3 Logan Pearsall Smith to Trevor-Roper, 19 July 1940, Dacre papers (DP), Christ Church, Oxford.

Hibernian Hotel, Dublin after being denounced as an English spy by Frank Pakenham (later Lord Longford). Oxford philosophers – A.J. ('Freddie') Ayer, Stuart Hampshire, Herbert [H.L.A.] Hart and Gilbert Ryle – feature more than Oxford historians. Trevor-Roper's journals are the work of a young scholar, of a frustrated office worker snapping at asinine superiors, of a countryman and nature-lover: he was the sort of sportsman who felt depressed in his chromium-plated hotel in Basra until on a bar-stool he met someone who had bred a pack of West Country basset hounds. These journals comprise a record of mental development. They show, and sometimes dramatise, the self-analysis, the intellectual discoveries and revisions, the repudiations and amusements, of a young historian in the making. They show an isolated, reflective intellectual wrestling with melancholy, isolation, doubt and dismay, and always in training for a sharper mind and a finer style.

The emotional chilliness, corrosive dissatisfaction, spiky resentment and seething aggression of Trevor-Roper's parents' household in Alnwick were reminiscent of the middle-class domestic torture chambers in the novels of Ivy Compton-Burnett. Rebuffed throughout childhood, he had a fixed determination as an adult to get in first with the rebuffs. Irony sheathed and armoured him against the world. Yet he was neither grudging nor joyless. These journals record his glee in the company of friends who were united by a high-spirited sense of absurdity.

Trevor-Roper was a studious yet rowdy undergraduate at Christ Church, Oxford in 1932–36. A prize-winning classical scholar, he converted into a modern historian who was awarded a first-class degree. Undergraduates were taught in individual tutorials, in which the undergraduate read aloud his essay, and had it dissected by the don. The best tutorials aimed at clarity, discrimination and rigour: the essays were often subjected to painstaking scrutiny, sentence by sentence; language had to be point-device; ideas were discussed unsparingly. This was not Trevor-Roper's experience with his Christ Church history tutors, Masterman and Feiling, whom he found uninspired. Nor did Trevor-Roper, as a Christ Church tutor himself, attach high value to tutorial teaching. He fostered some undergraduates, but did so either in the interstices of essay-discussion or outside tutorials, taking them to visit little-known jewels of country churches or recommending them as callers on Bernard Berenson at Villa I Tatti in Italy.[4] For others he did the minimum. Unlike Colin Dillwyn,

---

4 Information from Nicolas Tate (3 October 2005) and Mark Girouard (14 January 2011).

his predecessor as history tutor who had perished in the retreat to Dunkirk, he did not exert himself in teaching the most unpromising Pass pupils.

'The central educational feature of Oxford and Cambridge', wrote Trevor-Roper's Christ Church colleague Roy Harrod, 'is the unrivalled opportunities that the colleges provide for extensive conversation among undergraduates, who have an intense interest, appropriate to their time of life, in the central questions confronting mankind'.[5] This opportunity the young Trevor-Roper had seized, along with the opportunities to drink and hunt hard. From his undergraduate days he talked in the Oxford manner. There was no wandering or parroting in what he said. He needed the stimulus of conversation, or anyway of monologue, and as a young man seems to have talked his head off. There were Oxford dons – admired by Trevor-Roper – for whom it seemed almost as if the interplay of minds was deeper, more subtle, intuitive and enriching, than reading the best books. They found that a companion could be cross-examined, tested and made to think anew by a cool, teasing irony; but that a book never answered back with replies that made one re-think first principles or inferences. Often in the 1930s the philosophers J.L. Austin and Isaiah Berlin would begin talking after breakfast in the smoking-room at All Souls and, if there were no pupils to be taught, would still be talking together at lunch-time. Talk was not for Trevor-Roper an important method of work: he did his thinking alone, in his study, with a pen in his hand. These journals, as a solace for wartime exile from Oxford, are part of this process of analytic rumination.

Despite Trevor-Roper's enjoyment of dialogue – whether written, as in the case of Thomas Love Peacock's novels, or spoken, as in the *salon* assembled by his friend Logan Pearsall Smith – he surpassed himself in monologue, and discouraged interruption by holding up his hand like a policeman halting traffic. 'I rather like singing for my supper; what grates on my ears is the song of the other singers', Smith declared.[6] Trevor-Roper had a similar capacity for ironic self-appraisal: 'the beauty of conversation consists in the mute, attentive faces of one's fellow-talkers', he observes in these journals.[7] His journal entries served him not only as a substitute for good talk, but as a means to practise and improve his soliloquies. They are exercises in strengthening his

---

5 Sir Roy Harrod, *The Prof* (1959), 40.
6 Logan Pearsall Smith, *All Trivia* (1933), 146.
7 P. 40.

powers of clarification and concision. Repeatedly he provides lists of stylists whom he reveres: Stendhal, Peacock, Gibbon, George Moore, Pearsall Smith, whom he lists as his models at the start of the journals, are superseded in June 1942 by Bacon, Donne, Hobbes, Sir Thomas Browne, Gibbon and Moore. By December he is specifying Swift, Gibbon, Johnson, Flaubert, Apuleius, St Augustine, Donne, Milton and Browne.

Although these journals are dedicated to perfecting written words, and composed in emulation of literary masters, they are full of the talk of Trevor-Roper's mentors – H. W. Garrod, Gilbert Ryle and Logan Pearsall Smith – and written under their influence. Something must be said of what these men meant to him and his journals beyond his summaries in the 1946 entries 'Gilbert' and 'Logan died …'.

When in 1937 Trevor-Roper went to work on his study of Archbishop Laud as a Research Fellow of Merton, he found a congenial spirit in Heathcote Garrod, a hospitable elderly bachelor don with rooms at the heart of the college. Garrod was a universal rather than specialist scholar who had prepared scholarly editions of ancient classics, edited the correspondence of Erasmus, distinguished himself in the Ministry of Munitions, proved his expertise on Wordsworth and Keats, published his own poems and epigrams, compiled anthologies, been elected Professor of Poetry, and become an authority on ancient painted glass. Conversation in Garrod's rooms required as much ingenuity, and provided as much entertainment, as the games there of chess, bridge and dumb-crambo. He toyed with words, and upheld talk as an art. The love of literature, he believed, was best imparted in asides. His high quavering talk abounded in paradox, challenges and aphorisms; his provocations could appear abrupt, absurd, wanton, or offensive; and it endeared him to Trevor-Roper that the old man could be seen on most days exercising his dogs in the Oxford water-meadows. Otherwise Garrod seldom ventured beyond Blackwell's bookshop, where his portly figure stood stolid upon small pointed feet, his Augustan head crowned by a trilby hat worn back-to-front, his fingers clenching a cigar, as he scrutinised a book. 'He was', as another Merton polymath celebrated, 'one of those rich, uncommon personalities who have added an imperishable part to the Oxford heritage'.[8]

---

8 Sir George Mallaby, *Dictionary of National Biography 1951–1960* (1971), 394; *The Times*, 28 December 1960, 12c.

Garrod's observations and memories recur in these journals, but Gilbert Ryle, the linguistic philosopher, is quoted above all others in 'Gilbert says' or 'Gilbertiana'. After dining in pre-war Merton, Trevor-Roper had often visited Ryle's rooms in Christ Church for a long talk. He relished the dry wit of this urbane, laconic man, who moved and spoke with feline wariness. Ayer was sometimes present, too, but Ryle's combination of dialectic tension and conversational magnanimity – his brisk impatience tempered by occasional vast forbearance – especially attracted Trevor-Roper. Intermittently Trevor-Roper recruited Ryle to enliven the High Table at Merton: Ryle, a copious drinker, complained that the dons looked as if they drank nothing stronger than stagnant duck-pond water; Ryle's pleasure in country pubs, and ability to down pints in a gulp, was part of his attraction for Trevor-Roper. The two men opposed England's policy of diplomatic appeasement, and in November 1938 queued together to see 'Guernica', Picasso's picture of saturation-bombing in the Spanish civil war, when it was displayed in Oxford. In July 1939, during a typically ascetic summer vacation spent with his twin sister in Newcastle, Ryle read the proofs of *Archbishop Laud*: the acknowledgments of the published volume close with thanks to 'Gilbert Ryle, who, like Eve in Paradise, ranged through the whole wilderness, weeding out the solecisms, trimming the luxuriant phrases, and unmixing the metaphors'. Ryle and Trevor-Roper were companions on walks across Northumberland during the last fortnight of peace. When Hitler's forces invaded Poland in September 1939, they resolved to return to Oxford, driving through the night in Ryle's motor-car, taking turns at the wheel, and together rebuked by a policeman because their headlights were spoiling the blackout.

Before the war, then, Ryle taught Trevor-Roper how to hone his prose. Their late-night talks about linguistic philosophy intensified the younger man's interest in language and passion for clarity. Ryle detested writings or discussions that were vehement, unceremonious or bullying.[9] Trevor-Roper similarly detested the Christ Church drunk, S.G. Owen, for his conversational bludgeoning: as another don recalled of Owen, 'in short, staccato sentences devoid of any subordinate clauses whatever, and repeating after each full stop the subject of the sentence, he would tell the most improbable anecdotes, defend some preposterous thesis … or launch ferocious attacks on anything

---

9 Oscar Wood and George Pitcher (eds), *Ryle* (1971), 4.

or anybody that happened to enter his head'.[10] Ryle and Trevor-Roper wanted talkers who plumbed motives, divined character, and could reverse, pervert, confound and improvise far-flung ideas.

Michael Foster, Ryle's philosophy colleague at Christ Church, was nettlesome to Trevor-Roper because of his conversational dearth and love of privation (see the journal entry 'Fosterity' of 1947). Foster was defensive, taciturn, anxious to say nothing that might mislead; indeed a kill-joy who was apt to refuse to speak any opinion at all. 'Grave, austere, friendly, with a sort of suffering benevolence', Foster had an 'agonized conscience almost incapable of yielding one atom of compromise of any sort'. He was scandalised by Ayer's lack of religious feeling and by his import of Viennese logical positivism to Oxford, and blocked Ayer's appointment to a college fellowship saying that he was unfit to teach the young. Trevor-Roper, by contrast, was excited by the clarity and repudiation of metaphysics in Ayer's *Language, Truth and Logic*, which he read on publication in 1936. It was further to Foster's discredit, in Trevor-Roper's view, that he was devoutly religious and frugal. In 1948 he resigned his Studentship, and took the British Council chair in political science at Cologne, expecting to rehabilitate the youth of ex-Nazi Germany, 'but he found that instead of living in a hole with a tin roof, he was given rooms and a car and a secretary, and nothing valid to do'. Cheated of his chance of self-mortification, he returned to Christ Church, where a few years later he gassed himself at the start of Michaelmas term.[11]

The Oxford manner at its best – the phrase is a way of indicating the Oxford ideal of cultivating the decencies of human conduct – was personified by Ryle. 'We all present to other people, for the purposes of social life, versions of ourselves usually a good deal simplified, and edited certainly', wrote his colleague Geoffrey Warnock.

> Ryle was an outstandingly friendly, sociable, and (a word that particularly fits him) clubbable man; but I believe that he felt it proper, both for himself and others, to edit the public version, the version for the social uses of everyday, more austerely, more stoically, less self-indulgently and much more reticently than is usually

10 Robin Dundas, *Christ Church Record 1939–40* (nd), 6.
11 *Christ Church Record 1959* (nd), 3.

done ... Just as he thought it right and important that a writer should decide what versions (literally) of his work should be part of the public record, so, I believe, he thought it right and important that each of us should decide what version (metaphorically) of ourselves we wished to be visible and made available to others. That he preferred, both for himself and others, a fairly simple version, as little as possible demanding, or oppressive, or *difficile*, was a question of manners, not of metaphysical or any other high species of belief.[12]

Trevor-Roper, too, was a gregarious introvert, a man of tight emotional reticence, who edited and controlled the public version of his self as strictly as he cut and buffed his prose.

During the first fortnight of war, after motoring back to Oxford together, Ryle directed the Christ Church tutors who discarded their jackets to fill sandbags (their sandbag barricades were praised in the *Oxford Mail* as the most scientifically constructed in Oxford), while Trevor-Roper, who was on the staff of the Oxford University Officer Training Corps, awaited military orders in his rooms at Merton. There, at Merton, the college bursar, Ernest Gill, who during the previous war had served in Wireless Intelligence in Egypt, recruited him as a junior officer in the newly formed Radio Security Service, a section of MI8, the War Office's new communications department. The RSS was charged with tracing radio signals emanating from German undercover agents acting as head-beacons to direct German bombers to their English targets; but the only German agent active in England at the declaration of war in 1939 was controlled by MI5, and bombers were directed to their targets by back-beacons in Germany.

Gill was jovially impatient with pieties: in Egypt he had used the Great Pyramid as a mast for wireless interception; in Oxford he had jolted Merton by installing electric lights in its quadrangles; in *Who's Who* he listed 'rebuking sin' as his recreation. Finding that there was little useful to do in the RSS, he and Trevor-Roper, on their own initiative, working at night in the flat they shared in Ealing, decrypted the radio transmissions of the Abwehr, the German secret service. This breakthrough made enemies for

---

12 Sir Geoffrey Warnock in Gilbert Ryle, *On Thinking* (1979), xiv.

both men, who were equally dismissive of red tape, hierarchy and inter-departmental sensitivities, but established Trevor-Roper as an authority in specific intelligence work. 'By a series of accidents', he wrote in 1942 to Churchill's confidential adviser Lord Cherwell, whom he had known at Christ Church,

> I do in fact possess both a longer experience of, and a more inti-mate connexion with, the research, interception, and handling of German Secret Service W/T traffic. With Gill I built up a system, and evolved a technique, for doing this at a time when it was considered an improper and chimerical attempt. Now the system, as we founded it, is getting, by the methods we devised, over 5000 messages a week; and we can be reasonably certain that no major, or even considerable, development of the German sys-tem can take place without being detected and systematically taken by us.[13]

From Oxford to the Radio Security Service, in addition to Trevor-Roper and a young Christ Church historian, Charles Stuart, there came Gilbert Ryle in 1941 and a younger philosopher Stuart Hampshire in 1942.[14] The four men shared a small first-floor office designated the Radio Analysis Bureau where – Trevor-Roper sitting by the window – they analysed the de-crypts of the intercepted Abwehr wireless traffic. Ryle was the most helpful and access-ible to a young Signals officer at Arkley who often consulted their work and recalled the quartet mulling over job vacancies and promotional prospects in post-war Oxford during slack periods.[15] Trevor-Roper's group derided the solemn secrecy and self-important mystification which overcame intelligent men when they became involved in espionage. Victor Rothschild was a butt of their teasing: 'what a lot of trouble to take over a few snake-charmers', they told him, when he flew out to Abadan under a false passport bearing the name Dr Fish to investigate reports that German agents were plotting

---

13 Trevor-Roper to Lord Cherwell, 22 February 1942, Cherwell papers K295/1, Nuffield College archives.

14 Edward D.R. Harrison, 'British Radio Security and Intelligence, 1939–43', *English Historical Review*, 124 (2009), 59–93; see also Nicola Lacey, *A Life of H.L.A. Hart* (2004).

15 John Wright to Adam Sisman, 24 November 2010.

to explode oil-wells with booby-trapped teapots. Similarly, when Rothschild looked grave about the threat of German saboteurs in Central Africa, Ryle enjoyed telling him that the solitary agent to have reached Lake Chad had sent only one message to headquarters requesting an airdrop of Salvarsan to treat his newly acquired syphilis.[16]

At Arkley Ryle resumed his role as Trevor-Roper's incentive, guide and friend. In philosophical papers he coined new words, which English lacked but Latin possessed: reluctate, obstinate and vigilate as substitutes for reluctantly, obstinately and vigilantly. Trevor-Roper can be found playing similar learned tricks in these journals (pp. 61, 80, 288–89). It was with Ryle that Trevor-Roper discussed the stylistic power of asyndeton ('Ballads', November 1942) and other quirks of language. It is noticeable, though, and was probably regretted by Trevor-Roper, that his wartime contacts with Ryle, as with Hampshire and Hart, faded in post-war Oxford, although the four men worked in colleges within a few minutes of one another.

The office routine, staid report-writing and bureaucratic trammels of war work exasperated Trevor-Roper. He appreciated men like MI5's Guy Liddell, who was open, relaxed and intelligent; but despaired of the futile plotting by tense mediocrities who guarded their every thought and move. Some of his departmental superiors, who were formerly in the Indian police, required the thinking of their subordinates to resemble the left-right, left-right of a drilled march across a barracks square. They mistrusted, resented and repressed in their subordinates any impromptu show of initiative, speculation, originality and improvisation. Under this constricting discipline, Trevor-Roper needed a solace that would enable him to seek stylistic perfection in circumstances that were imperfect and unstylish, and to play with words, tease out ideas, plumb motives and divine character in ways that recalled the best of Oxford and gave temporary surcease from departmental drudgery. It was in this spirit – to assuage the austerity of his war work and to keep his literary intellect in trim – that Trevor-Roper began to assemble these notebooks.

They were compiled in emulation of the selections from Samuel Butler's notebooks published posthumously in 1912 and 1934. Another emulator of Butler was the solicitor E.S.P. Haynes, with whom Trevor-Roper spent a strange day in 1945 (see p. 259). In *The Lawyer's Last Notebook* (1934),

---

16 Kenneth Rose, *Elusive Rothschild* (2003), 77.

Haynes wrote of his and Butler's common inspiration in terms that apply to Trevor-Roper:

> Butler's pungency is largely due to a 'baulked disposition.' He had a real ardour for disputation combined with detestation of the herd and especially of the coterie which sheltered itself behind the herd. People like Oxford and Cambridge dons or Darwin and Spencer and Huxley appeared to his imagination as impostors who imposed their own fallacies upon the community and shirked discussion with real searchers after truth like himself.

Butler, and his votaries, including Haynes and Trevor-Roper, railed at the obstacles to clear thinking in England, where the deployment of rational arguments, resting on first principles and logic, jeopardised the success of most causes, whereas boneheaded muddle and hustings catchphrases advanced them. 'It is', continued Haynes, 'the resentment against this atmosphere of reticent compromise which throughout gives life and vigour to Butler's Notebooks – especially as they drove him into the solitude which so often develops hard thinking'.[17] All his life long, Trevor-Roper spurned reticent compromise, dynamited intellectual make-believe, and skewered pontifical egotists with his mordant ironical dialectic.

Haynes and Trevor-Roper met as Londoners. It was only during the war years that Trevor-Roper lived in the capital. During 1940, when the RSS was based in Wormwood Scrubs Prison, he shared a flat with Gill at 29 Mount Park Road, Ealing, in a house owned by the historian John Wheeler-Bennett. During the summer of 1940, while Trevor-Roper was away, a German bomb fell in the front garden of the Ealing house, which it wrecked. After Wormwood Scrubs Prison was hit by other bombs, the RSS relocated to Arkley, a Hertfordshire village near the north London suburb of Barnet (the postal address of the RSS depot, Arkley View, was PO Box 25, Barnet). Several commodious villas were requisitioned. A house called 'Oaklands' became the administrative section and orderly room. On the opposite side of the road, 'Scotswood' served as the mess. 'The Lawns', 'Rowley Lodge' and 'Meadow Bank' were used as billets for RSS workers.

---

17 E.S.P. Haynes, *The Lawyer's Last Notebook* (1934), 63–5.

The RSS community at Arkley was small and introverted: Trevor-Roper chafed at the predictable faces and conversations (see 'Breakfast time' of August 1943). He longed for his days off. As these journals record, he hitch-hiked to Buckinghamshire for the hunting; stayed overnight with Ryle at the Leander Club at Henley-on-Thames, where they drank bottle-deep potations; sometimes made the long journey to Northumberland; but mostly he took short train rides to London. In London he roistered with SIS friends such as the ebullient giant Aeneas Reay: once they drunkenly fell down the escalators at Leicester Square tube station. In 1941 he joined the London Library where he could vanish into the dark, narrow book-stacks and emerge with rare, recondite volumes for borrowing. By 1942 he was a member of the Savile Club in Brook Street, where he found affable companions and could write personal letters in peace. The Ivy restaurant was another haunt. Sometimes he was decoyed into dining with Catholic converts such as Frank Pakenham, or with literary men like Hugh Kingsmill, Malcolm Muggeridge, Stephen Spender and Philip Toynbee. Occasionally he found himself gazing sceptically at 'the great soap-bubble world of Mayfair'. Reluctantly he went to meet Cyril Connolly 'in his snobbish club, surrounded by earls and company promoters'.[18] And on some afternoons or evenings he gravitated to 11 St Leonard's Terrace, the home of Logan Pearsall Smith, the self-styled 'Sage of Chelsea'.

'I had a visit this week', wrote Smith, marking the red-letter day of their first meeting in June 1940, 'from the author of that excellent life of Laud – Hugh Trevor-Roper, who is in London in khaki, on some mysterious job connected with the war. He loves letters, and what pleased me, he loves my writing, and knows a good deal of *Trivia* by heart.' Smith found his visitor 'a charming, erudite young man' who impressed him by revealing that Milton had written his *Elegia Tertia* as a lament on Lancelot Andrewes.[19] 'I liked you before I saw you', Smith wrote to Trevor-Roper a year after their first meeting, 'feeling from certain turns in your use of words [in *Laud*] that you really were aware of the Platonic truth that words & phrases are the only things that matter; & that objects and actions are only gross & awkward & employ shadows of their meaning'.[20]

---

18 Trevor-Roper to Logan Pearsall Smith, 26 December 1943, DP. T-R long disliked White's.

19 Robert Gathorne-Hardy, *Recollections of Logan Pearsall Smith* (1949), 174.

20 Smith to Trevor-Roper, 26 June 1941, DP.

Smith was the scion of a Philadelphia Quaker family with a history of instability. His sister, Alys, who lived with him, was the earliest wife of Bertrand Russell, and still pining for him twenty years after their divorce. His other sister Mary had first married a failed politician, Frank Costelloe,[21] whom she left for the art historian Bernard Berenson. Smith was a capricious, timid, self-indulgent man who pretended to be rueful about his missed chances, but had a great conceit of himself. 'A refined and gentle-natured bachelor, with a pretty talent for turning out sentences and a taste for collecting bric-à-brac' – this was how he had struck Beatrice Webb. 'Behind the smile there is a deep-seated melancholy, due to a long record of self-conscious failure to become an artist of words. The world has proved too complex for him to grasp: he is perpetually breaking off before he has mastered even the smallest portion of it.'[22] Smith was a manic depressive, whose cycles seemed akin to seasonal affective disorder. Teasing, mischievous, voluble and unrestrained in his up phases, he could be cruel and vindictive when down. His nickname for Trevor-Roper was 'Derision'.[23] When he was young Smith flirted with Henry James, but Robert Gathorne-Hardy, who acted as his secretary-companion for many years, suspected him of being a virgin. In old age he liked to chatter naughtily about sex. He combined an agreeable inherited income with a disagreeable taste for manipulating people. Young men's affections he tried to fix by promising bequests to them. In 1942 he told Trevor-Roper that he was naming him as a principal beneficiary in his new will; but he rescinded this will three weeks before his death in 1946.

Trevor-Roper's devotion to Smith is evident in these journals. Years later he said, 'He was a wicked old man; but I like wicked old men'.[24] He had two breaches with Smith: he felt insulted (or perhaps compromised) when Smith offered to employ him as a paid holiday-companion in the summer of 1941; and in 1945 he left Smith's eightieth birthday party curtly, without a word of goodbye, after his host began a remorseless, boring interrogation, in front of spinster ladies, about his sexual experience (perhaps teasing him about the

---

21 'A good speaker, but he is a prig and a Roman Catholic, and wears cotton wool in his ears. This must have lost us at least 100 votes, & is a filthy habit': Diary of Marquess of Lincolnshire, 13 July 1899 (Bodleian, Oxford).

22 N. and J. Mackenzie (eds), *The Diary of Beatrice Webb*, II (1983), 211.

23 Smith to Trevor-Roper, 20 July 1942, DP.

24 Information from Blair Worden, 17 August 2005.

North African soldier who had made overtures to the young Trevor-Roper in the papal palace at Avignon). Afterwards, there were weeks of boycott by Trevor-Roper, while Smith expressed 'irritation at the way when my soul (if I have a soul) is like an open window to you, and all my failings apparent enough to your observation (and ironic comment), you keep on your mask in my company, & envelop yourself in enormous fig-leaves'.[25] Like Ryle, Trevor-Roper preferred the version of himself available to others to be under a simple cover, edited to extrude intimacies, and above all not *difficile*.

Foremost among the St Leonard's Terrace coterie were Smith's sister Alys Russell and the poet R.C. Trevelyan, who kept bedrooms in the house. Older *habitués* included the novelist Rose Macaulay and critic Desmond MacCarthy. Smith relished the company of bookish young men, and at different phases entertained Cyril Connolly, Robert Gathorne-Hardy, James Lees-Milne, Raymond Mortimer, John and James Pope-Hennessy, Stuart Preston and Paul Sudley – most of them, as the phrase went, confirmed bachelors. There are contradictory interpretations of Trevor-Roper's attitude to homosexuality: he had a laughing tolerance in some moods; but his younger brother Pat complained of Trevor-Roper's 'frowning disapproval' when in 1959–60 he started a household in Harley Street with his lover, the landscape gardener Edward Fitzgerald.[26]

Lees-Milne, who was recruited into Pearsall Smith's circle in 1943, was unenthusiastic when the two men first met at the hospital bedside of their mutual friend Stuart Preston. 'An old, frail man, of heavy, ungainly build', Lees-Milne noted. 'He may be a bore for he tells long stories "at" one, in a laborious, monotonous tone, laughing all the while and salivating a good deal.' James Pope-Hennessy, who was a seasoned visitor at St Leonard's Terrace, warned that Smith was tedious; but taking tea there a few months later, Lees-Milne was impressed. 'The old man coughs and spits incessantly. He is vastly entertaining … He has a splendid capacity for mockery and fun. And of course he has literary refinement; perhaps no other sort.'[27]

Rose Macaulay was the earliest of the set to whom Trevor-Roper was introduced. 'The lady professes herself as much a fan of yours as you are a fan of

25 Smith to Trevor-Roper, 17 October 1944, DP.
26 Letter from Carraigh Thompson, 23 September 2010.
27 James Lees-Milne, *Ancestral Voices* (1975), 166, 212–4.

her', Smith wrote in July 1940, lending Trevor-Roper a copy of her newly published Spanish Civil War novel, *And No Man's Wit*, 'as I think you will like the muted passion beneath the ironical surface'.[28] Her attraction for Trevor-Roper is clear from the 'auto-obituary' that she had written in 1936:

> Her novels and essays, if not widely read, appealed to certain thoughtful and well regulated minds. They were written in pure and elegant English, almost devoid of that vulgarity which degraded so much of the literature of her period, and inculcated always the highest moral lessons. Those who called her a flippant writer failed to understand the deep earnestness which underlay her sometimes facetious style ... She was accused of caring more for manner than matter, for words (in which she was morbidly interested) than for what they represented ... She was seldom bored by the spectacle of life, though, as she complained, the older she got the more barbarous and shocking this spectacle became.[29]

This 'auto-obituary' stimulated a fashion for self-analytical 'autopsies' beyond Smith's circle. Ryle in 1941 incited Trevor-Roper to write a 'Self-Appreciation' (pp. 50–53). The style and manner of the later 'Self-Revelation' ascribed to Stuart Hampshire (pp. 67–69) are so close that the section is best explained as an exercise by Trevor-Roper in ventriloquism.

The older *habitués* at St Leonards Terrace were walking dictionaries. As shown in her opusculum *Catchwords and Claptrap*, Macaulay shared Ryle's quest for verbal precision, and Smith's whimsical erudition about words and enthusiasm for new usages.[30] Trevor-Roper imported touches of linguistic philosophy into the old people's half-serious vocabulary games. 'Since you ... continue to coin words in Chelsea, let me inflate your currency by a few obols from a mint at Barnet', he wrote to Smith in 1944 after a talk with Ryle (an obol is a silver coin from ancient Greece). 'The first rule of this mint is that words should be self-explanatory, & should not depend on the membership of an esoteric clique, or the knowledge of its elaborate private anecdotes.' There was a 'second rule, or rather bye-law' stipulated by the 'Barnet cashiers', namely

---

28 Smith to Trevor-Roper, 19 and 29 July 1940, DP.
29 Rose Macaulay, 'Full Fathom Five', *The Listener*, 16 (2 September 1936), 434.
30 Rose Macaulay, *Letters to a Friend 1950–1952* (1961), 51.

'that the termination *-ousness* is ugly, & should be replaced, where possible, by the neuter *-um* (as odium and tedium for odiousness & tediousness – cf. delirium)'. He and Ryle offered the Chelsea old people several new coinages: *fastidium* ('also used, I have since discovered, by Roger North, in his *Lives of the Norths*'), *meticulum, impecunium, supercilium, ridicilum, deciduum, bogum*.[31] Smith forwarded this letter to Trevelyan.[32]

Trevelyan had long kept a room in St Leonard's Terrace where he slept a night or two each week. The younger brother of G.M. Trevelyan and of a libidinous socialist baronet who had been nominated Lord Lieutenant of Northumberland by Ramsay MacDonald, 'Bob' (also nicknamed 'Trevy') was a scholarly poetaster whose verse plays, dramatic and satirical poems, witty trifles, and classical translations had graceful meditative charm. Though his devotion to ancient Latin and Greek literature inhibited his creativity, and deterred readers, he never repined at his limited success. A Scholar-Gypsy, he was called by Max Beerbohm, who sketched him in 1941 tramping through the countryside: unmistakably a bookman when he was outdoors, but resembling a woodman when he was ensconced in his beloved library. 'His occasional brief flares of violent temper', wrote Desmond MacCarthy, 'only lit up the compassionate, anxious tenderness of his nature, followed quickly as they always were by an irresistibly gentle contrition'. MacCarthy believed that with their classical approach to literature, Trevelyan and the Chelsea coterie were beacons blazing out on a sombre age 'when education is becoming more and more utilitarian, when emotional and intellectual bewilderment tends to be more and more identified with profundity, and aesthetic pleasure with the psychological excitements of ugliness'.[33]

Before the Blitz Trevelyan had lamented that 'man's whole hard-won heritage of culture and wisdom' was jeopardised 'in this war-broken, disillusioned, hysterical world'.[34] Materially and culturally everything was getting smashed. In April 1941 a parachute mine exploded near Smith's house. His windows were blown in: shards of glass from the windows were still being found in his books when he died five years later. Alys Russell was trapped in bed beneath

---

31 Trevor-Roper to Smith, 21 October 1944, DP.
32 Smith to Trevor-Roper, 27 October 1944, DP. See also 'Vocabulary' (p. 61).
33 Sir Desmond MacCarthy, quoted in R.C. Trevelyan, *Selected Poems* (1953), xiii–xiv; 'Mr R.C. Trevelyan', *The Times*, 22 March 1951, 8d.
34 R.C. Trevelyan, *Rimeless Numbers* (1932), 15.

her bedroom door, which had been hurled across the room, until air-raid wardens rescued her. A month later Rose Macaulay's Marylebone flat was hit by incendiary explosives, and its contents burnt to ashes. She felt destitute without her library and papers, as Smith told Trevor-Roper with customary flippancy:

> Rose Macaulay has lost everything through enemy action, as we call it – clothes, manuscripts & all her books – she now faces the world with only a pot of marmalade & the clothes she stands in, trying to decide in what new character she shall begin life again. She says she is too old to be a street-walker, too patriotic to be a spy, too poor to set up as a Mayfair Jezebel. I have suggested social climbing, not in Hill St. or Mayfair, but on less frequented peaks, Denmark Hill or Muswell Hill.[35]

Under bombardment it seemed essential to the self-respect and discipline of the older people whom Trevor-Roper met in St Leonard's Terrace to insist on their commitment to England's 'hard-won heritage of culture' by continuing to celebrate the richness of the national language, protecting its rules, conning dictionaries, coining neologisms, parsing sentences, disputing grammar. Smith and his friends knew the corrupting force of slipshod or dishonest words: knew, too, the redemptive humanising power of scrupulous vocabulary. 'The great art of writing is the art of making people real to themselves with words', he insisted.[36] Trevor-Roper's talks in Chelsea about literary perfection, like his talks in Oxford and Arkley with Ryle about linguistic philosophy, inspired the style of these journals: Ryle and Smith were their living begetters, as Butler was their early inspiration.

If Ryle and Smith dominated the literary form of these journals, Trevor-Roper's life outside London, and away from Arkley, was crucial to their content. As they show, he had an intensely pictorial imagination coupled with a passionate susceptibility to landscape. 'Style', he noted in 'Health and Art' (December 1942), 'depends on experience and observation, since style needs imagery, and imagery must be drawn from life, from wild beasts in the forest,

---

35 Smith to Trevor-Roper, 1 June 1941, DP; Rose Macaulay, *Letters to a Sister* (1964), 120; Constance Babington Smith, *Rose Macaulay* (1972), 157.

36 Smith, *All Trivia* (1933), 149.

and storms at sea, and low-life in taprooms and circuses and at earthstoppers' dinners, and a relish and a recollection of these things, and a sympathy with them'. Sherry parties in St Leonard's Terrace did less to invigorate his style or intensify his sympathies than the formidable solitary walks which took him into storms, tap-rooms, remote farms and outlandish places.

'There are times when my thoughts, having been duly concentrated on the right spot, refuse to fire, and will think nothing except general misery' – the words are those of G.M. Trevelyan, but they might have been Trevor-Roper's. 'On these occasions', Trevelyan continued, 'my recipe is to go for a long walk. My thoughts start out with me like blood-stained mutineers debauching themselves on board the ship they have captured, but I bring them home at nightfall larking and tumbling over each other like happy little boy-scouts at play.'[37] Trevor-Roper, too, needed long, hard walks across rough country to subdue the blood-stained mutineers. Ryle, also, was a keen pedestrian, who eventually died after a long tramp along the Yorkshire coast. His philosophical papers abound with metaphors and similes drawn from walking. *Le Penseur*, his imaginary philosopher, strikes out on many paths: some well-trod; some dead-ends, and others leading into bogs or nettles; some forgotten or unexplored. *Le Penseur* paces ahead, scans for promising tracks, stumbles over difficult ground, staggers under a burdensome backpack of redundant equipment, probably meets an impasse, but ultimately, by perseverance or ingenuity, may find a viable path. It is similar for a historian like Trevor-Roper.

Many landscapes are portrayed in the journals, including the west of Ireland, the western marches of England and war-wrecked Germany, but chief of these are Northumberland and Buckinghamshire. 'In the great woods of Buckinghamshire is my spirit's home, and in Northumberland, in the valley of the Till', Trevor-Roper wrote after flying along the Mediterranean coast of North Africa on his way to India in March 1944.

Northumberland was Trevor-Roper's birthplace; and the town of Alnwick, with its ducal castle, remained his parents' home until their deaths. It is a county of ancient monuments: the Roman Wall built against the Scots, monasteries, abbeys, priories and friaries, forts, peel towers and castles, some of them still resplendent in their barbarous power. Together with Shropshire, it was the nearest that England in the 1940s retained of the old order. During the

37 G.M. Trevelyan, *Clio* (1913), 57–8, 69.

war years the great territorial families still held their land there: a Duchess of Northumberland reigned at Alnwick Castle (the young duke was away fighting like Hotspur); there was an Earl of Tankerville at Chillingham Castle; Middletons still at Belsay Castle; an Earl Grey at Howick; a Craster in Craster Tower (with another Craster, the Bodley's Librarian, in All Souls). Northumberland was a county for historians, with a hard terrain which yet cast a meditative spell. 'We walk all day on long ridges, high enough to give far views of moors and valley, and the sense of solitude above the world below', Trevelyan had written shortly before Trevor-Roper's birth. 'It is the land of far horizons, where the piled or drifted shapes of gathered vapour are forever along the farthest ridge of hills, like the procession of long primeval ages that is written in tribal mounds and Roman camps and Border towns, on the breast of Northumberland.'[38]

Trevor-Roper's devotion to the county's wild, empty hills, where stone walls took the place of hedges, provides some of the most memorable sections of the journals. To the east lay a windswept coast of dunes and sandy beaches. To the west, on what was then the border with Cumberland, lay the Pennines. To the north lay Trevor-Roper's great good place, the Cheviot Hills, that natural bastion on the frontier of England and Scotland. The rivers that flowed eastward from the Cheviots to the North Sea made him, he says, an ardent riverlover. The Till, with its winding course and humped-back bridges, enchanted him. One December afternoon he waded through its icy waters five times with a beagle pack. In 1943 his father leased five miles of fishing rights on the Till: Trevor-Roper, home on leave, was soon casting for trout. That June, too, he fished in the Aln until driven home at midnight by the mists.

If remnants of the Northumberland described by Trevor-Roper can still be seen or imagined, his Buckinghamshire is gone. Salden Wood, ancient woodland in the Vale of Aylesbury, through which Trevor-Roper joyously rode on a December afternoon in 1941, was targeted by post-war planners for a rubbish dump, and then bisected by a road during the development of Milton Keynes new town. 'Buckinghamshire', a woman who lived near Beaconsfield wrote in 1953,

> contains all of England – suburbia, industrial squalor, great estates,
> even valleys remote and rural where most of the families have the

---

38 Trevelyan, *Clio* (1913), 153–5.

same name. Some of the market-towns change little – coaching-inns and old-fashioned drapers surround the squares where the buses end their journeys. On market days [the town] is crowded, with stalls and village people. Waitresses run to and fro in the dining-room at the Bull; bus-queues line the pavements.[39]

This was a Buckinghamshire that Trevor-Roper was privileged to enjoy. Nowadays only inklings of that life remain. Wotton, that magical, secluded eighteenth-century house, seat of the Grenville marquesses and dukes of Buckingham, 'a golden pink central house flanked by lantern-shaped pavilions, behind delicate wrought-iron, golden-berried gates', looking out to sleepy Grecian temples by an unruffled lake, then owned by Trevor-Roper's friends the Beaumonts, where the Bicester & Warden Hill hounds used to meet, came close to demolition in the 1950s.[40]

Buckinghamshire meant so much to Trevor-Roper in wartime because, as these journals show, he was a dogged rider to hounds with the Bicester & Warden Hill and Whaddon Chase hunts. During the war, he later said, he was saved from going mad in Secret Service work by his treasure-hoard of free days when he could go fox-hunting, though the sport survived on a reduced scale and shorn of its scarlet flummery. In 1938, as soon as he had received his £40 advance from Macmillan for his first book, *Archbishop Laud*, he had attended horse sales at Leighton Buzzard, and bought a great love of his life, Rubberneck, whom he stabled at Quainton. Trevor-Roper's courage in the hunting field was rash given that he was so weak-sighted. 'There was no more pathetic, yet heroic, sight than Hugh Trevor-Roper, on his knees in a ditch, scrambling around trying to find his spectacles', recalled Lord Beaumont of Whitley.[41] Probably Trevor-Roper was the only man in the field carrying a pocket-sized edition of Horace. He wrote a dialogue in praise of fox-hunting which he tried to coax Cyril Connolly to publish in *Horizon*, the literary and arts review which nourished the minds and senses of the cognoscenti in the 1940s. For years he diverted himself during tedious moments of college meetings and university committees by doodling harum-scarum hunting scenes featuring Rubberneck, impetuous beagles and sardonic, rebellious basset hounds. Back

---

39 Elizabeth Taylor, *The Sleeping Beauty* (1953), 114.
40 Candia McWilliam, *What to Look for in Winter* (2010), 208–12.
41 In conversation with the editor.

in Oxford, after the war, he exercised a pack of hounds in Christ Church Meadow before breakfast until forced to renounce hunting after Rubberneck rolled on him and smashed his vertebrae in 1948. One of the comic characters in *Letters of Mercurius* (1970), Trevor-Roper's spoof letters of a seventeenth-century Oxford don, harks back to his strenuous winters in the 1940s: Euseby Todhunter M.F.H., of the Old Fox-Earth, Quainton, Buckinghamshire.

Trevor-Roper knew that he had a safe berth in England while contemporaries – Dillwyn, Field, Heathcoat-Amory, Lyell and others – were being shot down, blown up and drowned in the skies, battlefields and seas. His tribute to his friend 'Euston Bishop' (October 1942) places him in a generation that admired courage, extolled fortitude and valued resilience. He did not want to let life wash over him. He did not scurry away from risk. In June 1943 he thought of seeking a posting with the partisans in Yugoslavia. The exertions of fox-hunting kept him fit, mitigated his boredom with the stimulus of danger, and thus intensified his responses and perceptions. They contributed, too, to his developing sensibility as a historian.

In 1957, during his inaugural lecture as Regius Professor of Modern History at Oxford, Trevor-Roper warned against the humanities retreating into segmentation so specialised and remote that they lose all power to edify non-specialists. He sought to emulate Frederick York Powell, who had been appointed to the Regius chair sixty years earlier. 'His chief fame seems to have been that he left the Prime Minister's offer, owing to its external similarity to an income-tax demand, unopened in an old boot, until discreet enquiries from Downing Street led to its rediscovery', said Trevor-Roper, who hailed Powell as 'a universal man accidentally thrown up among our grim specialists'. Powell, he added, 'contributed impartially to the *Encyclopaedia Britannica* and the *Sporting Times*, was "as well acquainted with the boxing reports in the *Licensed Victuallers' Gazette* as with the *Kalevala* or *Beowulf*"', and dedicated one of his works jointly to the Dean of Christ Church and an old fisherman at Sandgate.'[42]

There is an exclamation of Pearsall Smith's in *Trivia*: 'What humbugs we are, who pretend to live for Beauty, and never see the Dawn!'[43] Trevor-Roper's journals, with their grateful celebration of the visible natural world, show that

---

42 Hugh Lloyd-Jones, Valerie Pearl and Blair Worden (eds), *History & Imagination: essays in honour of H.R. Trevor-Roper* (1981), 13.
43 Smith, *All Trivia* (1933), 151.

he felt this ardently. Northumberland moors, Buckinghamshire beech woods, the Cheviot Hills, the Vale of Aylesbury, Christ Church Meadow and the misty riversides of Oxford, formed the historical cast of his mind. The place-names where he hunted with the Bicester on Mondays – Marsh Gibbon, Poodle Farm, Gubbin's Hole, Piddington Cow Leys – and the Oxfordshire woods where he beagled – Hell Copse, Polecat End, Waterperry, Drunkard's Corner – provided the imagery drawn from life that he thought the basis of literary style. His relish for the guile and boasts of Northumberland poachers, his amusement at the quiddities of its gentry, his curiosity about old Cleveland huntsmen or Chilterns foresters, were, he felt, part of the training of any historian who was not bound to be a grim specialist. These notebooks show what has been forfeit in our intellectual life – and how much more that is precious there is still left to lose.

1940–41

In December 1939 Trevor-Roper, then a Research Fellow at Merton College, was recruited by Ernest Gill, the college bursar, as his deputy in the Radio Security Service (a department of MI8). During 1940 Trevor-Roper toiled for the RSS in a cell at Wormwood Scrubs prison, enjoyed the acclaim that marked the publication of his first book, Archbishop Laud, *and found a mischievous new mentor in Logan Pearsall Smith. He suffered debilitating sinusitis, and endured several operations. In May 1941 control of the RSS passed from MI8 to the radio communication section of SIS. Gill was demoted, and Trevor-Roper appointed as chief of the intelligence sub-section of the RRS, called the Radio Analysis Bureau. He was answerable to Felix Cowgill, head of MI6's Section V responsible for counterespionage, and to the deputy director of MI6, Valentine Vivian, for both of whom he felt mutinous contempt.*

At Vincent's, dining with abandon,
Blues surround me, Philip Landon:
With this grace my food I sweeten, –
'Eat, and (if you can) be Eton.'[1]

---

1 This sequence of squibs was written by T-R. Philip Landon (1888–1961), a bachelor law don and Fellow of Trinity 1920–1956, was a die-hard Tory who abominated progressive intellectuals and idolised hearty young noblemen. He was honorary treasurer of Vincent's, an Oxford club with sporting Blues as its members.

I am Elton, teaching here
History without a peer.
Why I'm here it is a mystery,
For I'm a peer without a history.[2]

———————

Duty, stern daughter of the Voice of God,
Had for her other parent Marcus Tod.
Virtue was born of mortals, her's the loss, –
Got by Sir David out of Lady Ross.[3]

———————

'Mid swallowtails and dragonflies
The gilded Bowra flits, and dies.
Long years unnoticed creeps the Dodds,
With centipedes and gastropods.[4]

———————

Are you rich and nobly born?
Is your mind by scruples torn?

———————

2 Godfrey Elton (1892–1973), Fellow of the Queen's College 1919–1939. Despite his obscurity, Elton received a peerage in 1934 on the recommendation of Ramsay MacDonald, whose son had been his pupil. He published a volume of MacDonald's official biography in 1939.

3 Marcus Tod (1878–1974), a tall, martial-looking Fellow of Oriel 1903–1947 and Reader in Greek Epigraphy, was an austere Presbyterian and life governor of the Bible Society; the stern outlook of Sir David Ross (1877–1971), provost of Oriel 1929–1947, and tutor in philosophy there 1902–1929, is indicated by the title of his book *The Right and the Good* (1930).

4 (Sir) Maurice Bowra (1898–1971), the flamboyant, gregarious Fellow and classics tutor at Wadham from 1922 had been disappointed when the less demonstrative Birmingham classicist E.R. Dodds was preferred for the Regius Professorship of Greek in 1936. Bowra was consoled by his subsequent election as Warden of Wadham (1938), Professor of Poetry (1946) and Vice-Chancellor (1951). Eric Robertson Dodds (1893–1979) had been sent down from University College, Oxford for his support of the Irish Easter rebellion of 1916. T-R came to regret Oxford's malicious reception of Dodds in the 1930s, and admired Dodds' *The Greeks and the Irrational* (1951).

Come hither! I can cure them all, –
Father D'Arcy, Campion Hall.[5]

––––––––––

I'm Lord Bishop Arthur Headlam.
I drive my flock to drink or Bedlam.
When I die, they'll sing Te Deum
In Gloucester and the Athenaeum.[6]

––––––––––

I am Feiling. To be sure,
My style is torturous and obscure;
'Tis not by Reason's sober light
One proves the Tory Party right.[7]

––––––––––

I think that I would rather dwell
Alone and in the Pit of Hell,
Than sit enthroned in the Heavens
With Lawson,[8] Jesus Christ, and Levens.[9]

––––––––––

––––––––––

5 Martin D'Arcy (1888–1976), a Jesuit priest and Master of Campion Hall 1933–1945, was the foremost English apologist for his faith; responsible for the Catholicism of several rich or noble converts.

6 Arthur Headlam (1862–1947), Regius Professor of Divinity at Oxford and Canon of Christ Church 1918–1923 and Bishop of Gloucester 1923–1945. 'Headlam often appeared brusque and insensitive', wrote Alwyn Williams, Bishop of Winchester: 'unsentimentality combined with a quick temper and a disregard of criticism often made him seem difficult'.

7 (Sir) Keith Feiling (1884–1977), Student of Christ Church 1911–1946, Chichele Professor of Modern History 1946–1950, founder of Oxford University Conservative Association (1924); his pupil Charles Stuart called his prose 'allusive, sometimes congested'.

8 Frederick ('Harry') Lawson (1897–1983), a loquacious Fellow of Merton 1930–1948, Reader in Roman Law until his appointment in 1948 as Professor of Comparative Law and Fellow of Brasenose.

9 Robert Levens (1901–1976), Fellow and classical tutor of Merton, 1927–1968, always kept an eye cocked, all too warily, on his pupils' examination results; sub-warden of Merton 1941–1942, compiled naval intelligence reports 1942–1944, and had Admiralty posting to Washington DC 1944–1945.

Explorers say, from expert knowledge,
That there are dons in Lincoln College;
Whence anthropologists foretell
That Jesus may yield Life as well.
We wait for Marett to unfurl
The secrets of the darkest Turl.[10]

————————

Toll, toll the bells in Keble College
For Wit and Freedom, Truth and Knowledge.
In that vast tomb their bones lie hid
'Neath dust and fust and must and Kidd.[11]

————————

Things that fascinate me: the luminosity of decay; pullulation; myths of great natural processes or cataclysms – the Creation, the Deluge, Adonis; the innocent freshness and wonder of the first day; the intrusion of daylight into dark places, σμερδαλέ' εὐρώεντα, τά τε στυγέουσι θεοί περ;[12] mermaids, nymphs, angels, and animate spirits of nature (not monsters or ghosts); the bottom of the sea; the Moon; cold empty wastes; twilit caverns; Jacob's Ladder; great rivers – Nile, Oxus, Ganges, Limpopo; intellectual life in the upper air; larks singing at heaven's gate (not nightingales); beauty squeezed out from tortured souls; bright flowers rooted in corruption; the earth seen from afar as a planet; the music of the spheres; distillations from the moon or stars; bright butterflies that feed on rotten meat; trees; the smell of low tide.

————————

I love reading Theognis: his bitter, introverted pride; his *snobisme* and homosexuality; his hatred of humanity and disgust with Life.

————————

10 Robert Marett (1866–1943), Fellow of Exeter 1891, and Rector 1928–1943, was the principal founder of the Oxford University Anthropological Society (1909). Exeter College stands on Turl Street.

11 Rev Beresford Kidd (1864–1948), Canon of Christ Church 1915, Warden of Keble College 1920–1939, examining chaplain to Bishop of Oxford, historian of early Christianity.

12 Horrifying, dank, hated by the very gods (Homer, *Iliad*, 20.65, of abodes in the underworld).

πάντως μὲν μὴ φῦναι ἐπιχθονίοισιν ἄριστον
μηδ' ἐσιδεῖν αὐγὰς ὀξέος ἠελίου·
φῦντα δ' ὅπως ὤκιστα πύλας 'Αΐδαο περῆσαι
καὶ κεῖσθαι πολλὴν γῆν ἐπαμησάμενος[13]

His views on getting drunk. His vindictiveness:

εὖ κώτιλλε τὸν ἐχθρόν, ὅταν δ' ὑποχείριος ἔλθῃ,
τεῖσαί νιν, πρόφασιν μηδέμιαν θέμενος[14]

He is the only readable Greek elegist, I think.

———

My life is a melancholy thing by itself, sad, bare, unlustrous: it is generally enlightened and enlivened by the reflected influence of my friends, so that often it seems to have a spontaneous gaiety of its own, – but wrongly, for it is only like a barren peak gilded by the light, the sun; when that is absent, it is a drear, cold lonely thing, as I now know, when all my friends are away, and I am ill and alone and introverted. Whose influence has warmed my life most? John Field,[15] who knows neither malice nor any indirection, who is so ingenuous and yet has such high and critical standards, who loves art and music and the sea, and who once told me the sudden truth that Religion is all very well for the old, and proved by his gay pagan sympathy that the young are better for dispensing with it? Or David Hawkins[16] (now killed) with his gay Regency poses? Or Arthur Stewart-Liberty?[17] These were the warming

---

13 Quite the best thing for dwellers in this world is never to have been born and never to have seen the rays of the piercing sun; but once born, to pass with all speed through the gates of Hades and lie under a heavy covering of earth (Theognis of Megara, fl Sixth century BC, 425–8). Standard editions give πάντων and ἐπαμησάμενον and put an acute rather than a circumflex accent on φύντα.

14 Put yourself out to cajole your enemy, but when you have him in your hand, pay him back, giving no reason (Theognis, 363–4). The accent on μηδέμιαν is wrong: it should be μηδεμίαν.

15 John Field (1915–1942), Charterhouse and Christ Church, 'a Soccer Blue and a man of irresistible charm'.

16 David Hawkins (1916–1941), matriculated Christ Church 1934, took third in PPE, RAF pilot officer killed in action over Norfolk.

17 Arthur Stewart-Liberty (1916–1990), Christ Church, served as a Major in the Royal Bucks Yeomanry before taking over an ancestral property, the Regent Street drapery store, Liberty's.

influences of my happy unthinking days; and then there are the cooler, more elderly stars, who bathe my barren peak in a more austere and intellectual glow – Lascelles Abercrombie,[18] at whose death I felt that the spring had gone out of the year, and now Logan,[19] whose light casts an upward shadow, so that this peak is sometimes irradiated in such a wise that it seems to point ambition heavenward.

Qui passo gli anni, abbandonato, occulto,
Senz'amor, senza vita: ed aspro a forza
Tra lo stuol de' malevoli divengo;
Qui di pietà mi spoglio e di virtudi,
E sprezzator degli uomini mi rendo,
Per la greggia c'ho appresso; e intanto vola
Il caro tempo giovanil; più caro
Che la fama e l'allor, più che la pura
Luce del giorno e lo spirar: ti perdo
Senza un diletto, inutilmente, in questo
Soggiorno disumano, intra gli affanni,
O dell'arida vita unico fiore.

Leopardi: *Le Ricordanze*[20]

[I spend years – loveless, alone, buried alive,
And growing bitter as a matter of course,
Cast among this pack of begrudgers. Here –
Because of whom I have to herd with –
I lose every last shred of civility,
Am stripped of every decent feeling,
And become a despiser of mankind
Whilst all the while my priceless youth –
More precious than any laurel crown,
Dearer than daylight or death itself –

---

18 Lascelles Abercrombie (1881–1938), lyrical and metaphysical poet, Fellow of Merton and Goldsmiths' reader in English at Oxford from 1935.

19 Logan Pearsall Smith (1865–1946), sedentary and malicious man-of-letters.

20 Giacomo Leopardi (1798–1837) wrote *Le Ricordanze* ('Memories') in 1829.

Takes flight. Sunk among miseries
In this inhuman place, living to no purpose
And lacking all joy, it's youth I lose,
The one and only flower that blooms
In this desert that we call life].

———————

Illness is a great thing: it induces celestial aspirations, and teaches sympathy and humanity to those who may have forgotten it. In my gay, unintroverted, fox-hunting and deep-drinking days, could I have sat still on a stone bridge over a running brook, all day, as I did in Cornwall in June 1940, reading canto after canto of Dante, when France had just fallen and England was at the brink of the precipice? No, in ordinary health, I should have been too active, enjoying heroic efforts, for such resigned, almost spiritual happiness in a world of toppling ruins. Or would I have thrilled, as I do, in reading poetry, when I come across that inexpressible lyrical *cri de coeur* that is in Shakespeare and Euripides and Leopardi? Was I not perhaps too exclusively fond of the drum-roll majesty of Homer and Pindar and Milton to appreciate, as I now do, this poignant beauty of the suffering spirit?

'A man who has not read Homer is like a man who has not seen the sea. There is a great object of which he has no idea.' (Bagehot: Lit Studies I. 255 (1891)).

———————

How furious I felt that day (Feb 1941) when Tom Armstrong[21] took me seriously to task and told me that I was being false to my own intellectual nature in going foxhunting and being such a snob and loving worldly rather than intellectual things. He accused me of this and more, and begged me to consider that I had an intellect and should be an intellectual and realise my intellectual vocation. My friends, he said, were disturbed at my evident wish to waste my talents in the pursuit of false values: to combine the tastes of a scholar and a country gentleman was possible in the 18th century, but

———————

21 (Sir) Thomas Armstrong (1898–1994), Christ Church organist 1933–1955, Student of Christ Church 1939–1955, conductor of the Bach Oxford choir, composer, Principal of the Royal Academy of Music 1955–1968.

now the two were incompatible; one must choose between them, and choose aright.

It was not because I was aware of the truth of these charges that I felt so bitterly hurt by them. It was because they had been true, but were true no more; and I was aggrieved that anyone I knew and liked as well as Tom Armstrong shouldn't have noticed my conversion, – shouldn't have noticed the burning contempt I entertained for the Feilings, the Eltons and the Bryants[22] and all the others whose intellectual standards were not prized for themselves but as a means to shabby success, – shouldn't have noticed my growing intellectual idealism, my growing distaste for high society without aristocratic ideals, – shouldn't have realised that my love of foxhunting is real, and unconnected with its social implications, which I despise.

———

Geoffrey Lamarque[23] once compiled a Roman history paper for Greats. One of the questions was, 'Illustrate the position of women under Nero.'

———

When I went up to Oxford, I was a pedant and a prig, as all successful Carthusians had to be. I had won numerous prizes, and had spent them on authorised good literature. Among them was a portentous anthology of English prose and verse, by a professor, in five volumes. In it was a passage from *Erewhon*, – the passage describing the crossing of the range; and this passage, which I read as a freshman, was the beginning of my emancipation from intellectual bondage. Seduced by the style (for I did appreciate style) I ordered more of the works of Samuel Butler;[24] and seduced further by his wit and humour (for I had preserved a sense of humour) I read them through and unconsciously opened my mind to his solvent ideas. I became an enthusiastic disciple and evangelist of Samuel Butler, and found co-religionists to keep the

---

22 (Sir) Arthur Bryant (1899–1985), prolific High Tory author of patriotic histories.

23 Geoffrey Lamarque (1913–1979), scholar of Oriel, joined Indian Civil Service 1936 and Commonwealth Relations Office 1957. T-R liked to visit London 'for a blind' with Lamarque: 'last time I dined in London with Geoffrey Lamarque, in the tube afterwards, I gallantly gave up my seat to a woman, and then discovered with surprise that I was quite incapable of standing' (T-R to Patrick T-R, 7 May 1937).

24 Samuel Butler (1835–1902), New Zealand colonist, novelist, painter, composer, atheist, satirist.

flame of my faith a-burning, – Ted Dorsch,[25] Jock Bills[26] and another wild Australian intellectual, Charles Jury.[27] I turned my back on the prim, traditional paths of classical learning, along which I was so profitably treading. And although now I regard Samuel Butler without veneration, a familiar figure of known weaknesses, he is nevertheless always to a certain degree sacred, for even fallen gods have a residual divinity; and though I may have explored his failings and quarrelled with his tastes, I cannot forget that he once saved my life.

———

In moments of silent meditation, sitting in the sun on hay-stacks or by river-banks, or roistering over pots of ale, or waiting by covert-sides, I am often astonished by the depth and extent of my learning. 'Hugh Trevor-Roper', I say to myself, when this bewildering revelation breaks upon me, 'you must be careful, or you will be buried, obliterated, beneath the burden of this stupendous erudition. Go slow! Be canny! In the interest of learning, you should devote more time to beagling, foxhunting, drinking, fishing, shooting, talking; or, if you must read, read Homer, Milton, Gibbon, who cannot harm the brain.'

———

My book

For style, read Stendhal, Peacock,[28] Gibbon's footnotes, George Moore,[29] and Logan Pearsall Smith's *Trivia*. The rest of literature is superfluous; but some useful pleasure can always be derived from secondary sources, such as the *Kai Lung Omnibus*, Bertrand Russell, and my own book on *Laud*.

———

25 Theodore Siegfried ('Ted') Dorsch (1911–1991), a Rhodes scholar from Adelaide arrived at Christ Church in 1934 and won a first in English 1936; schoolmaster at Winchester and Wellington before his election to the chair of English at Durham University.

26 Allan Maynard ('Jock') Bills (1906–1967), from Adelaide University, was a commoner of Christ Church 1934–1936.

27 Charles Jury (1893–1958), poet and essayist, MA Magdalen 1923, lived mainly in England, Italy and Greece 1919–1938, when he returned to Adelaide, where he was mentor to poets, dramatists, actors, painters and scholars.

28 T-R enjoyed the satirical dialogues and playful ideas in novels by Thomas Love Peacock (1785–1866).

29 George Moore (1852–1933), novelist and autobiographer.

I should add that the indispensable in this list are always changing.

Truth and Justice should be the guiding principles of a historian. But Truth need never be dull, and Justice should be done to persons as well as to theories.

From the precincts of ancient cathedrals I was greeted with a loud cannonade of heavy but superannuated shot; and in vicarages and chapter-houses there was an aggrieved bumbling, as of drones disturbed.

When I dip into my book on *Archbishop Laud* (and I dip into it almost daily) I am for ever discovering yet more exquisite beauties, lurking unsuspected among yet profounder truths.

The reading of an ecclesiastical historian must inevitably include so many dry polemics, dull sermons, pious fables, and other trash, that he must be excused if his writing is seasoned with an occasional grain of levity or scepticism.

————

In my comparatively religious days (*aetate* 21–22), I remember being attracted by some verses of, I believe, Newman, which I found in Plumptre's *Life of Bishop Ken*,[30] and which I now regard with complete lack of sympathy. They began:

> Had he not of joys his fill
> > Whom a garden gay did bless,
> And a gently trickling rill,
> > And the sweets of idleness?[31]

'Yes', I should reply, – unless, perhaps his felicity were to be improved by a little intellectual conversation and a little physical satisfaction, – by a roistering night, now and then, over a dozen of port, and a couple of days a week with the local foxhounds. But Newman unaccountably postulated entirely different pleasures to complete the picture – abstinence and flagellation, and similar discomforts, which I hope I shall always regard as totally superfluous to a civilised life.

And yet Logan Pearsall Smith tells me that flagellation is regarded by some as a delicious pleasure; and that all the *beau monde* go to a house not far from

————

30 Rev Edward Plumptre (1821–1891), translator of Sophocles and Dante, author of *Life of Bishop Ken* (1888).

31 In Newman's poem 'A Hermitage' (1834) the line reads, 'Had he not of wealth his fill'.

his in Chelsea, where, for a reasonable consideration, they can be privately flagellated.

Newman – what hateful spectres does not that name raise in my mind now! Asceticism, fanaticism, obscurantism, 'Revealed Religion', I hear a silver voice declaring (it is in his *Discourse on the Scope of a University Education*), 'furnishes facts to other sciences which those sciences, left to themselves, would never reach … Thus, in the science of history, the preservation of our race in Noah's Ark is a historical fact, which history would never arrive at without Revelation.' And, thin and scholarly, I hear the same voice, in the *Apologia*, declaring Newman's 'firm conviction that it would be a gain to the country were it vastly more superstitious, more bigoted, more fierce in its religion, than at present it shows itself to be.' The style in these passages is indeed the style of Newman, that chaste solemnity he learnt from the humane Gibbon; but the mind is the mind of Ignatius Loyola and Josef Goebbels, and all who have sought, by education, to prevent the young from learning anything. There are certain books which glow with luminous corruption. Newman's *Apologia* is such a book.

I don't often agree with Carlyle; but when he says that Newman had the mind of a half-grown rabbit, I do.

When the war began, and I waged it from Wormwood Scrubs, I thought it was lack of books that made me irritable and restless in my scanty moments of leisure; but this was wrong. And later Kenneth Morton Evans[32] attributed my sudden recovery, when I joined him over a glass of sherry or a bottle of port, to drink; but he was wrong. It is talk, I have now discovered, which arouses me miraculously from gloom to gaiety, without which my life sinks into melancholy and depression. To sit with some convivial old soak in a steaming tavern or subterranean dive; to learn, in summer, by a river-side

πὰρ ποταμὸν κελάδοντα, παρὰ ῥοδανὸν δονακῆα[33]

(a magic line!), while epigrams are hatched, in easy succession, by sunlight, champagne and pâté de foie gras; to expatiate within some resonant colonnade,

----

32 Kenneth Morton Evans (1909–1996), great-grandson of Queen Victoria's first physician *accoucheur*, inherited Llangennech Park near Llanelli in 1928. A pre-war amateur radio ham, he was recruited to MI8 and appointed Deputy Controller of the Radio Security Service in 1942.

33 By the roaring river, by the waving rushes (Homer, *Iliad* 18.576).

weaving around me a diffuse, iridescent tissue of ephemeral verbiage, – these are my most delicious pleasures, my image of life in Paradise, the sole elixir that can transmute, in an instant, a mood of despair into a world of perfect content.

Darwin's shooting

In his agreeable little autobiography, Darwin says, 'How I did enjoy shooting! but I think that I must have been half-consciously ashamed of my zeal, for I tried to persuade myself that shooting was almost an intellectual employment; it required so much skill to judge where to find most game, and to hunt the dogs well.'[34]

I was pleased when I came across this sentence; for it describes exactly the mental attitude which I developed in defence of my own favourite diversions of foxhunting and beagling. Indeed I once wrote a short essay to prove, at least to myself, the intellectual nature of the art of hunting.

What, I sometimes wonder, do monks and hermits catch, in their long, lonely vigils, when they fish, and fish, in the stale, murky depths of their untended souls? Silver, shining trout? No, but eels, perhaps, and flat creatures gorged with slime, and old boots choked and silted with decaying rubbish.

Classical scholarship

That great river which once rolled through the life of Europe, fertilising so many generations, and working so many mills and factories for the enrichment of the human mind, has now, like Oxus, lost itself in stagnant shallows; and dreary pundits, like wading birds, peck and grub in it for their unappetising fare.

---

34 *The Autobiography of Charles Darwin* (1929), 18. Darwin's father reproached him as a boy: 'You care for nothing but shooting, dogs and rat-catching, and you will be a disgrace to yourself and your family.'

Handel

The characters evoked by the music of Handel are like those in Botticelli's *Primavera*. They move in orderly pageant, with buxom tread, and each is obviously the better for half a bottle of champagne. They are like the horses of Erichthonius in Homer, which galloped on the tops of the cornstalks and did not break them, and trod upon the spray of the sea.

J.H.S.B.

I have a friend,[35] a young clergyman of strange views and character. His churchmanship is indecently low, – in fact he has admitted that only his snobisme (which is tremendous) keeps him from sordid chapel-divinity. Wearing a Bullingdon tie in preference to a dog-collar, he tends the uncultivated souls of the poor in Southwark with evangelical conviction, and disbelieves the Resurrection with such earnest piety that the Bishop of Southwark (from whose jurisdiction he is exempt) has forbidden him to preach in any church in his diocese. He hunts a pack of beagles, breeds sporting dogs, and runs a racehorse. And yet, with all this, he is the most deadly bore.

The prosperity of the wicked – that eternal enigma of the self-righteous and the unsuccessful.

Zu fragmentarisch ist Welt und Leben!
Leh will mich dem deutschen Professor begeben,
Der weifs das Leben zusammenzusetzen,
Und er macht ein verständlich System daraus;

---

35 John Harold Stanley Burton (1913–1993) graduated from University College with a theology degree 1935 and was ordained 1938. Head of Cambridge University Settlement in the Camberwell slums 1940–1943, RAF chaplain 1943–1946, hospital chaplain 1946–1954, then General Secretary of the Church Lads' Brigade.

Mit seinen Nachtmützen und Schlafrockfetzen
Stöpft er die Lücken des Weltenbaus.
Heine, Buch der Lieder, 1827.[36]

My Pleasures

My pleasures are food and wine and conversation, and hunting and shooting and fishing. And I like listening to solemn music, the stately and serene music of Handel; and walking, in May, through woods planted by 18th century dukes; and drinking fragrant morning-tea in bed, reading learned and elegant and worldly biographies about learned and elegant and worldly bishops.

But these pall. And, anyway, it's no good. Through the coloured haze of my complacent inebriation breaks a terrible warning voice, 'the Philistines be upon thee, Samson!' The dark ages are returning, in a single stride. So I find pleasure, like Petronius, in working hard and proving that, in unfamiliar fields, I can show the way.

My mind has undergone three revolutions of which it's conscious. The first was caused by the writings of Samuel Butler, which suddenly loosened, refreshed, and redirected its long misused engines. This was the most radical upheaval of the three, because the soil was quite unprepared for the shower that fell upon it; and it was some time before the exotic vegetation that shot up afterwards could be trimmed and gardened. This revolution happened in 1934, and the effects lasted till 1935–6 before they were completely assimilated.

The second revolution was in the summer of 1936, when I decided to do away with the metaphysical world, and, with it, the loose generalities and plausible labels that had counted for knowledge with me and got me my degree. Instead I decided to stand firmly on the ground, and grapple with, and master, the solid foundation of things. This was a more constitutional change,

---

36 Heine's *Buch der Lieder*, LVIII: The world and life are too fragmentary!/ A German professor will give me the solution./ Magisterially he puts life back together,/ Makes an intelligible system out of it;/ With scraps from his nightcap and dressing-gown/ He stops up the holes in the universe.

and was accepted quite firmly and consciously, as I walked one afternoon round the Christ Church Meadow. I can associate no teacher's influence with it; but it coincided with my rejection of theology and the beginning of my interest in the economic basis of history; and the period which opened with it reached its zenith, and sanction, in 1938, when the events of Munich crystallised and sharpened the thinking of us all.

The third revolution was in 1940, when I became a friend of Logan Pearsall Smith, under whose influence I discovered that this solid, austere research of the second period was, after all, compatible with a faith in literary style, – a faith which, somewhat neglected during the period of research, took root again and blossomed in the cracks and interstices of the rocky experience of the war.

The Conway Papers[37]

Henry More, urging Anne Conway not to increase her headaches by curious disquisition, says he speaks from experience, 'never man, I think, having been more pitifully rid and hackneyed with the witchery of speculation, than myself' (p. 76).

Sir Kenelm Digby, 'the Pliny of our age for lying',[38] was a first-rate letter-writer: 'These innocent recreations, which your Lordship mentioneth, of tabours and pipes, and more innocent dancing ladies, and most innocent convenient country houses, shady walks, and close arbours, make me sigh to be again a spectator of them, and to be again in little England, where time slideth more gently away than in any part of the world. Instead of your smiling happy English skye, I am here weatherbeaten with continuall winter stormes, for your smooth well-natured ladies, wee see nothing but rough-rided savage sea-calves:

---

37 *The Conway Papers: the Correspondence of Anne, Viscountess Conway, Henry More and their Friends 1642–1684*, edited by Marjorie Hope Nicholson, was published in 1930. It stimulated T-R's desire to write a history of the English ruling class, and introduced him to the *milieu* of Sir Theodore Turquet de Mayerne, whose biography he later wrote.

38 'The Pliny of our Age for lying' was Henry Stubbs' description of Sir Kenelm Digby (1603–1665), scientist, adventurer, author, diplomat, naval commander and lover. Digby was in Calais on a diplomatic mission (1647) when he wrote this extract.

for your delicious wines and curious foule, our diet is red puddle beere, made of brackish water and wood-dried malt, the flesh of seales, porpises and orkes, dressed with whale oyle, and our bread is made of tainted rye fished out of the bellies of some wrecked Holland hulkes cast away upon these sands' (p. 27).

'And I must again avouch, that the writing of books, when a man is not forced to it either by his place and profession, or obligation of conscience, so that he cannot be quiet in mind without so doing, is but a vainglorious piece of pedantry in comparison of the nobler sense of friendship, and his respect and natural love to his kindred and country' (More to Lady Conway, p. 163).

More's animadversions on a book against him: 'it is the most villainous libel for insolency and the ordures of language, for wrathfulness and maliciousness of spiritt, for the perpetual cavilling of its pretended reasonings that ever saw light.'[39]

More is quoted as having said, in a discourse on Valentine Greatrakes[40] 'that not only his own urine had naturally the flavour of violets in it; but that his breast and body, especially when very young, would of themselves in like manner send forth flowery and aromatick odours from them, and such as he daily almost was sensible of when he came to put off his clothes and go to bed. And even afterwards, when he was older, about the end of winter or beginning of the spring, he did frequently perceive certain sweet and herbaceous smells about him, when yet there were no such external objects near from whence they could proceed. Nay, he further tells us an extraordinary passage between himself and his chamber-fellow touching these matters …' (p. 124)

'Is not the whole consistency of the body of man as a crudled cloud, or coagulated vapour, and his personality a walking shadow and a dark imposture?' (p. 147)

———

At a crisis in the history of Rome, to ease the pressure, the authorities commanded all professors to leave the beleaguered city, but kept back a large

———

39 More refers to *Some Observations upon the Apologies of Dr Henry More for his Mystery of Godliness* (1664), by Joseph Beaumont, Master of Peterhouse.

40 Valentine Greatrakes or Greatorex (1629–1683), 'Greatrakes the Stroker', an Irish land-owner who believed that he could cure diseases by the stroking of his hand, was brought over to England in 1665 to treat Lady Conway's headaches.

number of chorus-girls. This seems a reasonable measure to provide for the necessary refreshment of the defending troops; but since history is more often written by professors than by chorus-girls, it has been most unfairly condemned.

Proust

A la Recherche du Temps Perdu – that great haystack of introverted snobbery.

Conversation

The beauty of conversation consists in the mute, attentive faces of one's fellow-talkers.

Moments

There have been memorable moments in my life, – moments when I have deliberately turned my back for ever on an old world, or suddenly, through a narrow aperture, glimpsed a new, and gone out in search of it. The first was when, at the age of fifteen, in my study at Charterhouse, I discovered Milton's Nativity Ode, and realised the existence of poetry. Another was in the same room, when I was construing Homer. Hitherto my progress had been slow; the forms were unfamiliar, the vocabulary new. Then quite suddenly, – it was in the 7th Odyssey, the passage describing the Gardens of Alcinous – I found that, at last, I could read it freely and easily and enjoy it. On I read, far past the appointed terminus, till late at night, fascinated; and all my leisure hours for long afterwards were spent in reading Homer, till I knew all the Iliad and Odyssey. In all the variations of my tastes and standards (and very few have lasted intact from my school days) I have never wavered in my passion for Homer and Milton.

And then there was that moment in the summer of 1936, when, walking round the Ch Ch Meadow, and pondering on the complicated subtleties of

St Augustine's theological system, which I had long tried to take seriously, I suddenly realised the undoubted truth that metaphysics are metaphysical, and having no premises to connect them to this world, need not detain us while we are denizens of it. And at once, like a balloon that has no moorings, I saw the whole metaphysical world rise and vanish out of sight in the upper air, where it rightly belongs; and I have neither seen it, nor felt its absence, since.

And again, two years later, when the events that preceded the Munich conference brought me in haste to Oxford, and I sat in the Merton Combination Room, and Guy Chilver[41] outlined for us all the principles of a sound British foreign policy, explaining, at great length, that in dealing with the problems of Czechoslovakia we must not allow moral considerations, which are alone valid, to be in the least affected, even to be supported, by strategic considerations, which are inherently immoral, etc. etc.; I listened to these follies with silent contempt and disgust, and I was aware at that moment that another balloon was vanishing for ever into the stratosphere, carrying with it, to their proper home, all those chattering disputants and dogmatists and nebulous left-wing humanitarian dons who, for twenty years, had made the word academic into a synonym for ridiculous.

'Language, Truth and Logic'

With the composure of a scientist proving his experiments, Freddie Ayer[42] first states his solvent principles, and then calmly watches while the whole metaphysical world, its cloud-capp'd towers and gorgeous palaces, slides majestically and obediently away into inevitable and predicted ruin.

---

41 Guy Chilver (1910–1982), classicist and Fellow of the Queen's College since 1934.

42 (Sir) Alfred Jules ('Freddie') Ayer (1910–1989), successively lecturer and research student in philosophy at Christ Church 1932–1944, was a wartime interrogator of German prisoners-of-war, British Security Coordination officer in New York responsible for organising agents in South America, and SOE agent in Ghana and Algiers.

Religion

Gilbert[43] defined it as 'the protest of man against the non-existence of God'.

Dreams

The working of the human mind is one of the most enthralling objects of study, and the symbols in which it expresses them in sleep have always fascinated me. Between the winter of 1935 and the spring of 1938 I recorded, on awaking, those which pleased or interested me; and at the beginning of the war, when I was destroying private papers, I found the document and here transcribe some of them.

A Flying Dream

In December 1935 I dreamt I was walking with Frank Fletcher[44] over downland country when we observed, flying above us in a large covey, numbers of hawks. They were at a great height, and flew in a steady stream, like migrant swallows. Frank suggested hawking, and immediately set the example. Shedding his 65 years like a garment, by the mere motion of his arms and legs, he rose suddenly through the air. I followed him. The sensation was delicious. Looking down through miles of space, I saw woods as specks and valleys as shadowy creases. There was no effort, no fear, but a serene satisfaction, an irrecapturable pleasure. By and by, we reached the level of the hawks, and swimming easily among them we continued our casual conversation, while now and then stretching out a hand to catch a hawk, wring its neck, and drop it to earth, confident of retrieving it later. The hawking was itself purely incidental, involving no pleasure or even conscious sensation. The flying was the thing.

---

43 Gilbert Ryle (1900–1976), Student and tutor in philosophy at Christ Church 1925–1968, Waynflete Professor of Metaphysical Philosophy (1945), succeeded G.E. Moore as editor of *Mind* (1947). He and J.C. Masterman were Southampton dockers during the General Strike shifting coffee, coconut, ketchup, ginger, typewriters, emery powder, oil stoves, horse hair and copper bars.

44 Sir Frank Fletcher (1870–1954), headmaster of Charterhouse 1911–1935, honorary fellow of Balliol 1924.

A Fragmentary Dream

In Dec 1935 I dreamt I was walking along the edge of cliffs overhanging the sea. They were very high, very steep cliffs, and it was a very wild sea, throwing up great clouds of spray that wettened the air even at the height at which I was walking. Suddenly, as I walked, I caught a fragmentary glimpse through the sea-haze. On a jutting, overhanging, perilous, giddy ledge, I saw, perched on the very brink and leaning over the unprotected rim, thousands of feet above the jagged rocks and breaking spray, a nursemaid and four children sitting in an improvised nest, like guillemots in the Faroe Islands. Within miles there was no other sign of life, and this sudden glimpse made a photographic impression on my mind.

A Glimpse of Australia

In January 1936 Bills, I dreamt, took me on a day-trip to Australia. We went to Sydney, and walked into the country. Within five minutes we were well out of sight of town-life. It was by the sea. Green hills rose up from the shore, and at their feet lay a beautiful stretch of rich, green, undulating turf, closely cropped by a few yellow-fleeced sheep. The air was unnaturally clear. Kangaroos were leaping about, and above our heads lively birds with bright yellow markings were tumbling playfully in the air. Bills said they were kiwi, and I believed him. I looked at the scene enraptured, thinking of those first European explorers, and the emotions of pleasure they must have felt when they discovered this idyllic land, a vast empty continent in the South Seas, all so green and temperate and fertile. But Bills understood my thoughts, and said it was very barren inland.

A Beagling Dream

In Feb 1936 I went beagling after frogs in a dream. Hounds put up a frog in a hedgerow, and it led them at a breakneck speed over several fields. The cry of hounds was much shriller than it is after hares, or even after rabbits. The kill was a very unpleasant sight; the frog was so smooth and green outside, but inside it was warm-blooded and steaming. I should add that it was as big as a hare. A second frog led us into the sea, near Brighton I think, and all the beagles were drowned. I didn't feel at all sorry about this, as I didn't want to see a second kill like the first.

A sad, allegorical dream

On 21.3.1937 I dreamt that I dined in the George with Hughie Hope,[45] and then we strolled (it was summer) along a path through a trim green park. On our right hand the grass bank sloped steeply downwards towards a stream fringed with reeds and overgrown willow-herb. It was still warm and sunny. Suddenly I saw a small, round ball, glassy and shining, which began to roll from before my feet down the slope, and came to rest among the willow-herb and flowering rushes at the water's edge. I knew what it was. It was my ideals, as yet unnamed and undetermined, but all, I knew, compact in that little glass ball. It hadn't rolled far away; it still glistened among the reeds; it was still retrievable. Should I retrieve it? Or should I let it lie where it had rolled, and continue my pleasant stroll, enjoying the compensations implicit in the loss of that dangerous treasure, – the delights of conversation and leisure and congenial society? For a moment I hesitated, undecided; then I thought no more of it, but continued to stroll along that pleasant path, in the warm evening air.

A Dream of Death

On 4.5.1937, after a fortnight's inactivity caused by mumps, I dreamt of my weak and helpless state. This was so lamentable that I saw a doctor, who told me that my body was worn out and finished with, though I would go on living for a few weeks yet. So I walked into the drawing-room at home and said casually, 'I'm dying'. Then I asked if anyone would help me to bury my now useless body, – quite nonchalantly and by the way, as I might ask if someone would care to come for a walk. Sheila[46] was lying on a carpet in front of the fireplace reading a novel. She said she wanted to finish her chapter. But Pat[47] said he'd help. So we went into his room and found a big, oblong reed-basket, the one Fonzo used to sleep in – and put my body into it, and then, since there was room to spare and no lid, we filled it up with earth, and Pat buried the whole affair in the garden. I continued to live, after this, a sort of ghost,

45 Hugh Hope (1914–1982) matriculated at Worcester College in 1933, served as an officer in the King's Royal Rifle Corps rising to the rank of Lieut-Col during the Mau-Mau rebellion; later member of the Hon Corps of Gentlemen-at-Arms.

46 T-R's sister Sheila (1912–1992), married Keith Price in 1942; Colin Kingham in 1972; and Sir Oliver Simmonds in 1979.

47 T-R's only brother Patrick (1916–2004), later a distinguished ophthalmic surgeon.

with a shadowy and conventional body, unequal to any kind of activity, but just enough to enclose my mind and convey it about. I had no feeling in it: I didn't possess it in any intimate sense; and I was unaware of any strength or substance in it. It was just a vessel to keep me from spilling for which I was to survive my body.

A War Dream

On 15.7.37 I dreamt I was taking part in a war. The scene was in France, – in Savoy, I believe, – and on the Duke of Buckingham's estate. Our enemies were French, but mostly fair-haired and blue-eyed and big. Four battles were raging, one in each corner of a big field. They were very small, almost personal affairs. The killing (which was all done with bayonets, or rifles used as clubs – there was no shooting) was slow, deliberate, and determined, and evidently followed some strict rules of precedent and rotation which I couldn't follow. The regular sequence of groans and thuds was sickening. But what alarmed me most was that everyone except myself was of such colossal stature and homeric prowess, while I was particularly weedy.

The enemy were prevailing. Their success in personal encounter was infallible. I saw a Frenchman killing one of us. Another man then approached the killer from behind and brought down his rifle on his head with a dreadful crash. The Frenchman crumpled up on the bank; but with his last strength, he rose again, by all other tokens quite dead, and gutted his assailant with a bayonet before finally collapsing.

Suddenly I found myself challenged by a tall, handsome man with a short golden beard. I supposed that my turn had come. He looked very strong, and his bayonet was already pointed at my belly. I rallied some supporters, but my opponent evidently thought this wasn't playing the game, for he gave me one severe 'Fellow-do-you-dare-kill-Caius-Marius' sort of look, at which I quailed, and thought better of it, and prudently withdrew, and

> Apart sat on a hill retir'd
> In thoughts more elevate, and reasoned high[48]

on all the personal horrors of war.

---

48 Milton, *Paradise Lost*.

This was a very vivid dream. No one spoke. It was just a slow, methodical, ineluctable process of silent slaughter on a stage so small that every death seemed premeditated murder. And the characters all had the air of generous, cultivated men, who hated the whole business. They were in the grip of an unrelenting, mechanical routine.

The Dictators

Though our modern dictators entertain us by their bombast and vulgarity, and maintain the high traditions of their class in other less engaging vices, they fall short, alas!, of the exorbitant pleasures, the outrageous, shameless orgies of debauchery, which are so endearing a feature of the more ancient and authentic tyrants. Hitler and Mussolini neither smoke nor drink, and although Musso sometimes allows himself a mild infusion of lime-flowers, for his stomach's sake, tea and coffee (those poisonous drugs!) he rigorously eschews. As for Hitler, cream-éclairs are said to be the limit of his indulgence; but of these, it is whispered, he has sometimes, when in convivial mood, been known to take one over the eight. When these two miserable creatures met in Venice, that city of ancient and exotic debauchery, did they feast with Lucullus and romp with Cleopatra? No: two plates of scrambled eggs, and early and alone to bed. O tempora, o mores! Shades of Sardanapalus and Semiramis![49] Where's Caligula, where's Nero, where's Elagabalus?[50] Has the long catalogue of luxurious Popes and Caesars tapered down to this, and the Seven glorious Deadly Sins shrunk to an inhibition?

---

49 Sardanapalus, the last great king of Assyria, was indicted in Greek accounts as cowardly, dissolute and effeminate. Semiramis was an Assyrian warrior princess vilified by Armenian writers as whorish.

50 Caligula (AD 12–41), Roman Emperor AD 37–41, a cruel despot; Nero (AD 37–68), Roman Emperor AD 54–68, remembered for his extravagance, iniquity and orgies; Elagabalus (AD 204–222), Roman Emperor AD 218–222, was reviled after his assassination at the age of eighteen. He imposed the worship of Baal upon his empire, married and divorced five wives, including a Vestal Virgin, and outraged the Praetorian Guard by treating a blond slave charioteer, Hierocles, as his husband. His relationship with an athlete from Smyrna and sexual passivity were equally offensive.

Since the beginning of the war, I have developed two dangerous tastes. I have nibbled at the delicious gingerbread of style, and bitten of the indigestible apple of Power.

Charterhouse

The worst harm Charterhouse did to my mind was to stuff it with what were likely to be the opinions of future examiners, that it could only disengage itself, and set out to discover its own, by lying fallow over the four years when it should have been the most active. At Oxford, for four years, I never thought and hardly read; my mind was closed, it neither sought nor found new experiences; it was insensible to every natural stimulant. Indeed, so empty was my life then that I can't remember what I did, except loaf and drink and win, without much effort, a regular series of lucrative academic prizes, – until, revolting against the tedium of this barren existence, I became, for a time, anti-intellectual through mistaking the nature of the intellectual world. And when I look back and think what I might have done, had I not been sterilised by academic complacency, – how I might have begun four years earlier than I did the fascinating exploration of the world of humanity and ideas, – when I recollect that there are some whose minds are stunted, whose mental *joie de vivre* is delayed, not for four years only, but for ever (I see them coming up to Oxford every year, dim paragons of reach-me-down orthodoxy), then my heart is filled with bitterness against my old school, and I wonder wherein it is better than education by Jesuits.

Tennyson

Samuel Butler was a philistine, and he led me, when he had me in tow, away from many altars to which I have since patiently returned, e.g. Tennyson. Of course Tennyson did write an infamous deal of rubbish, and I had had far too much of him at Charterhouse; so when I found the best authority in the world for scrapping him, I scrapped him, as I thought, finally, even persuading a little bookshop in the Turl, which wouldn't allow me anything for my prize edition of his poems, to take it for nothing.

It was Lascelles Abercrombie who, about four years afterwards, led me back by one of those remarks that first stick and then sprout in the mind. We were talking of dung; and he mentioned the old term for it in venery, citing from Tennyson,

> The slots and fewmits of the deer,

and going on to remark on Tennyson's wonderful rich vocabulary and exquisite choice of words, until I asked myself whether perhaps I hadn't been too precipitate in rejecting him on the mere command of a now dethroned prophet. So I decided to try him again, and began with the Lotus-Eaters. The rest was easy. O what treasures there are in those first two volumes, – Mariana, the Lotus Eaters, The Lady of Shallott, Break Break Break; no wonder if Tennyson seemed then a new giant, one to rank with Keats and Shelley. If only he had died young, like them! Unfortunately he lived to be 83, without gaining in profundity what he lost in freshness, and went on churning out the sort of stuff the British public expected in the dark ages of Queen Victoria.

The Christ Church manner, that assumption of effortless superiority, is said to be galling to those who weren't at Christ Church. But we can't expect the world to be run for the benefit of those who weren't at Christ Church.

My horse

My wild, irresponsible, rubber-necked racehorse is a creature after my own heart; and though it has frequently nearly killed me, and probably will kill me, all things are forgiven it, for its weaknesses are my weaknesses, and endear it to me. It is a snob. It revels in its speed and virtuosity. It loves showing off, and hurls itself, out of sheer *joie de vivre*, at the most impossible obstacles; and it doesn't care a twopenny damn when it takes a tremendous fall in consequence. It despises all dull and easy ways. It exhibits a malicious delight in the discomfiture of its rivals. And it never gives up.

Maxims

In my brief career of preaching and prophesying and battling with weak allies for unattainable ideals, I have reached a few conclusions to guide, if not to deter, any others who would seek, with worldly wisdom, to achieve unworldly aims:

1. Choose unattainable ideals, lest your allies reach them first, and they turn sour.
2. Always aim at perfection. In that race there is at least a consolation prize.
3. Preach to the critics with restraint, for they must be led to believe; but to the converted with fervour, for they must be driven to act.
4. Keep your eye on your goal, and even your indiscretions will lead you thither.
5. Do not, in the pursuit of your ideals, forget your standards.
6. It's an ineffective ideal that butters no one's bread.
7. When a man professes to share your ideas, it's usually to console you for his refusal to act on them.
8. A man cannot serve two masters, he should exploit them.
9. Reward your allies with the spoils, lest they seem to have had any higher motive in joining you.
10. Voices crying in the wilderness are like the music of nightingales: delightful to the casual visitor, but a great nuisance to the other birds.
11. Pursue truth. It is difficult to ascertain, inconvenient to hear, imprudent to tell. Could anything be more irresistibly recommended?
12. After a successful usurpation, the prudent man goes slow. He never withdraws.
13. In the blackest hour of imminent defeat, the wise man will be adding new details to his comprehensive plans for the exploitation of victory.
14. There are few things so exhausting as the conversation of highly placed fools.
15. Let the iron enter into your soul. The sensation is not disagreeable.
16. Power looks luscious on the bough, but, tasted, it is maggoty fruit. There are no such drawbacks to the sweet and solid satisfaction of revenge.
17. Snobbery, too, is a great consolation.

———————

There are three things on which I can get drunk: wine, the sound of my own voice, and flattery; and the greatest of these is flattery.

———————

Self-appreciation

When I was ill in bed, in Nov. 1941, I read to Gilbert Ryle the 'Self Revelations' by Bertrand Russell and Sir Hubert Miller printed by Logan in his *Golden Urn*.[51] Gilbert told me to go and do likewise. I did:

I like the world and its civilities, – wine and food, books, poetry, music and conversation. Books and educated society are indispensable to me. But I like the intellectual world to be alive, as in Paris and Peckwater, not dead, as in North Oxford and the Athenæum. I don't like learning isolated from common sense and the world, – it's pedantry; or dilettantism, which is slipshod, and therefore worse; or cranks of any kind. And I like hunting foxes and hares, and most country sports, and the country at all times, but especially in spring and autumn. I don't like moors and barren wastes, except in passing. I like woodland and pasture and plough, where one can know every field and brook and hedgerow, and observe the changing seasons and the work of men's hands. I like wild animals, and horses and dogs, but not pets. The petting of animals seems to me a morbid perversion.

I'm self-centred, but in a fairly free way. The world which centres upon me isn't just an extension of me. It's a real, gay, coloured world, full of independent life and variety, in which I am, of course, the principal, but not the only inhabitant. I like observing myself, as I observe others; but I don't take myself seriously. I like adventure, both mental and physical, and dislike routine. I'm pleased with my capacity for varied enjoyment, and expect others to admire it too; that's my chief vanity. In most things I'm a snob, – at least I've no use for people without high standards. I think nothing worth doing unless it's worth doing well. Sloppiness I detest, and shoddy work of any kind, and pandering to the taste of the public, or the level of the market. I consider it disgusting, a sin against the light. Socially I'm a snob, too; for living and manners are

———————

51 *The Golden Urn* was an ephemeral magazine, dedicated to the cult of perfection, privately printed in 1898 by Smith, his sister Mary Costelloe and her lover Bernard Berenson. Sir Hubert Miller (1858–1940) was a Hampshire baronet who leased the Palazzo Querini, Venice.

an art, and on the whole the upper classes have the best opportunities of perfecting it. Not that they do, – at least nowadays in their decay. When I live among them, and observe the lack of education and values amongst most of them, their dreary pleasures, and the sickening triviality of their lives, I despise them. At lawn-meets of the foxhounds I often recall Sir Walter Raleigh's lines,

> I wish I loved the human race,
> I wish I liked its silly face …[52]

but I can generally be reconciled by good port and flattery, and they give me both. Then I admit that they're not as bad as the average of other classes.

Pride is my chief fault, and will be my undoing. It calls me away from the bright world I so love and enjoy. Partly it's sheer joy in excelling; partly a more bitter and lonely emotion, – disillusion about other people, who seem to fall behind me when I enter their field. A few don't, and them I tend to regard as great men, putting them into niches and bowing before them, at least for a time; for I'm capable of devotion, though not of humility. I like to admire people, but often make mistakes in my choice. When I think of some of the former occupants of my niches, I shudder.

For all my self-confidence, I'm not self-sufficient. I need company; I demand recognition. Flattery and attention I love, and can always be won by skilful appreciation of them. And it's not just personal respect I want. I expect the outward badges and symbols of respect to be showered on me, and am annoyed if they're withheld. When they're awarded to me, I at once despise them. I boast a lot, but not of past distinctions. I'm not interested in them.

I'm quite unrepentant about my weaknesses. Some (like imprudence, ostentation, volubility, and the need for company) I neither conceal nor correct. I assume people would invent weaknesses for me, if they couldn't find any, and prefer not to trust their imagination. But I hate selfishness, and take great pains to correct it in myself, when I'm aware of it.

I have strong ethical views, and defend them with a quixotic, crusading spirit. For elementary justice and intellectual freedom (or perhaps I should say, against their opposites), and for my friends, I will fight with relish and abandon. But morals, – I mean the systems people make out of

---

52 Lines from 'Wishes of an Elderly Man' by Sir Walter Raleigh (1861–1922), Fellow of Merton College and Professor of English Literature at Oxford 1904–1922.

their repressions – I can't do with. Social and sexual conventions, religion, and all the apparatus of God and Sin, – these make an interesting psychological study; but when people attach importance to them, I don't argue, I flee.

When I have set my heart on achieving something, I rather enjoy the political manoeuvres it entails. I like fighting; I love victory; and I don't repudiate the exquisite pleasure of revenge. There is an impulsive, perhaps overbearing, element in my character. I generally seem to get my way, and am often embarrassed, lest this should have been by force. I don't admire strength of mind in others, only quality.

There is no branch of humane studies in which I am not interested, and I dislike exclusive specialisation within them. I love humanity, and its imperfections, better than all the abstractions of the philosophers. Religion, psychology, anthropology, fascinate me, – the haunted chambers of the human mind. In religion I'm a complete sceptic, though I could have been a pagan, – to allow of nymphs and fauns in woods and streams and hills is not, to me, a feat of credulity comparable to the acceptance of theological postulates. It's the mysteries of the natural, not of the supernatural world that enlarges my imagination. But the combination of ethics and religion seems to me a mistake. It makes ethics unplausible and religion prosy.

Metaphysical systems bore me. To subject life to formulas that can't be verified by reason or experience seems to me a form of suicide. Life, I consider, should be devoted to a vocation, that it may have meaning and purpose, and enjoyed for its own sake by way of reinsurance, and as a safeguard against fanaticism.

I'm naturally cheerful. I love laughter. I enjoy broad farce and rarefied nonsense. And then there's company. Next to a fox-chase, I love few experiences like a prolonged and congenial drinking-bout in a steaming tavern. But my nature is volatile, and I have bouts of melancholy, especially in loneliness, which, more than anything, I hate and fear. Personal relations mean a great deal to me. They're the only reality most of our lives have, except to ourselves. There's always plenty of company I despise, but the society of my friends I find delicious, and I always assume they find mine delicious too.

I'm very restless. Activity of body or mind is a necessity to me. It needn't be more than desultory activity; but the pleasures of complete idleness are unknown to me. I'm physically incapable of dozing. I don't daydream now, though I used to a lot.

As for conversation, a grain of malice, I find, doesn't spoil it for me in the least. It rather improves it.

I am instinctively a British whig. I believe in an élite (but not a static élite), for whom there must always be hewers of wood and drawers of water. The idea of equality, except equality of justice and opportunity, depresses me. The élite should have wealth as well as culture and authority, for though wealth isn't necessary to salvation, it's a great help; and surplus spending power is best entrusted to those who can spend it innocently and with distinction. I don't say the élite could come from our existing classes in society, – they're all unsatisfactory, and out of date. It would have to be created, – or rather, to assert itself. The Germans have a new élite, but not a nice one. It's neither innocent nor distinguished.

Talking of Germans, I don't like them. The world I admire owes nothing to them, – nothing whatever.

I don't like contemporary civilisation, and though I enjoy my life immensely, it's no thanks to the age in which I live it. The twittering twenties, the drab, introverted thirties, – I hate them. I look forward to the future with curiosity rather than confidence. I am confident only in myself.

I admire the Greeks, and the men of the Renascence with their insatiable intellectual ideals,

Still climbing after knowledge infinite,[53]

their almost physical gusto in intellectual matters, their love of life, their versatility, their scepticism, their grandiose and cultural extravagance. And of course the 18th century, with its elevated self-assurance, its complete and orderly world. Were I not so proud, so restless, so fond of shining in the eyes of the world, I could be happy living in a mansion in Ireland, where the 18th century (I'm told) isn't yet over, with a library, a French cook, an inexhaustible cellar, and a pack of foxhounds. But I hate being ineffectual, and I've no doubt I'd be back in London within a month.

---

53 Marlowe, *Tamburlaine*.

ClassicsDec 1941

There are some critics who make it a charge against certain great artists that they have no successors. It is a criterion which denies greatness to Homer, Virgil, Shakespeare and Milton; and that alone, I should say, damns it. Surely it is a proof of greatness so to have perfected a form or technique that posterity can do no more with it. Great artists must create their own forms; they won't be content with reach-me-downs. If they perfect them, they are among the immortals: the thing has been done for good; and their successors must begin elsewhere. So no good Greek poet would attempt epic hexameters after Homer, and Virgil, who, with infinite labour, mastered the Latin hexameter, left it an easy, and barren, exercise for Statius, Claudian, and schoolboys. I don't believe there's a single line in Claudian that Virgil might not have written; and Barrington-Ward[54] (he tells me) is continually confusing his own hexameters and Virgil's. By perfecting English dramatic verse, Shakespeare killed it for ever; and Milton did the same for epic blank verse. The embalmed corpses of all these have been scarecrows to deter imitators ever since, – holy scarecrows that terrify their worshippers; and this is the correct function of classics.

I think this truth was recognised by Samuel Butler when he wrote that Handel marked the climax of a musical development, – 'or rather, perhaps I should say that music bifurcated with Handel and Bach, – Handel dying musically as well as physically childless, while Bach was as prolific in respect of musical disciples as he was in that of children.' Which only means that Handel, by perfecting a form of music, made further development of that form impossible, and that Butler should therefore have known better than to write *Narcissus*; for *Narcissus* is to Handel as Claudian to Virgil, as John Philips[55] to Milton, as Cato and Sophonisba, and all the dreary wastes of 18th century dramatic poetry, to Shakespeare.

---

54 John Barrington-Ward (1894–1946), student and classical tutor at Christ Church from 1919, liked to talk of his own achievements, and would flush and glare if criticised. T-R thought him defeatist.

55 John Philips (1676–1709), an amiable aesthete who lived in Christ Church 1697–1707, wrote burlesques in Miltonic blank verse.

1942

'The strain of continually fighting with highly placed fools, combined with the rigours of the English climate, having proved too much for my health, I've come here to recover in the milder and less controversial atmosphere of Dublin', Trevor-Roper wrote to his brother Pat from Ireland on 25 February 1942. The Radio Analysis Bureau, now located at Arkley in Hertfordshire, comprised Stuart Hampshire, Gilbert Ryle, Charles Stuart and Trevor-Roper. Their office badinage, together with Trevor-Roper's visits to Logan Pearsall Smith in Chelsea, sustained his intellectual curiosity, honed his aesthetic standards and heightened his pleasure in the human comedy.

> Once did we hold the glorious East in fee.
> Then came Sir R. Brooke-Popham, K.C.B.[1]
>
> Anon., Jan. 1942

I was boasting of a political coup.[2] Gilbert said, 'Many a bull, emerging from a blood-stained china-shop, has congratulated itself on its Machiavellian diplomacy'.

---

1 Air Chief Marshal Sir Robert Brooke-Popham (1878–1953) resigned as commander-in-chief Far East on 27 December 1941, shortly before the fall of Singapore, and was blamed for the calamity in Southeast Asia.

2 The coup was doubtless on Christmas Day of 1941 when T-R was taken by Lord Swinton, chairman of the Security Executive, by car from Arkley to lunch at the Junior Carlton Club in Pall Mall, and unburdened himself of the frustrations arising from his intelligence sub-section of RRS, the Radio Analysis Bureau, being subordinated to the SIS radio communications section.

The Hebrews   Feb. 1942

They fascinate me, those old Hebrews, with their austere divinity and bestial practices, their sublime poetry and murderous passions, their love of nature and hatred of mankind. How brutality and beauty keep company through the pages of their bible. The old, vulgar, tub-thumping God of the Pentateuch, and the lyrical religious cry of Elijah and Amos. David charming Saul's madness away with music and lamenting for Jonathan, – and the lust, perfidy and cruelty of that petty Syrian king. Elijah enacting his Wagnerian dramas in El Greco scenery, and the petty professional revenges of Elisha and the sons of the prophets. I think of the great prophets, of Isaiah preaching his sublime faith in adversity, – and there is Ezekiel dreaming in gross images and dining on dung. I read the Psalms of David and the Book of Job, and all the magical and passionate poetry of that objectionable race; and I remember their tribal cruelty, their narrow, obstinate dogmas, their promiscuous gallantries with goats and donkeys. Had they no refinements, no curiosity, no innocent pleasures, no foibles, no tolerant scepticism? Did they know only the majesty and wickedness of the world, never its humanity? Had they never among them any rich, versatile, uncontroversial human characters? No Mrs Quicklys, no Falstaffs, no Mrs Gamps, no Jorrockses, no Piggs? Alas, none!

———————

'A scholar who means to build himself a monument must spend much of his life in acquiring knowledge which for its own sake is not worth having, and in reading books which do not in themselves deserve to be read.' (A.E. Housman in his memoir of Platt).

———————

The Bellocosi school   Feb. 1942

I was dining in Ch. Ch. on 27.11.40, on the evening when the news of our attack on Taranto came in, and conversation was about the Italian failure against Greece. Hilaire Belloc[3] was dining there too, with Frank

———————

3 Hilaire Belloc (1870–1953), poet, polemicist and Catholic apologist.

Pakenham.[4] What a wonderful fight the gallant Italians were putting up against a numerically superior enemy, he kept saying. Why, when the Italo–Greek war began (he didn't say who began it), the Italians only had two divisions in Albania. I asked why they had begun it then; but he didn't answer, merely repeating that the Italians, unprepared and outnumbered, were showing a courage and skill that was inadequately appreciated in this country, etc., etc., until his audience had dropped imperceptibly away.

Of course it was all because the Italians are popish and the Greeks aren't; but I had expected better casuistry than this from the new school of Paladins which the Holy Church, with the ingenuity of despair, has summoned to her aid. I had always thought of them as brilliant, indirect tacticians: men whose habitual platitudes are expressed in such a welter of startling paradoxes that even the fundamental truths of their Church seem, by comparison, not unreasonable. Instead, I found a plain fool.

———————

Buggers can't be choosers, as Robert Boothby[5] said, when Maurice Bowra was hesitating on the threshold of matrimony.[6]

———————

Ireland   March 1942

What delightful memories I have of my first visit to Ireland, in February 1942. How the inhabitants of that floating monkey-house clustered around us in Dublin, like pale, inquisitive ghosts around a mortal intruder, all eager

———————

4 Francis ('Frank') Pakenham, later 7th Earl of Longford (1905–2001) had as an under-graduate been thrown into a fountain at Christ Church by college hearties. He returned in 1932 as a lecturer in politics – nicknamed 'Polkinghorn' by his pupils – and was Student there 1934–1946. In 1940 he shocked his wife by converting to Catholicism without consulting her, and was henceforth a zealous proselytiser.

5 (Sir) Robert Boothby (1900–1986), exuberantly bisexual Tory MP and later life peer.

6 'He thought of marrying', Cyril Connolly wrote of Bowra, 'but I think his genius demanded an inner privacy which would never have tolerated the wear and tear of prox-imity'. Bowra proposed to Elizabeth Harman (later Countess of Longford) in 1928; to Audrey Beecham in 1936; and to Ann O'Neill (afterwards Rothermere and finally Fleming). Joan Eyres-Monsell (later Leigh Fermor) was a love of his life.

to protest their native brilliance, all bored stiff with their own pretensions, all anxious to gather scraps and titbits of information from the real world, from which, triply isolated by geography, neutrality and the censorship, they live as remote as the dwellers in Tristan da Cunha or the Falkland Islands. But it wasn't Dublin that so delighted me, – Dublin with its shrill envious provincialism, its priests and beggars, its shop-windows full of popish paste and superstitious furniture, its squalid slums, door after door each with the superscription 'God bless our Pope', leading up to the Loyola Hotel, its great monuments of English domination and oppression. It was in the country that three incidents happened which stand out in my memory, as the English public buildings in Dublin stand out from the coloured Celtic slums.

At Limerick, a town John Betjeman[7] described to me as like Harley Street set down in a bog, we called on one Stephen O'Mara.[8] He had been a rebel, I learnt, and had served his term; and now he had settled down comfortably to a lucrative bacon-monopoly, and lived in a stately white Georgian house of four storeys, crowned with an elegant balustrade, standing, detached and aristocratic, in a little walled park, with wrought iron gates and griffins on the gateposts, just across the Shannon. There we had tea, and our host bobbed about in a white coat, and gossiped and asked questions about England and the war. He plainly took us for spies, but was too polite to say so, – though he let it slip, in casual conversation, that he presumed the English government to be paying all our expenses. Limerick, he told us, took all its views on current affairs from a Sibylline oracle, an aged canon of the cathedral with Parkinsonian disease. (What kind of disease is that?, I asked. Not the sort of disease to have if you can avoid it, said Stephen O'Mara. It means, said Dickie,[9] that you can't keep still as long as you're in motion, and old men get it who sit too long in Bodley). This old canon, said O'Mara, was omniscient on three subjects, – the history of the world, racehorses, or the weather. He knew the pedigree of every racehorse foaled in his lifetime, and the exact state of the

---

7 (Sir) John Betjeman (1906–1984), poet and writer on architecture, was press attaché to Lord Rugby, the British representative in Eire, 1941–1943.

8 Stephen O'Mara (1886–1959) lived at Strand House, Limerick. A bacon curer, he was chairman of the Claremorris and Donegal bacon companies, a Sinn Fein fundraiser in the USA, Mayor of Limerick 1921–1923 and survived a murderous ambush by the Black and Tans at Clareconnel.

9 T-R was travelling with Richard Dawson (1918–1971), Eton and Christ Church.

weather on every day over the same extensive period. You'd only to ask, What sort of a day was it, Canon, on the 8th of May 1884, and he wd answer, 'Well, it was a damp, muggy morning, but it cleared up at noon, and would have been a fine afternoon but for a shower or two at teatime'. We often checked him; he was always right. This oracle had of course been consulted about the war, and 'after a preliminary bird's eye gallop over the whole history of the world', had uttered his findings. But these didn't strike me as being very profound, being oracular only in that they were unsupported by any reasoning.

Then there was the day I spent at Worlledge's house, Glenwilliam Castle, Ballingarry;[10] a house that took my fancy, and represents to me the ideal of an Irish manor-house, with its solid appearance, its peeling walls, its endless, twisted passages, its dim lights and sagging floors and ceilings, its great courtyard with a big clock-tower, like the yard of a château in Burgundy, full of horses and miscellaneous servants. And of course its wonderful situation. I stepped out in the morning, and there, on the left, was a rookery, and a natural lawn sloped gently down before me towards a pond; and looking, from the elevation of the site, through the buxom air, I could see on all sides only peaceful pasture bounded by hills over which I could imagine many a good fox-chase; and again I thought of what John Betjeman had written, in his delightful book, *Ghastly Good Taste*: 'Should a man wish to live in the 18th century, let him take with him what capital he has left, and buy one of those hundreds of empty Georgian mansions in the remote parts of Ireland. There, with his undulating park about him, the railway far distant, and never the sound of a motor-car near, he may drink himself to an honourable death, keeping his individuality alive.'

And finally I think of my last day in Co. Limerick, hunting with the Limerick hounds when I fell over a stone wall, jumping into a sunken lane, and cracked my head as I fell, with some force, on the stone wall on the opposite side. After a momentary eclipse I found myself lying on the grass verge, quite unhurt, full of high spirits, and eager to resume the chase; but a throng of people were standing around me, like a grim Druid cirque, holding their steaming horses, and saying, 'Don't let him move!' So I put my hand up to my head and found a pool of blood; and this, and the comments of the bystanders ('There's a great

10 Colonel J.P.G. Worlledge (d. 1957), a signals officer during the First World War and manager in the 1920s of a wireless station in Palestine, was appointed in 1939 to head the newly formed Radio Security Service (MI8), where he proved decent but not brilliant. He held this post until May 1941.

hole in his head', I heard one of them saying, and they all agreed, with modifications which seemed to emphasise, rather than diminish, the severity of my wound) persuaded me that I really must be hurt. So I allowed myself to be the object of various attentions, until I heard a solemn voice behind me saying, 'Someone go fetch the priest!' Here I protested. I drew the line at the priest, I said. But no; for before long, out of the corner of my eye, I saw the priest stepping briskly along, pulling elastoplast out of the more intimate recesses of his cassock: and behind him, at a more dignified hieratic pace, came his housekeeper, carrying a bowl of steaming water and a bundle of cotton wool; and after these ecclesiastical ministrations, I was taken away to a house and put on a bed in the dark. Of course I soon discovered that I wasn't hurt at all, and finally, breaking through the cocoon of elaborate injunctions, I was found eating a very hearty meal of sausages and eggs and bacon and beer and tea and toast in a conveniently placed country-house. But the Irish bush-telegraph had been at work, – for there's nothing so dear to the Irish imagination as death in the hunting-field, especially now, since an old gentleman of 88 had just broken his neck out with the Duhallow.[11] Dickie was having his horse shod in a neighbouring monastery when the news was brought to him that the priest was giving extreme unction by the roadside to his companion; and when we reached our hotel, and I sprang nimbly out of the car, a look of disappointed surprise seemed to lengthen the faces of the manageress and the head-porter, who had made ready my bed, and lit a fire in my room, and sent for the doctor, and were now waiting at the door to lift my body in.

Bach and Handel   March 1942

Bach and Handel – I always think of them together. They were born in the same year, and their joint anniversary was being celebrated when I was in Germany in 1935. And by thinking of them together I can think of the contrast between them, – Bach, that sedate Lutheran paterfamilias, whom I always envisage dining off beer and sausages, with his thirteen children like olive-plants round his table, and then pottering off to his parish organ to continue churning out that endless series of meritorious, but on the whole uninspired, exercises; and

---

11 The Duhallow Hounds, founded in 1745, hunt in the northwest of county Cork.

then Handel, alone, in Brook Street, walking rapt in the upper air, communing with immortal spirits; Handel retiring from human sight for 24 days, and then emerging with the Messiah full-blown, and going to Dublin to play it for charity; Handel managing a troupe of singers, as Shakespeare managed a troupe of players, both alike in their sublime mortality.

Ah, says Stuart Hampshire,[12] but there's no doubt in Handel, no *cri de coeur*, and I have to admit that it's true. Through the wounds of a broken heart, through the clefts of a cracked universe, great art does surely peep. But not Handel's. His is not of this kind, nor runs in this competition; for it is sublime, and sublimity has no room for doubt. It is the serene contemplation of one who sees humanity from the upper air, from such a height that its fears and sorrows, though sensed and interpreted, are but features of a various and majestic pageant.

All the same, when I hear the choir singing, with gay, reckless gusto,

> For wé like sheep
> Have er – er –erred and strayed,

I feel that Handel has perhaps too faithfully interpreted the spirit of the Anglican Church. And I think of my own cheerful expressions of contrition when my calculated irregularities are found out; as they sometimes are.

Self-mortification is the *coup de théâtre* of a wounded vanity.

Vocabulary

I said that abstract nouns ending in -ousness were a cumbrous impediment to our language, and advocated a more general use of the abstract neuter -um, as in te*diu*m, o*diu*m, con*tinu*um, re*siduu*m, de*cor*um, and other instances. So I suggested, as occasion arose, meticulum, obsequium, fastidium, supercilium, bogum, impecunium; and Charles Stuart added felicitously bibulum.

---

12 Stuart Hampshire (1914–2004), philosopher, Fellow of All Souls 1936–1940, military intelligence officer 1940–1945, Warden of Wadham 1970–1984.

Style

Style is the true elixir of life. Thoughts and theories and systems of knowledge die. St Thomas Aquinas was the Universal Doctor, – or was it the Angelic Doctor? – but I forget which, for he is now as obsolete as the mastodon. Only style could have saved him, as it has saved others, equally irrelevant to mankind, preserving them, as mammoths have been preserved, embalmed in the everlasting snow. But the poor old boy had no style. Whereas the Hebrew prophets, the Caroline divines, perhaps even Bossuet (though I find him unreadable myself), though they have outlived their significance, still have a compelling lustre. And so they float into our uncomprehending world, meaningless but majestic fragments of the past, like icebergs, detached from the frozen Pole, that drift into temperate seas.

My Mythology

The supernatural world bores me, bores me stiff, – since that day in the Christ Church Meadow when I watched it, with relief, disappearing for ever from my ken. But in the mysteries of the natural world I delight. My imagination loves to haunt great wastes and twilit spaces, and there are human characters, quite unsympathetic to me in the narrower sense, who yet fascinate me by their baroque minds or strange mental pilgrimages, – St Augustine, Dante, John Donne, Blake, El Greco, and Sir Thomas Browne. These bewitch me by their remote grandeur, like life at the bottom of the sea, or visionary habitations in the moon. In the mystical world I have my favourites too. Ghosts and monsters I can dispense with; abstractions I detest; and incubi and succubi are not necessary to my mental comfort. But an imaginary world without nymphs, fairies and mermaids is a thin, threadbare thing to me. Mermaids – not the drab seal-like portents of northern waters, but the sirens of the south – as often as they appear in poetry they enchant the very lines that enclose them:

> Io son, cantava, io son dolce serena
> Che marinari in mezzo il mar dismago.[13]

---

13 I am, she sang, I am the sweet siren/ who captivates mariners far out at sea (Dante's Dream of the Siren in canto XIX of *Purgatorio*).

And then there are the angels, the mute androgynous population of the middle air, the genial hangers-on of the remote, high-hat theological world, who lean occasionally from their spheres to influence one's destinies. In Italian paintings of the life of Christ – in Botticelli's *Nativity*, – how those angels, with their symbolic gestures, their coloured wraps, their pale, passionless faces, both exalt the secular and humanise the divine. When the bishops dropped belief in angels, I shook hands with Christianity.

The Secret Service

March 1942

How can I describe it? A colony of coots in an unventilated backwater of bureaucracy? A bunch of dependent bumsuckers held together by neglect, like a cluster of bats in an unswept barn? O for a broom, I cry, to drive them twittering hence! But expostulating voices say, No! for it is a consecrated barn protected by ancient taboos. And so another image rises in my mind, of the high-priests of effete religion mumbling their meaningless ritual to avert a famine or stay a cataclysm. And then I remember the hieratic indolence of those self-inflated mandarins, their Chinese ideograms, their green ink, their oriental insincerities, their ceremonious evasions of responsibility, their insulation from the contemporary world, and the right image has come, of Palace eunuchs in the Great Within.

Ivory Tower

March 1942

I have moments of disgust with the world, this weary treadmill of wasted effort – moments when I long for release from its injustices and disappointments, and sigh for a cool, cloistered shade where I may live the real life of devotion to an abstruse and shining ideal. 'O, for an Ivory Tower!' I cry; and at once my obedient imagination raises an Ivory Tower, like a mirage, before me, – well situated in a good hunting country, with a stately park around it, stables and cellars well-stocked, a stream of guests that come and go, and a spicy haze of malicious gossip clinging like a cloud to its battlements.

It is slightly derelict and peeling, perhaps; and a herd of elegant deer are nibbling round the deserted gazebo.

———————

Happiness   March 1942

> If it were now to die,
> 'Twere now to be most happy. For I fear,
> My soul hath her content so absolute,
> That not another comfort like to this
> Succeeds in unknown fate.

There are moments when these words of Othello come imperiously to me, demanding utterance; and I utter them. Not moments of actual exhilaration, for there is no time for such appraisal, but a little later, when the mind is beginning to disengage itself from the delight which it has not yet ceased to feel. I remember several such occasions in particular, all after hunting. Once I was riding back at dusk after a first-class hunt with the Bicester from Tittershall Wood, my face bleeding, my hat ribboned by bullfinches, my mare caked with sweat, and both of us plastered with liquid mud from splashing through the drowned water-meadows. I had had one or two falls in those big ditches, but at that time I subscribed to Kenneth Swann's doctrine,[14] that a day's hunting isn't a day's hunting without one or two cracking falls. I've forgotten the details of the hunt, but I recollect the pace, the blind, unkempt bullfinches, each with a great ditch on one side or both, the grey, melancholy winter landskip, with floods lying in the hollow fields, and then the death, at twilight, in the corner of a flooded meadow off the main road at Blackthorn, amid a small circle of steaming horses, and the doleful music of the horn, – most magical and solemn of noises when hounds are blown home on a grey winter's evening, as it is most stirring and cheery when it throws them into covert on a frosty morning.

And then there was that famous day when I thought I was too ill to hunt, having just got up the previous evening from a week in bed with the 'flu. But

———————

14 Kenneth Swann (1915–1944), Eton and Christ Church, rose to the rank of Major in the Hertfordshire Yeomanry and was decorated MC before his death in action after the Normandy landings.

I wrapped myself up and went, and we moved off from Marsh Gibbon as the dank fog was clearing, and hunted a fox for 20 miles with only one check, and that just long enough in which to drain a flask of whiskey, at Eustace's Gorse, till he went to ground at Quainton; and then a storm broke, a very deluge. But I was in the Sportsman by then, eating bacon and eggs, and drinking old beer to keep out the cold (for I had fallen into the brook, but had dried off again), and repeating those lines of Othello. Indeed, they seemed particularly apposite just then, for I felt that I might very well die when I got sober again; but, as I told Joe Bailey at the time, I didn't mind if I did die after such a hunt; and anyway, out of prudence, I was resolved to keep the dangers of sobriety at a distance. So I drove back to Oxford and drank whiskey in my bath, and never stopped drinking whiskey till dinner, when I had a quart of black beer; and then I went straight to bed with a tumbler of hot whiskey, and fell asleep, and hunted in my sleep till I awoke next morning, totally cured.

And I mustn't forget the last day of the season in 1939, when the Bicester hunted their fox to Swanbourne in the Whaddon country, and at one time Rubberneck and I climbed a tree, – at least, she got stuck between earth and heaven in a particularly stubborn bullfinch which we had taken at a gallop, thinking to break through. But when, after the noise of crashing timber, I lifted my head and opened my eyes, I found that, instead of galloping on with hounds over an open meadow, we were still in the thick of it; and climbing down I saw poor Rubberneck lodged up there in the branches like a bird's nest. It was with some difficulty that I got her down, and when I did she stood stock-still like an inanimate clothes-horse, her round, brown, race-horse eyes wide open, as if in a trance. But I pulled the thorns out of her nose and her knees and her shoulders, and mounted her, and like a whirlwind off she went, and never drooped till that great hunt was over; and then she hinted that she was lame, for she had an overreach and had cast a couple of shoes. So I led her limping back, singing my way from pub to pub, all the eight miles to Quainton; and at each pub I found a group of farmers celebrating the last and best hunt of the season, with deep and hilarious compotations, in which I joined, out of consideration to Rubberneck, that she might have a brief rest in her journey at these convenient halting-places.

But enough, for one hunting reminiscence leads to another, and unless I stop I shall anon be away, and it will be as vain then to try to stop me as to call back the Black-and-Tans when they have found a fox in the Penny-in-the-Slot at Oola, or John Milburn's beagles in the Cheviots, when they have winded the Peat-Hag hare.[15]

J.L.F. March 1942

During the fighting in Flanders, when familiar names began to appear in the Killed in Action columns of the papers, I said to myself that I must expect this, and consider myself fortunate if my more intimate friends survive, as particularly John Field, and Arthur Stewart-Liberty. Well, John Field is dead now, – at least his ship was sunk off Tobruk, and none knows what became of the crew; so of the bright influences that gave a lustre to my bare life, the brightest has been eclipsed; and after 25, I'm afraid, it's difficult to replace lost illuminations.

One of John Field's latest adventures was typical of him. He was wounded, and his ship sunk, in the battle of Crete; but he was rescued from the sea and taken to a hospital on the north coast of the island and given an anaesthetic. When he came to, the Germans had landed and captured the hospital; but he got out of bed on some pretext, and made a sudden dash for it. The German sentries fired at him, but missed, and when he had shaken off the pursuit he crept into a ditch and spent 24 hours there, sleeping off the effects of the anaesthetic. Then he slipped across the island, still in his pyjamas, to the south coast; found a small boat; made his way out in it into the Mediterranean; and was later picked up and taken to Egypt, where he recovered in hospital and rejoined his unit.

How much I owe personally and distinctly to John Field it isn't easy to say. I think he's the only one of my contemporaries whom I've put in a niche. For the characters we venerate aren't those whose qualities can be explained as the results, perhaps complex and oblique, but reached by known processes, of definite experiences. With these we sympathise, but our admiration goes rather to those who are what they are inexplicably, simply, by the direct work of nature. John Field was one of such. His generosity, his vitality, his tastes were all natural, unqualified and, therefore, infectious. The petty emotions

---

15 The Guyzance beagles, of which Sir John Milburn (1918–1985) was master, were hunted from a hamlet near Alnwick.

which he never entertained he could never understand. He wasn't interested in them. This quality of saintliness, the quality not of the Augustines, Dominics, or Loyolas, but of St Francis of Assisi, St Bernard of Clairvaux, St Francis Xavier; the quality that calls not for psychologists and interpreters, but for votaries and apostles.

Self-Revelation:
Stuart Hampshire   April 1942

I am not particularly interested in my own character, but I am passionately interested in my feelings and sensations, – not because they are mine, but as examples of their kind. I like to compare them with the experiences of the people I admire and envy. I believe that by effort and concentration feelings and sensations can be developed and exploited, and that it must be done. I am extremely introspective, and also vain. I loathe competition of all kinds, and consequently despise and reject its results, whatever they may be, even if they are favourable to me. I am not particularly vain about my intellectual abilities, and will admit to myself deficiencies in this respect without pain.

I am extremely lazy, and naturally a dilettante. I like eating, drinking, talking, reading books, listening to music, and looking at pictures. I am totally without ambition. I do not want to be rich, but I wish I had an unearned income, because I hate earning money. I am not a snob, except in the sense that I hate the English middle-class, particularly the upper middle-class, which I know so well. I do not want to have possessions, or a settled social position. I find it very pleasant and easy to be pleasant and sympathetic to people, but there are only three or four people whose death would cause me the slightest pain; I like friends as a periodical source of pleasure, but their disappearance does not affect me. I like people either because they are clever, or in some way physically attractive, – voices particularly either attract or repel me – or because they admire me and want to be an audience. I like gentleness, or the possibility of gentleness, above all other human qualities. I am prejudiced against successful and effective people.

I am absolutely and without qualification an escapist. I like all forms of escape from reality. I detest frankness, and calling a spade a spade.

I find complete satisfaction in three things, – being in love, reading books, and ordinary sexual pleasures. Without the first I would definitely prefer (though by a small margin) to be dead; the second is a nearly but not quite indispensable addition. I am not naturally monogamous, and slightly homosexual. I wish I were more homosexual, because I very much prefer the society of men to the society of women. I dislike manly men, and I despise old age in every form. I like boys.

I am extremely nervous and very sentimental; I often wish to weep, and sometimes do. I have moods of extreme elation. I am never shy. I repress and conceal as many of my emotions as I can. Outbursts, which have accumulated over a long period, are the consequences of this repression. I approve and feel exclusive and unqualified loyalties and corresponding hatreds. I am capable of great dissimulation, – that is one of my vanities. I am extremely vain about my capacity to perceive the moods and motives of other people.

I am extremely attached to, or repelled by, places – more than by friends or acquaintances – both for sentimental and aesthetic reasons.

I have no picture of what my life will be in ten, or even two, years from now. I do not look forward and make plans. But I love recalling the past in my mind, as much as I loathe returning to it in experience.

I loathe pain and unhappiness, and so far have avoided it with two exceptions: I was horrified when I saw how unhappy it is possible to be. I am not afraid to die. I know precisely in what circumstances I would commit suicide. I am very pessimistic about the world in general, and think optimism a sign of stupidity. I loathe Christianity and Christian emotion. I do not even understand the meaning of 'humility' and 'forgiveness'.

I like elaborate good manners and sophistication, and all forms of perversion. I dislike docility more than any other quality; that is why I find nearly all women unsatisfactory. I have a romantic belief in genius and great men. The theme in poetry which affects me most is that of transience – '*où sont les neiges d'antan*'.[16] The writer who satisfies me most is Marcel Proust; and Shakespeare's Sonnets alone among the great works of literature seems to me absolutely perfect and not boring; I am often bored by Shakespeare's plays.

16 Where are last year's snows? (refrain of François Villon's 'Ballade des Dames du Temps Jadis').

Rimbaud has a shrine, and of this I am ashamed; Flaubert has a shrine as a man: I would like to have been Flaubert.

I am a sentimental aesthete and only an intellectual by accident. I sometimes think I shall myself discover some important general truth, and I always behave as if I believed this. I am only interested in generalities, and not at all in facts.

I think Carmen is the greatest short story in the world, and I really prefer Racine's plays to Shakespeare's, because they have more gentleness and simplicity; I am ashamed of this also.

Every year I like fewer and fewer books and fewer and fewer people. But every year the pleasures of memory become more and more intense; also visual pleasures, and the pleasures of patterns of habit and routine.

I loathe all forms of Puritanism. I liked ordinary soldiers, because their attitude was usually expressed as 'fuck 'em all!', and because they had fixed and unshakeable loyalties. I like people to be dependent on me.

I want to live in a small space, and make marauding expeditions into the outside world at intervals when I choose. I am aware, but not ashamed of my quite abnormal immaturity.

I am not interested in action or men of action. I don't like public places or public faces.

There are only about six books in the world which excite me as intensely and as constantly as any great work of music. But there is so little music, and there are so many books. I loathe second-rate music, and I like second-rate books.

B-W

I'm afraid B-W's ideal of the vocation of a don isn't a very high one.[17] He once explained to me what a lot of work he had to do when first elected at Ch. Ch., in order to be ready for all likely contingencies. 'O yes', he said, 'it was some time before I was able to live on my fat'.

---

17 Barrington-Ward's vocation lay as a champion member of Oxford University Golf Club.

Literary Judgments   April 1942

Since the beginning of the War, I have revised all my literary values so completely that now I refuse to give any positive judgment on any work of literature that I haven't read, or re-read, since then. It's a delightful position to be in, – to have the whole of literature suddenly presented to one again, as it were, for the first time. What is the cause of this phenomenon?

Firstly, I think, Charterhouse, that skeleton in my cupboard; or at least Irvine.[18] I like Irvine. He has read and travelled and looked at pictures; he has a capacity for enjoying what he has decided to enjoy; and he always gives me excellent salads when I take lunch or supper with him. But as an educator he is a disaster. He says, with some complacency, that he is 'a full man', which means that he has done his reading, knows what he likes, and confines himself to that field of limited, but proved, enjoyment. That isn't in itself a fault, since (for all I know) he may have acquired his own taste for himself. But (what *is* a fault) he doesn't turn his pupils loose to graze even in his private field. He leads them up to every plant in it, tells them its qualities before they eat of it, and leads them on again before they have digested it. 'This is a good corner', he says, 'we shall spend some time here. Don't touch that, that's a buttercup – they don't agree with me; but here's a clover – eat it, for it is sweet and nutritive, as I will explain when you've finished it.' And so his pupils never acquire a taste of their own, or the standards by which they can develop one. They go up to the university with a borrowed, or rather imposed, and, what is worse, accepted and final taste, which they can neither escape nor extend beyond the limitations implicit in it. And after all, these limitations are great. For a schoolboy's taste is based, at best, on a feeling for brilliance of rhetoric, or majesty of style, or the evocation of visual images. The vast range of emotional experience, the finer subtilties of language, the infinite variety of character, are as yet unknown. These, when they come, bring new standards, which will lead to a gradual revision of earlier judgments, and a heightening of many former, and discovery of many new, pleasures – provided that those earlier standards have not been given, and accepted, with such finality that all further experiment is renounced. Irvine gave them with this finality.

---

18 Andrew Irvine (1881–1967), 'The Uncle', master at Charterhouse 1914–1946, housemaster 1927–1943, only taught books that he thought were first-class.

Secondly, the War, which, having for various reasons turned my attention back to literature, enabled me to make this discovery. Since the war began, I have re-read a great deal of literature, including all Homer, Pindar, Thucydides, Lucretius, Horace, and much of Dante, Shakespeare, Milton and Tennyson; and on nearly all of them I found my views so altered, the bias of my pleasure in them so changed, and that pleasure, often, so heightened, that now I expect the same experience with everything I re-read, and automatically doubt the validity of all my previous opinions.

This is, as I have said, a delightful position to be in. All the same, I do rather resent the waste of my earlier years, believing as I do (with a belief that almost preys upon me) that the imaginative faculties of man are gradually contracting from the age of about 25 onwards, and the possibility of revelation in the same measure receding.

Women   April 1942

In general, women repel me. I discovered this truth sitting on top of a bus that was taking me down the Haymarket the other day. The contemplation of my female fellow-passengers made me shiver. 'But they aren't all like this', I protested to myself, and I looked down into the street to make sure. Alas, they were no better; and in the restaurant, at lunch, I looked around me, and it was just the same. Without features, without grace, soft, shapeless lumps, like brown-paper parcels, or the wingless females of the less interesting moths, they repel without fascinating. I put this to Stuart Hampshire. 'They cumber the earth', he said, and remarked on their ugly gait and soft complaisant grimaces; to which I added other details, their foolish birdlike minds, their twittering voices. But then I thought of those women whom I so like, who belie their sex by possessing features and understanding the art of growing old; aged dowagers with aquiline faces, who sit erect and stately in their high chairs, giving orders to their servants, and disapproving the low standards of the age in life, taste and manners – the three arts of which women may, without impertinence, be a judge.

Bayle   April 1942

I read in Bayle that the pious bishop Aldhelm[19] used to cool and overcome his appetites by standing up to his neck in a pond at night. But his appetites do not seem to have been particularly formidable, since he also (I learn from the same source) took naked virgins into his bed, and then exasperated the Devil, and perhaps also the virgins (for, as Bayle observes, it's unlikely that they took the risk without being ready for the eventualities), by singing Psalms rather than continuing the process. And I understood also that the Empress Agnes, widow of Henry II, enquired of St Peter Damiani by an intermediary bishop whether it was lawful for a man, when in the act of copulation, to sing a Psalm; and received an affirmative answer, based on the statement of St Paul, in I Timothy, that God may be praised in all places.

De Quincey   May 1942

I've just read de Quincey's Confessions of an Opium Eater. It was M.E.[20] who introduced me to this delightful book. M.E. has high standards, an exact, lucid and discriminating mind, and a love of truth combined with ingenuous humility; but until May 1942 I don't think he had read any books, – I don't mean only that he had read no books that might have developed a literary taste, but that he hadn't read any that could have corrupted it either. A radio amateur's *vade-mecum* and a bird-book for the pocket probably constitute his sole forms of reading. His taste is consequently non-existent but potentially pure.

Well, one day in May 1942 he came into my office and asked if any of us had heard of a writer called Thomas de Quincey, and a book called his *Confessions*. Was it a good book? Did qualified judges regard it with favour, or with disfavour? He seemed relieved when Gilbert pronounced it first-rate, and Stuart Hampshire said it was the best English autobiography after Gibbon. 'I just picked it up in my billet last night', he explained, 'and I was so enthralled by it that I couldn't put it down'; and he went on to give an enthusiastic account of de Quincey's style. Now my silence, all this time, was considered

---

19 Aldhelm (d. 709), abbot of Malmesbury and bishop of Sherborne.
20 Kenneth Morton Evans.

a very curious exception to the general rule; and in the end I had to explain that I had never read a word of any work by de Quincey, – a revelation that was received with a good deal of surprise and complacency. 'In that case', said M.E., 'I must start your literary education at once'; and that evening a copy of de Quincey's *Confessions* was delivered at my billet, and I read it with unfailing delight, – the humour, the humanity, the verbal fancies and felicities, and the delightful exotic imagination, – I found M.E.'s judgment on it quite admirable.

On p. 317, I noticed, de Quincey says, 'I know not whether my reader is aware that many children have a power of painting, as it were, on the darkness all sorts of phantoms'. I had this power, if it is properly called a power, and can remember vividly how I used to be tormented for whole nights, as it seemed, by an endless kaleidoscope of brightly coloured symmetrical forms which moved against the blackness, constantly merging into, and re-emerging from, each other, until I was quite distracted by them. Once they had begun, no power seemed capable of putting a stop to them; and they generally came if I woke up in the night, rather than before I had gone to sleep.

S.I.S.   May 1942

I am sick of them, sick to death of them, that nest of timid and corrupt incompetents, without ideals or standards, concerned only with the security of their own discreditable existence, bum-sucking under the backstairs of bureaucracy. Weak men on the defensive, who will do and say anything through fear, they dread improvement, for improvement means change, and change may mean the shaking of a few old somnolent moths out of long undisturbed curtains and the brushing of cobwebs from dark, un-noticed corners. I would rather grill in the desert with unambitious idealists who have something to sacrifice, something to sacrifice it for, and willingness to sacrifice it, than sit here in the shade and watch the endless, meaningless, purposeless ritual of these Roman augurs.

Crecora   May 1942

I ought not to have omitted Crecora from my impressions of Ireland, that stone-built country house in Co. Limerick, with its heavy, Florentine gables, where Dickie and I stopped after a day's hunting; and at once two of the miscellaneous servants that hang about all Irish country houses came out to hold our horses, and we went in, and there was a great circular hall with green-and-white plasterwork on the walls, as in Trinity College, Dublin, and the Royal Irish Academy, and other 18th century brick houses. The height of the room, and its spare, tasteful furniture, gave an air of spacious civility to the place, – an island of culture in the pastoral solitudes. Truly my spiritual home is in Ireland, in one of those 18th century houses, like Crecora, that have not yet been turned into monasteries, or nunneries, or creameries, whose peeling walls and overgrown gardens yet preserve a pattern of antique stateliness and hospitality. They have libraries full of books – for lack of communications has forced their owners to discover the value of leisure, from which their English counterparts, with their cars, their conventions, and their cocktail-parties, so madly flee – and stables full of horses, and cellars full of drink. For of course there was plenty to drink in Crecora, and another casual servitor, emerging from the stable and donning a white jacket, brought it out for us, decanters of port and Irish whiskey, which we drank in good measure, being tired and wet. Fuller said that when hospitality died in England it gave its last groan among the yeomen of Kent; but its ghost still lingers in the country houses of Ireland.

———————

Stuart Hampshire doesn't like clubs. He says they're full of the musty smell of old age.

———————

Magic Lines   May 1942

When I read poetry, certain passages have upon me, as they had upon Housman, an involuntary physical effect. An electric thrill or tremor runs over the surface of my skin. I cannot prevent it, or produce it artificially, but I can elicit it again and again, automatically, by repeating again and again the lines that produce it. Once I went on repeating such a passage to see how often the same response would be elicited, and it took ten repetitions to exhaust the potency of the stimulus. But what, I asked myself one day in April 1942, is the quality that produces this effect? It isn't rhetoric, or dramatic power, or magnificence of style, or minuteness of observation, – although all these things inspire or delight me, they don't cause the same exquisite physical thrill. Is it anything that can be discovered or defined? So I began a great inquisition, and discovered it to be the quality I call 'the magic of single lines', a quality independent (it seemed when I looked at a few random examples) alike of the matter contained and of the style employed; for it seemed to be tied up with no common subject, no particular mannerisms of expression. Could it be the undefined quality of pure poetry? Inspired by the hope that I might define the undefined, I then began a great statistical survey, a domesday book of Magic Lines, that I might examine them all together, discover their common features, and comprehend them all in a single definition. Shakespeare and Keats, I found, are the richest quarries, with Milton a good way behind. Homer has only one certainty –

πὰρ ποταμὸν κελάδοντα, παρὰ ῥοδανὸν δονακῆα[21]

unless we include another in which the conventional epithets give, by accident it would seem, a magical effect

ἢ γὰρ μάλα πολλὰ μεταξὺ
οὔρεά τε σκιόεντα θάλασσά τε ἠχήεσσα[22]

Lucretius has a few magic lines, like

Per loca pastorum deserta atque otia dia;[23]

Virgil practically none – he nearly always just fails through preciosity. But before coming to conclusions, here are instances taken systematically from Shakespeare, and a few chosen more at random from Milton.[24]

Shakespeare

in shady cloister mew'd
To live a barren sister all your life,
Chanting faint hymns to the cold fruitless moon.   MND

---

21 By the roaring river, by the waving rushes (Homer, *Iliad* 18.576).

22 Because many indeed are the things between us – shadow-clad mountains and silence-shattering sea (Achilles at Homer, *Iliad* 1.156–7, about himself and the Trojans).

23 Through the deserted haunts of shepherds, and the divine places of their rest (Lucretius, *De rerum natura*).

24 T-R noted a hundred extracts; only a sample is reproduced here.

Night's candles are burnt out, and jocund day
Stands tiptoe on the misty mountain-tops.   Romeo & Juliet

Is there no pity sitting in the clouds
That sees into the bottom of my grief?   Romeo & Juliet

           O here
Will I set up my everlasting rest,
And shake the yoke of inauspicious stars
From this world-wearied flesh.   Romeo & Juliet

Comfort's in Heaven, and we are on the earth,
Where nothing lives but crosses, cares and grief.   Richard II

           On such a night
Stood Dido with a willow in her hand
Upon the wild sea banks, and waft her love
To come again to Carthage.   Merchant of Venice

           ditties highly penn'd,
Sung by a fair queen in a summer's bower
With ravishing division, to her lute.   Henry IV pt 1

To turn and wind a fiery Pegasus
And witch the world with noble horsemanship.   Henry IV pt 1

To this worm-eaten hold of ragged stone.   Henry IV pt 2

And to relief of lazars and weak age,
Of indigent faint souls past corporal toil.   Henry V

Five hundred poor I have in yearly pay
Who twice a day their wither'd hands hold up
Toward heaven, to pardon blood.   Henry V

When time is old, or hath forgot itself,
When waterdrops have worn the stones of Troy,
And blind oblivion swallowed cities up.   Troilus & Cressida

Again in complete steel
Revisit'st thus the glimpses of the moon.　　　Hamlet

O that this too solid flesh would melt,
Thaw, and resolve itself into a dew.　　　Hamlet

This goodly frame, the earth, seems to me a
　　　sterile promontory.　　　Hamlet

O timid soul, that struggling to be free,
Art more engaged!　　　Hamlet

As mad as the vex'd sea, singing aloud,
Crowned with rank fumiter and furrow-weeds,
With burdocks, hemlock, nettles, cuckoo-flowers,
Darnel, and all the idle weeds that grow
In our sustaining corn.　　　King Lear

The murmuring surge,
That on the unnumber'd idle pebbles chafe,
Cannot be heard so high.　　　King Lear

Bare ruin'd choirs, where late the sweet birds sang　sonnet 73

Milton

Over some wide water'd shore
Swinging slow with sullen roar　　　Il Penseroso

calling shapes, and beckoning shadows dire,
And airy tongues that syllable men's names
On sands, and shores, and desert wildernesses.　　　Comus

Wondering tell
Of Babel, and the works of Memphian kings.　　　Paradise Lost

> Who shall tempt with wandering feet
> The dark, unbottom'd, infinite Abyss?   Paradise Lost

> From their blissful bowers
> Of amaranthine shade, fountain, or spring,
> By the waters of life, where'er they sat,
> In fellowships of joy   Paradise Lost

> O dark, dark, dark amid the blaze of noon,
> Irrecoverably dark, total eclipse,
> Without all hope of day.   Samson Agonistes

> But now with head declin'd,
> Like a fair flower surcharg'd with dew, she weeps.   Samson Agonistes

Having collected all these instances together, I now see what this quality is. It is the concentration within a small compass of emotional and imaginative experience. Homer and Milton, two of my favourite poets, have it comparatively rarely, because, although their imagination is no less than that of Shakespeare, it is more diffuse in its presentation. They lead us through their worlds, – Homer through his serene pastoral and maritime world, with its unruffled humanity and divinity dividing the possession of nature, Milton through his baroque, exotic, vast, twilit world – by hand, pointing out the details with almost professional skill, till the accumulation of detail has built a complete picture in our minds, and we know where we are. But Shakespeare doesn't accommodate his genius thus to the slowness and gradualness of our perception; he shows us the whole world in a single sudden glimpse; and it is the capacity to concentrate in a single glimpse the vast world of emotion or imagination which other poets patiently point out to us that makes magic lines. It is a capacity of concentration in two elements, – concentration of perception and of expression; and where Virgil fails is in the former, – he has not the range of either imagination or feeling to give body to his art, and therefore his stylistic miracles, since they convey neither intensity of lyrical feeling, nor vividness of imagination, are always, to me, somewhat watery and pretty. Shakespeare, although (very unlike Virgil) he was a careless writer who 'never blotted a line', has this double faculty to an astonishing degree. He penetrates to the remote world of the human fancy, to the elevated world of passionless philosophy, to the buried world of the human heart, and the mysteries that he finds there he brings back not in meaningless fragments, nor in tedious complexity, but concentrated and compressed in a crystalline bubble, which he tumbles carelessly before us as a casual stage property.

Autobiographies   May 1942

There are two kinds of Autobiographies, – Confessions and Reminiscences. Now reminiscences should be written in old age, – they don't deal with a single life in the first instance, but with a variety of historical and social incidents which derive a certain unity by their impact upon a single life. But Confessions, which deal with the impressions and development of a single personality, should be written at 30; for it's only the early years of an individual that are psychologically and humanly interesting – the years when the mind, under a series of influences, is seeking, in this or that form of experience, or in this or that philosophy, a pattern whereby to regulate its course through the years that follow, when external influences no longer excite so powerfully, and the mind is closed to new revelations. Perhaps, on this theory, I should have made the age for writing confessions earlier than 30; but few men have a decent style much before 30, so it's a safe choice. I will even admit (provided the interval isn't misused, by the writer's either over-dramatising his early years, or narrating them in a spirit too different from that in which they were experienced) that a man may postpone the actual composition of his confessions to a later date; but the history itself shouldn't carry the author beyond the age of 30.

I'm aware that the greatest of English autobiographies is an exception to this rule, but then Gibbon's autobiography is neither memoirs nor confessions, but a history of the development of *The Decline and Fall of the Roman Empire*, and is therefore outside my jurisdiction. On the other hand de Quincey's *Confessions of an Opium Eater*, George Moore's *Confessions of a Young Man*, James Joyce's *Portrait of the Artist as a Young Man* and Winston Churchill's *My Early Years* (all admirable works) conform obligingly to my rules; as does Newman's *Apologia*, which, although I won't allow anyone to admire it, is still of psychological interest as a study in exceptionally morbid vivisection.

The Legacy of Religion May 1942

What good has Religion done in the world, I sometimes ask myself. And at once I think of intellectual bondage, of Jesuitical education, of hypocritical professions, of vindictive cruelty, and the crass, incompetent apathy of parasitical priests. But these hot, immediate emotions soon pass off, and I find myself repeating a rolling series of hypnotic polysyllables which, but for religion, might never have existed to make the human tongue worth manipulating: Anchorite, Baptistery, Basilica, Canonical, Cardinal, Carmelite, Catacomb, Catechumen, Chasuble, Cloister, Commination, Consistory, Conventual, Coenobitic, Corybant, Dithyramb, Ecclesiastical, Encyclical, Enthusiast, Epiphany, Eremite, Eucharist, Evangelist, Exegetical, Genuflexion, Gnostic, Gymnosophist, Heresiarch, Heterodoxy, Hierarchy, Homoonsian, Iconoclastic, Idiorhythmic, Inquisition, Litany, Liturgical, Missionary, Monastic, Mystagogue, Paradise, Pentateuch, Propaganda, Psalmody, Quadragesima, Quasimodo, Reliquary, Septuagint, Seraphim, Supererogatory, Tympanum, Ultramontane, – let alone all those eloquent sects and heresies, – Manichaeans, Maronites, Nestorians, Circumcellions, – like the sands of the sea for number. Can football, can cricket, can winter-sports, cocktail-bars, or philandering – can even foxhunting or falconry produce a constellation of vocables that can twinkle in the presence of these?

The Bogs of Ireland June 1942

When Dickie and I were walking in Connemara from Leenam to Clifden, we came to Kylemore nunnery, whence it was our purpose to strike across the hills direct to Clifden – a distance of about 8 miles; but we found no living soul in the nunnery-precincts, to whom we could apply for precise directions, except the old gardener; and as he heard our intention, his jaw dropped and his eyes popped, and he implored us earnestly, with many highly secular oaths (such as always flourish best in the neighbourhood of cloisters and churches), not to think of any such thing, for there were bogs and loughs and treacherous morasses and Jesus only knew what else up in those hills, for none of the natives would ever venture thither to find out, but many a fine young man he had heard tell of, who had rashly attempted the passage and never been seen again. The vehemence of his entreaties almost persuaded us to go round by the road, but it was a long way round, so we decided to take a second opinion; for that old man, we said, has obviously never been up the hills, and to him, as to all primitive valley-dwellers, they are another element, involved in a mist of superstition, the haunt of bog-dwelling banshees and leprechauns, as foreign as the peaks of Olympus to the lowlanders of Greece. So we walked on till we came to a house in the valley, surrounded by trees. It seemed deserted at first, but as we approached it we heard the sound of rather ragged religious chanting – it was just like that scene in the *Odyssey* when Eurylochus and his companions,[25] exploring the enchanted isle, lit upon a clearing in a dell, and found a trim house in it, and Circe singing therein as she plied her loom; only our Circe wasn't responsible for the singing, which came from indoors, nor was she plying the loom, but scrubbing the conventual undershifts at a laundry-table outside the back-door of the house; for she was a nun, and a pretty young nun too, and it was hither, evidently, that the whole colony had temporarily swarmed from their castellated Victorian-gothic citadel on the hillside. She seemed a bit abashed, when I addressed her, and ran indoors; whereupon the singing ceased for a moment, and then went on again, and she came out, affable and unabashed having (I presumed) obtained a dispensation to speak to us. But when we spoke of going across the hills, she looked at us in horror, as if we were creatures whom things mortal moved not at all; for having swallowed the camel of the True Faith, who was she to strain at the gnat of the quaking bogs in the hills of Connemara? 'Great green places', she assured us, 'that you never do see till you be in them, and then down you do go' – and here she made a demure ecclesiastical duck to indicate engulfment – 'and up you never do come'. She recommended us to the steward's boy for confirmation, and he gave it, for certain sure; but by this time our faith was beginning to wear thin, and in the end we struck up the hills as we had intended, and came, before long, to a herd's cottage; and the herd, being a dweller in that cool, sceptical, upper element, uninhibited by the superstitions of the valley-dwellers beneath, was surprised when we spoke of the possibility of bogs in his heritage. 'Sure', he said, 'there were none at all'; and he was quite right, for we traversed the whole eight miles or so of moor without ever wetting our shoes in those murderous but mythical swamps.

––––––––––––––

25 Eurylochus was Ulysses' mutinous companion who did not taste Circe's potions.

Art and the Counter-Reformation   June 1942

Why did Italian painting fail with the Counter-Reformation? Is there a distinctive character in Counter-Reformation religious art? Is a contracting ideology, like that of the Counter-Reformation, necessarily incompatible with art? What of El Greco? These were the large questions which Dickie Dawson and I were ventilating, as we walked from the grove of Delphi (in Connemara) along the valley of the Glenummera. But I had no doubts, for my theories fit all facts and emerge with effortless infallibility from the swamps and quagmires of the most complex problems. There are, I said, forms of art, which hold in perfection (once perfection is attained) but a little moment, because, once they are perfect, the impulse to use them excites no response save in the second-rate artist; so that although some great artists are pioneers, whose constructive achievement, though great, yet leaves the possibility of some further progress to their successors, the artist who perfects a form makes it final and obsolete, and has therefore no successors. Now this, I said, happened in Italy. The Florentine school, the Venetian school, could have no successors in their own traditions, and their epigone must either break away, as El Greco broke away from Venice, and, ignoring the giant figures who lowered like forbidding schoolmasters from the days of the Renaissance, looked back to the Byzantinism of his Levantine home, or, like Raphael, pick for jewels, like a jackdaw, among existing masterpieces. If there is no specifically Counter-Reformation art, I said, that is because the Counter-Reformation was a deliberate limitation of the human spirit, after the intoxicating liberation of the Renaissance, at a time when the forms of art then discovered had all been brought to the dead end of perfection. There was neither the impulse to make new discoveries, nor room for further development of the old.

Canon of Style   June 1942

The sole warranted masters of English prose style now are: Francis Bacon, John Donne, Thomas Hobbes, Sir Thomas Browne, Gibbon, George Moore. This canon is final, and supersedes all previous final canons.

Apparitions   June 1942

I've always been interested in apparitions since that night in the early summer of 1938 when I saw one myself. It was an elemental, Felix Ingham[26] told me afterwards, – a very frightening apparition, like a great black gorilla, with long arms hanging straight down from its stooping shoulders; and it sidled slowly round my bed, from foot to head, always facing me, until it was out of my sight. But I knew it was still there, leaning over me from behind, had I dared to look round at it. I adjured it several times, in a loud voice, to go away. 'What do you want?' I asked it, and getting no answer, 'Paulus', I said, 'what are you doing here?' But still it said nothing, so I shouted, 'Go away, Paulus!' and then I put out a hand, gingerly, and turned the light on, and looked round, and it had disappeared. My general scepticism was outraged by this apparition, for certainly I hadn't slept at all, although I must have been declining into drowsiness or I wouldn't have given it a name. But what my thoughts were about before I saw it I don't know, for sudden fear at its appearance drove them completely away.

This incident made me seek to rationalise apparitions, and it was while I was in camp with the Life Guards that I achieved my theory. For the mess of the Life Guards at Pirbright, having been a mortuary, was said to be haunted, and there were some well-authenticated stories about it, – how a young subaltern, sitting there late and alone, had suddenly rushed out in terror, and absolutely refused to return; for although he had seen nothing (unlike a sergeant, who had a similar experience, but who explained his emotion by an undefined horror which he claimed to have seen), he had become aware of a baseless but compelling fear which had driven him out of the place. And I had a dream, too, while with the Life Guards, which suggested some psychological possibilities to me, and contributed to my theory.

The study of dreams shows us that real physical sensations are often incorporated into them, and sometimes end by waking us up. But in these cases, instead of the sensation breaking in upon the dream, the dream seems to lead naturally and inevitably to the sensation. Thus a noise, that is a natural incident in the dream, will develop into an alarm-bell, etc., which will wake us up. In other words a shock, which would shake us rapidly from one mental

---

26 Felix Ingham (1912–1992), scoutmaster of Standlake sea scouts, proprietor of an Old Bond Street travel agency specialising in Alpine sports.

state into another, is prevented by the unconscious working of the mind, which interposes an explanatory fiction to act as a mental shock-absorber; and this interposition is done so rapidly that time seems not to exist, but the shock, when it is consciously appreciated, seems to follow after the fiction which has been called in to explain it. Suppose then, I asked myself, that a sudden sensation of fear was to assail the mind in a similar drowsy and imaginative state. Would not the mind then unconsciously interpose a similar fiction, which would seem to explain this emotion? And may it not be that there are certain places which are invested with an atmosphere that causes, in sensitive (or, as we say, psychic) people, the emotion of fear, just as some places have an atmosphere causing melancholy, or exaltation, or religious awe? I believe that there are such places, – we call them haunted places on account of the phenomena which our minds create in order to explain the emotions of fear which they inspire. Our minds naturally respond to this atmosphere more readily at night, when the critical faculties are drowsy, and the imagination is loose, and darkness makes it easier to people the air with phantoms; and since the atmosphere of a single haunted place is constant, the minds of different people will supply similar phantoms to excuse the fear it causes.

So I elaborated my theory, and it seemed very good, and I explained it to Dickie Dawson over a bottle of claret in Clifden, Connemara. 'But why', he asked, 'are there no delightful apparitions, evoked to explain sensations of delight and exaltation, such as are also inspired by certain surroundings?' 'Because', I said, 'emotions of fear are caused, or at least assisted, by the circumstances of loneliness and darkness, which work upon the imagination, and help it to breed phantoms. But feelings of exaltation are encouraged rather by daylight and conviviality, by conversation and champagne, and such circumstances, which are less encouraging to the visionary fancy; or by works of art, which are themselves apparitions of delight, and need no airy coadjutors. And besides', I said, 'though rare, there are such apparitions. Saints and great artists have seen them, men who, in the clear solitudes of the intellectual world, in gardens and upon mountain-tops, and when life has dawned after long inward struggles, have seen, suddenly, the heavens opening, and have smelt the smells of Paradise. But we worldlings' (and we ordered another bottle of claret) 'are more likely to see elementals'.

Frank Pakenham   June 1942

Frank Pakenham is a wonderful character. His behaviour is constant only in that it is quite unpredictable. A fall on the head in a steeplechase, and he became a socialist overnight; a biff on the nose from one of Sir Oswald Mosley's praetorians, and Frank is a Roman Catholic. And now it is Anglo-Irish relations of which he has become the sole and jealous custodian.[27] 'I've been engaged for more years than I care to remember in improving Anglo-Irish relations', he assured me, and added (what no one doubts) that he took them very seriously. I'm afraid I've never been able to learn what improvements Frank has actually achieved in this line, as I haven't yet found anyone, in England or Ireland, who takes his activities seriously; but certainly he preaches the gospel of Mr de Valera very insistently, and he is now struggling with the obsolete Irish language in order to be the better armed in his hazardous encounters. For like all frightened fanatics, Frank has discovered a vast and diabolical Plot against his chosen people. On the one hand he sees holy Ireland, a sixth-century Arthurian land, where the saintly de Valera, unversed in the wiles of the world, and protected only by Frank in shining armour, innocently fondles the milk-white hind of the Roman Church; and on the other hand, half-hidden in sinister twilight, he sees the Conspiracy, vast and complex, supported by infinite resources, and organised with devilish malice, ingenuity and resolution. Why the leader of this great conspiracy should be myself, who have never expressed any views on Irish politics, or been to Ireland before this year, I don't understand; but that is the role for which I've been cast in this private melodrama, – a sinister figure of vast power and inscrutable

---

27 This is amusing but inaccurate. Pakenham worked for the Conservative Research Department 1930–1932, and was a leader writer on the *Daily Mail*, before returning to teach at Christ Church. His conversion to Labour was a slow process begun by his wife, who was a socialist. He resigned from the Carlton Club as late as 1935 after publishing a book, *Peace by Ordeal*, sympathetic to Irish nationalism and Eamon de Valera. During the 1935 general election, at which his wife stood as a Labour parliamentary candidate, he was election agent to A.P. Herbert, who was elected as Independent MP for Oxford University. Pakenham was beaten up in the Carfax Assembly Rooms, Oxford by Mosley's Blackshirts in 1936 (suffering concussion, two black eyes and injured kidneys) but this had no part in his conversion to Catholicism in 1940. Together with a visit to Hitler's Germany, his beating led him to join the Labour Party, become Labour councillor for Cowley in 1937 and Labour parliamentary candidate for Oxford City in 1938. He was sent as Ministry of Information delegate to Dublin in 1939, but failed to woo de Valera.

purposes; and whenever my cloven foot touches the enchanted island, then the true knight Sir Pakenham must put on his magic armour, and prick forth to the rescue of St Valera and the milk-white hind.

I first got a hint of this interesting hallucination shortly before I went to Ireland for the first time, in February 1942. 'Frank, I'm going to Dublin next week', I said to him over the telephone; 'hadn't you better come and lunch with me tomorrow and give me the low-down?' There was an embarrassed silence, and then, 'As a matter of fact, I won't', a cold voice responded, somewhat uncomfortably; 'Dublin's one of the few places where my credit's still fairly high, and I'm not going to ruin it by sponsoring an obvious spy.' I laughed at this sally, but no, it wasn't a sally. Frank was quite serious. 'Oh, come, Frank', I said, 'I'm only going to escape from the war for a fortnight and get some foxhunting'. But it was no good. 'Of course you'll have a cover', he said, rather contemptuously; and when I suggested that anyhow he should come and lunch with me, and we would never mention Ireland, he still refused. 'If you're going to Ireland', he said, 'I'd rather not be connected with you at all'. And lest I should be in any doubt about his attitude he warned me that the Irish would soon know all about me, that I couldn't escape their detectives, and that British intelligence officers had been murdered in Dublin before now.

Well, I went to Ireland, and wasn't murdered, but greatly enjoyed my visit, and made friends, and decided to go again on my next leave; and it was on this second visit, when Dickie and I were lunching at the Unicorn, that I saw Frank walking into the restaurant with a guest. Of course I waved genially from my seat, but all I got in reply was a Parthian glance of horror as Frank shepherded his guest to the most distant corner of the room. I wasn't going to allow this, so when I'd finished my lunch I sauntered mischievously over to his table, smiling affably as he shrank in his chair, like a rabbit before an advancing weasel, and we chatted, and then I left him. 'Of course you must see that you put me in a very awkward position, recognising me in that restaurant', he said afterwards, in England, when I was teasing him about it. 'But Frank, I don't see …' 'Well, you can't see very far in that case', he retorted impatiently, – for of course it was as clear as noonday to him that notorious spies, shadowed everywhere by the sleuths of de Valera and the Milk-White Hind, have a duty not to involve pure-hearted Paladins in their sinister penumbra by recognising them in public places. Of course if I would obtrude myself, what else could Frank do but wait till I had gone, and then explicitly dissociate himself from me and my nefarious activities, – indeed, explain to his guest (an official of the Irish government) that it was in spite of his emphatic discouragement that I had insisted on visiting Ireland on this mischievous mission? And how long had I been there? For all he knew I had been there ever since February, lurking in the shadows, weaving the intricate web of the Conspiracy. And since I had told him when and where I should be back in Dublin, that he might come round and take a drink with me, perhaps I ought not to have been so surprised, on our return from Galway, when Dickie and I were beaten up at midnight, in the Hibernian Hotel, by a posse of four armed policemen, who posted themselves at strategic positions in our bedroom, and cross-examined us on our movements, and turned our luggage inside outward, while they hunted for firearms, and read all our letters and papers, and confiscated our undeveloped films, and noted the names of our friends mentioned on cards or correspondence. It was all very entertaining, and when I returned to England I enjoyed myself thoroughly teasing Frank about it. Poor Frank got quite alarmed at times, and confessed a great deal out of fear; but of course it would never occur to him that it might be in the least irregular for an employee of the British government (he works in the Ministry of Labour) to denounce a friend and colleague to a neutral government as a British spy. 'And besides', he insists, 'you know perfectly well that you are a spy. Of course you'll lie and say you aren't – I'm not blaming you for it – it's your duty to lie – but you can't persuade me that anyone like yourself goes to Ireland for any purpose so frivolous as a holiday.'

Perhaps it is my book on *Archbishop Laud* that has convinced Frank of my dangerous views. He read it when he was in bed in 1940, having been shot in the bottom by a fellow Home Guard, and told me that it made his gorge rise. (It's true that he also said it was about the same standard as Gibbon; but that, the highest praise I could ever hope to hear, was, for him, an expression of disgust.)

S.I.S. June 1942

There are only two classes of men in the British Secret Service, – those who protect their incompetence by neurotic secrecy, and those who screen it with bombastic advertisement.

R.D.T.-R.   June 1942

I've never met my cousin Dick Trevor-Roper of Plâs Teg,[28] but whenever his name drifts into my ken it is attached to some exploit showing a proper spirit of enterprise and adventure, – either controlling an extensive underground betting organisation as a schoolboy at Wellington, or speedtrack-racing, or climbing the outside of skyscrapers (if this story isn't apocryphal), or disgracing the name of Trevor-Roper by being cashiered from the Regular Army, or rehabilitating it by brilliant exploits in the R.A.F. I expect he's an awful bounder really, but among my drab and dreary relatives, who emerge occasionally from sordid suburbs or faded spas, he beacons from afar, and helps me to bear the burden of my name. So I look with relief from them to him, as one lonely mountain might eye another across a flat and featureless waste.

Saints   July 1942

We were talking of saints as a phenomenon in humanity, and Logan spoke of their essential simplicity, how they grow like the flowers, unconscious of themselves, carrying sweetness and innocence and gaiety impartially wherever they go; and when they die, their bodies don't corrupt, but sweet odours possess the air, as happened (I have read) at the death of Sir William Roper, the son-in-law and biographer of More. And the names of Jesus, and St Anselm, and St Bernard of Clairvaux, and Sir Thomas More were mentioned; and perhaps St Francis Xavier should have been added, and others. And indeed they are a delightful company, walking indifferently through the world, neither preaching nor prophesying, but speaking casually, as if unaware of the giant consequences that attend their words. But I couldn't study them at leisure in my imagination, for they were ousted from it by a long procession of gaunt, forbidding men, tall, hieratic figures in copes and mitres, with hard, angular features, like El Greco's picture of St Augustine. St Augustine was there, and I presume the others included St Paul and St Dominic and St Ignatius

---

28 Richard Trevor-Roper (1915–1944) was killed on RAF operations over Germany. His ancestral home in Wales, Plâs Teg, was later bought and restored by T-R's brother Pat.

Loyola, but they all looked the same, and they repelled and fascinated me. They were saints too, but of another kind, – men whose hot, turbid natures express themselves painfully through a tangled complex of emotions which their struggling intellects have crystallised into an elaborate system of symbols interfering, like an encrusted deposit, between them and the natural world; and who, at a crisis in their lives, under the stress of some psychological shock, have suddenly discarded this great apparatus of symbols, and replaced it by another, equally elaborate but yet harder and more coercive than the last; persecutors, inquisitors, doctors of the Church. For such is the conversion of these old saints, as also of Tertullian and John Donne. And I thought that our terminology is at fault, if we use one word to comprehend *both* these and the former, to whom we should confine the term 'saint' if it is to have any meaning, calling the latter by some other name.

O had you perfect eyes, organs to pierce
Into that chaos whence this stifled verse
By violence breaks: where glow-worm like doth shine
In nights of sorrow, this hid soul of mine;
And how her genuine form struggles for birth
Under the claws of this foul panther earth:
That under all these forms you should discern
My love to you in my desire to learn.

George Chapman [1559?–1634]

A Party

Whither, O Lord, shall I flee? I cried to myself, for bores encompassed me around; there was Arnold Lunn[29] on my right talking of Alps and Popery and Latin America, and Stephen Spender[30] on my left, eating octopus, and, opposite

----

29 (Sir) Arnold Lunn (1888–1977), Alpine mountaineer and skier, inventor of the slalom and Catholic convert.

30 (Sir) Stephen Spender (1908–1995), poet, co-editor with Cyril Connolly of the magazine *Horizon*.

me, Philip Toynbee.[31] But why am I so impatient? I asked myself. Only 90% of what Lunn is saying is demonstrably silly, the remaining 10%, though laughably platitudinous, is quite sensible. But examining the matter I realised that sense or silliness were quite irrelevant; it was the fact that I knew in advance everything that he would say on any topic that made his statements so appalling when they came; and I remembered that conversation with H.G. Wells had been a similar experience. This then, I said to myself, is the real quality of the bore, predictability of response. It is this that has turned Shaw and Wells from prophets into the deathless bores of our age; and armed with this ready criterion I began discovering in my friends the incipient symptoms of the disease, – poor old Rowse,[32] for instance, – we all know exactly what he will say on any topic, he has said it so often already. And what of myself? I asked, inconsequently, – when I speak of, say, Charterhouse, or the Secret Service, or the upper classes? ... but better the conversation of Lunn or Spender than such unhealthy introspection; so I allowed myself to listen to a discourse on the necessity of theology, and the topography of Zermatt, and merely wished I was sitting a little further up the table, next to Frank Pakenham, who had invited me to this absurd party; for at least no one can predict the responses of that engaging, if random, character.

———————

Gilbert described the New Bodleian architecture as 'Selfridges on top of Sing-Sing'.[33]

———————

Things that repel me   July 1942

I have mentioned the things that fascinate me. There are things that repel me too, and in a physical way, so that I shudder involuntarily before them:

---

31 Philip Toynbee (1916–1981) had been a history scholar at Christ Church in T-R's time and was the first Communist to be President of the Oxford Union. He was a book reviewer and disruptive drunk.

32 (Alfred) Leslie Rowse (1903–1997), Fellow of All Souls, Oxford 1925–1974, was a self-infatuated, prickly historian of Tudor England, whom T-R enjoyed baiting.

33 Gilbert Ryle's remark refers to Gordon Selfridge's department store in Oxford Street and to the square-bottomed extension to the Bodleian Library built in 1937–1940 to the design of Sir Giles Gilbert Scott. 60% of its book-stacks were in underground cells.

insipidity; deformity of any kind; softness – physical or intellectual squashiness; formless, sentimental women – they make me think of overripe pears; smooth, oleaginous men; deliquescence; the petting of animals.

1940

Awoken the other night by the long-unfamiliar sound of bombs descending, I decided that really I must destroy my diary for the year 1940; for it contained a good deal of very secret matter which ought never to have been entrusted to it. But before doing this, I read through again the chronicle of that memorable year in our history, and was astonished at the serene, effortless confidence with which we accepted, and reacted to, the most colossal disasters. Had we paused to think, we would have seen that we had been defeated, and that the value of further resistance was questionable; but this intellectual process never occurred to us, and we survived. The Norwegian fiasco was redeemed by the fall of Chamberlain and his friends ('for I have my friends'). When France fell, I merely reflected that we had no more speculative allies, and I knew where we stood. How I rejoiced, lying in a Cornish hospital, at the Copenhagening of the French fleet! And on Sept 11th I read with pleasure that Göring now spends his days on the French coast, looking at the English cliffs through his field-glasses, –

> A king sate on the rocky brow
> That looks o'er sea-born Salamis.[34]

But there was another kind of confidence, too, which I detected in my diary with a wry and disillusioned smile. For it was sadly obvious that in those days I had faith in the purpose and methods of our bureaucracy. How often, and how bitterly, have I since reflected on its failings.

And always present through that fatal year, now in the background, now in front, flooding and obscuring everything, was my illness. How often did I think I saw a means to recovery in another operation, or another hospital, only to revert, disillusioned, to my former state; until, after two of the former, and six of the latter, I settled into a dreary despondency in which all the

---

34 A description of Xerxes before the naval battle at Salamis (480 BC) from Byron's *Don Juan*.

reflexions and emotions that vary and adorn life seemed smothered in one universal gloom. All delights and interests seemed to have flown away, and I thought of Hesiod's tale of Pandora, how, when her box was opened, and all the gifts of the gods dissipated, Hope alone remained perched like a butterfly on the rim, to tease mortals with unreal promises; and sometimes I have abandoned even hope, and fallen into the deepest depression and despair, from which only a conscious intellectual effort, and a determination never to submit to depression or despair, have raised me temporarily up. Reading that diary I am convinced that the year 1940, and particularly the months from July to December, was the most miserable period of my life; and it was very miserable. ἠλιβάτοις ὑπὸ κευθμῶσι γενοίμαν[35] – how many times that cry of the fugitive from despair was uttered in its many forms; but there were yet a few momentary bubbles of delight that broke through that gloomy marsh, and find expression in a few brief pictures that I read with pleasure and relief: Frank Pakenham camping out from the Army, in bed on his own sofa, and reading a bedside book of 600 pages of crude Roman Catholic propaganda; a dinner with the Crawhalls[36] which ended with our going to the kitchen at midnight, and there finishing, cold, the chicken we had begun, hot, four hours previously; a walk in Hulne Park,[37] when 'I noticed, what I must often have seen, but have never remarked before, – how beautiful are birch trees on a heath in May. I noticed them on Brislee Hill, and they looked like puffs of green vapour frozen still, so delicate was the foliage. Against the pinkish-brown background of dead bracken, they looked like a Chinese painting on silk.' And how, in Cornwall, I walked from Paul to Lamorna through the fields. 'It was warm and sunny, and the air was laden with smells of hay and hedgerows; ὦσδεν πάντα θέρευς μάλα πιόνος, ὦσδε δ' ὀπώρας;[38] and yet it was bright and fresh and clear from the open land and the sea, so that it was verily a delight almost beyond the imagination to be alive, and certainly beyond my recent experience, when continued ill-health in Wormwood

---

35 Oh to be hidden in the depths of some abyss! (chorus at Euripides, *Hippolytus*, 732).

36 Mrs L.H. Crawhall lived at Holme House, Lesbury, and was probably the daughter-in-law of Joseph Crawhall, the Northumberland wildlife painter. One of the Crawhalls captained Alnwick cricket club.

37 Hulne Park and Brislee Hill both lie on the outskirts of Alnwick.

38 Everything had the scent of plenteous summer, the scent of ripe fruit (Theocritus, 7.143). Standard editions give πάντ' ὦσδεν θέρεος. T.-R., presumably quoting from memory, changes the order and rescues the metre by changing θέρεος to θέρευς, which is an alternative form of the genitive.

Scrubs has caused me reluctantly to harbour the most melancholy thoughts. So I sat above the Lamorna valley, intoxicated with these pleasures, and read a couple of cantos of Dante, and then went unwillingly back through more flowers and summer smells to Mousehole and Penzance', and found that on that morning (for it was June 14th) Paris had fallen. And then I was arrested as a spy in Cornwall, at the point of a double-barrelled sporting gun levelled at me over a road-block improvised in my honour, and hauled before the police of two villages, which gave me pleasure; and there was my visit to Trewinnard, that solid, spacious Queen Anne manor-house,[39] in lonely pastoral surroundings, whose negro mistress, Mrs Ellis, of British Honduras and Blackpool (she owned the Hotel Royale at Penzance too), 'a fat, friendly, and garrulous lady, told me of her evacuees, and the exact dietary on which she fed them, and enlarged in minute and repellent detail on the burst blood-vessel in her husband's stomach, – the clots of blood he vomited, and how she, by skilful massage, had secured their egress by the rectum instead'. And then, after long series of hospitals, an aimless, hopeless period of disappointed and despondent waiting, I shook hands with doctors and nurses, and returned to London, and there, going to my flat, 'found the stairs hanging like a cobweb in the burnt, roofless building, while in what had been our drawing-room the tops of chairs projected like islands from a sea of roof, rubble, and miscellaneous wreckage'; but all the Londoners were so bright and cheerful among the blitzes that to be among them seemed like a holiday. And finally there was the great act of faith, when I decided 'that if I sit and analyze my condition, and investigate what I can do and what I can't, I must admit myself equally incapable of intellectual work and physical activity; and it's only by doing both that I can do either'. So I planned to do what I had thought I would never do again, and go hunting. I gave myself two months to get fit to sit a horse, and then, wrapped in clothes and stayed with flagons, went out with the Bicester, and behold, it worked. And on the second day out, on Boxing Day 1940, with the Whaddon, 'Sidney Meyrick rode through the Claydon Brook, and his horse disappeared entirely from sight, but re-emerged on the other side, festooned with water-reeds and coils of ooze-laden wire from Davy Jones' Locker.' When I read these passages from that now destroyed volume, I felt that there were glimpses of light even in the blackest period of my personal life.

---

39 Near St Erth in Cornwall.

The Value of Literature

"'… As for me (said Fox),[40] I love all the poets." And well did they repay his affection. They consoled him for having missed everything upon which his heart was set, and to the attainment of which the labour of his life was directed; for the loss of power and of fortune; for his all but permanent exclusion from the privilege of serving his country, and the opportunity of benefitting his friends; even for the extinction of that which Burke,[41] speaking from a long and intimate knowledge of his disposition, most correctly called "his darling popularity." At the time when, for the crime of maintaining that the Revolution of 1688 had placed our constitution upon a popular basis, he had been struck off the Privy Council and had been threatened with the Tower; when he never went down to Westminster except to be hopelessly outvoted, or looked into a bookshop or print-shop without seeing himself ferociously lampooned and filthily caricatured, there was yet no more contented man than he throughout all that broad England for whose liberties he suffered. He could forget the insolence of Dundas,[42] and the chicanery of Sir John Scott,[43] while intent upon the debate which Belial and Mammon conducted in a senate-house less agreeable to its inmates even than the House of Commons of 1798 was to the whigs; and although it was less easy to efface from his recollections the miseries which were endured by humbler patriots than himself, yet the wrongs of Muir[44] and Palmer[45] and Wakefield[46] and Priestley[47] lost some

---

40 Charles James Fox (1749–1806) was hated by George III and spent nearly thirty years in Whig opposition.

41 Edmund Burke (1729–1797), Whig oracle until his crusade against the French Revolution estranged him from Fox and made him an apostle of European conservatism.

42 Henry Dundas, 1st Viscount Melville (1742–1811), Pitt's Home Secretary 1791–1794, hated Jacobinism.

43 John Scott, 1st Earl of Eldon (1751–1838) introduced legislation against traitorous correspondence and radical conspiracies as attorney general 1793–1799; later Lord Chief Justice and Lord Chancellor.

44 Thomas Muir (1765–1798), parliamentary reformer, was arrested for sedition in 1792 and sentenced to fourteen years' transportation to Botany Bay. Escaped but died of wounds.

45 Thomas Palmer (1747–1802), Unitarian minister who, for correcting the proof of a handbill issued by the Society of Friends of Liberty at Dundee, was convicted of treason in 1793, sentenced to twelve years' transportation to Botany Bay and perished on his return voyage.

46 Gilbert Wakefield (1756–1801), Unitarian minister who was imprisoned 1799–1801 as author of a seditious pamphlet.

47 Joseph Priestley (1733–1804), chemist, controversialist, librarian to Lord Shelburne, preacher at Hackney Gravel Pit 1791–1794, when he was obliged to move to Pennsylvania.

of their sting to one who could divert at will the current of his indignation against the despot who imprisoned Tasso[48] and the roysterers who affronted Milton. And whenever things were for a moment too hard on him, – when he returned to his country home fretted by injustice and worn by turmoil, – his wife had only to take down a volume of *Don Quixote* or *Gil Blas*,[49] and read to him until his mind was again in tune for the society of Spenser and Metastasio.'[50] (G.O. Trevelyan, *The Early Years of C.J. Fox*, 303).

Mornington Crescent

We spoke of Mornington Crescent, and Gilbert said he had never seen anyone get out of, or on to, a train in that underground station. Indeed Mornington Crescent, if such a place really existed (which is questionable), was most probably the sort of lost world whither aged elephants retire to die. And thereupon, being slightly inebriated, he evidently had a vision vouchsafed to him; for he went on to say that possibly moribund tube-trains went thither as to a cemetery, when they felt their days drawing to a close; and no doubt an intrepid explorer might light upon their gloomy sepulchre, a twilit place, full of dead tube-trains in varying degrees of decomposition, – some but dusty bones, some still fixed in the grip of rigor mortis, some but newly arrived and composing their limbs in decent postures of demise.

Mythology

I said that the races of modern Europe have no mythology. They have heroic cycles perhaps – Charlemain, Siegfried, Robin Hood – but no general pantheistic conceptions that can be invoked to irradiate any incident in life or nature.

---

48 Alfonso II, Duke of Ferrara imprisoned the poet Torquato Tasso (1544–1595) for seven years in the madhouse of St Anna.

49 The picaresque *Gil Blas* by Alain-René Lesage (1668–1747) was translated into English by Smollett.

50 Pietro Trapassi (1698–1782), the pastoral poet 'Metastasio', introduced melodrama to operatic plots.

That is what makes the Greek world so delightful to me, – the perpetual intermingling of the human and the divine which makes poetry possible; and the lack of it in Western civilisation can only be supplied by recourse to the ancient Greeks. Logan then spoke of the Japanese, and taking up a volume of memoirs by Sir Thos. Hohler,[51] read an account of the address made by the victorious general to the spirits of the dead after the battle of Tsushima. I didn't like being driven into the arms of the Japanese at this stage in our history, so I suggested the Irish instead; but Logan said I couldn't sell the Irish to him, – they had borrowed too much money from him which he had never seen again.

But again, not long afterwards, when Gilbert and I were walking along the Thames at Henley, and I was in an extraordinarily happy mood (as I generally am when I have been drunk the night before), I thought of this great hiatus in our modern world, and wondered how I should begin to supply the starved soul of England, ahungering for spiritual refreshment. The Thames at Henley is a handsome river, rolling majestically past meadows and parks, temples and peacock-haunted groves, broad and smooth, fringed with weeping willows and lovely plants – blue peppermint and pink rosebay, all the things that make rivers especially delightful to me; and I exclaimed to Gilbert that, had the Greeks possessed such a river, they would have peopled it with nymphs, and invested it with divinity and divine associations, as they did Eridanus or Scamander, for lack of any decent streams in their own mainland; and I thought of Odysseus' address to the river of the Phaecians at whose mouth he landed.

Why shouldn't I begin my new mission with potamolatry, choosing the Thames for my first god, sweet Thames that is so beautiful at Kelmscott and at Eynsham, that has seen so many gay evenings at the Trout and idle days in Port Meadow, that flows so demurely between its poplars in Binsey meadow, so majestically at Henley, so historically in London? I would make the Thames to Englishmen (I said) what the Rhine is to the Germans, and the Volga, I understand, to the Russians.

But a few days later I was home in the north, and when I looked on Tweed again in his glory, all the associations of that ancient river arose in my

---

51 Sir Thomas Hohler (1871–1946), author of *Diplomatic Petrel* (1942), was *en poste* in Tokyo at the time of the Russo–Japanese war, during which the Czar's fleet was destroyed by the Japanese victory at Tsushima.

mind, and my artificial affection for the Thames had somehow all melted away.

’Εβρε κάλλιστος πόταμος παρ’ Αἶνον
ἐξίησθ’ ἐς πορφυρέαν θάλασσαν
Θρᾳκίας ἐρευγόμενος ζα γαίας[52]

The Road to Xanadu

My ballads are nearly always produced in certain conditions – when I have been drunk the night before on an excess of choice wines, and wake up in the morning at early dawn, with a delicious sense of exhilaration and content. Then the birds are singing, and everything (after my early evacuation) is delightful; and it is in this state that the divine afflatus most infallibly descends upon me. When I was staying with Gilbert at the Leander Club (which provides all the physical prerequisites of inspiration),[53] I enjoyed such a state, and I told Gilbert as we glid along the Thames in a dinghy, that all the lineaments of a ballad were peeping obscurely forth from the twilight, but that its exact form was not yet clear. Gilbert had been telling me of John Bell,[54] late high master of St Paul's, a great exponent of Aristophanes, who had once been mystified, as he strolled along a country road on the morning after a feast, by the spectacle of giant pyramids of dung, – horse-dung in character, but Pegasean in dimensions, such as no mortal horse could have laid. The heaps seemed to become larger as he went on, the dung-balls themselves to increase in volume and solidity, and long he pondered over this rural enigma, until he overtook a troupe of circus elephants on the march, upon whom the laxative properties of a fresh vegetable diet had not worked in vain. I said it was a pity the Aristophanic element had been driven out of English literature since the 17th century; why shouldn't we restore it? Then Gilbert's mind wandered, for he babbled about bullrushes and things, and asked if there were really such

52 Hebrus, who fairest of rivers issue forth past Aenus into the surging sea as you roll through the land of Thrace (Alcaeus, fragment 45.1–4).

53 The Leander Club at Henley-on-Thames (founded 1818) is the oldest non-university rowing club.

54 John Bell (1890–1958), High Master of St Paul's School 1927–1938, where he instituted Russian classes.

things as scented reeds, for he had never smelt one. And then he fell asleep in the dinghy; and suddenly the muse of poetry awoke and sang, and I copied down at her dictation, and it was the poem for which I had been waiting, a ballad about Cole-Adams and the Hanslope sewage system,[55] beginning

An architect stood in Hanslope Park
In a scented water-closet,
And he sang this strain as he pulled the chain
And flushed away the deposit:
'Slide, sewage, slide, gurgle and glide,
Down the bed Cole-Adams has built you,
Past sweet-scented reeds and flowring weeds
With never a block to silt you.
And many a nymph, by your fragrant lymph,
Shall sing to her sisters, Hark
To the ripple that runs from the well-sucked bums
Of the lords of Hanslope Park ....'

And it was similarly on a summer morning, after a convivial night of claret and port-drinking, when I awoke early and, lying in bed, heard the birds greeting the dawn outside my bedroom window, that I was inspired to immortalise my battles with Cmdr Travis,[56] and to use for that purpose the most immediate incidents of the occasion:

A raven croaked in Bletchley Park,[57]
– O sit praesaga avis![58] –

---

55 Walter Cole-Adams (1891–1971), architect, was Worlledge's assistant in the Radio Security Service. Hanslope Park House, a seventeenth-century mansion in Buckinghamshire, housed the Foreign Office's first radio station (1939) and remains the communications security department of SIS.

56 Commander (Sir) Edward Travis (1888–1956), was in charge of security at the Government Code & Cypher School during the 1920s, replaced Denniston as operational head of GC&CS at Bletchley 1942, and headed its successor, GCHQ, until 1952.

57 Bletchley Park had been bought in 1883 by Sir Herbert Leon, who enlarged and remod-elled the house in a displeasing medley of Victorian Tudor and Dutch baroque styles. After Lady Leon's death, the estate was sold to a speculative builder who intended to demolish the house and erect a housing estate in the grounds; but in 1938 Sir Hugh Sinclair, head of MI6, paid £7,500 of his own money to acquire it for use by the secret service. It was occupied by GC&CS from 1939.

58 O let it be a prophetic bird!

'I hear the sounds of morning – hark!
The chough, the chiffchaff and the lark!
Too long have we outstayed the dark!
    Come with me, brother Travis!

'We gloomy creatures of the night
    Have little time to stay;
Our doings will not bear the light,
Left unprotected to the spite
Of peewit, pipit, tit, and twite, –
    Come, Travis, come away!'

Commander Travis lay in bed, –
    He listened, and he heard.
He drew the blankets o'er his head;
'That voice was heard before,' he said,
'When Denniston[59] packed up and fled –
    O, blast the bloody bird!

But Page[60] and Twinn[61] and Birch[62] and Knox[63]
    Cried, 'O divine avis!'[64]

---

59 Alexander ('Alastair') Denniston (1881–1961) won a bronze medal for hockey at the 1908 Olympics, served in Naval Intelligence 1914–1921, was operational head of GC&CS 1919–1942 (described in *Who's Who* as 'late Head of a Dept in the Foreign Office'), retired from SIS in 1945 and taught French and Latin in Leatherhead.

60 (Sir) Denys Page (1908–78), classics tutor at Christ Church 1932–1950 and active in wartime deciphering of enemy signals at GC&CS Bletchley, was elected Regius Professor of Greek at Cambridge in 1950 and Master of Jesus College, Cambridge in 1959.

61 Peter Twinn (1916–2004) read mathematics at Brasenose and joined GC&CS as an assistant to Dilwyn Knox in 1939. The first English cryptographer to read a German Enigma message in 1940, he succeeded Knox as head of the Abwehr Enigma section at Bletchley, 1942. Director of Hovercraft at the Ministry of Technology; awarded a London University doctorate for his study of the jumping mechanism of click beetles.

62 Francis ('Frank') Birch (1889–1956) worked in Naval Intelligence 1916–1919, Fellow of King's College, Cambridge 1915–1934, lecturer in history 1921–1928, left university life to become a playwright, theatrical producer and actor, joined Bletchley's naval section 1939 and headed German naval section.

63 Dilwyn ('Dilly') Knox (1884–1943), classicist and Fellow of King's 1909–1922. As a cryptographer in Naval Intelligence in the First World War, he broke the German navy's flag code. Afterwards, instead of returning to Cambridge, he worked at the GC&CS under Denniston. In the Second World War, he ran a cryptographic section at Bletchley monitoring Abwehr wireless traffic.

64 O divinatory bird.

Their sections thronged the gates in flocks,
And sang, 'Finita est longa nox!
Ave cornicis grata vox!
   Vale, Commander Travis!'[65]

Conversation

I was staying with Gilbert in the Leander Club, at Henley, and we listened to the conversation of four members at the dinner-table beside us. Finally Gilbert said, 'That is true conversation. In no Oxford Common Room could such perfection be attained as that.' For without effort, or strain, or interruption, or monopoly, they had passed from French impressionist painting through Polish war decorations and King Amanullah of Afghanistan[66] to baroque architecture and Bosnian water-closets.

Places   Sept 1942

How happy some places make me, Ireland for instance, and Otmoor, and many places in Gloucestershire and Northumberland, and now Coldingham, where I stayed with John and Nim Church[67] in that delightful house of theirs which discovers itself, like the gingerbread house in the story, quite suddenly, at the end of a long ride in a wood. There I would take the dogs out, with or without a gun, and walk out of the wood and over the moor; or I would go to the top of the wood, and from the eminence there would overlook a vast distance bounded by the Cheviots on one hand and by the Lammermuirs on the other, and in front by the sea. In that clear air, all the autumn colours stood out, the colours of golden corn standing in the fields, or stubble-fields dotted with cornshocks, or green pasture, or moor in heather-flower; and there was a pastoral loneliness, that most exquisite loneliness, that Lucretius so happily describes.
   Per loca pastorum deserta atque otia dia,[68]

---

65 The long night is over, hail with grateful voice, Farewell Commander Travis!

66 Amanullah Khan (1892–1960), a westernising King of Afghanistan 1919–1929 who was deposed by reactionaries.

67 John Church and his wife lived some miles north of Alnwick in Berwickshire.

68 Through the deserted haunts of shepherds, and the divine places of their rest (Lucretius, *De rerum natura*, 5, 1387).

that is emphasised rather than broken by the noise of rooks and pigeons and curlews. And I had the same sensation, the sensation of physical delight in places, when cub-hunting the other day with the Bicester in Tittershall Wood. I arrived late, having hitch-hiked early in the morning from Aylesbury on a milk-lorry, and saddled and bridled my mare at the Crooked Billet, and as I rode up to Tittershall, the whole wood was ringing with a rising and falling note, as of seagulls around a ship, the cry of hounds hunting hither and thither through the covert. It was a beautiful morning in September; the trees were heavy with leaves; the autumn flowers, willow-herb and scabious, were out in the woodland rides; and the berries of bryony and woody-nightshade hung in the hedgerows. There again I enjoyed that delicious sensation, which is one of the choicest pleasures, that rapture that Izaak Walton meant when he quoted,

> whence I know not,
> I was that instant lifted above earth
> And possess'd joys not promised in my birth.

Sept 1942

Rideout[69] is to me the embodiment of the plutocratic spirit. Not that he is a plutocrat himself, – that is unnecessary; to embody the spirit of aristocracy it isn't necessary to be a duke. One day at lunch we were talking of A.L. Rowse's autobiography, and I spoke of the shrill, vulgar, boastful, hysterical, over-dramatised, and often irrelevant outbursts which frequently intrude in that otherwise prim narrative, whenever Rowse remembers his bugbears. 'Just what you would expect from the lower orders', said Rideout, sipping impassively at his Montrachet, – 'you only have to bump into them in your motor-car to discover that'.

---

69 John Rideout (1912–1950) was a scholar of Charterhouse and classics exhibitioner at Christ Church who did not take an Oxford degree but transferred to London University where he obtained first-class honours in oriental languages and became a lecturer in oriental languages. He was unfit for war service and taught Japanese to British officers destined for the Far East. Professor of Oriental Studies at Sydney University 1948–1949, and then Professor of Chinese Studies in Hong Kong, where he died. A scholar of high philological acumen, with a brilliant gift for turning Chinese classics into clear English.

ʿΑλιευτικά[70]   October 1942

Logan was telling me about impending conversions to the Church of
Rome in high or intellectual society (I forget which), and he observed that
the Roman Church had recently improved its methods in the apostolic art
of fishing for the souls of men. Not long ago, he said, their methods were
coarse and unskilful; they set night-lines for gross, unappetising creatures,
and plied dragnets and seines in sluggish backwaters; and often what they
caught weren't fishes at all, but old miscellaneous garbage that stank less if it
were left alone. But recently they have changed all that; for while they still
left their coarse fishermen posted on mud-banks to hook eels (and he named
a missionary to whom such tasks were most regularly assigned, who dressed
like a layman and got drunk with the vulgar in low resorts), this was now
by deliberate choice, one specialised branch of their various and elaborate
art. On every reach and tributary of the great river of society now stands
the angler most appropriate to it. In the drawing-rooms of Mayfair suave,
fashionable sophists – and he spoke of a salon-sermon Cyril Connolly[71] had
attended, in which the priest had spoken eloquently on the tragedy of modern Greek, a language which, he seemed suddenly to remember, to its many
beauties, had one fatal drawback – 'it has lost its infinite. What a terrible
thing', he went on, after an aching and significant pause, 'for a language,
or a people, or a human soul, to lose its infinite!' And then there are the
refined dry-fly fishermen who, with hand-tied flies and private virtuosity, fish
the classic chalk-streams of Oxford, – men like Fr D'Arcy, S.J., that subtil
practitioner ...

But here I felt that he was trespassing on my experience, so I took over the
conversation from him, and, pleased with his piscatorial metaphor, told how
I had once spoiled one of Fr D'Arcy's Oxford fishing-parties, and, at the same
time, lost all my snob friends, and become an outcast from the holy fleshpots
of Campion Hall. For there was a time, when I was at Oxford, when I used to
be invited to dine quite often in Campion Hall, and drank choice wines there,
and spirits late into the night in the senior common room, with Fr D'Arcy,

---

70 On fishing. This is the title of a didactic poem in hexameters ascribed to Oppian.
71 Cyril Connolly (1903–1974), editor of *Horizon* magazine 1939–1950.

and Fr Woodlock,[72] and Sir Edwin Lutyens[73] and Sir Ernest Swinton,[74] and Tom Boase.[75] Those were gay symposia, and I remember how a timid Jesuit would poke his head into the room at intervals saying, 'Father, it is compline', or sext, or whatever the holy office might be; but Fr D'Arcy would wave a hand through the convivial haze, saying, 'Dispensation! Dispensation!'; and the decanters would clink again, and this trifling interruption be forgotten. And sometimes Fr D'Arcy would take his guests to see the artistic treasures of his spider's web – for he understood the catholic doctrine of the shop window, τὰ αἰσθητὰ ἱερὰ τῶν ἀναισθητῶν ἀπεικονίσματα καὶ ψυγαγωγά,[76] or words to that effect, and was an old hand at wheedling objects of rarity and vertù 'for his poor house' out of the well-endowed. There were pictures and statues and vestments to be seen, and sometimes with pious relish he would open a long, flat drawer, and point to an elaborate, but faded, garment preserved in mothball, and say, 'a chasuble' – or a nighty or whatever it was – 'of St Edward the Confessor', – pronouncing the last words affectedly, as if in Spanish, or in Shakespeare's manner, 'Good even to my ghostly confessor'. And Jesuits used to write letters to me in those days, which they don't now, and sign themselves 'yours ever in Christ'; but the 'ever' was apparently a formality.

Well, it was in those days that I was once invited to dinner by Dawyck Haig[77] to meet Paul Maze,[78] a Frenchman, whom (I understand) his fellow

---

72 Francis Woodlock (1871–1940) entered the Society of Jesus in 1899, professed logic, psychologist and ethics at Stonyhurst College until 1921 when he became special preacher and lecturer in the Jesuit community at Farm Street; an omnivorous reader, theological essayist and popular commentator.

73 (Sir) Edwin Lutyens (1869–1944), architect of New Delhi and Campion Hall.

74 (Sir) Ernest Swinton (1868–1951), pioneer of tank warfare, ghost of Lloyd George's memoirs, director of the Citroen motor-car company, Major-General in the Army and Chichele Professor of Military History at Oxford with a fellowship at All Souls 1925–1939.

75 Thomas Boase (1898–1974), art historian, Fellow of Hertford 1922–1937, worked in wartime GC&CS at Bletchley, President of Magdalen College, Oxford 1947–1968.

76 Holy things accessible to the senses represent holy things inaccessible to the senses and draw the soul to them. T-R is quoting from memory Ps.-Dionysius, *De ecclesiastica hierarchia*: τὰ αἰσθητῶς ἱερὰ τῶν νοητῶν ἀπεικονίσματα καὶ ἐπ' αὐτὰ χειραγωγία καὶ ὁδός (see G. Heil and A.M. Ritter, *Corpus Dionysiacum II* (Berlin, 1991), 74.7–10).

77 George ('Dawyck'), 2nd Earl Haig (1918–2009), godson of the French empress Eugénie, prisoner-of-war in Colditz, painter and Borders gentleman, whose sister married T-R in 1954.

78 Paul Maze (1887–1979), fashionable painter of the racing at Goodwood, rowing at Henley and yachting at Cowes.

social climbers often meet on the crowded staircases of the aristocracy. I happened to be dining elsewhere, with David Hawkins, that night; but after dinner we went round to Dawyck's rooms, and I noticed a faint whiff of sanctity as we climbed the stairs in no 5 Tom Quad; and sure enough, when we entered the room, there was Fr D'Arcy, holding forth in honeyed tones to a number of slightly inebriated young aristocrats, who included Dawyck, and Peter Wood,[79] and Gavin Astor,[80] and others whom I have forgotten, for they were very forgettable. He was talking of art, which was understandable, for Dawyck has some skill in watercolours, and Paul Maze is a painter, too, in the intervals of social climbing. The others were of course at sea, but they felt that they were at sea on a very distinguished vessel, and took what was given them with humility. Now Fr D'Arcy's views on painting, I noticed, were not casually or artlessly expressed, for he was slowly, and unobtrusively, but firmly leading the conversation whither he would have it go; and before long he was saying that art does not ultimately consist in the expression of personality, or the discovery of a platonic archetype, or in accuracy of portraiture, or virtuosity of technique, as some heretics foolishly maintain, but in the choice of a subject. For instance, he said, and he would soon produce arguments to support his statement, a religious painting is a higher form of art than a secular painting, and this regardless of the manner in which the idea is expressed.

It was here that the débâcle began, and, to do him justice, it was Paul Maze who began it. Scenting, I suppose, a competitor in Fr D'Arcy, a rival siren singing for the same social supper as himself, he boldly dissented from this tendentious opinion; and I, partly because I was slightly inebriated too, and therefore wanted some fun, and partly because I was disgusted by the shameless tactics of the holy man, and the evident success with which he was developing them, dissented with him. 'In the Louvre', expostulated Paul Maze earnestly, 'there is a picture by Salvator Rosa (or whoever it may have been) of the crucifixion of Jesus Christ, and beside it is a picture by Rembrandt, of

---

79 Peter Wood (1916–1942), Master of Beagles at Eton and Christ Church, joint master of the Exmoor foxhounds as an undergraduate, author of light verse and comic opera, trainee architect in Beaconsfield, killed in action in Egypt. His friendship with T-R was chilled by the latter's rudeness about Catholicism.

80 Gavin, 2nd Baron Astor of Hever (1918–1984), married Dawyck Haig's sister Irene in 1945. As Life President of Times Newspapers, he recruited T-R as a director of Times Newspapers in 1974.

a joint of raw meat ...' 'A far less hackneyed topic', I interposed, and dwelt for a while on the relatively unexploited artistic properties of butcher's meat, particularly sausages, offals, and the like. Besides, might not art be said to consist in evoking, by imagination, the divinity, the majesty, of ordinary things?' But when I ceased, I noticed that the temperature of the room had suddenly sunk. Gone was the warm, convivial glow. There were frozen looks from some of the shocked young aristocrats, who thought, it seemed to me, that the imaginary corns of a Jesuit were sacrosanct. I had thrown a pebble, it seemed, into the pool, just when Fr D'Arcy had tied the appropriate fly, and, from a convenient alder tree, was preparing to cast it. There was a plop, and a ripple; the trout had fled; and the angler was not at all pleased with the visitor. Then the aggrieved silence was broken by a yet more devastating sound. It was from David Hawkins. If I had thrown a pebble into the stream, he had detached a few yards of the bank, and sent it tumbling down into the water with a terrible, reverberating splash. I forget the remark. I don't think it was either witty or profound; but it made further fishing in that water impossible. Fr D'Arcy remembered that it was time for compline or sext, and this time saw no need for a dispensation. He took his leave with infallible suavity, shook hands with all, and was escorted to the gate. Since that day I have never been invited to Campion Hall; its holy wares are no longer displayed to me; Peter Wood, with whom my relations had already begun to cool, never spoke cordially to me again; Gavin Astor, too, seemed to think I had gone a little far in dissenting from so holy a man; and Jesuits have never written to me since with their devout salutations.

October 1942

Often, out hunting, when I am cantering down a woodland ride with hounds panting at my horse's heels, or when I watch them lapping at standing water on the way home, or crashing through the undergrowth after a fox in covert, I think of Homer's great images of beasts in the forest; and on my summer walks in woods and fields I am often reminded of the charm given to Dante's metaphors by his minute observation of birds and flowers; and the other morning, while cub-hunting in Charndon Wood, it occurred to me to wonder whether perhaps, in our great cities, in London, Detroit, or Stalingrad, there are not people who can have no conception of the world from which these images are drawn, to whom the phenomena of wild life are the tedious ritual of an esoteric world from which they are excluded. I remembered that not long ago Eve Aitken had taken a goat to London in a tube-train, since other transport was unavailable; and at King's Cross a conductress, seeing this strange, almost heraldic animal led into her subterranean kingdom, thought it was a breed of dog, – this being presumably the only quadruped that had hitherto penetrated, from above ground, into the lamplight and ozone of her nether catacombs. But then I wondered whether the world of these people might not have its own mysteries, and its own esoteric poetry, from which I am excluded, – a poetry drawing its images and its symbolism from cafeterias and petrol-pumps and gasometers and factory-sirens, strip-work, telephone-exchanges; and gambling machines, and all the plugs, switches, and gadgets of a mechanised world. Could it be that this is modern poetry, and the reason I so dislike it, – because it is the emotional language of an esoteric world I detest, – the hieroglyph, as Samuel Butler would say, of a lost soul, or rather, of a whole civilisation of lost souls?

Geoffrey Baskerville   Oct 1942

My views on historiography have been influenced casually and indirectly, by A.L. Rowse, whose insistence on readability, combined with his example of historical method, ended for me the old haggling debate, 'Is history an art or a science?', and by Geoffrey Baskerville,[81] whose single book on monks, with its brilliant research and scholarship, combined with scepticism and wit, humanity, detachment, and genial malice, seemed to offer a new future for historiography, clogged at present with slipshod hackwork and ponderous

---

81 Geoffrey Baskerville (1870–1944) became a naval cadet on *HMS Britannia* at Dartmouth in 1884 and a midshipman in 1886, but left the Royal Navy in 1890. Read history at Christ Church, and obtained a first in 1898. Appointed a history tutor at Keble in 1899 and librarian in 1906, but was obliged to relinquish both posts in 1914 (reputedly because of sexual indiscretions). He inherited Crowsley Park near Henley-on-Thames. His reaction to his young donnish visitors may be gauged by his aside in *English Monks and the Suppression of the Monasteries* (1937): 'if a "man's man" is a detestable type of clergyman, a clever and conceited young don is an equally hateful type' (p. 126).

miscellanies. In an altogether remoter, and cooler, climate sat Firth and Tawney, and perhaps Hammond, distilling their vast and precious wisdom from the multiple, elaborate cells of their deep rich minds; but it was Rowse and Baskerville that I most wanted to know, for those were priests, hid in hieratic mystery, but these were gay, worldly acolytes of my Temple of Fame, whose brilliance and vitality appealed to me – the hot Celtic character of Rowse, his unusual career, his baroque mind, his complicated prejudices, and Baskerville's curious situation, his unfortunate academic fate, and the unique praise awarded to him by the young T.E. Lawrence.

Poor old Rowse! I know him so well now, – he has become a comic, with his bugbears and his self-dramatisation, his egotism, his transparency, his endless journalism. Still, Goldsmith[82] was a comic, and a genius too; and I think Rowse is only incidentally absurd, that he still keeps the old standards I first recognised and admired in him.

The other day I was staying at Henley, at the Leander Club, with Gilbert, and we walked over to see Geoffrey Baskerville, a stranger hitherto to both of us. We found his huge park, remote, silent, and deserted. A herd of deer was nibbling under the trees, and trooped elegantly away at our approach; and in the centre of the park stood a great red-brick country house, built in the reign of James II, and completed in the next century, perfect in design, a monument of ancient opulence and taste. From it seven great avenues of elm-trees stretched starwise into the distance; and nothing could be seen in any direction but rolling parkland, and trees, and deer; nothing heard but rooks and wood-pigeons. The front door was locked, but we found a side-entrance, and were led up bare kitchen stairs to a room full of books and eccentricities, where Geoffrey Baskerville received us. He was living in one corner of the shuttered house, for the Canadian soldiers had left, after emptying his cellars even of the Imperial Tokay which his father had bought in Ischl in 1865, and the BBC had not yet come in. He greeted us with old-world courtesy, spoke of the visitors, mainly antiquarian clergymen, whose occasional visits enlivened his isolation, and asked us to stay to tea. Then he pulled an antique bell-rope, and went out to forestall the housekeeper who, with her sister, were the only domestics left in that great house, and ask her, apologetically, if this were not too much trouble. We had tea in an empty bedroom, and I asked

---

82 Oliver Goldsmith (1728–1774), poet and dramatist.

him if he were writing another book. He replied that he was supposed to be writing a parallel volume on the English secular clergy in the 16th century, but he seemed dubious about it, as did Gilbert afterwards – his last had got him into such trouble, he said, especially with the Jesuits. At one time he had feared they would put poison in his food; all because of his cracks at their great Panjandrum, Cardinal Gasquet.[83] Then he spoke of the difficulties of keeping up his great park, how he was afraid he might be forced to put down his deer, and of course he had no servants or gardeners, but fortunately his friend Lord Macclesfield[84] had the right to present to a ward [nominate an inmate] in a home for the aged at Ewelme; and anyway the days of private parks were numbered, – this would undoubtedly be turned into a public park for the citizens of Reading. Was this the man, I asked myself, who had written that robust, genial, sceptical book, *English Monks and the Suppression of the Monasteries*, this shy, hesitant and bewildered anchorite, with his clerical visitors, his collector's fads, his fatalist resignation? Only once did I detect any trace in him of the Baskerville I had so admired, – when I said that ecclesiastical history shouldn't be taken too seriously, and he answered that no history should be taken seriously. However, on the way back I recollected that such disillusion is a common incident. The Cyclops knew it when he met Odysseus –

ἀλλ᾽ αἰεί τινὰ φῶτα μέγαν καὶ καλὸν ἐδέγμην[85]

Logan experienced it with Matthew Arnold, and Max Beerbohm with Walter Pater; and Garrod[86] tells me that he felt it with all the dons of Balliol when he went thither as an undergraduate.

---

83 Francis Gasquet (1846–1929), Prior of Downside 1878–1885, wrote a massive defence of the monks, *Henry VIII and the English Monasteries* (1888–1889). He was created Cardinal in 1914, appointed as archivist of the Holy See in 1917 and Vatican librarian in 1919.

84 George Parker, 7th Earl of Macclesfield (1888–1975), chairman of Oxfordshire County Council 1937–1970, succeeded Lord Bicester as Lord Lieutenant of Oxfordshire 1954. Ewelme almshouses were founded in 1437 by Alice Chaucer, granddaughter of Geoffrey Chaucer and wife of William de la Pole, Duke of Suffolk. The Suffolks made Ewelme – sheltered in a valley of the Chilterns – into a model village of its day. The rosy red-brick almshouses housed thirteen poor men under the care of two chaplains.

85 But I always expected a man tall and handsome (Homer, *Odyssey* 9.513).

86 Heathcote William Garrod (1878–1960), tutorial fellow at Merton since 1904, classical scholar, literary essayist, poet.

Euston Bishop   Oct 1942

In October 1942 I stayed with Euston Bishop,[87] whom I hadn't seen for many years, and he told me his history during the war. He has always been an invalid; he has chronic asthma which sometimes completely prostrates him; and he has an infirmity of the legs which makes him permanently lame, able to walk stiffly, but not to run. At Oxford he was always under the care of Girdlestone.[88] He explained that he had tried, on the outbreak of war, to get a commission in the Guards, or, failing that, in the H.A.C.;[89] but, being rejected because of his ill-health, and not relishing the alternative of a commission in the Pay Corps, for which alone he was declared eligible, he gave up thought of serving as an officer, and contrived to go to France with the B.E.F.[90] as a private. He went through the Flanders campaign as driver-batman in Gen. Montgomery's divisional headquarters, and, after our defeat there, was evacuated from la Panne; but his ship was blown up in the Channel by a bomb dropped down the funnel, and Euston lost his hunting-horn in the shipwreck. This was his principal complaint; for he was himself rescued and brought back to France, which he left for the second time from Dunkirk with the demolition-party. Then, he spent nine months in hospital with an accumulation of diseases, and, on recovery, wangled a transfer to the R.A.F. He was appointed intelligence officer, and sent out to Egypt and Cyprus, where he got sandfly-fever, and was invalided home. In England he went to hospital again with pneumonia, but now he was out again, and having contrived again to wangle his way past the doctors, had got transferred as a pilot to a night-fighter squadron. Meanwhile, till his next orders came, he was bicycling and 'busing daily to Hungerford to work voluntarily

---

87 Euston Mannin Bishop (1917–1987) joined the staff of the Institute of Contemporary Arts, 1962. His uncle Euston Salaman (1871–1916) married a Miss Wertheimer painted by Sargent; his cousin Merula Salaman married Sir Alec Guinness.

88 Gathorne Girdlestone (1881–1950), an old Carthusian son of a Canon of Christ Church. After surviving a motor-cycle smash he dedicated his life to the care of crippled children and was an inspirational leader at the Wingfield-Morris orthopaedic hospital near Oxford. As a Christian he believed in healing by the power of love as well as surgical skill. An expert on tuberculosis of bones and joints, Nuffield Professor of Orthopaedic Surgery at Oxford University and Fellow of New College, Consulting Orthopaedic Surgeon to the Army and Radcliffe Infirmary, Oxford.

89 Honourable Artillery Company.

90 British Expeditionary Force.

in a factory there; but this the Air Force authorities discovered and firmly forbade.

As I elicited each detail of this admirable career from him, I decided that here was someone who had lumped all considerations of pride, waived all advantage of wealth, and triumphed over all the obstacles of infirmity, in his determination to live dangerously. He told me that he had thoroughly enjoyed being a private soldier (he had risen to the rank of sergeant) and liked the privates with whom he served; they were much more honest than his friends, he said – they always returned the money they borrowed, which, after living in the society of Peter Wood and such, was a surprise to him, – as I could see they would, since his freedom from pride and side is so natural and simple, no complex masochism as with T.E. Lawrence. I went to bed that night chastened; I thought of my own misery in 1940, and since, and the indulgence I had allowed myself in illness and depression; and I resolved, and hope I shall keep my resolve, never again to complain of ill-health, or to excuse myself on its account.

Ballads   November 1942

I told Gilbert the ballad of Sir Pakenham, –

> Don Pakenham de la Mancha
> Has gone on a crusade:
> The bees sing in his bonnet,
> He waves his two-edged blade;
> And his emblem of the Double Cross
> Is gallantly displayed.

He complained that the narrative was insufficiently consecutive; so I had to explain to him the essential qualities of a ballad. A ballad, I said, is a lyric poem, and hasn't the elbow-room for continuous narrative or the formal monotony of interludes, digressions and conventional lines that an epic poem has. It must be short (long ballads, like 'John Gilpin', are dull; the best old ballads, like 'Sir Patrick Spens', 'the Wife of the Usher's Well', and 'True Thomas', as given in Aytoun's collection – far the best – are short and compact); and it must be vivid, a succession of vivid pictures implying continuity rather than exhibiting it. This entails the different formalities of ellipsis, asyndeton, concentration, and indirect inference, – just as it also requires elaborations and variations of metre. Compare, for instance, Pindar's lyric version of the voyage of the Argonauts with any epic narrative, and observe the way Pindar ignores the strict sequence of time, hopping selectively from incident to incident, and leaving the inessentials, and the continuity, to imply themselves. Or take a good modern ballad, Kingsley's *The Sands of Dee*

> O Mary go and call the cattle home …

Observe how much is omitted, and yet implied, in that short poem. There is no introduction; we start in the middle and imply the beginning. Nor does Kingsley ever tell us that Mary was overwhelmed and engulfed by the tide, or that boats went out to search for her, and fished her up dead. All he says is,

> The rolling mist came down and hid the land
> And never home came she

and the next stanza is the exclamation, presumably, of one who has fished up some dubious mundungus from the sea, mundungus which, it is agreed, isn't salmon. And then he says that they rowed her back to her grave beside the sea, and we know that it must have been Mary, and she must have been drowned. Nor does he explain that Mary's ghost is believed, by the credulous vulgar, still to haunt that desolate tidal waste. A postscript of two lines,

> But still the boatmen hear her call the cattle home
> Across the sands of Dee

is enough; the rest is inferred. And so in the Ballad of Sir Pakenham, I said … but Gilbert didn't seem to be convinced by my deductions.

The Bicester Monday country   November 1942

The Bicester Monday country has, to me, associations of romantic dreariness. To call it wet, or even waterlogged, savours of meiosis; rather it is an archipelago of forlorn islands in a vast extent of bogs, and poached lanes, and flooded meadows, and continuous duck-ponds. The very place names speak of its nature – Marsh Gibbon, Poodle Farm, Gubbin's Hole, Piddington Cow Leys. Beginning in the flat fenlands of Otmoor, where I have so often beagled, knee-deep in water, and where I used to walk, in summer, along the causeway, to watch the redshanks that bred there, till the bombers drove them away, it embraces the floods of the river Ray, which I have often swum out beagling, and where the colours have so captured my fancy, bright and liquid, like a water-colour painting, still wet; and so to Marsh Gibbon, whence I had that most famous foxhunt of all time, a twenty-mile run, on a misty morning, with a fall into the brook, and where the almost mythical hunt of the South Oxfordshire hounds ended that day in 1911, I think, when, going home after a blank day, they found a fox at Woodeaton, accidentally, and hunted him through the night till they killed him at Marsh Gibbon, and the hounds got home at one o'clock next morning, – and where I once spent most of a cold, foggy December night, in 1935, with Peter Wood and Euston Bishop, in one of the three village duck-ponds into which Peter had driven me; and so it continues through the marsh-bound fields of Gawcott and Hillesden, with its splendid fifteenth-century church and great avenue, all half-forgotten in the midst of the fields, to the vast winter floods of the river Ouse, which I once saw Tom Lines,[91] a local farmer, swim out hunting, though they were a mile wide, and the river Ouse was somewhere in the middle, only he knew where. I don't often hunt in the Monday country, but when I do, it's generally memorable, as on that famous Marsh Gibbon day, or when I hunted on Otmoor in a blinding snowstorm, and our progress, according to my diary, was like the retreat from Moscow; but I've often ended up there, and the circumstances are nearly always the same. It is evening, on a Thursday, and we've been hunting the big woods, and a fox goes suddenly away from Charndon Wood as dusk falls, and hounds are on his brush, and nothing will stop them; so away we go through the gathering darkness in a westerly direction, and the scent becomes stronger, and the cry of hounds dwindles fainter ahead, and the fences get bigger and wilder, great tangled bullfinches with double ditches brimful of stale water, and the grey fields are streaked with pale, silvery floods that glint warmly in the darkness. Is that the horn? I ask myself, and gallop towards the sound through the drowned meadows. But no; for there it is again, and it is the lowing of some forgotten, benighted cow. Finally I draw aside to a dead deserted village,

---

91 The Lines were yeoman farmers at Newton Longueville and Newport Pagnell.

and with great difficulty summon to a cottage-door one of the dwellers in those desolate regions. Whether they are web-footed, as in parts of New Guinea, I have often wondered in vain; but certainly in the village of Noke, on Otmoor, they have variable numbers of fingers and toes, and other sinister irregularities. But this isn't Noke, it's Poundon, they tell me; and at the sound of that name my heart sinks, for I know I must ride ten miles back through the darkness. But then I cheer up, remembering that afterwards I shall drink potations bottle-deep in the Sportsman, and through the convivial fumes my image of the Bicester Monday country shall once again assume its fabulous shape, and I shall tell tales of my adventures there, tales like those of Sir John Mandeville or Sinbad the Sailor, when they returned from their imaginary voyages;[92] or like those of the mendacious Procopius,[93] who speaks of Britain in his day as an island lost in Cimmerian darkness and populated entirely by ghosts, whither the people of Brittany sailed on ceremonial missions to deposit their dead.

Images   November 1942

Like Lord Kelvin,[94] I can't understand anything that I can't present to my imagination in a pictorial form; and when I comprehend anything vividly, it's always in the terms of some visual image; which is one reason why I so admire the writers of the Jacobean and Caroline age, with their rich, elaborate fancies, Bacon, and Donne, and Milton, and Sir Thomas Browne. And therefore it is that I always think of the corrupt racketeers of the Secret Service – Gambier-Parry,[95]

---

92 Both Sir John Mandeville and the travel tales set in the Holy Land and Asia, which were attributed to him and circulated after 1356, are imaginary. Sinbad the Sailor is a character in Alexandre Dumas' novel *Le Comte de Monte-Cristo* (1844).

93 Procopius of Caesarea (d. after AD 562), historian of the Byzantine wars, whose memoirs decry Emperor Justinian.

94 William Thomson, 1st Baron Kelvin (1824–1907), Professor of Natural Philosophy at Glasgow University 1846–1899, scientist and inventor.

95 (Sir) Richard Gambier-Parry (1894–1965) worked in the BBC's public relations department until required to resign after his divorce, then as sales manager of Philco radio company, recruited by SIS in 1938 for radio work, Brigadier 1942, organised propaganda broadcasts to Europe from Whaddon Hall, Director of Communications to the Foreign Service 1947–1955, lived at Milton Keynes and in retirement was President of Bletchley Conservative Club and annual speaker at the Bletchley police dinner.

Maltby,[96] and all – as giant fungus, soft and yellow, flourishing in the dark clefts of a rotten tree; and the dithering, fraudulent old women of it, the Vivians[97] I mean, as flea-raddled old bats hanging precariously by one toe in a dark, unswept corner; and Maltby in particular, when he swivels his vast, blotchy, smirking face round the table at our committee meetings, puts me in mind of one of those baboons on Monkey Hill, exhibiting to all in turn their great iridescent blue bottoms, and sometimes it is a performing sea-lion that his clumsy, irrelevant antics call to mind on those occasions when, as Dick White[98] says, 'he turns his belly to the spray'; and the whole institution seems to me on some days like a Roman circus, full of expensive and exotic monsters; on others like the mythical upas tree of the Eastern Spice islands, beneath whose spreading shade no life can flourish. And so I was pleased when Stuart Hampshire likened old Dundas[99] to a vulture, appearing suddenly and inevitably from nowhere wherever there was any emotional carrion to be found, for I saw the picture at once, in all its lineaments, before me. Poetry too I love wherein the vast efforts of the imagination are compressed and rendered lucid and visible to the inner eye by this lively symbolism, as in Aesychlus, and in that wonderful poem of Rossetti's where all is seen from the high window of Heaven, – this earth spinning in the void below like a fretful midge, and the curlèd moon, like a little feather, fluttering far down the gulf, and the souls of lovers mounting up to God like thin flames, or going down to the deep wells of light, and old prayers, granted, melting each like a little cloud. The study of images, too, as illustrating the characters of their users, delights me. Miss Caroline Spurgeon has made such a study of Shakespeare's imagery,[100] and shown thereby the fastidium of Shakespeare, who hated bread,

---

96 Edward ('Ted') Maltby (1904–1981), son of a director of Barclay's Bank, was recruited in 1939 to run the Foreign Office's radio station at Hanslope Park and replaced Worlledge as head of RRS (MI8).

97 Colonel Valentine Vivian (1886–1969) joined SIS 1923, first head of MI6's counter-espionage unit, Section V, targeting the Comintern 1925–1939, when he became deputy director of the service.

98 (Sir) Dick White (1906–1993) was a pupil of Masterman's at Christ Church and at his mentor's instigation was recruited as a MI5 agent in 1935. He was head of MI5 1953–1956 and head of MI6 1956–1968. His wartime friendship with T-R proved lifelong.

99 Robin Dundas (1884–1960), Student of Christ Church 1910–1957, was a fretful, prurient bachelor who interrogated undergraduates on sexual habits and quandaries.

100 Caroline Spurgeon (1869–1942), Chaucer scholar and author of *Shakespeare's Imagery* (1935).

and was nauseated by dirt and grease, & disliked untidy clothes, and loved mute animals, all except slobbering, fawning spaniels, which he hated, as I do. And Logan has shown the somewhat meagre and finicky taste of Jeremy Taylor in this respect,[101] whose fancy played on the intricate patterns of light & water as, I think, did that of Apollonius of Rhodes;[102] and I have noticed how attractive the unattractive, austere, baroque character of St Augustine is in this particular, for he evidently loved the country and wild creatures too, and the subtilties of light and colour.

Paul Maas[103]

He is not to be confused with Paul Maze, the painter and social climber. He is a German classical scholar of elephantine learning and no taste who recently arrived in Oxford with his useless baggage of tedious erudition at the invitation of his fellow exile Fraenkel.[104] Denys Page has described him:

> If you study the infinite classes
> Of boring irrelevant asses
> And ask, Who is he
> At the top of the tree?
> The answer is obvious, Maas is.

---

101 *The Golden Grove,* Smith's selections from the works of Jeremy Taylor (1613–1667), was published in 1930.

102 Apollonius of Rhodes (3rd century BC) told of the search for the Golden Fleece by Jason and the Argonauts.

103 Paul Maas (1880–1964) was a scholar of Byzantine literature, Greek metre and palaeography. As an eighteen-year-old seminar student he corrected Wilamowitz. Expelled from his chair at Königsberg by the Nazis, he came to Oxford, where he never taught in the university, but advised the university press. His favourite meal was sauerkraut and chocolate, but in England he became an immoderate lover of porridge.

104 Eduard Fraenkel (1888–1970), a German Jewish classicist, was forbidden to teach when the Nazis took power in 1933. Elected to a Fellowship at Trinity College, Oxford in 1934, he held the Corpus chair in Latin (1935–1953), and pioneered the use of the German seminar method in Oxford. Fraenkel was furious when T-R included a swipe at his pedantry in his inaugural lecture as Regius Professor of Modern History (1957).

Stancliffe Hall   Nov 1942

In my directory of scrambler telephones I noticed, the other day, the name of J.C. Sterndale Bennett,[105] head of the Far Eastern section of the Foreign Office; and at that name a host of associations and recollections crowded before my mind, images from my childhood, a period so mute and drab that my naturally cheerful temperament rarely dwells upon it. For Sterndale Bennett occupied the next bed to mine at Stancliffe Hall, and shat in it nightly, thanks to the overdoses of liquid paraffin in which he indulged; and he beat me, aetate 9, in the only boxing-competition which I have been forced to enter, and was in other ways associated with me.

Wordsworth says that, after visions of delight in childhood, shades of the prison-house begin to close round the growing boy.[106] But my personal experience is just the reverse. My childhood was miserable; and looking back on it after the real happiness I have so often experienced since, I can recollect no real pleasure before the age of 16, when I began, bit by bit, like a hatching chick, to chip and peck my way out of the enclosing eggshell, and discover the gay, coloured world around me, and the stars above. Till then, it had all been silent, patient, unobservant indifference, protected by a self-created barrier of reserve, and only interrupted by occasional misery. And then, at Charterhouse, I began, quite suddenly, to discover that after all I wasn't seriously mocked or despised, that my refusal to play games wasn't really charged against me, and that, for the first time in my life, I was being regarded as a human being, to be treated with civility, not as a child, to be snubbed and apologised for. So I began to enjoy life at Charterhouse more than life at home, and accepting enthusiastically its standards, so novel and kindly, became a prig, but a prig with a capacity for pleasure that has since grown and grown, and more than compensated me for the delights of childhood which I never knew.

But the most miserable period of my life, the sole period that is always vivid to me in its deadening wretchedness, is my year at Stancliffe Hall, my first private school, in Darley Dale, near Matlock. It was an old-established school,

---

105 (Sir) John Sterndale Bennett (1895–1969), deputy commissioner general in Southeast Asia 1950–1953 and head of the British Middle East Office 1953–1955, was not at school with T-R. Sterndale William Bennett (1916–1998) may have been.

106 William Wordsworth (1770–1850), 'Intimations of Immortality', part v.

with traditions jealously preserved from the time of Dotheboys Hall, and I was sent there because some distant relative had been there in the last century; but I can recollect nothing of its architecture, or the country in which it lay, or indeed any of its external features, so enclosed was I in my own misery for the four terms that I kept there. I didn't love my home, but how I cried every time I left for Stancliffe Hall! The long corridors that stank of slop-pails and stale fish night and day; the cold mutton, all solid white fat, like lumps of chalk, and the catsmeat, smelling and full of tubes, that we were given to eat; the Scott's Emulsion that was ladled out to all of us by the matron when there was influenza in the school – in a bone spoon that served sixty boys and was never washed between the first mouth and the last; the protests we vainly made against the slovenly habits of the dormitory-maids who wiped out jerries and tooth-glasses with the same rag, so that the latter always had a haunting fragrance of stale wine; and my most vivid and regular recollection, implicit to me in the very name of the place, the dreary ritual of tea, when we all stood in the cold, flagged lobby, and tea was served from a great urn, so hot (to disguise its tastelessness) that we had to dilute it from the cold-water tap in the lobby sink to make it drinkable. So we stood around, sipping this insipid brew, while a master whom we called Twitch (I forget his real name, but his initials were T.W.H.) auctioned the slices of bread-and-butter which were all that there was to eat – 'A second slice for A1' (the top form), he would announce, and then read the form list, and each boy would approach the table in turn, and take a slice; and so on. I think everyone got two slices, but the supply rarely, if ever, allowed a third slice for all. Finally, I remember those long evenings in bed, before lights out, and the dreary church-bells, which always seemed to toll their most doleful sequence at that time of night, making misery more miserable by the formless, melancholy thoughts they always aroused in me. After four terms, I was taken away, and when I was told that I wasn't going back, I cried inconsolably for a whole afternoon – not indeed because I loved the place, but because I now felt callous to its misery, and could face the continuance of it, whereas to go to a new school would be to start all over again, which would be more than I could endure. But it wasn't, for this time I went to a better school, of which I have no such memories.

There are only two special incidents which I recall from my experience of Stancliffe Hall – my early loss of faith, and my first book.

Perhaps I expected too much of the Almighty on the first of these occasions, – but then our school scripture lessons consisted solely of readings from the more highly coloured books of the Old Testament, and the local rector had an eloquent sermon which he used to preach in the school chapel, the authentic tale of two small boys who, on a country walk, had disputed, pro and con, about the existence of God, till God, in the rector's certain knowledge, had terminated the dialogue with a thunderstorm and the descent of a tree on the head of the heterodox boy. Thus educated, I saw nothing unreasonable or improper in imitating Elijah and the Priests of Baal, and subjecting the Almighty to a simple empirical test.

I collected stamps in those days, and I was sensible of the absence from my collection of that triangular Cape of Good Hope stamp which was the glory of my fellow philatelists. Since I lacked the resources to supply this deficiency myself, I put my trust in the Lord, of whose wonderful works I had heard so much; for if God had condescended to disconcert the regularity of the solar system for Joshua, he would surely collaborate with me in filling a serious lacuna in my stamp-album. So I took an ordinary 2d stamp to bed with me and tore it to shreds, and prayed fervently, and resolved that if, in the morning, it had not been changed into an intact three-cornered Cape of Good Hope stamp, according to my detailed and explicit injunctions, I would have no alternative but to abandon belief in a God whose magical powers had plainly become obsolete. My incantations over, I stowed the shreds under my pillow, that God might not complain of lack of time and privacy for his conjuring-trick, and went, with difficulty, to sleep. On awakening in the morning, I groped eagerly under my pillow to verify the miracle. I was disappointed, of course, at what I found there; but I accepted, without flinching, the intellectual consequences of my experiment, and that morning God was silently dropped from my universe, to which he has never returned for more than brief and temporary visits.

The other incident was the appearance of my Bible of Ghosts, which was very popular in the school. It was a complete natural history of ghosts, subdivided into their genera and species, with full descriptions and illustrations – something like Edward Lear's illustration of plants (the manypeeplia upsidedownia and polybabia pyramidalis, etc), or Lewis Carroll's insects in *Through the Looking Glass*. I can only remember the Skittywakky Ghost, which issued out of mouse-holes, and wore elaborate head-dresses, like Queen Mary.

Classical and Baroque

I was dogmatising about style, and saying that perfect style is lucid and effortless, the expression not of simplicity but of complexities mastered and at rest; and at once I saw it before me, a still, translucent sea, deep, smooth, and serene, but beneath which a diver would find coiled and tangled forests of weeds, and submarine deserts of broken rocks and shipwrecks and dead bones, and coral labyrinths, and green caverns, and darkness, and subaqueous slime; but all these would be far below, deducible, not seen, under the smooth, glassy surface. But even before I had finished my generalisation, while I was still illustrating it with the classical names of Swift and Gibbon, and Johnson, and Flaubert, I saw the same scene at low tide, the water breaking over rotten, barnacled hulks and twisted spars, and gurgling up dark, tortuous caverns, and forming pools that reflected the whole sky in their narrow compass, with star-fish and sea-anemones in them; and there were gulls and cormorants and kittywakes about, and whelks and sea-urchins and hermit-crabs under the weeds and stones; and I realised that of course I was forgetting those wonderful baroque writers, Apuleius,[107] and St Augustine and John Donne, and Milton, and Sir Thomas Browne.

I was riding back from hunting yesterday, December 8th, with General Micklem,[108] and as we passed through Whitchurch, we met a bent and shapeless figure that came shuffling towards us, old and squalid, of infinite decrepitude, and all trussed up in rags for the winter. He was a local nomad, I learnt, who lived in a chicken-house; and I was beginning to pity him, if pity can apply to those who can be scarcely be included in any of the categories of humanity, when he drew level with us, and the General greeted him, and asked how he was. 'Like the morning star', he answered gaily, and shuffled on. (Of course he must have been Irish, as Gilbert reminded me afterwards; and of course he must really have said, 'Sure, it's like the morning star I am, your

---

107 Lucius Apuleius (Second century AD), born in Numida (now Algeria), author of the earliest entirely extant Latin novel *The Golden Ass*, a picaresque tale in which the dignified, ludicrous, voluptuous and horrible swiftly succeed each other.

108 Either Brigadier Ralph Micklem (1884–1977) or his brother Brigadier John Micklem (1889–1952).

honour', only I must have misheard him at the time). Indeed I was wrong to pity him, I said to myself afterwards, when, stayed with flagons by the hospitable general, I was trotting happily along the Oving road; for it's true, he can't be classed as humanity, he transcends it, a pure, poetic soul. And I thought of the Greek chorus who, in a song of exquisite beauty, wished that God might turn them into feathered fowls, and insert them into a flock of poultry, far from tragic humanity, – a happiness to which this old boy seemed to have attained in his philosophic chicken-house.

Mysteries   Dec 1942

The classical commentators and the religious historians are always telling us of the high purifying ritual of the Eleusinian mysteries, and the ennobling austerity of the Mithraic ceremonial. But it won't do. For I have eaten from the timbul, I have drunk from the symbal, I have been initiated into the mysteries; I have been a Freemason and a member of the Secret Service; and I have had enough of esoteric societies.

Woods and Streams   Dec 1942

Woods and streams and hills, how I do love them! It is among them that I feel capable of some of the intensest pleasure I know, and their images in literature and art evoke in me the image of that same felicity. Inevitably, I think of the South Oxfordshire woods where I have beagled and foxhunted, Studley Wood, Oakley Wood, Shabbington Wood, Hell Copse, and Waterperry Wood with its curiously named features, Polecat End and Drunkard's Corner; and the Bicester Woods, Tittershall and Doddershall, Ham Wood, Grendon, and the 'Big Woods' par excellence, that spread all the way from the Quainton hills to Charndon. And often I think of the great beech-woods at Stokenchurch, memorable to me for one association only, the day I beagled there with the New College & Magdalen Beagles, and the cry of hounds, as it rang echoing among those smooth, columnar boles still haunts me, so loud and clear was it, and infinitely reduplicated, like a canon in music, Bach's Goldberg canon perhaps, so complex, and yet regular in its rising & falling pattern. It seemed as if we were hunting in Westminster Abbey, or York Minster, or any great gothic cathedral; which is one of the things I have always wanted, but am never very likely to do.

Well, yesterday I knew such felicity; for I went out hunting with the Bicester at Ham Green, having caught a passing lorry at Apex Corner as dawn was breaking, and on my way thither I came across a stream, and in the cold, white light of a December dawn it had an unearthly beauty, as in a background by Leonardo, pale and white, like a long, sad jelly trailed across a waste land; and seeing it, my mind at once lit upon Shakespeare's line

> Gilding pale streams with heavenly alchymy.

Of course, I reflected, it was of the change from this colourless early morning to the lively, sunlit landskip that Shakespeare was thinking: for by daylight we never really see a pale stream, but at dawn water is always a sad and pallid element.

I arrived at Ham Green far too early for the meet, but it was a mild morning, and I walked abroad, and the fields were still dewy and the bare woods black, dead black, against the white morning sky; and I sat on a gate, my senses dwelling on the scene, and read in my pocket Horace of the pastoral world of Calabria, and Liris, now Garigliano, the silent stream, and Galaesus, and the creaking oakwoods of Garganus. But later, in the early afternoon, when the colours were up, we checked during a merry hunt, and I paused on the top of Finemere Hill with all the world beneath me; and there, before and below me, like a vast, undulating smoky-brown sea, stretched the Big Woods; and the pleasure of that sight remains with me, so that I really ought to include December 12th 1942 among my recorded days of undiluted felicity.

Health and Art   Dec 1942

Poor old Rowse says somewhere in his autobiography that he regards the old ideal of *Mens sana in corpore sano* as arrant nonsense and a contradiction in terms, or words to that effect; for when he rides his hobby-horses he does ride them with whips and spur. He prefers to believe that bodily health and intellectual force are incompatible things, and that art springs from the limitation of experience. Well, I suppose it's a tenable view for such as want to hold it, and for sure, since Flaubert and Leopardi were invalids, there's something to give a smack of taste to the weak, insipid soup of Wackenroder[109] and Proust. But I'm on the side of the Elizabethans, and Goethe, and St Aristophanes, my patron saint, and all whose philosophy is founded on experience, or, at least, on a bottom of common sense which presupposes experience. I'm for Gibbon and Surtees, not these etiolated continentals. Why even style depends on experience and observation, since style needs imagery, and imagery must be drawn from life, from wild beasts in the forest, and storms at sea, and low life in taprooms and circuses and at earthstoppers' dinners, and a relish and recollection of these things, and a sympathy with them. But who can draw a good image from private wards and clinking bedpans and cut flowers and demure white sheets and undertones, an unillumined world, without seasons, without laughter, where even a fart is an austere medical symptom only? But of course poor old Rowse hasn't any style, and perhaps he is thinking not of intellect or art but of sensitivity; and that, of course, is quite a different thing.

Salden Wood — Dec 1942

I was hunting with the Whaddon the other day, Dec 29th, from Mursley, and we were riding through the remote solitudes of Salden Wood,[110] and just as I was coming to the end of a ride, where it disembogued into the open fields, I observed, what was new since last year, a small cluster of wooden huts, and people, armed with kitchen-utensils, moving to and fro among them. 'A gypsy settlement', I said to myself; and if a tone of familiarity seemed to exist between the gypsies and the members of the hunt, well, we had had a very enjoyable chase from Mursley, and that always inspires a feeling of classless benevolence. While I thus mused and rode on, one of the gypsies ran up after me and asked whether I would have some cake, suggesting plum-cake, Christmas cake, or gingerbread; and what would I drink? Cherry-brandy? Cherry-whisky? I was still boggling at this unexpected wayside hospitality when another woman

109 Wilhelm Wackenroder (1773–1798), German romanticist.
110 Salden Wood, near Mursley, in the vale of Aylesbury, was an ancient Buckinghamshire woodland.

appeared with a tray of tempting drinks, and pyramids of rich cake followed, and the whole field was served. I ate my plum-cake, and drank my cherry-whisky with grateful relish, for it was an icy-cold, clear day, and the whole incident seemed to me like a scene from Don Quixote or the Arabian Nights, for who else, on a normal day's hunting, in the dead winter of a war-time year, has been unexpectedly refreshed with these luxuries by strange hermits living alone in the wild woods forlorn? I thought of the English settlers who were first entertained by the bewildered denizens of Virginia and Tahiti; and of Circe, whose enchanted refectory was also in a clearing in a dell; and of the fable of the Gingerbread House, for that, too, stored with entertainment, lay hidden in a solitary wood. Of course I made enquiries, and found that they weren't gypsies at all, but Mr & Mrs Harry Roberts, the owners of the wood, who, when their house in London was bombed, had retired hither and built themselves huts to live in by day, while at night they withdrew to Mursley. All their interests, too, had been transplanted to Salden Wood. I was shown the greenhouses they had erected, where orchids and other exotic flowers still bloomed, – and they entertained there so well that lunch in Salden Wood was likened to lunch in the Ritz; and their servants had come with them, such as were left, 'although of course', Mrs Digby Whitehead[111] explained to me, as if this part of their conduct required some apology, 'they don't keep them in livery here'.

The South Oxon had a good day, too, about Xmas, Col. Ashton told me.[112] Having killed two of Lord Harcourt's Japanese deer in Nuneham Park,[113] they went away in a cloud of stink and mud-spray, and huntsmen, whips and all the field were left nowhere. Nor were they ever seen again that morning, or that afternoon either; but at 8.0 p.m. it was rumoured that benighted wanderers on Shotover had been alarmed by a pack of ghost-hounds streaming in

111 Grace Ross, wife since 1925 of Digby Compton Whitehead (1874–1950).

112 Samuel Ashton (1888–1968), an old Christ Church man, was master of the South Oxfordshire Hounds 1920–1924 and cousin of Lord Ashton of Hyde, master of the Heythrop. His two sons were T-R's beagling companions.

113 Nuneham, seat of William, 2nd Viscount Harcourt (1908–1979), had been commandeered by the RAF as the Central Interpretation Unit for air surveillance photography. It was sold by Lord Harcourt to Oxford University in 1948. Since 1993 it has been used as the Global Retreat of the Brahma Kumaris World Spiritual University.

full cry through the blackout; so an expedition went forth in the dead night, he said, to fetch them back to the kennels at Stadhampton, and whether they were all yet recovered, he couldn't say.

———————

At a Christ Church Governing Body Meeting, when the investment of college capital was being discussed, someone advocated the general principle of investment in land, since for 300 years this had always proved profitable. 'But you must remember', interposed Hutchinson,[114] the Treasurer, 'that the last 300 years have been a very exceptional period'.

———————————

S.G. Owen

S.G. Owen was a character I hated.[115] Of course he had his defenders. Old scouts had uncontroversial tales of the incidents which gave him the title of 'D.T. Owen', – how he was once discovered, well in liquor, sitting in Mercury, with a jerry on his head, protesting he was a mushroom;[116] and when I knew him, those who had known him earlier all agreed that he was now a more mellow, less cantankerous figure than he had been. But even then he was a selfish, greedy, bigoted and conceited old man, who believed that a classical student of Christ Church was entitled, from his narrow eminence, freely and stupidly to insult the world. When Dr Gibson[117] once brought a guest to dine at High Table, and a Student turned up who had forgotten to sign on, Owen forced

———————

114 George Thomas Hutchinson (1880–1948), Treasurer of Christ Church 1910–1945, died of a heart attack while hunting with the Heythrop. 'A hard man, Sir', a college servant declared after his death.

115 The classicist Sidney George Owen (1858–1940) still ate at Christ Church after his retirement in 1926, for he liked plenty of victuals and drink. 'His simplicity was virile but almost maidenly,' said Dundas.

116 Mercury is an ornamental pond in the centre of Tom Quad, Christ Church.

117 Alexander Gibson (1875–1950), a lively, hospitable man nicknamed 'The Gibber', was T-R's physician. A Christ Church M.D., interested in cardiology and diseases of the spleen, the moving spirit of the Dunn School of Pathology, Fellow of Merton, Nuffield reader in morbid anatomy, consultant physician at Radcliffe Infirmary, author of *The Physicians' Art* (1933), a keen observer of wild birds and wild flowers, he possessed the equanimity which his friend Osler said was the requisite of a good physician.

Gibson to take his guest elsewhere, since Masters of Arts, he said, must in all circumstances come after Students. He hated Housman, whose arrogance he shared. In a review of Owen's *Juvenal*, Housman wrote that 'Mr Owen's innovations, so far as I can see, have only one merit, – which certainly, in view of their character, is a merit of some magnitude: they are few'; and elsewhere he spoke of Owen as an editor 'who uses his MSS as a drunken man uses a lamp-post: not to illuminate his path, but to conceal his own instability'. Owen retaliated when Housman, on some extraordinary impulse, published in *Hermes*, without introduction or explanation, an annotated collection of Latin references to various sexual perversions. 'He couldn't have known so much about them', said Owen, 'if he hadn't practised them all'. Such are the elegantiae of scholars.

Gilbert and Colin Dillwyn[118] shared my dislike to Owen, and one day, meeting him pottering round the Parks, with a stick and a drop on the end of his red nose, Colin suggested that he should be pushed into the river to drown. It would take very little force, he said, to dispose of an old man of well over 80; no one was looking; it would soon be over; and when the body was found, it would be presumed that the old boy had slipped up unobserved, or fainted with age at the water's edge. But in fact Owen was allowed to live on for another year; and then, one afternoon, when he returned from his potter round the Parks, he said to his servant that he felt tired and would take a nap. So he lay down on his sofa, and she bundled him up in his rug, and prepared to depart; but he called her back, 'Mary, I think the whisky-decanter is nearly empty – you might order another couple of bottles'. Then he closed his eyes and died.

---

118 Colin Dillwyn (1912–1940), research fellow at the Queen's College 1934–1935, returned from historical research in the West Indies to succeed Feiling as history tutor at Christ Church in 1936. He had a gift for assimilating masses of knowledge at top speed. He was one of the young reformers, including Ayer and Ryle, who in 1939 sought to laicise Christ Church by changing the statutes to permit the appointment of a secular head. He was killed in the Dunkirk retreat, while serving with the Oxfordshire & Buckinghamshire Light Infantry.

1943

In 1943 Trevor-Roper's departmental superiors, Cowgill and Vivian, who found him incorrigibly insubordinate, expected that he would be disciplined or dismissed after making direct approaches to Lord Cherwell, the Christ Church physicist who was Churchill's adviser on weaponry and tactics. Instead, in May, the Radio Analysis Bureau, the Radio Security Service intelligence subsection led by Trevor-Roper, was removed from the ambit of the SIS radio communication section and brought under the aegis of Sir Stewart Menzies, head of MI6. Trevor-Roper was promoted to the rank of Major. Ryle and Pearsall Smith, with their witty provocations and unwavering excellence of mind, remained the chief redemptive influences in Trevor-Roper's wartime existence. Northumberland, hunting men and Rubberneck provided his other consolations.

Retrospect   January 1943

I've just been reading my diary for 1938, and it gave me a shock. Did I do any serious work then? I asked myself. But of course I did, I quickly reassured myself, for I was compiling my book on *Archbishop Laud* (though there is very little to indicate that in my diary), and all critics have commented on the astonishing amount of work it incorporates, and the amazingly short time in which it was done. All the same, could I not have done even more work, or at least sought more varied experiences, travelled more, developed more interests, cultivated other friendships? For that is an irrecoverable period, into which too much of experience, actual, intellectual and emotional, cannot be poured. At least such is the conviction that grows oppressively upon me, and the lines of Rubén Darío

> Juventud, divino tesoro,
>> Ya te vas para no volver![1]

toll in my mind like a maddening, repetitive bell. But from that diary I get the impression that I did nothing but hunt foxes and hares, and dine out, and drink, and talk, and exercise my horse on Sundays, and go to occasional race-meetings, and enjoy low-life, and exercise hounds in the sweet early air on summer mornings. And the amount one drank in those forgotten days of cheap and plenteous wine! Never less than three bottles of claret or burgundy, or two of port, between two people, to keep conversation going after a convivial dinner. There was no introspection then, no hesitancy or doubt (there is none in my book either), I was always in over-brimming health (as I needed to be for the violent life I led), and I was always happy. And yet looking at the chronicle of that life now, I wished I had been less happy then, for I saw the justice of Tom Armstrong's criticisms, which I so resented when they came, two years later, and I saw the truth of Halifax's aphorism, 'Content is to the mind like moss to a tree; it bindeth up so as to stop its growth.'[2]

Gilbertiana

In Common Room an earnest discussion was going on with some visiting undergraduates, when someone held it up saying, 'but what is the difference between the soul and the intellect?' The question was referred to Gilbert. Without waiting a moment, or lifting his eyes from his glass of beer, Gilbert answered nonchalantly, 'The intellect is that part of you with which you read books other than the Bible'.

---

1 Youth, divine treasure,/ You are leaving never to return!: opening lines of 'Spring-Autumn Song' by Rubén Darío (1867–1916), poet and Nicaraguan diplomat, whose life was wrecked by alcoholism.

2 George Savile, 1st Marquess of Halifax (1633–1695), author of *The Character of a Trimmer*.

Gilbert described Philip Landon as 'one of those Etonians who have joined the school as an old boy'.[3]

Someone in our office said that Steedman, of M.I.6, and Curry, of M.I.5, were researching on some subject together. 'Steedman and Curry collaborating to produce intelligence?' exclaimed Gilbert. 'It's like two mules trying to breed.'[4]

The Americans   Jan 1943

Herbert Hart[5] and I were speaking despairingly of the Americans, – these callow, touchy, boastful, flatulent invaders, who seem to think themselves, as politicians, a match for the case-hardened double-crossers of struggling, tortured Europe. Will they never see, I protested, that they are only great children, pampered children of the rich, among experienced and desperate sharpers? Will they never admit that Europe, though torn with immemorial conflicts, is still the foundry of the world's ideas, while they are fresh from their luxurious nursery? But Herbert likened them to the Romans in the second century B.C., when they overran the East; and they look on us, he said, as the Romans looked upon the Greeks, miserable people, scratching about subtleties and upsetting the peace of the world. What interest have they in the ideas that divide Darlan from de Gaulle?[6] Now I had recently been reading

---

3 Landon (see note 1, 1940–1941), who had attended a newly founded school for the sons of naval officers near Tavistock, venerated Etonian undergraduates.

4 Steedman has not been identified. John ('Jack') Curry (1887–1970), a MI5 officer specialising in counter-subversion, was seconded in 1943 to MI6's new unit monitoring Communist penetration and espionage in foreign countries.

5 Herbert [H.L.A.] Hart (1907–1992) was a Fellow and philosophy tutor at New College, Oxford, Professor of Jurisprudence 1952–1968 and Principal of Brasenose 1973–1978.

6 Jean-François Darlan (1881–1942), who had been assassinated in Algiers on Christmas Eve, was appointed *Amiral de la flotte* commanding the entire French navy in 1939, and deputy to Pétain in the collaborationist Vichy government in 1941. The confirmation of Darlan in the post of French High Commissioner in North Africa (November 1942) by the American general Dwight Eisenhower outraged General Charles de Gaulle (1890–1970), leader of the Free French forces.

Mommsen,[7] and I saw in terrible detail the picture he had suggested, – those sudden vulgarians of the west, like a fresh, loud, frothy heedless tidal wave, deluging the brilliant but atomised republics, the 'ancient, famous states' of the old world, and burying their splendid past in universal banality.

It nearly broke her father's heart
When Lady Jane became a tart;
But blood is blood, and race is race,
And so, to save her parents' face,
They bought her an expensive beat
From Asprey's down to Grosvenor Street.

Charles Stuart and Herbert Hart feel strongly about characters like Vivian and Maltby in S.I.S., whom, puritanically, they find morally repulsive and disgusting. But I'm afraid I can't; nor, I think, can Dick White. To me, these characters are so incredibly remote, so far beneath the most indulgent condescension, that I can no more entertain serious feelings about them than about the parasites in the plays of Plautus; whom they resemble in other respects too, – for without them the comedy would be unremitting tedium.

'In some respects', said Gilbert, in course of a conversation on Socrates, 'Socrates was rather a Joad'.[8]

---

7 Theodor Mommsen (1817–1903), Roman historian and archaeologist, Prussian parliamentarian and jurist, whose scholarship combined minute precision with bold generalisations.

8 Cyril Joad (1891–1953), head of the philosophy department at Birkbeck College, London, became famous on the BBC radio Brains Trust programme. Labour parliamentary candidate for the Combined Scottish Universities constituency, his hopes of a barony were dashed when he was convicted of travelling without a railway ticket in 1948. Short, tubby and shabby, with piggy eyes and a bristly beard, he was conceited and lecherous, and described sexual desire as 'a buzzing blue-bottle that needed to be swatted promptly before it distracted a man of intellect from higher things'.

Northumberland   March 1943

O these endless dichotomies that torment the wavering soul! Must every road that I follow immediately branch in two before me? Love of the remote pastoral solitudes that give me so intense a pleasure, and love of intellectual conversation and society that seem incompatible with them; restless vitality & love of life, and yet delight in indolence & contemplation.

Every time I think of Northumberland, this problem faces me, for of course there's no intellectual life in that delightful county, no salons or conversazioni or exquisite pedantries, but I love the place, and have the happiest memories of it, and of particular parts of it especially. That great stretch, for instance, north of Belford, where the high, lonely moors are separated only by a narrow strip of green pasture from the flat grey sands and the sea, in which are Holy Island and the Farne Islands, with their seals and sea-birds of every kind. The air is clear there, and fresh from the sea, and I remember once hunting a September fox there, with Roly Milvain's hounds[9] – just Roly, Tom and myself – a nine mile point from Belshill to the top of Kyloe; and as I rode back, I marvelled to see that whole long stretch of countryside coloured and variegated by the cloud-broken autumn sunlight, as it picked out and enhanced, through that bright, transparent air, the purple, the green, the yellow-grey, and the blue. And once we hunted a fox there, all along the wet tidal sands of Budle Bay, in the twilight, and as I rode back, an old farmer told me of the coastal foxes there, that have little or no scent, being in and out of the water so often; and how the Percy once killed one of them a hundred yards out to sea, swimming towards Holy Island, and all the pack swimming after it. When killed it sank, and Kinch rode out till the sea-water was over his boots, and lowering his crop by the thong, hooked it up from the bottom. And then there's Eglingham, and the Kimmer loch, and Beauley, and Chillingham, where between fox-hunting and beagling and coursing I know every inch of the country and am yet unsated. In Chillingham Park I have ridden after a fox straight through the herd of wild white cattle, and they hardly stirred, so docile had they become with winter feeding; and beagling there with John Milburn, I once had to

9 Roland Milvain (1880–1960), of Eglingham Hall, Alnwick, was master of the Percy foxhounds 1910–1921, and thereafter hunted his own pack.

go through the Till five times in an afternoon in December, – but drink is a preservative against all consequences.

———————————

The River Douro   March 1943

Rose Macaulay[10] is going to Portugal, and, in discussing her projects, she mentioned the Anglo–Portuguese port-families on the Douro. What a thought for the passionate potamolator like myself! I saw the whole picture at once, – a series of fine villas with ample pleasure-grounds sloping down to the golden river Douro whose vineyards, ever since the days of the Methuen Treaty,[11] had yielded their steady yearly increment to those proud dynasties of Dow and Cockburn, Grant and Fonseca. I thought of the great Thames-side country-houses of the 18th century English aristocracy, with their orchards and lawns, regattas and water-music; of the robber-barons and robber-bishops with their castellated fortresses on the Rhine and fabulous gothic nympholepsy; and of Ausonius' Moselle, sliding softly past the villas where the 4th century Gallo-Roman nobility, like Horace Walpole, polished and polished their careful epistolary style. And since Mirko Rot, a Yugoslav Jew from Novisad,[12] who had some useful intelligence about the German secret service in Sofia, happened to have arrived in Lisbon, I at once applied to be flown thither to interrogate him, which was approved. But alas! Mirko Rot was an indiscreet and voluble creature, unfit for secret employment in that centre of the European spy-web; so the plan was changed, and he was flown back to London instead, to be interviewed there. But at any rate, my vision of the Douro was thereby preserved unbroken.

———————————

10 T-R often met the novelist (Dame) Rose Macaulay (1881–1958) at Pearsall Smith's house. Her book on Portugal was published in 1946.

11 An Anglo–Portuguese treaty of 1703, negotiated by John Methuen during the War of the Spanish Succession, with extensive commercial clauses.

12 Mirko Rot (alias Imre Rot and Michael Rath) was a clothier of Hungarian antecedents who escaped from the Balkans in 1942 by bribing an Abwehr officer and signing up as a German agent. He was transferred from Portugal to Camp 020 for interrogation.

I'm afraid the Beveridge marriage, like the Beveridge report, is taken rather profanely in Oxford, where Maurice Bowra referred to it as 'the Purification of the Blessed Virgin Mair'.[13]

Eavesdrops   March 1943

Once, talking with Gilbert, I had said that literature needed a new form, since the old are all trite and weary. Plato gave it a new form with his philosophic dialogues, and St Augustine with his *Confessions*, and Montaigne with his *Essays*, and Pascal with his *Pensées*, and Samuel Butler with his *Notebooks*; and the Pastoral and Picaresque novel were new forms at one time; and now it's time for another; but what should it be?

At the time I could think of no answer, neither could Gilbert; but since then I have read some of the admirable eavesdrops which M.I.19 collect, with the aid of a Dictaphone, from our prisoners of war, and I have decided that the overheard conversation, with its artlessness, its purposelessness, its irrelevant digressions, its tantalising interruptions, is perhaps the form which I have been seeking.

Of course it mustn't be entirely artless; one must start by selecting one's victims; and my victims were the two captured Panzer Generals, Crüwell[14] and Ritter von Thoma.[15]

Gen. Crüwell is a very worthy man, and a Prussian. He is sensible and realistic, as all must be who have lived through a great revolution; but he is timid, and dares not add to the physical discomforts of captivity, the mental

---

13 Sir William Beveridge (1879–1962), Director of the London School of Economics 1919–1937, Master of University College, Oxford 1937–1945 and architect of the Welfare State. On 15 December 1942, a few days after publication of his epochal report 'Social Insurance and Allied Services', he had married his recently widowed cousin Jessy Mair, an overbearing, moody and unpopular woman.

14 Ludwig Crüwell (1892–1958), commander of the Afrika Korps, was captured in Libya on 29 May 1942 when his aircraft landed behind British lines because of pilot error.

15 Wilhelm, Ritter von Thoma (1891–1948), a tank commander who deputised for Rommel in North Africa, was captured on 4 November 1942 when his tank was immobilised during the Battle of El Alamein. He was a prisoner-of-war at Trent Park, Barnet and subsequently at Wilton Park, Beaconsfield, where his leg was amputated in 1945.

discomfort of accepting his own logic. He doesn't like the Nazis – they tried to murder him on June 30th 1934 – but he likes defeat less, for he has four children. Time and again, in conversation with German air-force officers and U-boat commanders, he would check himself, as the tenor of his own arguments become clear to him. 'No, no, as a prisoner of war I say to myself, I believe in victory to the last; otherwise I would go mad.' 'It *must* work, or it will be the end of Germany for centuries.' 'But people *can't* collapse internally, the S.S. are too sharp; they would shoot them all.' So he would pull himself up, and refusing to continue the dangerous discussion, would digress to other topics, – the impotence of the other generals, the brilliance of his Serbian campaign, the undue favour shown to the German Air Force, the bad advice taken by the Führer, the fatal wealth and obstinacy of the English. And then Churchill, a wonderful man, far greater than Roosevelt. Of course no one expected the English to go on fighting in 1940 – it was madness – but this Churchill, oh if only he would die! The Führer, in his recent speech (and I admit it was in bad taste) called him a drunkard. Dare we hope – could it be that the Führer has reliable secret information on the subject? Supposing Churchill were to die of drink, – but alas! he has a constitution of iron – think of the work he does, and all those strong cigars he smokes! Poor Crüwell, between his intelligence and his timidity, he is a pitiable figure. How gladly he grasps again at some more promising topic – his capture of Belgrade, for instance, a brilliant campaign, comparable, to its advantage, with the best of Hannibal's, – but there's a fly in the ointment, too – all those unjust charges of looting made against him. Why, from that princely castle in which he made his HQ he took nothing for himself, he protests, not even a picture. Of course he requisitioned 18000 bottles of wine from the cellars for his division, but what is that among so many? A bottle per man to celebrate a great victory – nothing! And then came the news of the battle of El Alamein, and the occupation of French North Africa; and then, a result of the battle, he was joined by a new prisoner, Gen. Ritter von Thoma.

Gen. von Thoma is a very different character. A Bavarian, a well-educated man, of strong character, shrewd perception, and trenchant expression, he has moved fearlessly and uncompromisingly in the great world. 'I am not, and never have been, a Nazi', he states; and unlike Crüwell, he has given no hostages to the future; for he is a bachelor. 'It's all very well for you to say that', wails poor Crüwell in answer to one of his frank statements, 'but you haven't got four children'.

So these two old professionals talk on together, exchanging memories and verdicts. How they both detest Rommel,[16] arrogant, vain, obstinate, vulgar and incompetent! and Nehring[17] – 'if he comes here as a P/W, I shall go mad'. Halder,[18] he was a good man, but now he's sacked. How badly they've treated the old generals – that shocking Fritsch affair,[19] staged by Heydrich,[20] was the beginning of it all – and how many of them have been killed in Africa, and in that mad Russian venture![21] And then there are the party-bosses, the Bonzen, who alone have profited from the revolution, upstarts now living in huge palaces and paying no taxes, men like Christian Weber,[22] the uncrowned King of Bavaria. A coarse fellow, says Thoma, I knew him well. He was a stable-boy to Fränkl the Jew horse-dealer from whom all officers used to buy their horses in the old days, and now he owns a huge racing-stable, having bought the Aga Khan's and the Rothschilds' horses, and a country-house at Leutstetten,[23] built in the middle of the war, and stables and loose-boxes at Deichselfurt, his beautiful Bavarian estate, which are a horses' paradise – I've never seen any loose-boxes like them, except in Tetuan, where the sheikh keeps his sacred horse. Even the ruling politicians aren't free from von Thoma's merciless tongue, – Hess[24]

---

16 Erwin Rommel (1891–1944), one of Hitler's most successful commanders before the El Alamein defeat.

17 Walter Nehring (1892–1983) had been succeeded by Crüwell as commander of the Afrika Korps in March 1942. He ended the war as commander of the First Panzer Army.

18 Franz Halder (1884–1972), Chief of Army General Staff until 1942, was involved in the abortive military plot against the Nazi leadership in 1938. T-R later praised Halder's account of Hitler's relations with his military commanders for its objectivity and accuracy.

19 Werner, Freiherr von Fritsch (1880–1939) was falsely accused by Himmler and Göring of homosexuality and forced to resign as Commander-in-Chief of the German army in 1938. Acquitted by a court martial; killed in the siege of Warsaw – the first German general to die in combat in the Second World War.

20 Reinhardt Heydrich (1904–1942), 'the Blond Beast', pre-war head of the Gestapo, was blamed by Himmler for the failure of the Fritsch affair. As wartime Reich Protector of Bohemia and Moravia, he chaired the Wannsee conference which settled the extermination of European Jews.

21 Both Crüwell and von Thoma had served with distinction in Operation Barbarossa. The latter led the tank advance on Moscow.

22 Christian Weber, a former stables groom who became an obese, beer-swilling President of Munich municipal council, and was one of the most financially corrupt of the Nazi bosses, was killed in the Bavarian uprising of 1945.

23 A village near Munich where the Bavarian royal family had stabled their horses.

24 Rudolf Hess (1894–1987), Hitler's deputy, strangled himself with electrical cord in Spandau prison, aged 93, after 45 years' incarceration.

has a Messiah-complex and will only eat vegetables planted at full moon; Hitler surrounds himself with coarse drinking companions, always the same. He can't sleep any more at night, and has ever wilder attacks of rage, – in Munich they call him *Teppichfresser*, carpet-biter.[25] You're romancing, protests the incredulous Crüwell, but no, Thoma goes on, it's quite true, he lies on the floor, and snaps around like a mad dog. And then those absurd architectural fantasies of his, that 'House of German Art' in Munich, – a glorified public latrine! – he built it on a notorious marsh, spending a million and a half marks on the cement-piles alone – pure megalomania and the worst monstrosities of the Reich chancellery in Berlin are all his own inventions. 'My dear fellow', expostulates Crüwell, 'es ist ganz schrecklich was Sie alles sagen!'[26]

But best of all is Thoma's description of Göring, and Göring's country palace at Karinhall.

'Is there any truth', asks Crüwell, 'in the story that Göring has bought himself a house in Stockholm?' 'Yes', replies Thoma, 'and on the Riviera, and at Capri. All on the grounds of state representation. I'll tell you something about Göring – I knew he went in for all these things; but Heliogabulus …'[27]

When I lit on this passage, a new image presented itself to my mind. I saw Göring, not now standing on the Channel coast in the summer of 1940, and looking daily through his glasses at the chalk cliffs of Dover, but Göring riding in a chariot drawn by naked virgins, Göring introducing new, exotic religions into Berlin and lascivious dances and barbarous music, 'whilst the gravest personages of the state and the army, clothed in long Phoenician tunics, officiated in the meanest functions with affected zeal and secret indignation'. But unfortunately Crüwell hadn't heard of Heliogabulus, so Thoma switched off to tell how he was driving out with Generaloberst Model …[28]

Crüwell: He's mad!

---

25 The journalist William Shirer, in *Berlin Diary* (1941), reported that in Munich in 1938 he heard a covert anti-Nazi call Hitler *Teppichfresser*, or carpet-eater. Thoma's use of the phrase vitiates Sir Ian Kershaw's suggestion that Shirer misunderstood German slang meaning 'climbing the wall'.

26 Everything you say is really terrible!

27 Elagabalus: see note 50, 1940–41.

28 Walther Model (1891–1945) was known as the *Frontschwein* (Front-line pig) because of his foul language and crudity. He specialised in defensive battles of attrition, with high casualties on both sides, and was notorious for his chaotic disruption of chains of command. Hitler called him the saviour of the Eastern Front.

Thoma: Yes. I said, 'There's the Reichsmarschall!' He was standing there in the distance like a great white stone pillar. I saw the Maharaja of Kapurthala[29] in Venice a few years ago, and Göring looked just like him, only he had no turban. He was dressed completely in white silk – a white silk shirt such as the Doges used to wear, with big puffed sleeves, and over that a hunting-coat of white patent-leather, and a white silk tie fastened with a clasp as big as your thumb, with one blue and two yellow diamonds, all sparkling; and then (I'm not exaggerating) a huge buckle as big as an octavo volume, made of gold, with sapphires and rubies, on his wide belt. On his head he wore St Hubert's stag, with a swastika of gleaming pearls set between the antlers.

Crüwell: How is that you get on so well with the Führer?

Thoma: Because I speak Bavarian dialect. That's the whole secret of it: I speak to him in Bavarian. I know Jodl[30] very well too – they told me that he cheered the Führer up – I knew him when he was a private. I knew Göring in old days too. Only ten years ago Göring was living in quite small official quarters in the Badischenstrasse in Berlin, and there wasn't a single piece of furniture that wasn't mortgaged to his creditors. That was only ten years ago, and now he's the richest man in Europe. But they say he suffers a lot from depression …

And now let us turn to the richest man in Europe in his country retreat.

Thoma: I was in Karinhall once. Göring has very fat fingers, and he had to hold his hands like this – he had rings on – I'm not exaggerating, – he had a blue diamond the size of your finger-nail, which must have been enormously valuable; it would probably have cost half a million marks. I've heard that a lot of these jewels came from that big jeweller's in the Place Vendôme in Paris. Then he had rings with huge emeralds and rubies in them – he could have lived comfortably for the rest of his life on the proceeds of one of them. We stayed there from 10.0 a.m. till 4.0 p.m. We had a conference, and at 3 o'clock he gave us soldiers' ration-sandwiches. He himself disappeared into his private quarters. I told Generaloberst Jodl that he seemed to live very simply. We actually had ordinary soldiers' ration-sandwiches. Then Göring invited us to have a look over Karinhall. Brauchitsch's son was there[31] – he

---

29 Sir Jagatjit Singh Bahadur (1872–1949), Maharaja of Kapurthala since 1877.

30 Alfred Jodl (1890–1946), Chief of Operations Staff of the German army, 1939–1945.

31 Walther von Brauchitsch (1881–1948) succeeded Fritsch as Commander-in-Chief of the German Army in 1938. A weak leader and ineffectual strategist, he was promoted Field-Marshal but dismissed by Hitler in 1941.

was his adjutant for a long time. I believe he's a major now; he was an Oberleutenant then.

Crüwell: Oberleutenant der Luftwaffe?

Thoma: Yes. Next day Göring had completely different rings on. He appeared as Reichsmarschall, but in a fancy uniform, light blue, and carrying his Reichsmarschall's baton, a very valuable thing, – you could buy a large country house with it. It was made of pure gold and ivory, and had the crest of the Luftwaffe all over it, as it might have had the Prussian eagle. A grotesque thing, with enormous jewels on it, that sparkled and flashed. Then we had a look over Karinhall. I'm very interested in antiques, and this was the finest, most sumptuous, and most elegant place I'd ever seen. His so-called work-room is like a medium-sized church, with huge oak-beams and *ausgesucht*[32] works of art. *Ausgesucht* in every respect – you could see straightaway that we had conquered France. He has got his art-gangsters who go everywhere. Göring's and Hitler's art-gangsters have been pretty busy in Italy. I know that for a fact, because I know these people. Money doesn't matter, – it all counts as 'state representation'.

Crüwell: Does he really appreciate these beautiful things?

Thoma: I can only tell you what Brauchitsch told me. He said, 'Today is Sunday, and today our Reichsmarschall will be running round changing the position of his pictures, and saying, "We'll hang this Rubens here today, and the Van Dyck there tomorrow." He keeps on changing them round.'

Crüwell: Is that a kind of snobbery, or what?

Thoma: No, he gets a curious sort of pleasure out of it. He has things of incredible value. I've never seen such tapestries. Of course they came from Vienna. I recognised the Viennese Gobelin tapestries at once.

Crüwell: But they come from the Hofburg?

Thoma: Yes, from the Hofburg. He had everything you could think of. When I was there, a major of the Luftwaffe arrived from France, and said, 'I've just arrived with the Junkers, and at last we've got those damned Gobelin tapestries'. There's a family called Markiewicz in Lyon. The husband lives apart from his wife, and he had two late Gothic Gobelin tapestries well-known in the history of French art. They are the most valuable tapestries in the world. They are 8 or 10 metres long, and 5 metres wide, depicting the most beautiful hunting scenes, and the colours look as though they'd been painted yesterday.

32 Exceptional.

Their value must run into millions of marks. Göring got to hear of them through his art-gangsters, and went methodically after them. The wife was negotiating with Göring to sell the tapestries, and had more or less come to an agreement with him, when the husband found about it, and immediately presented them as works of art to the French state, so that they should remain in France. As there were great difficulties about it with the French state, Göring not only got in touch with Laval,[33] he even told old Pétain[34] that he must have those tapestries. At all events, they were sent over with Laval's consent, and they had just arrived that day. Göring was just like a beaming art-collector. The tapestries were hung provisionally in a huge room – the finest tapestries I've ever seen.

Crüwell: Does Göring actually live in Karinhall?

Thoma: As a rule. He told me himself that he's happiest there. But the tapestry room: one wall is without exaggeration twice the size of this wall here, and the whole wall is one large glass window. He has one famous picture from France of the Marquise de Pompadour walking through a meadow, dressed as a shepherdess. He has old Roman bishops' staves, and Augsburg work,[35] and all the fine things that the world can offer. It reminded me of the Kaiser Friedrich Museum. He's got a lot of things from there too, – for instance the famous *Man with the Golden Helmet*.[36] He doesn't pay any taxes – it's all done through a limited company under the guise of State Representation. Surely you know that none of the Party Bosses make their tax-returns as we do? They don't make any at all – they have their own tax offices. It's such a swindle, the way it's worked – I'm only telling you what I know to be true from the fellows themselves. They told me that a Gauleiter only pays a fraction of what you and I pay. Their taxes don't go through the ordinary channels.

And then those rooms! The Reichsmarschall told us to take a look over everything as we wanted, and Brauchitsch actually said, 'This is just the everyday stuff; the really valuable things are in the huge bomb-proof safes under

---

33 Pierre Laval (1883–1945), pre-war French Prime Minister and again (as a Nazi collaborator) 1942–1944, was shot by firing squad while vomiting from the effects of attempted suicide by cyanide.

34 Philippe Pétain (1856–1951), Field Marshal and French head of state 1940–1944.

35 Augsburg was the richest city in sixteenth-century Germany, famed for its jewellers, goldsmiths, wood-carvers, sculptors in bronze, and baroque decorative arts.

36 Painted by Rembrandt.

Karinhall'. One of his own art-gangsters told me that you could reckon the value of the works of art at Karinhall at between 250 and 300 million gold marks. And to think that ten years ago he hadn't a chair to call his own! That's what you'd call a step up in the world. The things are absolutely marvellous!

Crüwell: Does he work at Karinhall every day, or does he go to Berlin?

Thoma: He only goes there when he must. When you go to Karinhall in the Schorfheide, you come first to the gateway. Then you drive five or six km till you come to a sort of farm, where the company of guard troops live, and where the A.A. guns etc are. And then you come to this colossal building, all covered with camouflage-netting of course. He has a library like the Vatican library, all domed. Then he has a conference-room, every piece of furniture perfect. His desk is about 8 metres long and 2 metres wide, made of thick mahogany, in Empire style, but with the new emblems, – the Luftwaffe badge, for instance, and the Luftwaffe Storm-Trooper's badge, and of course the swastika, all inlaid bronze. It's wonderful! And on it he has two big baroque candelabra, and an inkstand all in oynx, and a long ruler of green ivory studded with jewels. Karinhall is the most lovely place I've ever seen.

Crüwell: Does Göring give the impression of being nervous?

Thoma: Not at all. Of course he's enormously fat, – that's the result of the wound he got on the 9th November 1923, which caused a glandular change. He has a tremendous appetite – he doesn't eat, he gorges, enough for ten men. I don't grudge it him, because one feels that he lives for this sort of thing! He's like someone from the time of the Medici.

––––––––––

The Medici indeed, those cultivated and discriminating princes! No, but the Roman millionaires, Mummius[37] and Verres,[38] Crassus,[39] Lucullus,[40] and Hortensius,[41] and the rest, who sacked or ransacked the cities of the East to stuff their palaces with its treasures, and bedizened the lampreys in their

---

37 Lucius Mummius Achaicus (fl 147 BC), consul who plundered Corinth and Thebes.

38 Caius Verres (120–43 BC), Roman magistrate notorious for his rapine as governor of Sicily.

39 Marcus Linnius Crassus (*c.* 112–53 BC), slave-dealer, silver-mine owner, and governor of Syria.

40 Lucius Licinius Lucullus (*c.* 118–56 BC), consul and victorious general in the Mithridatic war.

41 Quintus Hortensius (114–50 BC), orator.

fishponds with golden earrings in their exorbitant ostentation! They had their art-gangsters!

So I read on in these fascinating documents, so unscrupulously obtained, and began to like these two old generals, and to hope (since they have so plainly hinted their wishes), in spite of the new conversations it would occasion, that Rommel and Nehring are not closeted with them, if they are brought back from Africa in bondage.

An Enigma   March 1943

The problem of happiness, and the purpose of life, why do these two irrational, insoluble enigmas so pester me, night and day?

It's no good looking for happiness, you won't find it thereby. It eludes direct search, and only turns up incidentally, and unawares. And anyway, is it a boon to covet, since content, like moss upon a tree, smothers what it embraces? Is it not better to remember, as Mommsen wisely, though perhaps not originally, says of Hannibal, that whom the gods love experience both great happiness and disappointment? And is there not in this bitter-sweet mixture, to a fastidious palate, a more exquisite flavour than in the unheightened taste of ordinary felicity?

I count Winston a happy man according to my definition, – at least so far. σκοπέειν δὲ χρὴ παντὸς χρήματος τὴν τελευτὴν κῇ ἀποβήσεται.[42] Him surely the gods love, for he has lived fully and learnt widely; he has learnt the bitter taste of disappointment from long experience, and has discovered its antidote in life and literature; and the sweet, intoxicating taste of success he knows also. In his exile he wrote, like Clarendon, a great work which Destiny itself seemed to have reserved particularly for him; and his exile lasted long enough for him to complete it; and then the prophet was summoned from the wilderness to save his country, and, it seems, he has saved it; not, unlike Lloyd George, leaving rancour and recrimination in his wake, but healing divisions, obliterating enmities, forgetting injuries. Must not a man who has

---

42 But one must gauge how every matter will turn out in the end (Solon to Croesus at Herodotus 1.32.9).

fared thus bless God, as Henry More expressed it, to all Eternity for that Lick of Bitterness he has experienced in this present life?

Genius, poor old Rowse has said – it is to me the one memorable remark in that pussycat autobiography of his – is the one saving phenomenon that illuminates and redeems the else drab and meaningless story of mankind. And genius and happiness rarely go together. *Ingenio caput et plantae caeduntur.*[43]

And yet there have been men of genius who have been happy in the ordinary association of the word, without any lick of bitterness; men who quietly cultivated an attainable ideal, and quietly attained it, – an Olympian, not a dionysiac felicity; Gibbon, Haydn, and of course Horace.

Logan said, 'One man is born to do the world's work and win its prizes, and another to sit apart, quietly observing; and each, when they meet, despises himself'.

Macaulay   March 1943

I was reading Macaulay, and on the same day alit by chance on two passages in which he touches on the unfortunate topic of homosexuality – or unisexuality, as poor old Farnell called it, when he too, with equal embarrassment, felt called upon to explain it away in a note upon Pindar.[44] In Jacobite pamphlets, says Macaulay, William III 'would have seen that the unalterable affection which he felt from his boyhood to his death for three or four of the bravest and most trusty friends that ever prince had the happiness to possess, was made a ground for imputing to him abominations as foul as those which are buried under the waters of the Dead Sea'; and of Frederick the Great he says that 'he was accused of vices from which History averts her eyes, and which even Satire blushes to name'.

'Now really', I exclaimed, 'how can we hope to understand these Victorians?

---

43 Lead cleverly and spread carnage.

44 Lewis Farnell (1856–1934), lecturer in archaeology and comparative religions, Rector of Exeter College 1913–1928, a politically and socially repressive vice-chancellor of Oxford University 1920–1923, edited Pindar's *Works* in three volumes (1930–1932). He was severe in style, Victorian in outlook, a worrier, highly strung, a good talker but impatient listener: 'his sincerity sometimes gave offence.'

An enclave in the midst of our history, they are more remote from us than the Red Indians, or the Trobriand Islanders, or the Bushmen of Australia! Macaulay was an educated man; he had read the Greek classics; and there is hardly a Greek writer who doesn't take the phenomenon of homosexuality for granted – Herodotus, Theognis, Pindar, Aeschylus, Plato, Theocritus, Plutarch – they all either relate or ennoble it. Had Macaulay read the classics in vain, that he reacts to an interesting psychological phenomenon as if he were a provincial nonconformist grocer?' Charles Stuart said it was all humbug, for sure; and he told me that Macaulay had once been approached by the geologist Sir Charles Lyell,[45] who wanted his support against the fundamentalists, and had replied that while he accepted his logic, he would not come out in support of his conclusions. For public purposes, the world was still created in 4004 B.C. Now this double standard of the Victorians, said Charles, is to me part of their charm. To them homosexuality was in the same category with religion; educated men might contemplate it freely, but their public reactions must be orthodox. But Stuart Hampshire wouldn't agree; he insisted that Macaulay had read the classics, as he read all literature and most of history, in vain.

Logan & A.L. Rowse

Rowse asked me to introduce him to Logan, of whose works, he said, he was a great admirer, and of the *Life and Letters of Sir Henry Wotton* in particular, a book he would fain possess, were it not too expensive for him to buy. I boggled at the responsibility of introducing a shrill exhibitionist to a venerable and fastidious sage, but Logan said, 'Yes, I will see him *once*', so I arranged it. 'He won't bring you butter in a lordly dish', I warned Logan, who likes judicious flattery from his visitors; 'he will choke you with great gobbets of gross, insipid, fulsome lard; and when you recover your senses, you'll find that he's pocketed the two volumes of *Sir Henry Wotton*, and that his praise has changed to boasting, as loud and as tasteless, but more prolonged'. Still Logan said he would risk it; for Rowse, he said, is a man in a false position, a proletarian who has succeeded in gate-crashing the serene citadels of light and

---

45 Sir Charles Lyell, 1st baronet (1797–1875). In *The Antiquity of Man* (1863) he endorsed Darwin's theory of the origin of species.

learning, and I'm in a false position too, an American refugee, a Philadelphia Quaker, who have fetched up in English society, and it is we alien settlers in an unfamiliar world, not the familiar natives of it, who see its subtle half-lights and iridescences, and draw the greatest pleasure from such contemplation; like Byron, he went on, – a cad who happened to fall into the English nobility, or Disraeli, who might have been the Vizier of an oriental court, but somehow became the leader of the solid country-gentry of Victorian England, and Dante Gabriel Rossetti, another alien aesthete in the smug Victorian gloom … ('Rowse in a false position?' expostulated Gilbert when I told him of this conversation, – 'why he's back where he began – back from Christ Church in the Cornish village of All Souls'. But that was afterwards, and irrelevant).

'Well', I asked Logan when I next saw him, 'and how did you fare at his hands?' 'It was awful', he replied, 'and just as you said it would be. His flattery was gross, outrageous, an insult to me; I felt as virgins are said to feel when they are raped. At first I was indignant, and resisted the outrage, – but after a while – dare I confess? – I found it wasn't so unpleasant after all, and, if I ceased to reluct, could be quite enjoyable. And then he angled for *Sir Henry Wotton*, but I wouldn't rise; and then, for two hours and a half, he boasted.'

'And were you impressed with him?', I asked. 'No', he said, 'for do you know, though he is a good historian, I found that he hasn't read any history. He has never heard of Gregorovius.[46] Milman's *History of Latin Christianity* wasn't even a name to him.[47] Why I don't believe he has even read Gibbon …'

I realised that of course Logan was right, and I had known Rowse for some years without realising it; for herein Rowse is typical of modern Oxford historians. He lacks the large, European background that the historians of the last century had, that Tawney[48] and Hammond[49] still manage to preserve. There

46 Ferdinand Gregorovius (1821–1891), a Prussian whose twenty years of research in Italy produced an authoritative history of medieval and early renaissance Rome and works on medieval Athens.

47 Henry Milman (1791–1868), Fellow of Brasenose and Canon of Westminster, wrote a *History of Latin Christianity* (1855).

48 Richard Tawney (1880–1962), Christian socialist, professor of economic history at London School of Economics 1931–1949, author of *Religion and the Rise of Capitalism* (1926). In 1953 T-R published an *opusculum* pulverising Tawney's historical interpretation of the English gentry 1540–1640.

49 John Hammond (1872–1949), Honorary Fellow of St John's 1937, *Manchester Guardian* journalist 1919–1945, author with his wife Barbara of a trilogy on the English labouring poor 1760–1832.

is neither breadth nor depth in him. He is provincial, – a good provincial journalist. He has not read the classics.

Dream April 1943

Recently I dreamt – I don't know what I dreamt; but in the course of my dream, I saw a painting by, I understood, Botticelli, and it was a painting of angels making merry in the sky; but it wasn't the theme that struck me, for of that I have no details in my memory; it was the background. For the artist had painted the picture as if he had stood, not upon the ground, looking upwards, but himself on a level with his angels, up in the middle air; and far below lay a landskip more desolate & enchanting than ever I have seen from tower or mountain-top, a vast, dreary, unpeopled waste, over which great floods lay spread in formless patterns, coiling aimlessly this way and that in long arms and reaches over the grey treeless waste; and between it and the clear, bright air where the angels were holding their celestial conversazione, there wheeled, like drifting flakes of snow, a cloud of wild swans, with wide rings and necks outstretched, looking ever downwards, so vivid that I thought I could hear their heavy pinions whirring – the symbol of life, midway between the dead world and eternity.

Rideout April 1943

Rideout is one of my oldest friends; I have known him since Charterhouse; but my relations with him are still formal, public, and intellectual, such is the high wall of self-bred reserve with which he protects his complex and vulnerable mind from the contact of society. Cool, fastidious, and intellectual, he left his parents' house at the age of 14, and lived, during his holidays from school, with his more sympathetic housemaster. When he went up to Oxford, he was always mature with learning and what psychological suffering I can only guess, and none influenced him. He was given a set of poky rooms on the top floor of the Meadow Buildings, hideously furnished, and with choco-late wallpaper. Rideout eyed them with the serene contempt of the aesthetic aristocrat; and for the next week, artisans were busy altering and renovating; a grand piano was brought up the stairs in pieces; Rideout's fine collection of rare books and Sung porcelain was installed; repapered in cream, the rooms seemed twice the former size; and in that eyrie of fastidious taste, Rideout, like a serene Chinese mandarin, read his Apuleius, his Gibbon, his George Moore, and drank his exquisite blend of Oo Long and Kai Mun tea.

He was indifferent to the spacious society of Christ Church. The aristocracy he regarded with aristocratic disdain; for the grubby Westminster scholars who shared his staircase, and gathered in each other's rooms for mutual admiration and cocoa, he entertained, and expressed, summary disgust. A few athletes only, having no foothold of common ground with him, had no reason for quarrelling with him, and with them he maintained a casual, Olympian intercourse. Dons he ignored. Barrington-Ward, seeing in him the most accomplished Latinist of his year, urged him to take the Hertford; but Rideout, who knew his psychological inability to take examinations, refused, and failed twice in the Pass Mods Latin papers. Neglecting all the paths of orthodoxy, he read theology to justify his residence, and devoted his time to the study of Chinese. The college authorities said he was 'a bad buy'.

There was a streak of masochism in his character. For long a misfit, he had made a felicity of his insulation, and seemed even to enjoy the rebuffs of the vulgar, to which he had reduced himself insensible. He never told his scout that his Sung pots had any value, and always expected to learn, one morning, that 'that green saucer', or 'that plaster horse', had come to pieces in somebody's hands. He gave to a casual friend, on his wedding, the Doves Press Bible from his collection, and was thanked, by the unappreciative recipient, for 'the Nonsuch volumes'. And then there was his friendship with Doggett.[50]

Doggett came from Surbiton. He was middle-class, and proud of it. No one ever influenced him, for he was already quite satisfied that the bourgeoisie of Surbiton in general, and the Doggetts in particular, represented the final zenith of culture, on which no advance was possible. Short, stout, red-haired, aggressive, and infinitely untidy, he moved among the proud élite of Christ Church confident that he, not they, represented the central tradition of the college. For 'Doggett's coat and badge' the bargees of London annually compete

---

50 Arthur Doggett (1911–1982), an old Carthusian like Rideout and T-R, was a Christ Church scholar 1930–1934, and later a solicitor.

along the Thames; but the coat of this Doggett, disintegrating with age and wear, and only precariously held together by dirt, would never have tempted even the least fastidious bargee from his malodorous backwater. The censor once suggested to Doggett that he might well buy a new gown, since his own, purchased at third hand, was now far in decomposition. Doggett thanked him for his advice, but ignored it, and went firmly through his university career in rags, relieved only by a heavy gold chain, the symbol of his class and aspirations. On one occasion Doggett's rooms were smashed by inebriate aristocrats, and Lord Normanby,[51] after throwing most of the furniture through the window, deposited a large, fresh turd on Doggett's carpet. But grieve not for the wounded pride of the poor scholar. To him the nobility were a class to be pitied, a depressed caste, born to be outwitted by the sound, solid and triumphant bourgeoisie. Undismayed, he surveyed the wreckage of his rooms, and then, seeing a few unvalued items of furniture which had escaped the notice of the perfunctory marquis, he soon reduced them to fragments too, and tossing them into the ruins, added them, at a greatly enhanced price, to the already considerable bill for damages presented to the now sober peer. But I think there is no truth in the tale that Doggett preserved the turd in a sealed and labelled jam-jar, until the exhibit was purchased back, at a fancy rate, by the humiliated nobleman.

And yet Rideout cultivated this bear, – without, of course, influencing him in the least. Every Thursday, Doggett dined with him at the Great Table, swilling his burgundy like beer; and if, by chance, Rideout should have forgotten to invite him by Thursday morning, Doggett would come into his rooms and sit there firmly till he remembered. After dinner, in Rideout's rooms, picking up some rare and precious edition, Doggett would rend the uncut pages with his thumb, and leave grubby finger-prints in the margins; and as he splashed milk and sugar into his Oo Long, saying defiantly that all tea was just tea to him, he would dogmatise about foreign fads, and knock his cigarette-ash into a Chinese vase of priceless celadon ware. Or perhaps the two would go out to

---

51 Oswald Phipps, 4th Marquess of Normanby (1912–1994) was sent down from Christ Church after two terms for desecrating a Belisha beacon (1931). As a German prisoner-of-war 1940–1943, he taught the Braille alphabet to blinded prisoners, as described in his article 'Blinded War Prisoners', *The Times*, 19 Nov 1943. He joined the Labour benches in the House of Lords in 1948 (the sole Labour Marquess and perhaps only Labour member of White's), but resigned the whip in 1950.

a cinema, or for a walk together; and as they passed through Canterbury gate, the Christ Church squirearchy, gathered there to go out beagling, would mock at that incompatible pair, – Rideout, tall, thin, pale, and loping; Doggett, squat, brisk, and portly, – as they went out, discussing at hopelessly different levels of conversation, topics on which they could not hope to inform each other.

———————

Gilbert said of Frank Taylor[52] that he wasn't bright enough to be a fool; 'a fool flirts with Error; Taylor fussily paws the backside of Platitude'.

————————

Mythologies   April 1943

I was walking along the Thames at Henley, where always the same thought occurs to me, of this great river flowing wasted through our national life, nymphless, unstoried, unvotaried; and I thought of the myths of the Greeks, who, more than any other people, could work that imaginative alchemy which transmutes primitive phenomena and psychological patterns into a rich poetic mythology; of the tales of Bellerophon, and Perseus, and Meleager, of Demeter and Persephone, of Orpheus and Eurydice, of Hylas, and the Argonauts, and the river of Lethe; of the Cretan myths of Theseus and Ariadne, of the Labyrinth, and of Minos and Rhadamanthus, Kings of the Dead; and particularly of the myths of Troy. The heroic cycles of the Greeks who sacked Troy are grubby affairs, – Oedipus, Heracles, Agamemnon, with their sordid passions, murders, competitions and disgusting banquets; but the city they conquered, a city, clearly, of a far higher culture, was overwoven, at least afterwards, with a texture of far more elevated, sophisticated legends – of its founding by Poseidon and Apollo, of Amphion, of Tithonus, of Laomedon, Ganymede, the horses of Erichthonius, the judgment of Paris, Helen, and Cassandra. And I observed how the memory of that great and fabulous city,

———————

52 Frank Taylor (1890–1960), a serene New Zealander, came to Oxford in 1918 after being wounded out of the war, obtained first-class honours in medieval and modern languages, was a Student of Christ Church from 1922 and tutor in modern languages. T-R called him 'a man of scholarship, taste and irony' (letter to Berenson, 12 Jan 1950).

long ago destroyed, ran through all Greek literature, like a great river that fertilises a whole land, and the poets of Greece had come to drink of its waters, and had stayed to build their temples along its edge; and I suggested that perhaps the Greeks had never forgiven themselves the sack of that queen of the cities of Asia, and that heroic cycles are perhaps often the expression of such a psychological trauma as this; observing in evidence how the Romans had never freed their literature of the incubus of conquered Greece, how the ghost of conquered Rome haunted the barbarians of the Dark Ages, and how the cycle of Roland and Oliver and Charlemain was a relic of the expedition against the more civilised Moors in Spain. But Gilbert, who always punctures my generalisations, reminded me of the Arthurian cycle and the mythology of Ireland, which are the idealised residue of defeat; so I had to modify my theory slightly, so as to include these also.

Remorse   April 1943

It's worse and worse; it's more than I can bear; I wish I were dead! I've just read my diary for the year 1936, and so mortified was I at what I found there, that in bed that night I could not sleep for many hours, but like Dido and Medea, and other famous insomniants of whom I read in Virgil and Apollonius, lay tortured by restless thought and nagging remorse, and those years of my life that seemed to me at the time the happiest of all, now seemed like a crystalline bubble that had rolled behind me, and which I would not now stop to recover if I could. Even one or two gay recollections of old-fashioned nights, of empty champagne-magnums sailing down from the top windows of the Gridiron Club to burst in Carfax on Kenneth Swann's birthday; of a beagle-dinner that ended with 'Jim Ashton[53] throwing boot-trees, a decanter of sherry, and a coal-scuttle through his brother's window panes into the quadrangle, Arthur Stewart-Liberty delivering noble speeches in Peckwater and lassoing the intervening censor with interminable rolls of sanitary paper, while Geoffrey Lamarque

---

53 James ('Jim') Ashton (1915–1991), first whip of the Christ Church beagles, took a third in history in 1936. He put the coal-scuttle through the window of John Ashton (1912–1975), also whipper-in of the Christ Church beagles, who took a second in history in 1934 and was bursar of the Ditchley Foundation 1958–1962.

(ignorant of unmentionable goings-on in his digs) was putting a fresh egg in the bed, and hiding the pyjamas, of Peter Wood, and Rice swam helplessly round in Mercury';[54] of the end of an evening when 'I took a hunting-horn and went round the college, while trundling porters, with heavy tread, followed the elusive note; but ever like some nimble grasshopper, I pooped where they least expected me, and finally slipped away, with one last merry blast in Holywell, which drew nightcapped heads from every window along the street, to haven in my pillow'; or of that degree-night when Mrs Ross acquired immortality by intervening in our merry symposia, – even these incidents in my education seemed at times, on re-perusal, a loss of intellectual opportunity.

S.I.S.

Stuart Hampshire observed that S.I.S. values information in proportion to its secrecy, not to its accuracy. They would attach more value, he said, to a scrap of third-rate and tendentious misinformation smuggled out of Sofia in the fly-buttons of a vagabond Rumanian pimp than to any intelligence deduced from a prudent reading of the foreign press. And of course he's quite right.

Impotency & Genius   April 1943

Logan, as old men do, was ascribing all the manifestation of human behaviour to one cause; and this time it was impotency, which, he said, makes men doubt more than ever the reality of their existence, and seek to prove it to themselves by obvious and lasting self-expression. Now Hitler, he said, is impotent of course, and Ruskin was, and I forget who else, but I'm sure he didn't run dry for lack of examples (George Moore, and William III, I dare say); and he spoke of this 'goblinism', as he called it, this besetting belief that all sometimes feel, of their own unreality, but which those who extend and perpetuate themselves by breeding imagine that they have disproved. And

---

54 Arthur Rice (1915–1944), Christ Church, took a second in history in 1938 and was killed in action.

I wondered whether perhaps it were true, and I thought of Euripides, who twice at least formulated the thought

$$\text{τίς οἶδεν εἰ τὸ ζῆν μέν ἐστι κατθανεῖν}$$
$$\text{τὸ κατθανεῖν δὲ ζῆν κατὼ νομίζεται}^{55}$$

Was Euripides impotent? *Quaere plus de hoc*, as Aubrey says.[56] But Norman Douglas, in his *Fountains in the Sand*, I think, suggests that all progress, all creative genius, comes from an intersexual element, which isn't quite the same thing; and recalling Shelley and Napoleon, and others, I think it a more satisfactory explanation.[57] Pater too, – though where and why I don't know – affected a taste for remote, diaphanous androgynies; I expect Logan would say he was impotent too. But the whole question raises tempting vistas, a vast endless *quaere plus de hoc*.

———————

The Welsh Guards tried to make Gilbert join the Guards' Club, 'but I was too old to be had that way', said Gilbert. Then they asked him to supply a motto for that institution. He gave it them: 'Promotion recollected in senility.'

———————

My great work

The more I think of the subject of my great work, *A History of the English Ruling Classes*, the more I like it. I shall begin with the silent, patient, nibbling rat-faced country landlords and lawyers of early Tudor days, slowly surveying, undermining, and circumventing their predestined parcels of abbey-lands;

———————

55 Who knows whether life is death and death is regarded down below as life? (Euripides, fragment 638). T-R probably knew this from a commentary on Aristophanes's *Frogs*, where the verses are parodied at 1477–8. The accent on κατὼ is wrong: it should be κάτω.

56 John Aubrey (1626–1697) used this notation when a statement in *Brief Lives* needed further investigation.

57 T-R met 'that old *roué* Norman Douglas' (1868–1952) amidst the 'decayed *rentiers* and social casualties' of Capri in 1949 (letter to Berenson, 12 Jan 1950), and backed his application for a Royal Literary Fund pension. *Fountains in the Sand: Rambles among the Oases of Tunisia* appeared in 1921.

and then I picture this same class, raised by revolutions in agriculture, industry and commerce from parochial squireens into the splendid renaissance gentry of Elizabethan and Jacobean times, those cultivated stylists who held elevated conversation among the terraces and fountains and colonnades of their elegant Palladian houses – Sir Walter Raleigh scandalising the conventional by bold discussions at Cerne Abbas;[58] Sir Francis Bacon with his infinite speculations, his ambiguous pleasures, his elaborate discourse in the gardens of Gorhambury; Lord Bridgewater holding the first performance of *Comus* at Ludlow Castle;[59] Sir Kenelm Digby, airing his fantastical notions abroad and longing to be back in the 'most innocent convenient country houses, shady walks, and close arbours' of England;[60] John Aubrey with his seraphical notions of chemistry, and his friend Colonel Long,[61] whom the Muses did accompany, as he rode out with his hawks and spaniels; Carberies and Conways with their pastoral salons in Wales and Ireland. But the Puritans did them in, and the next age is less speculative and refined – the age of the hard-headed, stuffy grandees of the Revolution, 'those mercenary souls' as King James II called them, who were determined that no quixotic principles, no oblivion of business or politics, should lose them their estates, and whose letters to the Prince of Orange, as a commentary on the springs of political behaviour, are as revealing as those of their ancestors to Thomas Cromwell when the monasteries were a-tumbling. Well, their prudence paid them good dividends; for next we see them under the Georges, secure in their vast wealth and insufferable arrogance, advertising their varnish of culture and tolerance, and legislating the riches of half the world into their pockets; and, like the Roman millionaires, they are for ever building vast palaces with detached wings

---

58 Sir Walter Raleigh (1554–1618) retired to his estate at Sherborne after his banishment from Court, and entertained the Cerne Abbas circle of astronomers, mathematicians, philosophers, scientists, poets and sorcerers known by the ominous name of the School of Night.

59 Ludlow Castle was the official residence of John Egerton, 1st Earl of Bridgwater (1579–1649), Lord President of Wales 1631–1642. His daughter Alice was benighted in a forest while travelling to Ludlow, thereby inspiring Milton's *Comus*, which was first acted there with three Bridgwater children taking leading parts.

60 Sir Kenelm Digby (1603–1665), a founding Fellow of the Royal Society, discovered that plants needed oxygen, but believed that wounds could be healed by sympathy.

61 Sir James Long, 2nd baronet (1616–1692), colonel of the royalist horse, FRS, MP, Gentleman of the Privy Chamber, Wiltshire landowner, amateur scientist, naturalist. Described by his friend John Aubrey: 'Good swordsman, horseman: admirable extempore orator, great memorie, great historian and romancer; great falconer, for insects exceeding curious.'

and resonant colonnades, to humiliate their rivals & embarrass their descendants, palaces in formal parks studded with columns and nymphs and gazebos, palaces not to live in, but to house their treasures and soothe their pride. And then there is the gay, irresponsible aristocracy of Napoleonic and Regency days, like the Cavaliers and the Renaissance bishops, never so splendid as on the eve of their collapse; and thereafter, through the thick Victorian gloom, we can see strange, hieratic figures, like Roman augurs, winking at the dreary ritual of their deferential masters, the triumphant bourgeoisie. And finally the champagne age, the loud, bounding, commercial aristocracy of Edward VII and P.G. Wodehouse,[62] cosmopolitan and exotic, Oriental Sassoons,[63] American Astors,[64] the Indian Aga Khan,[65] the last mutation of this long fantastic history of a class now dead as the mammoth and the mastodon. And with what epilogue shall I end? With the Countess of Carlisle[66] emptying the cellars of Naworth Castle into the River Eden – surely in those pipes of port & claret the ichor of the old nobility, after all its nine lives, was shed voluntarily away? Or with Lady Talbot de Malahide sitting on a summer's afternoon in her castle gardens, and tossing the unpublished letters of Boswell, one by one, as she read them, into the gardener's bonfire, lest revelations that had left her unmoved might shock, or corrupt, that drab purity of posterity?[67] Or with Lord Lonsdale, his coal-mines nationalised, his castle bare, his race-horses sold, his yellow-liveried flunkeys dismissed, his packs of hounds disbanded,

---

62 (Sir) Pelham Grenville Wodehouse (1881–1975), author of 120 comic novels.

63 An mercantile Jewish family, originally settled in Baghdad and Bombay, whose members stormed English society. Sir Albert Abdullah Sassoon's granddaughter married the Marquess of Cholmondeley.

64 The Astor fortune derived from New York rents: the family acquired a viscountcy in 1917 and a further barony in 1956; its descendants married into several English ruling-class families.

65 Sultan Mohamed Shah, Aga Khan III (1877–1957), a direct descendant of the prophet Mohamed's daughter Fatima, succeeded as 48th Imam of the Shia Ismaili Muslim sect aged seven. An Anglophile, who was the only person outside the Royal Family to hold four Grand Crosses of different orders of knighthood; a lover of horseflesh and beautiful women, his son had married Lord Churston's daughter.

66 Rosalind, Countess of Carlisle (1845–1921) was a fanatical Temperance campaigner. Several of her descendants, including Philip Toynbee, became alcoholics.

67 James Boswell's manuscripts came to Malahide Castle near Dublin by the marriage of his great-granddaughter to Richard, 5th Baron Talbot of Malahide and 2nd Baron Talbot de Malahide (1846–1921). After her death, Lord Talbot married, *en secondes noces*, a busy philanthropic widow who winnowed the manuscripts before their sale in 1927 to Americans.

wearing out his faded splendour in a villa in Surrey?[68] Or with Lord Halifax, mumbling superstitious anilities and garnishing his country-houses with bones?[69] Or with a bare recital of their great houses, now put to public uses, or pulled down, or peeling tenantless, those mausoleums, those cenotaphs, of a vanished race? 'How many noble families have there been whose memory is utterly abolished, how many flourishing houses have we seen which Oblivion hath now obfuscated?' And how pleasant, having launched the book, to be attacked by sensitive peers, and decaying snobs in Cheltenham and Sidmouth, and tuft-hunting dons, for suggesting that it is all over, just as I was attacked by querulous clergy about *Archbishop Laud*. Already I can hear the rotund expostulations of Philip Landon, the indignant snorts of Michael Maclagan,[70] the pained demurrers of William de Geijer[71] and indeed that is not the least of the attractions of the subject.

A.L. Rowse

Did I say that I had once admired Rowse? It seems incredible. More & more, as I recoil from his grasping, ungenerous, peasant personality, his base, transparent methods of currying notice and publicity, his shameless egotism, his

---

68 Hugh Lowther, 5th Earl of Lonsdale (1857–1944) had a tax-free income derived from coal-fields, iron-mines and farmland of nearly £4,000 a week in the 1880s. An inferiority complex made him a fantastic boaster who craved the adulation of race-course mobs and lived with ruinous ostentation. Famous for his stables, private orchestra, huge cigars and yellow carriages with liveried postillions, he was described by Lord Ancaster as 'almost an Emperor and not quite a gentleman'. When his depleted resources forced him to leave Lowther Castle forever, in his yellow Daimler, in 1936, he went to earth like an old fox in the Stud House of his stables at Barleythorpe, Rutland – not a Surrey villa.

69 Charles Wood, 2nd Viscount Halifax (1839–1934) was a connoisseur of old ghost stories, who appeared in the hunting-field at the age of 93. He devoted much effort to defending Anglo-Catholicism in England, and to promoting the reunion of Rome with Canterbury.

70 Michael Maclagan (1914–2003), a Christ Church man with whom T-R served in the Oxford University Officers' Training Corps, later a Fellow of Trinity College, enjoyed dilating on the peerage, and became Richmond Herald at the College of Arms.

71 William de Geijer (1889–1954), first-class honours in history from Trinity College, Cambridge, on staff of League of Nations secretariat 1920–1921, employed on government service 1939–1945; proud of being stepson of Lord Abinger and brother of Rouge Croix Pursuivant at the College of Arms.

gross disregard of the conventions of tact & civility, he has drifted into the regions of my contempt. And now I've finished with him.

He asked me to write a book on Marlborough and the Grand Alliance for a series he is to edit, a series, he said, that would capture historiography from trashy female novelists, and, mingling *utile dulci*,[72] would compare with the best volumes in the Home University Library. I considered the subject; I liked it; I thought I would do it; and I was envisaging a book rather better than Lytton Strachey's *Elizabeth & Essex,* when Hodder & Stoughton sent me their contract, and I read of a series, 'Teach Yourself History', a set of manuals in yellow boards, to be sold on railway-stations to mugging but conscientious artisans. So I wrote to Rowse and explained that I had evidently misunderstood him when he described the scope and nature of the series, and wished to be excused, since I would be out of tune with my public and therefore couldn't write a good book. And now, in answer, I have received four pages of abuse – boastful, hectoring, rude, condescending abuse, – and four pages of it; and Raymond Mortimer[73] tells me that he received a similar letter when he ventured to criticise Rowse's autobiography in a review; and Cyril Connolly that he too received a letter of mingled boasting and cringing demanding a favourable notice of that same pussycat autobiography, and a letter of abuse for rejecting Rowse's contributions to *Horizon*; and Logan showed me a letter he had received from this Rowse, shortly after his visit, a letter of sickening adulation and egotism. Logan said he couldn't acknowledge it for disgust, and dropped it in the wastepaper-basket. But I suppose I must allow him talent, – a talented shit.

Advice to historians

You may read all the documents in the world, but without sense you will not be right, and without style you will not be read.

A good book is like an iceberg. Four-fifths of it is never seen.

---

72 The useful with the agreeable (a quotation from Horace).

73 Raymond Mortimer (1895–1980), literary editor who later shared a house in Dorset with T-R's brother.

A binge

The doings of the previous night were hard to explain away; to Gilbert they were hard to recollect. 'Did Reay[74] and Bertie Eugster[75] come here?' he asked, as he surveyed the unaccountable place in which he had woken up. 'Yes', I answered. 'How did we get here?' 'We walked.' 'And did *I* walk?' 'Yes.' Gilbert was silent; then 'I remember quite a lot', he remarked objectively, 'until I raced Bertie Eugster over a pint of beer. After that there will be certain gaps in my autobiography, which will have to be supplied from external sources.'

The Valley of the Restless Mind[76] April 1943

I went home to Northumberland at the end of April this year, and finding that Father had taken the Harehope fishing, five miles of the most beautiful fishing in the world, of the river Till, that enchanted river, thither I went, day after day, and fished with wet fly for trout and grayling; and when the fish were not rising, it was enough, I could taste the ecstasy of the place; for the water was clear, the weather fine, the trees, not yet in full leaf, were all in flower, sallow, weeping willow, and slender birch-trees, and the birds sang in them; and through that bright, translucent air the Cheviots loomed across the intervening landskip of cornfields & meadowlands. I thought of Horace at Tivoli and in Calabria; of the Ancient Mariner's hidden brook

> In the leafy month of June
> That to the sleeping woods all night
> Singeth a quiet tune;

---

74 Aeneas Mackay, 13th Baron Reay (1905–1963), was a toweringly tall nobleman with whom T-R fell down the escalators of Leicester Square underground station when they were drunk. He was a boon companion to T-R, who visited his house in Selkirkshire and Dutch castle, and wrote a tribute in *The Times* when Reay died.

75 General Sir Basil Eugster (1914–1984) graduated with a third in history from Christ Church, 1936; Irish Guards survivor of Narvik campaign, 1940.

76 Phrase from a medieval Latin love-song borrowed as title of Malcolm Muggeridge's sexually morbid novel of 1938.

Of Laurence Binyon, 'the last of the perfectionists', whom I had met at tea with Logan a month ago, just before his death;[77] – what felicity those poets had enjoyed, withdrawn from noise and all ambition, in places but half as beautiful as this! But still I could not exorcise from my mind the problem that, like a maddening, irrelevant bell, intrudes unseasonably upon its peace, – the problem of the meaning and purpose of life on this aimless planet, the problem of happiness in this valley of the restless mind. Is it genius, as some, and notably Pindar, have held, that gives a significance to the otherwise drab record of human existence, –

> ἐπάμεροι· τί δέ τις;
> τί δ' οὔ τις; σκιᾶς ὄναρ
> ἄνθρωπος· ἀλλ' ὅταν αἴ-
> γλα διόσδοτος ἔλθῃ,
> λαμπρὸν φέγγος ἔπεστιν ἀν-
> δρῶν καὶ μείλιχος αἰών.[78]

But genius is by definition exceptional; with Homer and Shakespeare we cannot compete. Is it then contemplation – the enjoyment of rare, exquisite, neglected pleasure? But why do I torment my poor intellect thus? I kept asking myself, for is not this perfect felicity, to fish for trout in the river Till, in springtime, with the trees in bloom and the birds singing? But alas, these palliative assurances get me nowhere; like the stellar system, my doubts go on for ever, aimlessly revolving; no charm will still them, no formula explain them into rest; it is Necessity, against which even the gods strive in vain.

---

77 Laurence Binyon (1869–1943), poet and British Museum curator, had died on 10 March. 'I didn't see him often, but we used to correspond, picking fleas, like friendly apes, from each other's fur or writings. But the thought that he was there, raking up leaves in his garden, or translating Dante in the big library of his little farmhouse in Berkshire, made England, made the world, seem a better place to live in. He was the last of a noble line of lovers of perfection, Milton, Wordsworth, Pater (Pater for all your pishes) & Robert Bridges' (Pearsall Smith to T-R, 14 March 1943).

78 Creatures of a day: what is anyone, what not? Man is a shadow in a dream; but when sunlight comes by the gift of the gods, men glow with radiance and life treats them kindly (Pindar, *Pythian* 8.95–7).

1. Hugh Trevor-Roper *circa* 1940

2. Gilbert Ryle –
Le Penseur – in his
Oxford rooms

3. Logan Pearsall Smith –
the Sage of Chelsea – in his
library overlooking the
Royal Hospital

4. H.W. Garrod – a Merton friend whom Trevor-Roper cherished – with war-time visitors

5. S.G. Owen, Christ Church's drunken bully whom Trevor-Roper hated

6. John Barrington-Ward, the complacent Christ Church classicist

7. Michael Foster, the austere Christ Church philosopher

8. Mercury, the ornamental pond in Tom quad, at Christ Church, where S.G. Owen once sat with a jerry on his head, protesting that he was a mushroom, and into which Arthur Rice was thrown during a rag

9. Tom Tower glimpsed from Peckwater quad, where Arthur Stewart-Liberty lassoed the Christ Church Censor with rolls of lavatory paper. 'I like the intellectual world to be alive, as in Paris and Peckwater, not dead as in the Athenæum', wrote Trevor-Roper

10. H.W. Garrod's room in Merton, where the talk abounded in paradox, aphorisms and provocations

11. Charles Stuart, the Christ Church historian

12. Stuart Hampshire listening to Isaiah Berlin

13. Frank Pakenham

14. Rose Macaulay

15. Chillingham, Lord Tankerville's castle in Northumberland where
Trevor-Roper's friend Dicksie Marshall went poaching in the park

16. Bewshaugh, the remote Northumberland sheep farm where
Trevor-Roper dossed for a night in 1945

17. The lake at Wotton, where Trevor-Roper went for meets of the Bicester hunt. He felt ecstatic when once he saw the whole pack swimming across the lake

18. 11 St Leonard's Terrace, Chelsea, where Trevor-Roper coined neologisms and capped quotations with Pearsall Smith

The Etruscans   May 1943

Logan was reading to me his recollections of Henry James and George
Santayana and Sir Walter Raleigh; and as he read, in his ivory tower in
Chelsea, those anecdotes of elaborate leisure and esoteric conventions, an
image arose before me, of Etruscan priests elaborating, with infinite solemnity,
in an unintelligible language, their long, formal flummery. The image pleased
me, so that my attention strayed, as it sometimes does, especially when I have
heard it all before, and I thought of Mommsen's description of the Etruscans,
and their ritualistic observances, which he describes, somewhat summarily, as
'pious nuisances'. And why not? For Henry James, I murmured inaudibly to
myself, was a very tiresome fellow. But I took care not to voice such a heresy
to Logan.

Morton Evans

M.E.'s manner is quiet, his speech soft, but his mind is ice-clear; and when
he spoke of Maltby his words, said Gilbert, were a gentle dew of sulphuric
acid.

'But how can I?' protested Stuart Hampshire, when I suggested that he should
engage in conversation with Vivian, 'I've no common ground with him at
all!' 'It's not necessary', interposed Gilbert, 'he'll just drip on, like a washerless
tap'.

I was giving a felicitous account of Gilbert's conversational method. 'But
surely', interposed a worthy person, addressing himself to Gilbert, 'you adapt
your conversation to your audience?' 'No', said Gilbert remorselessly, 'I adapt
my audience to my conversation'.

Introspection

May 1943

Stuart Preston[79] said he wanted to write a self-revelation, but didn't know how to begin. It's quite simple, I said gaily; you take off all your clothes; you hesitate for a moment at the brink; and then you plunge headlong into the cool, deep waters of introspection. Of course it's a bit frightening at first, for the water is cold and numbing, and when you open your eyes you find yourself in a strange world of darting, elusive fish, waving tentacles, seaweed and coral caves. And you can't stay there long either; you just reach out and grab what you can, and then you rise, panting, to the surface, and scramble to the bank to recover your breath and see what you've managed to collect. Not that it looks so attractive out of water; the sea-anemones, the mermaid's hair, the iridescent, shimmering water-weeds, they all look sad and bedraggled out of their element. Still, you have discovered a new world that you can revisit for longer and longer periods, a fascinating under-water pleasure-garden (for of course I was carried away again by my metaphor), where you can swim, open-eyed, among submarine forests, and coralline labyrinths, and fronded caverns, and watch the bright, flickering fishes, the swaying polyps, the quaint crustaceans, the barnacles and giant sponges; and there still lower there are dark and sinister regions to probe, regions of mystery and fear, where a ghostly, phosphorescent twilight now and then reveals hideous, Freudian monsters heaving and uncoiling in their ancient slime.

But I'm afraid my enthusiasm wasn't infectious on this occasion; for when I looked at Stuart Preston, he seemed much less eager to dive into those cool, refreshing waters than he had been before I described these allurements.

Stuart Preston

May 1943

But who is Stuart Preston? An American, a Bostonian, Harvard-bred; politely rich, a member of the Knickerbocker Club, a friend of all that's elegant and

---

79 Stuart Preston (1915–2005), formerly a curator at the National Gallery of Art in Washington and later assistant cultural editor at the *New York Times* (1949–1965), came to London with the US Army in 1941. He had high social ambitions, was entertained by Lady Desborough at Panshanger and Lady Colefax in London; his ubiquity is immortalised by Evelyn Waugh's character 'The Loot'.

cultivated in New England; and he crossed the Atlantic as a sergeant, with all the right introductions, intent to please. Handsome, charming, and polite, he succeeded from the start. It is said he keeps a card-index of conversational topics appropriate to those whose friendship he seeks, and rehearses them carefully before each interview. At all events, the effect was wonderful. One by one, the great houses of England, faded with war and neglect, glowed again at his approach; their untended gardens smiled anew; frosts thawed where he trod; portcullises dropped, barbicans opened, battlements ceased to frown, and Stuart Preston passed into earthly bliss in each in turn. In the literary world, too, he fain would shine. Harold Nicolson[80] sent him to Raymond Mortimer. Through Mortimer he got introduced, as a passionate admirer of Logan and George Santayana, to Logan; and finding from Logan what would please Maurice Baring, he wrote appropriately to Maurice Baring, and was accepted in Beauly Castle, Inverness.[81] Nothing resisted him; he had discovered a magic talisman, and every door swung open at his approach. He fell ill. 'The all-conquering American charmer', Logan wrote to me, 'is in hospital from an indigestion of lobster-salad, and champagne, and iced coronets'; but he soon recovered, helped by the attentions of Queens of Society and Arbiters of Taste, and was as irresistible as ever. I met him often; he flattered me exquisitely; and discriminating, well-directed flattery is nectar and ambrosia to me. But even his admirers noticed sometimes that this fastidious devotee of Santayana and Henry James, this collector of rare volumes and connoisseur of Agostino di Duccio,[82] was a trifle catholic in some of his tastes. He stayed for several days with Chips Channon,[83] and that made one think. And the insides of the books he mentioned seemed often less familiar to him than their titles.

I'm not sure when his decline began. John Pope-Hennessy[84] maintains that it was the Poetry Reading, that solemn occasion when Lady Dotty

---

80 (Sir) Harold Nicolson (1886–1968), diplomat and man-of-letters, was then an MP and Governor of the BBC.

81 Maurice Baring (1874–1945), diplomat, man-of-letters and Catholic convert, who was incapacitated by Parkinson's disease, had lived since 1940 at Eilean Aigas, under the care of his fellow Catholic Laura, Lady Lovat. Beaufort Castle at Beauly was another Lovat house in Inverness.

82 Fifteenth-century Italian sculptor.

83 (Sir) Henry Channon (1897–1958), a camp, sybaritic American social-climber and MP.

84 (Sir) John Pope-Hennessy (1913–1994), Renaissance art historian and museum curator.

Wellesley[85] was so sadly inebriated, and was carried out blowing kisses to the Queen. For this function, he says, Stuart Preston was given a 12/6d, not a 25/-, ticket; and after that climacteric, his career was plainly on the wane. With me, his fall was sudden and complete.

There are times in our lives when we seek (*o pectora caeca!*)[86] to protect ourselves from the irresistible evidence of our own senses. We see it advancing in strength, but seduced by pride, or alliances, or sclerosis, or other prejudice, we throw up walls and barricades against it, and man them, and fortify them, and shout defiance for a while. But the charade cannot be kept up for long, and as the enemy draws near, our hastily erected defences, like the walls of Jericho, suddenly tremble and collapse. So it was with me. Against the dawning truth that Stuart Preston is a pretender, a humbug, a fraud, a bogus Boston snob, I constructed elaborate walls, with crenellations and round-towers, loopholes, machicolations, and redoubts, and dared the evidence from behind them. But when he suggested, at tea with Logan and Rose Macaulay and Lady Berwick[87] (our conversation being about the great unreadable of literature) that Lucretius was one of them, they wobbled; he hadn't read Lucretius, he hastily added, when he saw my face fall; but could he ever, I wondered, have read Santayana, of whom he professed himself an admirer. And in Sloane Square, a little later, when I was walking back with him, they collapsed. For he said ... but my pen cannot repeat the solecism he there committed; suffice it that, when I looked over my shoulder in Berkeley Square, clouds of dust and pillars of smoke were still rising from the rubble of those walls; and that the

---

85 Dorothy Wellesley (1889–1956), whose husband succeeded as 7th Duke of Wellington in September 1943, was asked to recite her poetry at a reading held in the presence of Queen Elizabeth in aid of French war charities at the Aeolian Hall, New Bond Street on 14 April 1943. Other poets reciting their work included Edmund Blunden, T.S. Eliot, Walter de la Mare, John Masefield, V. Sackville-West, Edith Sitwell and Arthur Waley. Sackville-West tried to keep Wellesley sober, but her charge insisted on visiting the lavatory five times within 45 minutes: 'Dotty', cried Vita, 'you can't possibly want to go again!' After ruthless measures to prevent her from accosting the Queen, the imminent duchess plonked herself down on the Bond Street pavement screaming.

86 The full lines, from second book of *De Rerum Natura* by Lucretius, mean: 'Miserable minds of men, in what darkness of life, in what dangers, you spend this little span of years.'

87 Edith Hulton (1889–1972) had been brought up in Venice, and in 1919 married Thomas Noel-Hill, 8th Baron Berwick, whom H.A.L. Fisher, Warden of New College, called 'ignorant and foolish' (diary, 11 April 1916). She was a benefactor of the Bodleian library and the Ashmolean Museum.

noise of their ruin startled friends of mine chasing their birds of pleasure as far away as the Isle of Dogs, and Wapping Old Stairs.

All this I told to Logan, but he, blind and infatuated as he was, would not have it, and I said I would give this humbug another chance; so when he wrote to me inviting himself to lunch, I responded, and he came. This time his fall was final. The asparagus was delicious, green and soft from tip to root; but with his knife he detached the tip only, and left the rest. Half a pint of beer was still shimmering in his tankard when it was taken away. The gull's egg which he took he nibbled and left. Trembling, I offered him port, a delicious vintage, soft as flattery. Yes, as always, he complied. When he got up he had left half a glass.

———

June 1943

'And how is that bold, speculative intellect D.D.S.P. getting on in America?' I asked Walter Bell[88] at lunch the other day; but it did not seem that Vivian was making history during his transatlantic visit. 'And does he send no masterly reports?' I asked. 'He sends cables to Curry', said Walter, with malicious relish. Now the name of Curry seems to have a magical, maientic effect upon Gilbert. 'Cables to Curry?', he repeated, lowering his glass of port. 'It's like posting love-letters up the arsehole of a camel.'

———

'I thought it my duty', Gilbert was explaining, 'to accept a glass of port'; and Bertie Eugster remarked how conveniently Gilbert's sense of duty always came to the aid of his inclinations. 'Of course', said Gilbert; 'one owes it to one's self to salve one's conscience'.

———

88 Walter Bell (1909–2004), former MI6 officer under cover of passport control at British consulate in New York, intelligence analyst in London of reports from USA (1942–1945), post-war MI5 officer monitoring decolonisation. Isaiah Berlin thought him 'a nice man, a little boring'.

My Boasts June 1943

Logan was boasting; they were all boasting; why should I alone remain modest and silent? So I opened my lips and boasted too. 'Do you know', I asked, 'that my name has been mentioned with praise in the *Journal of the Society of Master Glass-Painters*? And that I have been invited by an Anglo-Catholic missionary in Bloemfontein to collaborate with him in compiling an illustrated missal for use in nigger Sunday-schools? And that I share with Desdemona the distinction of having kindled sexual passion in the bosom of a Moorish soldier – in Avignon, in the Palace of the Popes?' They didn't know; and after telling them these truths I felt my self-respect greatly increased.

Nel mezzo del cammin di nostra vita ...[89] June 1943

I went home to Northumberland again in June, when the grass was long in the verges, and the wild briar blossomed in the hedgerows, and the air was laden with the scent of hay and of meadowsweet; and every day I went out to enjoy these things, fishing up the Till by day from Old Bewick Bridge, where the monkey-flower and the forget-me-not were in bloom, and the meadow cranesbill and the biting stonecrop, all along the river, and the water-ranunculus, like a milky way, straggled down the shallow reaches, and the fragrance of trodden peppermint and wild thyme rose from my feet as I cast overstream into the deep pools under the willow-trees; and at night I fished the Aln, in Hulne Park, with wet-fly, until midnight had passed, and suddenly, the air becoming cold, I would look up and see a white mist creeping down the river-valley, and among the dipping of rats I would put up my rod and walk home, three or four miles, through the damp film of dew. How happy I was in that brief interlude! I thought of Dick White, how he had designed to give up his work as a civil servant, at which he is so successful, and retire, on an exiguous pension, to live in idleness, sailing his boat among the island creeks of Alderney. 'Just what I feel about Northumberland, or Ireland', I had said

---

89 Canto 1 of Dante's *Inferno* begins, 'In the middle of the path of life I found myself in a dark wood'.

to Gilbert, when he told me of this fact; but 'No', he had answered, 'for Dick would be happy in Alderney, but in Ireland, or Northumberland, you wouldn't, and you know it'. Of course I knew it; and why wouldn't I? Because my mind has no rest, tortured by those irrelevant problems, those gadflies that disturb its summer happiness.

In the midst of these doubts I got a letter from Logan. 'I am rather under the impression', he wrote, 'that you are taking a pause or holiday to consider your future and your fate, to decide what you want to make of your life, what are your real wishes, and how you can best attain them …' 'Now how did he know?' I asked myself indignantly, forgetting the transparency of human reservations; but indignation didn't solve my problem, and I read on; 'I take it you are about 30 – a turning-point in life, when one has more or less to decide on the future path one wants to pursue. Here we are in life; something has got to be done about it; one has ventured on various paths which have seemed to lead to nothing; snatched at fruit which has turned sour; knocked at doors which have either remained shut, or, if they have opened, have led into what seemed likely to be prisons, or penitentiaries, or bordels, from which one must flee to save one's life …'

It's quite true; I'm 29; and those are my sensations. The world, which I have so enjoyed, seems now dull, insipid, tasteless; gone are the days, the happiest days of my life, when, in the most beautiful rooms in Oxford, overlooking the Christ Church Meadow, I was writing my book on Laud (would it had been a better book); when I went foxhunting in Buckinghamshire, and beagling in Northumberland & Oxfordshire, and drinking & talking, drinking & talking with the friends I have now lost and can never replace. Well, those days are past, and now

> How weary, stale, flat and unprofitable
> Seem to me all the uses of this world!

Dramatising, as always, my predicament, I thought of those among the great whose crisis came also at this time; of St Paul and St Augustine, grim figures, tortured by sterile learning, and seeking, amid those flinty rocks for a simpler path; of Dante, who, at 30, contemplated Heaven and Hell, and never looked on earth with the same eyes afterwards; of Sir Thomas Browne, who seemed at 30 to have outlived himself and to begin to be weary of the sun; 'I have shaken hands with my canicular days; I perceive I do anticipate the vices of the age; the world to me is but a dream or mock-show, and we all therein but pantaloons and antics to my severer contemplations.' I thought of Samuel Butler, who, at 30, heard these pugnant words, '*Et maintenant, monsieur, vous allez créer?*'[90]

Shall I, like Horace, retire to the country, to this Northumberland perhaps, which I so love, there to polish style, to hunt and fish, and aim ambitiously at an unattainable literary perfection? But I thought, too, of Wordsworth, who also retired to the country to worship an ideal, and there, for lack of society and intellectual stimulus, became a dowdy, platitudinous, egotistical, moralising bore.

But these circuitous cogitations lead nowhere, I exclaimed to myself; what is needed is some sharp external blow to direct the aimless thoughts. Should I plunge into a life of action, madly seeking the stimulus of force? Should I ask to be sent to Yugoslavia, to live with the rebels there, in their woods and caves? For S.I.S. had sent a man thither, called Stuart,[91] who had been killed on landing, so there was a vacancy in the establishment. Then there are some who can only realise their desires in death, like Byron, and young Richard Hillary,[92] the Byron of our age. Should I court death, for at least that is better than taking one's own life dingily, in a garret or gunroom, in despair of life and its purposeless, vertiginous calm?

How happy was Gibbon, who could live untroubled by such thoughts, executing a life's work in perfect peace! How happy is Gilbert, whose temperament has never experienced the anguish of intellectual self-division, who makes his cracks morning and evening, and goes on uninhibited, now drunk, now sober, from day to day! How happy the labourer, who breeds and conforms and thinks not, who looks neither forward nor backward, but goes singing to his grave!

I did not solve this great enigma, – partly of course because it's insoluble, but partly because I got a telephone message from Barnet to return early to

---

90 And now, sir, are you going to create?

91 On 28 May 1943 W.W.Y. ('Bill') Stuart of SIS and (Sir) F.W.D. ('Bill') Deakin (1913–2005) of SOE parachuted into Montenegro to work with Tito in waging guerrilla warfare. Stuart was killed, and both Deakin and Tito wounded, when German aircraft strafed partisan headquarters at Mount Durmitor on 9 June. Deakin got a first in modern history at Christ Church in 1934, was a Fellow and history tutor at Wadham 1936–1949 and Warden of St Antony's College, Oxford 1950–68.

92 Richard Hillary (1919–1943), RAF pilot and author of *The Last Enemy* (1942): see entry of Oct 1943 (p. 180).

duty. But Gibson has bidden me consider my health, and I intend to take the whole month of September off; and then perhaps I shall make a choice among these tangled perplexities.

Meanwhile, I'm becalmed.

June 1943

In her childhood, Marjorie Madan lived at Chillingham Castle,[93] and loved the place, and the Cheviots, and the river Till, as I do, with a nostalgic affection. When I gave her some trout I had caught there, and had brought down with me by the night-train to London, she told how, at the age of 10, she had first fallen in love with a young man whom she had seen fishing on the Till. 'This', she had said to herself, as she precociously analysed her emotions, 'must be the state they call love'; and she delivered herself unconditionally to it. But some days later, looking from the castle window, she saw the same young man playing tennis with a girl, and at once (she says) she fell on the floor and bit the carpet in despair; and then, recollecting herself, 'I suppose', she gravely philosophised, 'that this must be the state I've read about called jealousy'. 'And now', she added, 'every time I fall in love, I think of the first time I fell in love, by the river Till, at the age of ten, and of my jealousy, and biting the carpet at Chillingham'.

Books June 1943

'And books', I asked myself as I stood in Blackwell's shop in Oxford one day, surrounded by fat volumes on Soviet Russia and the Virgin Birth, and thin volumes on Education and Democracy, earnest pamphlets, flimsy novels, yellow manuals, reprints, Americana and all. There seemed no end of them. And what is in them all? Learned sawdust – vapour trash. And there were historical

---

93 Marjorie Noble (1896–1987), wife of Geoffrey Madan, was granddaughter of Sir Andrew Noble, the Newcastle armaments manufacturer, who leased Chillingham Castle, the Northumbrian seat of the Earls of Tankerville, from 1900 until 1907.

works too, lives of saints, and lives of kings, and lives of conquerors and politicians and administrators, and chronicles of wars and politics and movements and revolutions, – all the accumulated mundungus of all the centuries of man, stirred this way, stirred that, and smelling now thus, now thus, as the stirrer stirred. Must I add to these? I asked myself; spend perhaps a whole lifetime to increase this great Sargasso Sea by one wisp of seaweed? *Vanitas Vanitatum!* And over & around me, in the hidden background, in the Bodleian, in the New Bodleian, in the Radcliffe, I was aware of the unseen, oppressive, brooding presence of myriads of musty tomes, hundreds of tons of them weighing me down with their stifling, persecuting bulk. A feeling of hot spiritual claustrophobia overcame me, as in childhood, when I was besieged by a great herd of panting cows; and I turned and left the shop in disgust.

Palermo   July 1943

The Allies had occupied Palermo; and as we spoke of the news, a dim, spiritual spinster, of clerical background and faded artistic tastes, remembered that it was in Palermo that she had visited a monastery, and had been lured by her monastic guide down into a subterranean cloister or catacomb. Not having read Norman Douglas on *Southern Saintliness*, she had evidently expected to look at moral tapestries knitted by devout and charitable nuns, and interwoven with improving platitudes; but this was not at all what she found there. Faint and jittering, she was helped out from a long gallery where hung in order, like flitches of bacon, each in his decaying robes, the corpses of some macabre order of monks. Each, as he died, had been hung up on the wall, and there they still hung, some freshly dead, the maggots still dropping from their yellow flesh, others white, grinning bones, swathed in tatters, others fragmentary bundles of dust, like old bluebottle-flies slung in an ancient cobweb; but none too old, none too rank, to serve those grinning, demented monks as a salutary, refreshing reminder of mortality, a fragrant foretaste of everlasting life. My thoughts ran back to Garrowby, when I stayed there with Peter Wood, and a grinning, illuminated skull peered at me all night through the curtains of my four-poster, lest I should omit to ruminate on futurity; but to Gilbert it had other associations. 'Like Oriel Common Room', he said, 'on a guest night'.

The Two Voices   July 1943

Gen. Ritter von Thoma was speaking of Göring and his extravagant, ostenta-
tious way of life. This luxury, he was saying, is now essential to the man, it has
become part of him; he is like one of the Borgia ...

'I don't care', interrupted Gen. Gerd Bassenge,[94] a prisoner in the Tunisian
débâcle. 'Let him sit on a golden throne if he likes; let him stick golden peacock's feathers in his arsehole if he thinks it suits him. But what I can't forgive
him is the mess he's made of the German Air Force.'

Important disputes   July 1943

I have read somewhere, but I forget where (Martianus Capella, I think is the
authority) of two grammarians, Terrentius and Galbungus, who argued for a
fortnight about the vocative of *ego*; and in Lacy Collison-Morley's *Italy after
the Renaissance* (1930, p. 289) I read of two Tuscan cavaliers who disembow-
elled each other in a duel over the respective merits of Tasso and Ariosto.
Before dying both duellists confessed that they hadn't read a line of either.

And in Oxford, one day recently, Garrod showed me a life of old Darwell
Stone, the late Puseyite luminary, by F.L. Cross, showing that the old questions that troubled 17th century divines (whether angels had beards, how
many angels could stand on a point of a pin, and of what sex they were)
were burning topical problems compared with those still gravely disputed
by the casuist of Puseyism. I opened the book at random, and read a letter written by Stone in 1918 in answer to the question whether war-bread
might be validly consecrated. It was a long, learned & serious letter; & Stone
ended by saying that he must enquire into proportion of beans mixed in
the bread.[95]

---

94 Gerhard Bassenge (1897–1977), First World War fighter ace, commander of Stendal
parachute school 1937, captured at Methelin in Tunisia on 9 May 1943 and a prisoner at Trent
Park from 16 May 1943 until 1946; repatriated 1947.

95 Darwell Stone (1859–1941), Anglo-Catholic theologian and principal of Pusey House,
Oxford 1909–34, author of *The Faith of an English Catholic* (1926), and subject of F.L. Cross's
Darwell Stone, Churchman and Counsellor (1943).

I mentioned this to J.C. Masterman.[96] 'What nonsense!' he exclaimed; 'I thought you could consecrate a ship's biscuit, if you got down to it.'

———

A Jesuit once praised certain remote members of my family to me, because, he said, they had turned Roman Catholic and given all their wealth to the Jesuits. I felt less enthusiastic about their virtues, and so, when I told him, did Gilbert. 'One should sacrifice everything to religion', he said devoutly, 'except cash'.

———

To the boasts of others I am not normally attentive; but if they are seasoned with a little flattery of me, I can listen for ever.

Drink & conversation, how I love them! Other people's drink, and my own conversation.

———

The Victorians   July 1943

I was dining in Merton, with Garrod and Wilkinson[97] and Nichol Smith.[98] We spoke of early recollections, and when asked what were the earliest public events they recalled, Garrod remembered Gladstone's Midlothian campaign of 1880, Nichol Smith the Tay Bridge Disaster of 1879. A feeling of dank, bewildered gloom overcame me, as if I had entered a prehistoric sepulchre, full of bats and mustiness, and witnessed the resurrection of the dead. And

---

96 (Sir) John Masterman (1891–1977) had been inattentive as T-R's history tutor at Christ Church; chaired MI5's 'XX' Committee during the war.

97 Colonel Cyril Hackett Wilkinson (1888–1960), Fellow of Worcester 1918–1958, a man of whimsical opinions and martial aspect who commanded the Oxford Officers Training Corps and was Delegate of Military Instruction for the University Police. As a lecturer, 'he scarcely held the attention of young hearers for his love of English literature was not confined to any particular purpose'.

98 David Nichol Smith (1875–1962), Fellow of Merton from 1921, Merton Professor of English Literature 1929–1946. 'I found Nichol Smith, sitting, like Dr Syntax, in his fine Rowlandson study, deploring the decay of sense & orthodoxy ... his mind inhabits an upper storey of one of those gaunt Edinburgh houses of the 18th century, where Hume philosophised cannily in the sedate library, while the housemaid emptied the *pot-de-chambre* from a still more elevated window' (T-R to LPS, 11 Sep 1944).

yet, I reflected, they aren't old, – the active head of the French state today is a quarter of a century older than either of them. I projected my mind into the past to see what I could remember. I could remember the Borgias – they were but yesterday. Justinian I knew, and Mohammed, and Charlemain, and Julius Caesar, and the tyrants of Sicily. Certain even of the Pharaohs seemed humane and familiar to me. But however I might pierce or overleap the intervening centuries, I could not reach to that prehistoric age which these men remembered, when Queen Victoria was middle-aged, and mammoths and mastodons frisked and trumpeted in the swamps of Kensington and Kew, the days of Gladstone and Disraeli, Tennyson, Kingsley, and Herbert Spencer.

Nebulones   August 1943

I like those gay, casual Etonian figures among whom much of my Oxford life was spent; I like the recollection of them; and now that they have gaily and casually got themselves killed in this war, the memory of them always brings pleasure to my mind. There was Mark Pilkington,[99] who made my term with the Life Guards into a holiday, with whom I enjoyed many a mocking hour, and who inspired the same infectious devotion in his English troopers and his Abyssinian tribesmen. And now Antony Lyell,[100] who was killed in Tunisia, and has just been given a posthumous V.C. for his last exploit, – destroying, single-handed, with the bayonet, an enemy machine-gun nest. I can't think of him without pleasure – a tall, smiling, cavalier figure, with his high spirits and

---

99 Mark Pilkington (1914–1942), Eton and Christ Church, was killed while fighting with the Long Range Desert Group in Libya. 'With his good looks and his peculiar lazy charm, Captain Mark Pilkington, the Life Guards, passed for one of the most fortunate of men. His sense of humour and his dislike of pretension made him no friends among the pompous and the aggressive. He had a queer, almost fey gentleness and fineness of character, which he covered by a vague, desultory manner. Mark Pilkington was a most hardy and gallant soldier, as was recognised by all officers and men who served with him in the patriot guerrilla forces in Abyssinia' (*The Times*, 15 June 1942).

100 Antony, 2nd Baron Lyell (1913–1943) graduated from Christ Church with a science degree. As an officer in the Scots Guards, he was killed on 27 April at Dj Bou Arara. The award of his posthumous VC, with a description of his leadership, gallantry and self-sacrifice, was published in *The Times* of 13 August 1943.

Rabelaisian quatrains, mocking now the formal snobisme of Dean White,[101] now the careful pomposity of his more serious contemporaries. Well, death immortalises these figures at their most attractive hour; this the meaning of the Greek phrase that the favourites of the Gods die young. I make no bones about their loss, no claims for their reprieve. They are immortal spirits, not human companions, spirits whose influence is separable from such accidents as absence or death.

> The earth hath bubbles as the water hath,
> And these are of them.[102]

Image   August 1943

I was in a genial, forgiving mood; it seemed to me that we were winning the war, in spite of S.I.S. 'It will solve itself', I said. 'As each area becomes really important, it will have to be given to Philby, and thus, in the end, he will control all, and Cowgill[103] and Vivian and the rest will drop uselessly from the tree, like over-ripe plums.' But a different image was in Reilly's mind.[104] 'No', he said, and there was bitterness and hatred in his voice as he went on, 'they will hang on and batten still, like lice in the folds of a diseased dog's ear'. And then he described to me, from his days in Persia, the reality from which this brilliant image of S.I.S. was drawn.

---

101 Very Rev Henry White (1859–1934), Dean of Christ Church from 1920. 'So long as we have the Cecils and the Percys, Christ Church can hold up its head among the colleges of Oxford,' he told the undergraduate T-R. Roy Harrod wrote that White's voice trembled with pleasure at mention of a duke: 'for him dukes were an important and honoured part of the establishment of Church and State, for which he prayed sincerely.'

102 Shakespeare, *Macbeth*, act I, scene 3.

103 Felix Cowgill (1903–1991), head of MI6's section V responsible for counterespionage. Guy Liddell wrote (diary 17 July 1943) that while MI5 'regarded Felix as a loyal and hard worker, we found him an infernal nuisance and thoroughly uncooperative'.

104 (Sir) Patrick Reilly (1909–1999) had befriended T-R while a Fellow of All Souls (1932–1939). He joined the diplomatic service in 1933, served in the Ministry of Economic Warfare 1939–1942 and had wartime posts in Algiers, Paris and Athens. T-R visited him in Moscow in 1957 after his appointment as Ambassador to Russia, and rejoiced at his appointment to the Paris embassy in 1965.

A compliment   August 1943

A young officer came into Freddie's office in S.O.E. 'I'm Ayer', said Freddie. 'What Freddie Ayer?' 'Yes.' 'I used to attend your lectures', said the young man, and then, said Freddie, as he recounted the incident afterwards, he paid me a great compliment, for he went on, 'and for *six years* I believed what you said – until hard facts made it impossible to believe it any longer'.

Fr Beck, S.J.   August 1943

At Campion Hall, in the days when I was still admitted to those holy flesh-pots, I used to meet a drab, skinny, melancholy Jesuit, Fr Beck,[105] a Hegelian philosopher, whom Fr D'Arcy disliked, but found useful, I think, as foil at those devout junkettings. The decanters clinked, those worldly old Jesuits gabbled gaily on to their rich secular guests, Fr D'Arcy puffed the blue fumes from his long ragged cheroot and pronounced his dispensations from the tedious routine of devotion; but Fr Beck sat there solemn, silent and macabre, a skeleton at the feast, his head projecting from his heavy priestly costume like the skull of a haddock from a newspaper-wrapping, and if he spoke, it was only to refuse, in dreary, sepulchral tones, an offer of port, or cigars, or conversation. I sometimes wondered what he was thinking of, – a barren wonder, for of what does a haddock think, when it is already unconscious, or dead?

But then, one day, – O regenerative spirit of love that springs even in the unpromising soil of Hegelian tea-parties – Fr Beck cast eyes on Miss Joachim, the philosopher's daughter,[106] and saw that she was good; and about the same his ratiocinative faculty was quickened to fresh discoveries, and he found flaws in hitherto accepted doctrines. The inspiration of St Ignatius, the dialectic of the blessed Bellarmine, the infallibility of the Pope, the mission of his Order, all now seemed to him imperfectly proven; and having first (for he was a prudent man) secured the promise of a philosophical fellowship in Magdalen College, he peeled off, and tossed away, the unhygienic garments of his order,

---

105 Leslie Beck (1906–1978), pre-war Jesuit and Fellow of Magdalen, author of works on Descartes, joined the Political Warfare Executive in 1940, and ran its French department.

106 Ursula Joachim (1909–1968), daughter of Harold Joachim, Wykeham Professor of Logic at Oxford, married Beck in 1938.

and I next saw him walking at great strides round the Christ Church Meadow, in baggy flannel trousers and an open shirt, wielding a great walking-stick, which he whirled with one hand, to encourage the frolics of a large Alsatian dog, while on the other arm leant the admiring Miss Joachim.

And now scene III in the Metamorphoses of Fr Beck. It is the end of the fourth year of the war, and Freddie Ayer was sent to P.W.E.[107] to an interview with the grandest of all its functionaries. 'Mr Beck?' asked the watchman incredulously, 'but have you an appointment?' 'Yes', said Freddie, and he was taken under guard from ante-room to ante-room, and kept in play by secretaries and assistants, and finally the word was given, a silent, valvular door was opened, and he was led into a large, comfortable room, where, at a polished table, sat the regenerate Fr Beck, controlling, from this centre of that sinister spider's web, incalculable forces throughout the world. Perhaps even now, like the Jesuits of the 16th century, he was assassinating great princes, over-toppling distant governments, through his far-flung intellectual machinery. What chance wave had tossed this poor dead fish into so high a cranny, so strange a posture? It was useless to ask, but after their business, Freddie ventured to make a philosophical crack. Fr Beck was impatient of such trifles. 'I've not thought of philosophy for four years', he said drily, and touching a bell with a long, bony finger, he told his secretary to show Freddie out.

'We need Evelyn Waugh in this world!' I exclaimed, when Freddie had finished his narrative, – and it is a thought that often recurs to me, for all Africa and its surprises, its jungles and cannibals, its totems and witch-doctors, are not so fantastic as Whitehall in wartime – but I added that Beck himself would certainly be unaware of the fantasy of it, and probably derives no relish or mirth at all from contemplating his own metamorphosis.

'No', said Gilbert, 'we can be sure he remains what he always has been, an unimportant minor rodent'.

———————

Breakfast time   August 1943

It's at breakfast at my billet that the air is most heavily charged with spiritual thunder; and at breakfast-time I'm never in my most robust conversational

———————

107 Political Warfare Executive.

form. How should I evade the storm? I ask myself, when that formidable prophetess descends kipperwards, fresh from some new nocturnal revelation, either vouchsafed in a dream, or culled in the long vigils from the pages of the philosopher Ouspensky.[108] Shall I explain finally and firmly that I not a Christian; that I don't believe in natural rights or the importance of a vegetable diet; that the errors of the Fundamentalists don't need labouring to me; that I don't see salvation in the Wisdom of the East, or hope in the prophecies of the Great Pyramid, or explanations in the submerged continent of Atlantis; that I don't believe all lucidity to be shallow, or the profound always meaningless, or shepherds the wisest philosophers; that I don't think Civilisation is going up and up, or that it bears a fixed relation to morals, and will reach its zenith in a parliament of women; that I don't believe we're hovering on the frontier of a new psychic dimension, or that the body is an irrelevant clogging burden whose importunate demands we will one day be able to satisfy with unsubstantial nutriment, so that we can walk barely touching the ground; that I don't believe in the Powers of Evil, or that the world is full of Wickedness and Woe, or that all life is vibration, and all history a spiral, or that the Suffering God is the key to the Cosmos, and that vaccination and bloodsports are Sin. But no, it would be no good, no good at all. So I just smile sweetly and prevaricate by passing the toast; or explain that I was brought up in a different school of philosophy; and I can listen without pain to the lamentations which these manoeuvres excite, that is a tragic and terrible sight to see a young man flitting like a headless butterfly over the Eternal Verities. But how I agree with the old Duke of Northumberland,[109] that at breakfast a gentleman doesn't talk, he only eats!

Dicksie Marshall   Sept 1943

He is a great character,[110] the best fisherman in Northumberland, probably the best shot, and quite certainly the most notorious poacher. He never goes

----

108 Peter Ouspensky (1878–1947), an exponent of Gurdjieff's esotericism, whose works included *The Fourth Dimension* (1909) and *A New Model of the Universe* (1931).

109 Alan Percy, 8th Duke of Northumberland (1880–1930), coal-owner and polemicist, lived at Alnwick Castle.

110 Richard ('Dicksie') Marshall (1888–1969) lived at Anstead, Northumberland.

abroad without first putting his .22 rifle in the back of his car; for who knows but he might espy a partridge sitting in someone's stubble-field at 300 yards, or a pheasant perched on someone's wall by the roadside? His indifference to the tedious minutiae of *meum* and *tuum* in the sporting world has involved him in temporary trouble with most of his landowning neighbours by now, and he frequently deplores their unsportsmanlike habits of padlocking their boats, or omitting to put down pheasants, or failing to stock their depleted rivers. But, on the whole, his activities are too notorious to be taken seriously, and his ingenuity is equal to most occasions, – even when Colonel Bridgeman's keeper surprised him fishing Colonel Bridgeman's lake from Colonel Bridgeman's boat which he had with difficulty unmoored.[111] Only with Lord Tankerville did he have a serious row; 'For five minutes I told him what I thought of him', he told me, 'and never repeated myself once'. And anyway, Lord Tankerville is a crank.[112]

I went shooting with him at Henlaw the other day, and a very enjoyable day it was; for the dearth of partridges troubled me less than it troubled Dicksie. On the way we passed Bellshill, and Dicksie was reminded of a tragedy enacted there when Constance Grey gave a shoot. 'When we reached that covert', he said, 'she lined us all up and said, "Now I want everyone to be very careful here; there's a Chinese golden pheasant in this covert; you can't mistake it, it has a tail six feet long. It must not be shot." Well', he went on, 'we took up our posts, & the beaters went through the wood, and I saw an ordinary hen-pheasant coming at me; so I opened up with a withering fire, and it tumbled over in the air and fell; and as it fell, it was like a rainbow falling, and I knew I'd done it. So when the gamekeeper came up I said, "I've shot a hen-pheasant", and pointed in exactly the opposite direction; but the man's blasted retriever found it out, and it was quite true, its tail was six feet long. I was very unpopular. I didn't even dare to go to the house for a drink afterwards. Poor lady', he added, after a pause, but without much evidence of contrition, 'she had fetched it all the way from China, to cross it with one of her cock-pheasants. But I didn't give it time for that.'

---

111 Hon Henry Bridgeman (1882–1972) rented Harehope Hall, near Alnwick before buying the Fallodon estate.

112 Charles Bennet, 8th Earl of Tankerville (1897–1971) dedicated his life to protecting the only British herd of pure white wild cattle, which roamed the park at Chillingham. They almost perished in the winter of 1946–1947.

As we ate our sandwiches on the moor at Henlaw I had told Dicksie of my arrest in Ireland, but he said he could go better than that, for he had been expelled from Mexico under article 33 as a pernicious foreigner, – but the President of Mexico had escorted him back again within a fortnight; and he described the scene when his enemies were summoned before him by authority. They fell on their knees, and begged him to intercede, for the authorities were going to shoot them; but Dicksie is a humane character. 'I don't want them shot', he said, 'I know who they are, and they're not such bad fellows at all. Just flog them tonight, and flog them again in the morning, and that'll do for me.' The fate of the man who had poisoned Dicksie's bitch in Mexico was similar. Dicksie offered the police 100 Mexican dollars if they caught him, and by next day they had hunted him down and brought him back, & he confessed to putting arsenic in a meat-ball to poison the bitch. Thereupon Dicksie started counting out the cash; but the *Jefe* of the police interposed, saying, 'Señor, we're very hard up at present; make it another $100 and we'll hang him for you'. But again Dicksie's humanity prevailed. They had done a good job of work, he said, and for that he gave them another $50; but as for the culprit, let them shambuck him tonight, and rub salt in the wounds overnight, and shambuck him again tomorrow, and that would do.

I asked him about the pack of hounds he had hunted in Mexico, for it had a great reputation. How were they bred? 'Penitentiary-bred', he said, 'from the blood-hounds that had been used to track runaway niggers; and the best of them came from a couple of blue Pennsylvania hounds that ran down the man who murdered the sheriff of San Antonio, Texas, and took him in 48 hours, a hundred and fifty mile away, across the Rio Grande. Their fault was that they wouldn't cast, always going back to where they lost the scent; but I bred that out of them', he said, 'while keeping their noses, and where any pack of English hounds had lost their fox, I'd bet £100 my hounds would take up and kill him'. 'And what did you hunt?', I asked. 'Not foxes', he said; 'they all lived up trees; but lynx and tree-bear, and for an all-day hunt the timber-wolf, or, best of all, the coyote. Oh, there was no lack of quarry; we'd hunt anything, – anything, but peccary – they killed too many of my hounds.'

So he went on, describing his 20 years in Mexico, the best country in the world, he said, till the Americans came and spoilt it, & drove him back again to Northumberland where his family had lived, his old uncle, whom I remember hunting over the Chatton Moors, looking like a little tailor on his half-clipped pony, aged 88; and his father the colonel, who was cut off in the bloom of his youth by a hunting accident, and him barely 70, on those same moors. And now Dicksie keeps up the family tradition, shooting and fishing promiscuously over the fields and in the water of his vainly protesting neighbours; an admirable character.

Sept 1943

I sat in the bar of the inn at Osmotherley with the earth-stoppers and second-horsemen of that delightful district, and someone spoke of Bobby Dawson.[113] Who was he? I asked; and at once a dozen beer-mugs were lowered heavily on to the table in horror at my ignorance. But it was no good my pretending to know, and so they had to explain that Bobby Dawson was the most famous man in England, after John Peel, and that he hunted the Bilsdale hounds for sixty years; and one by one, from every corner of the bar, successive voices added new details to the gradually forming picture of this great character: how he rode so much that his horse had a hollow in its back in which he carried his lunch while out hunting, and in which a crow (said one, but another said it was a jackdaw) built its nest; and how, when he died, aged 85, all the neighbourhood subscribed to buy him an ornamental tombstone with a fox's mask and crossed hunting-whips carved upon it. But the parson wouldn't allow these profane emblems within holy ground, so Bobby Dawson was buried in the churchyard, but his tombstone was set up in the pub, where I could still see it, if I would go to Chopgate and call on Will Ainsley, the publican, who is also Bobby Dawson's successor as master and huntsman of the Bilsdale Hounds.[114]

Of course I went to Chopgate, and called on Will Ainsley, and he showed me the tombstone, and told me about the hounds. They are trencher-fed, he explained, and he doesn't hunt them until October, else the high-growing bracken cuts up their mouths; but he goes on hunting into April, peace or war – will I not come over in March, and get a horse from Tom Fletcher, and let him know, so that he can fix the meets accordingly. What sort of a

---

113 Bobbie Dawson (1816–1902), huntsman of the Bilsdale hounds for 60 years.
114 William Ainsley (1893–1953), huntsman of the Bilsdale hounds, was landlord of the Sun Inn at Chopgate, a village high in Cleveland.

country is it? I asked. Well, it's a rough country, but Will Ainsley has killed his 240th fox there, 49 of them last season, with his 8 couple of hounds; and the only real danger is jet-mines, disused and overgrown, in these Yorkshire hills. Poor Frank Morris, huntsman of the Cleveland – never was there so unfortunate a huntsman, he sighed, with every bone in his body broken out hunting, so that he'll have to retire after the war, and him barely 70, – well, poor Frank Morris' last accident was a fall down a jet-mine, and although they got him out again after a while, it took a couple of cranes to fetch his horse out ...

O happy Bilsdale hounds to have two such huntsmen as Bobby Dawson, now a legendary hero among the moor dwellers of North Yorkshire, and Will Ainsley, the priest of his cenotaph! Of course I will go there in March, jet-mines or no jet-mines.

The Return of the Monasteries   Sept 1943

I went to Ampleforth, too, when I was in Yorkshire, with a letter from David Mathew[115] in my pocket, strolling over the Hambleton Hills from Osmotherley on a bright September morning to Hawnby and Rievaulx and down the Rye valley and across the Duncombe moor; and reaching Ampleforth about tea-time, I looked up and down for guidance amongst those miscellaneous buildings, till I espied a black hat stirring in a vegetable garden. I addressed it, and, like Thetis arising from the sea-waves, a figure in monkish clothes, but with the encouraging face of an Irish horse-coper, rose from behind a row of beans. I asked after the abbot, to whom my letter was addressed, but the abbot was away, and the Irish monk (for he did turn out Irish, and Father Placid Dolan[116] was his name) took me in charge. Where was I from, he asked. From

----

115 David Mathew (1902–1975), Catholic chaplain to London University 1934–1944, auxiliary bishop of Westminster 1938–1945, apostolic delegate to the British colonies in Africa and Archbishop of Apamea 1946–1953.

116 Joseph Dolan (1878–1954) read mathematics at Oxford in 1900–1904, and took the religious name of Placid after his ordination in 1905. He was mathematics master at Ampleforth, 1904–1941; kept bee-hives and an aviary; a photographer, gardener, naturalist and poetry-lover.

Northumberland, I said; and that reminded him of days spent fishing on the Whitadder, and he went on to praise the local trout-fishing, on the river Rye. And at that moment the image I had formed of an Irish horse-coper floated away and was replaced by another image of an old monk, with his black hat and his winking face, crouched in the rushes by a riverside, gaffing a poached salmon. But while my fancy was thus at play, he had pressed me to stay at the monastery, and I was given a suite of rooms reserved, I discovered, for visiting bishops, furnished with many crude but edifying pictures, and a prie-dieu with a cushion of rubber-sponge, lest I should excoriate my knees in prayer.

After tea, while the hospitable monks amused themselves at vespers and sext, I strolled over to Gilling castle, where the Fairfaxes had once lived, popish lords; but now (after an interregnum when various bubble-families, including the Hunters, had owned it) the monks had got it, and had turned it into a preparatory school for Ampleforth; ironical change, for Ampleforth itself had started as a dependency of Gilling, the Fairfaxes having built there a small house for their retiring popish chaplain in the 18th century. It was on this house, and this old man, that the Benedictines of some French abbey, fleeing from the French Revolution, had suddenly descended, like a summer swarm of bees, *anno* 1800 or thereabouts; and finding the place good, they had stayed there, and grown rich, and begun its transformation, by piecemeal accretions in every known style of architecture, into this large and opulent monastery, with its 900 acres of farmland and endowments and capital, and its dependent satellite at Gilling.

A beautiful house it was, set in a beautiful place, a small castle exquisitely converted by Vanbrugh,[117] with long projecting wings, rounded at the ends, and an 18th century pediment, and a battlemented balustrade, and a court-yard and clock-tower beside it. And Gilbert Scott,[118] in his adaptations, had not impaired its beauty; and the Gardens were still in flower, and rooks cawed eternally about it, proclaiming its pastoral loneliness. And as I looked at it I was aware of the reversal of history that is taking place in our time; the return of the monasteries. Four hundred years ago they fell, and their lands and great houses, after a period in the hands of bubble-speculators, gravitated into the

---

117 Sir John Vanbrugh (1664–1726), architect, dramatist and Clarenceux king-at-arms.

118 Sir George Gilbert Scott (1811–1878), restoring architect at Ely, Hereford, Lichfield, Ripon and Salisbury cathedrals, and at Westminster Abbey, whose renovations provoked the founding of the Society for the Protection of Ancient Buildings.

possession of the private families who, for four centuries, ruled England, and ruled it, on the whole, well. But now their day is over, and their houses, their old castles and abbeys, their Palladian houses and classical houses, one after another, after a brief term in the hands of bubble-magnates, are falling back again into public ownership, to ministries and to corporations, as schools and as institutes, even to monasteries, like this Gilling.

Of course it's very patriotic of their owners to accept their burdens, and pay their taxes, and surrender their inheritance like this; but it isn't the virtue of a ruling-class. Commissars don't behave like this, nor Gauleiters. Only today I read that Ribbentrop[119] has switched an aeroplane-propeller factory over to building furniture for one of his palaces, and that Axmann[120] has made a war-factory divert its resources to building him a house. And indeed is it a virtue at all? *Pendant que la paresse et la timidité nous retiennent dans notre devoir, notre vertu en a souvent tout l'honneur.*[121]

Holy Island   Sept 1943

It was early morning and I stood on the wet sands of Beal, the most lonely, waste, forsaken spot on that beautiful Northumbrian coast. The gulls cried overhead, or picked for lug-worms and sea-vermin on the glistening grey sands that seemed to stretch away for ever. Three miles ahead, across the tidal flats, lay Holy Island; and on either hand, half-sunken in the mud, like the skeletons of camels that are said to mark the ancient caravan-routes of the Libyan desert, lay the rusty wrecks of cars that had tried to cross those three miles and had failed – whether because their wheels had stuck in the soft ooze, or because the incoming waters had overwhelmed them, as the waves of

---

119 Joachim von Ribbentrop (1893–1946), partner in a *Sekt* (sparkling German wine) business, became a Nazi Party member 1932, German Ambassador in London 1936–38 and Foreign Minister 1938–1945. Sentenced at Nuremberg to be hanged, he took 17 minutes to die in the noose.

120 Artur Axmann (1913–1996) succeeded Baldur von Schirach as youth leader of the Nazi Party in 1940, and retained this post until the war's end. His arm was amputated on the Eastern Front in 1941. He heard the shot that killed Hitler, and left the bunker with Bormann.

121 While laziness and timidity keep us within the bounds of our duty, our virtue absconds with all the honour (a maxim of Rochefoucauld's).

the Red Sea had engulfed the chariots of Pharaoh, who similarly misread the omens, I do not know. And therefore my first sensation if simple, wide-eyed delight in the lone majesty of the place was superseded by another, less impersonal feeling. Oh to live in Lindisfarne! I thought, in that rock-perched castle that winks at Bamburgh over the intervening gulf, as the towers of Sestos and Abydos eyed one another across the Hellespont; to live there exalted and alone, inaccessible to importunate visitors. An army of bores might land the sands of Beal; they might stretch out their hands *ripae ulterioris amore;*[122] but for the six hours of high tide they would clamour in vain; and even at low water, three miles of gray, water-dappled and sometimes treacherous sands, dotted with the wreckage of too ambitious cars, and marked at each mile by windy crows'-nests for tide-trapped pedestrians, might have a deterrent influence on the more unwieldy and slow-footed among them.

The Last Enemy Oct 1943

Staying with George Ward[123] at Cirencester, I found myself disputing with him the merits of Richard Hillary's book, *The Last Enemy.* An unhealthy book, he had said, bad for morale; one shouldn't dwell on the details of mutilation and pain; it's not fair on the other chaps; it might make them waver in the trenches. So I mocked him, and bade him distinguish between art and recruiting-propaganda. And anyway, who has ever been deterred from action by the fate of others? Has the bad driver, or the criminal? When then the fighting man? So I reasoned; and then I went quietly and read the book, to provide against a counter-attack on the weakest spot in my argument; for I hadn't read it before.

An attractive book I found it, representing to me the Oxford I like to believe in, – a gay, sceptical, tolerant, enquiring, unshockable world, enjoying experience for its own sake, and unimpressed by proprieties and slogans.

122 *Tendebantque manus ripae ulterioris amore*: they were holding their arms outstretched in love towards the further shore (a phrase from Virgil's *Aeneid*).

123 George ('Geordie') Ward, 1st Viscount Ward of Witley (1907–1988), Commoner of Christ Church 1936, Wing Commander in the RAF 1942, Secretary of State for Air 1957–1960.

But experience has proved this inadequate in the end. Must I then accept his conclusions? I asked myself. 'Yes', replied a crowd of ghostly inquisitors. 'But I haven't been shot down into the Thames estuary', I protested, 'nor hurtled through life at the rate of sixty years *per annum*'. And then, recollecting in this connexion my argument that we are not deterred by the warning example of others, I went further, and concluded that the lessons of experience are valid only to those who have suffered the experience; and since Hillary's experience was extraordinary, his conversion was valid for himself only. And not only Hillary. Like the albatross from the mariner's neck, they fell away from my emburdened mind, all those stormy introverts, with their crises and conversions, St Paul, St Augustine, Loyola, John Donne, – of what significance are they to us, who have not trodden the same hot and prickly desert paths as they? They are no guides for us, who are not travelling in the Arabia Infelix of their exotic souls; but we may watch them, as we watch the antics of Hollywood stars, or Indian fakirs, or Methodist preachers, and deduce what we will about the infinite variety of human behaviour. Or we may read, as art, the expression they give to their experiences; their confessions, their apologias, their testaments, the odysseys of their intellectual pilgrimage, the mirrors of their chameleon souls. Further than that they are to us irrelevant. *Il faut cultiver notre jardin.*[124]

The Great Whaddon Row   Nov 1943

I was staying with the Wheelers at Whitchurch,[125] before hunting with the Bicester; it was after dinner; I was alone with Mr Wheeler; and it seemed a good opportunity to hear the complete tale of the great Whaddon Chase row which, for twenty years, had split the solid-seeming society of Buckinghamshire to its foundations. So I reminded him of our unfinished conversation on the way back from Botolph Claydon one hunting day, and he agreed to resume the topic, and animate, with circumstantial details, that spectre which still

---

124 We must cultivate our garden (Voltaire, *Candide*, chapter 30), meaning, in this context, We must work with what we have.

125 G. Wheeler of Whitchurch was a friend of the huntsman-artist Lionel Edwards, author of *The Wiles of the Fox* (1932). His wife may have been Grace de Courcey Wheeler (1908–1960).

haunts so many country houses in the district. After a pause, therefore, in which he probed silently into the vast backward abysm of Time, 'Let us go back forty years', he began, 'to 1901, when I first hunted with the Whaddon. There were two packs of hounds in the country in those days, the Rothschild staghounds at Ascott, and the Whaddon Chase at Whaddon. Both showed good sport, and they worked in well together; for the staghounds drove all the foxes into the coverts, and the foxhounds hunted them out again. Now the Whaddon Chase was the family pack of the Selby-Lowndes;[126] the old squire owned it, and Bill Lowndes was field-master; and very good sport he showed for several seasons. But the Lowndes were a poor family, as things went, and, frankly, they lived by the pack, which they hunted as parsimoniously as they could, mounting the servants cheaply, and taking as big a subscription as they could, and always refusing a committee, or any audit of the accounts; for as long as they showed good sport, and the subscribers were satisfied, whose business was it how the Selby Lowndes administered their property? Unfortunately there came a time when the subscribers were not satisfied.'

For after a while, Bill Lowndes thought of reducing still further the expenses of the establishment by disposing of his huntsman and hunting the hounds himself; and then the trouble began, for the sport began to decline, and the voice of discontent arose, and over many a bottle of old port the demand for a hunt committee and more regular management was heard. But then the war came, and Bill Lowndes joined his regiment, leaving the hounds to one Murray[127] to hunt; and when the peace was restored the situation had crystallised; for Murray had quarrelled with the Lowndes and had gone over to the dissidents, who had formed up behind Lord Dalmeny;[128] and since the Rothschild staghounds had been disbanded, Dalmeny had the Ascott kennels

---

126 William Selby-Lowndes (1836–1920), of Whaddon Hall, Stony Stratford, and his eldest son William Selby-Lowndes (1871–1951). The latter was a Buckinghamshire magistrate, chairman of the Country Gentleman's Association and the Grimsby Seine Fishing Company. The family had little money, but were entitled to quarter the arms of Plantagenet, Pole and Neville.

127 Possibly John Murray (1863–1943), Master of the Wrest Basset Hounds in Bedfordshire.

128 Harry Primrose, Lord Dalmeny (1882–1974), whose mother was a Rothschild, succeeded as 6th Earl of Rosebery and 2nd Earl of Midlothian in 1929. Master of the Whaddon Chase Hounds 1923–1933, joint Master 1934–1940; chairman of White's, 1934–1936 and 1938–1945; Secretary of State for Scotland, 1945.

at his disposal. All that was lacking was a pack of hounds to put in them, and with money this was easily come by.

There was a man Nell,[129] he went on, who, during the war, had hunted part of the Duke of Beaufort's country, and, being a good kennel-man, had bred an excellent pack; and this pack Dalmeny bought from him, and taking advice from Boddington, whom he imported as huntsman from, I think, the VWH,[130] he drafted into it a number of hounds from the Berkeley, and made a first-class hunting pack. And now the battle was fairly joined, for, four times a week, from the kennels of Whaddon in the north country, under Bill Lowndes, and from the kennels of Ascott in the south country, under Dalmeny, there issued two rival packs of fox-hounds, both, like the Popes and Antipopes of Christendom, claiming to be the authentic Whaddon Chase, and advertising in *Horse and Hound* under that name, and drawing each others' coverts, and sometimes even meeting in the field, and hunting each others' foxes; and this happened throughout the season of 1920–21, but neither side abated a jot of its claim to be the one and only legitimate Whaddon Chase Hunt.

And how did the division go? I asked.

Well, he said, the north where the Selby-Lowndes' property lay, stood by them, but in the south, where Rosebery and the Rothschilds were the great landlords, Dalmeny had his following; and of course his was the better pack. The dividing line was at Winslow, and for long the village of Winslow, like some medieval free city havering between the Emperor and the Pope, hesitated in its allegiance; but first the McCorquodales,[131] and then the Lambtons,[132] opted for Dalmeny, and after that the small fry followed obediently in their wake.

And was it a hard-and-fast division? Must everybody choose one side or the other? Or were there neutrals and trimmers who hunted with both packs?

Oh, it was a serious matter, said Mr Wheeler; if I had gone out with Bill Lowndes in those days, I would have had to face many black looks in

---

129 Herbert Nell (1876–1952), of Chipping Sodbury, was the Beaufort huntsman 1905–1910.

130 Will Boddington. The hounds of the Vale of the White Horse hunt were kennelled at Cirencester.

131 Norman McCorquodale (1863–1938), of Winslow Hall, Bletchley, High Sheriff of Buckinghamshire 1909.

132 William Lambton (1867–1943), of Redfield, Winslow, High Sheriff of Buckinghamshire 1926.

Whitchurch. Everyone went with one or the other – except Dick Cruise;[133] but he was always rather a pirate. And I thought I noticed a tone of disapproval in his voice, when he admitted that Sir Richard Cruise, ophthalmic surgeon to His late Majesty, had broken the rules of ideological warfare, and trafficked openly with both sides.

And how did it end? Well, it didn't end altogether, for like the religious conflicts of the sixteenth century, it still arouses black passions in Buckinghamshire bosoms; but in 1921, it seems, the Masters of Foxhounds Union sent Lord Galway[134] down to arbitrate, and he called a meeting of the farmers and covert-owners, and stopped Dalmeny hunting; but Bill Lowndes he allowed to continue to the end of the season. And thereafter he forbade either of them to act as master of the Whaddon Chase for three years, that passions might have time to cool – vain hope, for hunting passions are of sempiternal duration. Meanwhile Dalmeny got his nominee, Lord Orkney,[135] accepted as master for that period, and after three years succeeded to it himself, Bill Lowndes refusing to recognise the successful usurper, or to let him draw any of his coverts – until 1938, when age had cooled his blood somewhat, and hounds were admitted to some of the outlying coverts of the estate.

And what happened to Lowndes and his pack? Well, Lowndes was a prudent man, and although he wouldn't recognise Dalmeny and his pack, he sold his own hounds to him at a huge price, and then withdrew on the proceeds to hunt a strange pack in Kent …[136]

So these local passions simmered on, and then came another war, and Rosebery (as Dalmeny had become) tasted the delights of hunting a pack of hounds in war-time, when the rich subscribers had melted suddenly away,

---

133 Sir Richard Cruise (1876–1946), Surgeon Oculist to King George V, was famed for his success in operating on cataracts. In the First World War he devised a visor of light chain-metal to protect the eyes of troops engaged in trench warfare and perfected a method of reconstructive surgery that enabled the contracted sockets of blinded soldiers to be fitted with false eyes. He married a Selby-Lowndes stepdaughter and divided his time between Wimpole Street and a house at Shipton-cum-Winslow; a bold hunting man, winner of steeplechases, connoisseur of wine and amateur of painting.

134 George Monckton-Arundell, 7th Viscount Galway (1844–1931), Master of the Grove Hunt 1876–1907, 'a good performer across a stiff country', author of *A Pack of Foxhounds* (1925).

135 Edmond Fitz-Maurice, 7th Earl of Orkney (1867–1951), the first peer to marry a Gaiety Girl, Master of Whaddon Chase Hounds 1920–1923. Despite their Irish surname and Scottish title, the Orkneys had been settled in Buckinghamshire for centuries.

136 Bill Selby-Lowndes's brother was Master of the East Kent Foxhounds 1900–1930.

and the glory of it had departed, and misliked it exceedingly; so he quietly resigned, and withdrew to Scotland, and Harold Morton[137] took over the pack. As for Lowndes, he is a prudent man, and when the Secret Service descended like locusts on the green fields of Buckinghamshire, and Col. Gambier-Parry, purged from the BBC, creeping unscathed from the crashing ruins of Philco Ltd, cast his eyes on the pilastered splendour and shady pleasaunces of Whaddon Park, Col. Lowndes was not unwilling, *moyennant une petite consideration*,[138] to give him the use of it. So now the chapter is ended, the rift almost closed; the protagonists have withdrawn; Whaddon has a new squire, the hounds a new master and new huntsmen; and thrice a year, in Whaddon Park, the *Most Secret* files are stuffed away, the clinking decanters are brought out, and amid the breezy bonhomie of an old-established bucket-shop, the Whaddon hounds meet again at their eponymous mansion.

December 1943

Am I mad? I sometimes wonder, at those winter daybreaks, when I hitch-hike forty miles to go hunting with the Bicester, and sometimes even with the Whaddon Chase – not seriously mad, of course, but just a little touched in the brain, like Frank Pakenham, for instance, or poor old Rowse. I wondered it today, as I shot, coatless and shivering, along the Watford by-pass, in the back of a charitable but icy jeep. I had only come out of hospital three days ago, after a hunting fall on my last excursion, and I had only had four hours' sleep since last night's debauch, and now icicles were forming on the end of my nose; for it was very cold, and when dawn broke, and light leaked into the sky, even the fog couldn't disguise the fact that the country was all overfrosted. However, I went on, – if there was no hunting, I could always go on to Oxford, I said to myself, for drink and gossip, – and in Aylesbury I alit at a lorry-drivers' pull-up and warmed myself with a cup of tea by the fire; and then, as my last driver drew up at Ham Green, the fog ceased, and there was Johnson, in his pink coat, jumping a broken-down old gate off the road, and all the hounds

---

137 Major Harold Morton (1894–1972), a City director, was Master of the Whaddon Chase Hounds 1940–1947, High Sheriff of Buckinghamshire 1943, chairman of Aylesbury Conservative Association.

138 For a small fee.

behind him, and Tom sending them on after him, all on the way to the meet at Wootton. The sun shone through the tatters of dissolving mist; the black branches were beaded with rime; and on the other side of the road, Morn Simms was leading Rubberneck out of the stable of the Crooked Billet. I was not mad; these moments of ecstasy are my reward; and I can always count on their occurrence, thus or thus. One day it was the sight of a ride in Chinkwell Wood, all white with snowberries; on another, it was the whole pack, in full cry, swimming the lake at Wotton; the music of hounds in the woodlands, the autumn flowers in cubbing-time, the naked woods in winter, the very dreariness of the Bicester Monday country, – in all of these there is a delight that will compensate me for any discomfort in the getting of it. Why, even the pleasure of that famous hunt from Marsh Gibbon (since malice, too, is among the intellectual pleasures), was improved when I rode that bounder Freddie Courtney into the brook, and left him there, gurgling revenge.

A bye-day

I went out yesterday to hunt with the Bicester at Charndon Wood, but it was a full moon, and the frost had come, and from Aylesbury I rang up the kennels, and they said no, it was too hard, they couldn't go. So remembering that it was rent-audit day at Merton, when the tenant farmers turn up to pay their rent and consume, with the Warden and Fellows, great quantities of capons and burgundy and port, stopped a friendly lorry-driver, who, having been second whip to the Exmoor hounds, appreciated my predicament, and went on to Oxford to join in those rustic and learned compotations.

Hunting and divinity, how well they sort together in my mind! I must own to a weakness for sporting parsons; for those unapostolic characters I read of in Nimrod and elsewhere;[139] for parson Jack Russell, and the hundred Devonshire clergymen who rode to hounds once a week in his day;[140] for

---

139 Charles Apperley (1779–1843), a Shropshire hunting squire, used the pseudonym 'Nimrod' for his sporting memoirs, which T-R felt were written in 'cold, snobbish prose'.

140 John Russell (1795–1883), breeder of fox-hunting terriers, parson of Swimbridge, Devonshire 1832–80 and rector of Black Torrington 1880–83.

the clergyman whose advertisement Arthur Young read in the newspaper: 'Wanted, a curacy in a good sporting country, where the duties are light and the company convivial';[141] and reaching back into the 17th century, for the learned bishop Wilkins, who got his first promotion through beagling, and the pious archbishop Juxon, who, untainted by the scruples of 18th century bishops, combined the horn and the mitre, and scattered a puritan prayer-meeting by hunting a fox through Chipping Norton churchyard.[142]

As to that, Biffy Holland-Hibbert[143] told me that he once got into trouble for jumping into a churchyard, when the Bicester were in full cry; they said it was outrageous to the dead; which I thought inconceivable until I was myself shoo'd out of the Oxford crematorium by a scandalised custodian in course of a gay hunt from Woodeaton Spinney with the South Oxon. Fantastic indignation! I thought to myself as his *cri de coeur* died away behind me; and as I rode home from the Wick I tried to rationalise his extraordinary conduct. Why, when I am dead, the very thought of a fox-chase in full cry streaming over my maggoty remainder will be as refreshing dew to my poor wilting spirit, as it fiddles away in some inconspicuous corner of the celestial orchestra. But it was no good; the mind of that odd janitor of the dead evidently worked on different principles from mine.

The Missionaries   December 1943

One day I will make a study of the Missionaries. Not, of course, those tiresome Scots who pressed Evangelical tracts on the happy cannibals of Central Africa and the South Seas, and were sometimes eaten for their pains, thus passing into eternal bliss; but those even more extraordinary characters who, in the critical and wellnigh fatal climacteric of our history, believed themselves personally chosen by God to save our civilisation, and to save it by surrender: Neville

---

141 Slightly misquoted from *Travels in France* (1792) by Arthur Young (1741–1820).

142 John Wilkins (1614–1672), natural philosopher and Bishop of Chester; William Juxon (1582–1663) hunted a pack of hounds in Gloucestershire between his deposition as Bishop of London in 1649 and restoration as Archbishop of Canterbury in 1660.

143 Wilfrid Holland-Hibbert (1893–1961), land agent of New College 1923–1958, estates bursar of Merton College 1932–1960, presided over the college's rent-audit day, and attended the feast with T-R.

Chamberlain, Sir Horace Wilson, Sir Nevile Henderson, Lord Runciman.[144] What general law of history can account for the sudden emergence of these uninspired prophets with their extraordinary convictions? Is it an universal, or merely an English phenomenon? Analogies fail, for in all our history, I think, we have only once had a government as bad as that; and I'm sure Lord North never thought himself inspired. But Chamberlain, with his 'leave it to me', his 'Peace in our time', his 'this time he has promised to *me*', certainly did. And poor old Henderson tells us that when, in his appropriate backwater in Montevideo, he read the telegram offering him the embassy at Berlin, he knew that he was unequal to the job. So what did he decide? That it was a clerical error? That he ought to refuse? No. His trained mind at once concluded that Providence (whose ways are inscrutable) must have selected him as a blind instrument for the redemption of mankind. So he went to Berlin, and gazed with wide, uncomprehending eyes on the Roman magnificence of Karinhall. How different from the modest comforts of Sleasby Hall, Lincs! But did it occur to him that this new world in which he was a missionary was as remote from the English tea-parties of Lincolnshire & Montevideo as the potlaches of Red Indians or the cannibal feasts of the Solomon Islands? That he was at sea, and that perhaps even Providence and Mr Chamberlain were at sea also? No more than such a heresy occurred to Lord Runciman, as he posed for the photographers, 'the man of the moment', reading a Chatham House manual on Czechs and Germans in his first-class carriage on the way to Prague to save the Czechs; or to Sir Horace Wilson as, blissfully ignorant of history, diplomacy, and foreign affairs, he stepped jauntily into the aeroplane to fly to Berlin and diddle Hitler.

How shall we account for it? Is it that the old, incomprehensible, hairy, portentous, frock-coated, taboo-ridden English liberal democracy was as sublimely self-confident in retreat as when Gladstone and Palmerston, Cobden and Bright had led its irresistible advance? Or should we seek psychological

---

144 Appeasement's chief proponents: Neville Chamberlain (1869–1940), Prime Minister 1937–1940; Sir Horace Wilson (1882–1972), head of the Civil Service under Chamberlain; Sir Nevile Henderson (1882–1942), British Ambassador in Berlin 1937–1939; Walter Runciman, 1st Viscount Runciman of Doxford (1870–1949), whose diplomatic mission to Prague betrayed the Czechs in 1938 and prompted Sudeten Germans to sing, *Was brauchen wir'nen Weihnachtsmann, Wir haben unser'n Runciman!* (What do we need Father Christmas for, we have our Runciman evermore!).

parallels among the inspired tinkers of the Commonwealth, and the jabbering saints of the desert? Or in poor old gaga Pétain? – but no, for that would explain nothing. I wish I thought Keith Feiling would throw light on this baffling enigma in the official life of Chamberlain which he is compiling from documents supplied by Mrs Chamberlain and the table talk of the surviving missionaries; I wish I even thought he would write a book like Purcell's *Life of Manning*, and surreptitiously supply the reader with pins to puncture his own panegyrics. But alas! he won't.

Gibbon and Newman   December 1943

That Newman based his style on Gibbon seems to me one of the paradoxes of literature; for really there is no parallel between them. Gibbon's style is firm, spacious, and technically faultless; like a stately eighteenth-century house, the mansion of an English duke. Massive, elegant, and exact, it will stand forever among its pastoral grounds, its trim gardens, its harmonious fountains, with sleek hunters in its courtly stables, and peacocks strutting in its well-proportioned colonnades. But Newman's style, though classical, though stately, is of an altogether different kind. It is majestic, but deliquescent, – an old eighteenth-century mansion in Ireland, derelict and forlorn among the silent, superstitious bogs and hills. The walls bulge and gape, the ceilings sag, the windows are cracked and cobwebbed, the stucco is peeling; the rosebay seeds on the crumbling cornices; bats hang in the unswept state-rooms; the lawn has grown to hay; goats clamber over the deserted gazebos; the park-wall has tumbled down, and arbutus and fuchsia have overgrown its ruins; the great gate has disappeared, and in its place between the armorial gateposts swings an old iron bedstead.

December 1943

It is a casual method of travel, the way I go out hunting, stopping passing cars and lorries, till I meet my horse trotting forward towards the meet; but a sociable method, whereby I meet many representative members of the great road-going confraternity. The other day it was a farm-worker who had been second whip, I think, (or was it a second horseman?) with the Heythrop hounds, and told me many admirable anecdotes about a late master of that pack, which I ought to have chronicled before they faded, as they have faded, from my memory; how he cared nothing for the society of his own class, but sat up all night with his chauffeur or his groom, playing cards and drinking whisky; and generally he would lose money, but sometimes he had his winning days too, and then he would win all the stud-groom's wages from him, and have to give them back again; until the day came when either he must give up his bottle of whisky a day, which would kill him, or go on drinking it, which would kill him too; as it did; for he sensibly chose the less troublesome form of extinction.

And today it was a forester, who was on his way, he explained, to cut timber in one of the great Claydon woods. O sacrilege! I exclaimed to myself; and then he enlarged, all the way to Aylesbury, on his views about the cosmos, which were tiresome and strange. Still, when he said that they didn't include teetotalism, I warmed slightly towards him. That was impossible, he said, in his job, out all days, in all weathers, in the woods. He had to drink beer to keep out rheumatism, lumbago, cramp, chills, aches, spasms, and all such episodes of sylvan life. In fact, for this reason, he never drank less than ten pints of old ale in the middle of every day. An admirable character! I thought; let him cut down all the woods in Buckinghamshire. And then we came upon a sort of gypsy pantechnicon; at least I might have called it a pantechnicon till then, but never since; for he called it a didicoy – a Berkshire word, he explained. Berkshire be hanged! From now on let it be a full member of the English language!

Ireland

Through all our history she clings to us, a poor, half-witted, gypsy relative, defying our improvement, spoiling our appearances, exposing our pretences, an irreclaimable, irrepressible slut, dirty when we are most clean, superstitious when we are most rational, protesting when we are most complacent, and when we are most prosaic, inspired. Of course she really needs a good whack on the bottom; but I have fallen in love with her, from the moment I saw her; her inconsequent behaviour, her pretty speech, her delightful fancy have seduced my wits away; so what's to do? I know I ought to admire the Russians, their gigantic feats of organisation and propaganda; their collective women black-smiths; their triumph over nature, reaction, and arithmetic; their enormous beliefs and appetites; their unanimous virtue. But try as I will, my eyes are always diverted from that distant, impregnable Amazon by a dirty and melodious little gutter-snipe singing a tragic-comical ditty in my own backyard.

And Irish writers, how they saved our language, when it was worn thin and colourless by the use of centuries, and kept thin and colourless by the habits of journalism; kept thus for ever, it must have seemed, like Byzantine Greek; for the English didn't care; it was easier to knit in one colour than in many, especially now that only one shade of wool was to be had in the market. But there came others in those days, foreigners who looked on our language and literature from without, Yeats and Synge, George Moore and James Joyce,[145] for whom those simple Saxon words had a freshness and a mystery forgotten by their native users, and unrolling the worn and faded tapestry of the past, they uncovered fresh, gay patches, and making themselves material thereof, and going about the country to gather the dying art of speech, they wove according to their own native designs coloured stuffs that put all the former workmen to shame. And therefore though strangers, let them have a niche in the Temple of the English Tongue; like those Africans, Apuleius and Augustine,[146] who recreated their Latin language in its long sterility.

The novel

Surtees I can read, and Sir Walter Scott, and Stendhal of course, and Flaubert (but is he a novelist?), and possibly one or two others; but few enough for me to generalise and say that the novel is a form of literature that deters and discourages me. Is this a gap in my constitution? I sometimes ask myself, when I have to admit in conversation to having faltered in the midst of Trollope and blenched at the frontispiece of Tolstoy; but no, I quickly answer myself, for the novel, after all, is not an essential ingredient of literature, like poetry or prose; there is nothing eternal in it; it is but a form, one of many, a fashion

---

145 All Irish-born.
146 Both Apuleius and St Augustine of Hippo were born in Numidia (now part of Algeria).

of a period, as romances of chivalry of the late Middle Ages, or Messianic prophecies of a certain period B.C., or didactic poems of the Alexandrine era, or characters and acrimonious theology of the 17th century. So novels are the fashion of the nineteenth century; before that there were picaresque romances to be sure, like *Don Quixote* and *Gil Blas* and the tales of Defoe and Fielding, Smollett and Sterne, but not novels; and after that there are psychological problems and transformed autobiographies, and all the literary maggots that have been bred in the decomposing body of the novel, but not novels; but the nineteenth century is the age of the novel and of the great novelists, the age of Balzac and Stendhal and Flaubert, of Walter Scott and Jane Austen, of Dickens and Thackeray, Trollope, Surtees, and Hardy, of Tolstoy and Turgeniev and Dostoievsky; the age when even second- and third-rate writers aspired to greatness through the novel, Victor Hugo and Dumas, Meredith[147] and Ouida;[148] so that even now people cannot realise that it is a dead form, dead as the blank-verse tragedy or the *sententiae* of Solomon, dead of perfection, that fatal distemper, and that its death has left a great gap in literature, crying out for a new form to come and fill it.

Freddie Ayer told me how he had been sitting the other night in the Gargoyle, and seeing Sir William Beveridge and Frank Pakenham discussing the social millennium over their cocktails there, had joined them and had been pressed by Frank to come and dine with him at the Café Royal in a few days' time.[149]

And what did you discuss? I asked, knowing that dinner with Frank Pakenham must include some enjoyable absurdities.

'Well', said Freddie, 'we had some soup, and when it came, Frank said suddenly, "Are your views on religion the same as they were?" So I said "Yes"; and he said, "Do you believe in the divinity of Christ?"; and to that I said "No", for the direct question made polite evasion impossible. Then he said, "What do you think of him then?", and I said, "Well, I believe there is some evidence

---

147 Victor Hugo (1802–1885) and George Meredith (1828–1909) were both poets who turned to novel-writing; Alexandre Dumas (1802–1870) was a playwright who resorted to historical novels.

148 Ouida, pseudonym of Marie-Louise de la Ramée (1839–1908), author of 45 escapist novels.

149 Ayer was a habitué of the Gargoyle, a smart Soho drinking-club with a mirrored ball-room based on a Matisse design. Pakenham was Beveridge's personal assistant, 1941–1944.

in Tacitus to suggest that he did exist, so I'm ready to believe that." And then we had some steak, and ate it for a time in silence.'

But the silence doesn't seem to have lasted long, for soon Frank was asking Freddie whether he ever read the Gospels.

Regularly, said Freddie, who sometimes subordinates veracity to convenience in material questions.

I'm so glad of that, said Frank, beaming earnestly over his steak. And when do you think they were written?

As far as I can remember, said Freddie tentatively, I was given to understand that they were compiled some time in the second century AD.

Mere German criticism! exclaimed Frank indignantly; and a thin spray of cauliflower descending on the tablecloth emphasised his condemnation of those jacobinical heresies.

So the meal continued, and the doctrine of the Incarnation was ventilated over the herring-roes on toast, and the mystery of the Virgin Birth over the coffee and liqueurs, and Freddie gave up evasion and sought to transfer the discussion onto a philosophical plane, and they discoursed widely, until a waiter, observing that this was a conversation capable of infinite extension, drew Frank's attention to the hour, all other diners having long departed, and the restaurant being about to close. Then Frank paid the bill ('I must give him credit for that', said Freddie, doubtless thinking of the less fortunate experience of Freddie Birkenhead,[150] whom Frank recently lured to dinner at the Ritz and then left there alone with Fr D'Arcy and the bill), and they went out, and long and late Frank led Freddie up and down the street, earnestly expounding the important truths of the Holy Church. And when tarts swooped out of the penumbra of Regent Street crying 'Come home with me, duckie!' Frank would settle upon them a glazed, impersonal eye, till they retired again into their shadows, the doctrine of the Atonement ringing strangely in their ears. Finally Freddie said he must catch a tube-train; and the evening ended with Frank standing on the steps of the Piccadilly Underground station, calling after him, as he descended, 'Well anyway there's hope, – you do read the Gospels'.

When I told this tale to Charles Stuart, he said that now at last he could understand my detached and tolerant attitude towards the activities of Frank Pakenham.

---

150 Frederick Smith, 2nd Earl of Birkenhead (1907–1975), biographer and T-R's lifelong friend.

1944

In January 1944 Trevor-Roper turned thirty – it felt a significant birthday – and later in the year had the promise of a post at Christ Church after the war's end. During March and April he visited North Africa and India. The deaths in action of his combatant rather than desk-bound contemporaries continued to trouble him.

Venatica   March 1944

Poor old Whaddon hounds! Their history has been an epitome of political development: a long, unimportant, almost static existence, as the establishment of a family of country squireens; then a period of bitter faction and struggles, ideological passions, swelling ambitions, and civil war; then the golden age after victory, the age of Peter Farquhar[1] and Boddington, on which the fading memory of the sportsmen who tasted it, and of the bewildered rustics who saw it pass, still loves to dwell. But everything that glows holds in perfection but a little moment; the inter-acting stresses of the two-party system are the necessary foundation of all great achievement; absolute victory is a treacherous basis for success; and now what spectacle is afforded by the Whaddon hounds in their wartime decline? They creep out from Aston

---

1 Sir Peter Farquhar, 6th baronet (1904–1986), joint master of the Tedworth foxhounds 1927–1931, Meynell hounds 1931–1934, Whaddon Chase hounds 1934–1938 and Portman hounds 1947–1959.

Abbots on hunting days,[2] a dejected, dispirited troop, lamenting that there is no fog or frost or snow to keep them indoors; and if by chance an outlying fox should skirt them in the fields, they piously avert their eyes and noses, and the field hastily preoccupy themselves with unimportant talk; for of all things they are most determined to avoid a hunt.

So now the season is over, and for six months my notebooks will be free of these tiresome anecdotes; but I must first cast a backward glance at the Whaddon huntsman,[3] an old buffer of 65 or 70, whom they found after some difficulty last summer, and who might have been some use to them, had they found him 30 years ago, and had he not also fallen on the flat early in the cubbing-season, cracking himself up on an electric pylon, and never appeared out again till the end of January, when the poor old Whaddon Chase were already thanking God that the season was over for unenterprising hacks.

Still, he had his past to live on; since for 25 years he had hunted the Rome foxhounds, rattling bagged foxes through the Pontine Marshes, and often, so he explained, running them to ground in the Roman catacombs. It's true, he admitted, he employed catacomb-stoppers, but the stoppage wasn't always effective; twice he had seen a kill in the catacombs, and often he had gone through them with torches in search of hounds lost in those nether sepulchres of the Eternal City.

March 1944

At least, I said to myself, as I made my way to the suburb of Algiers where they had found me a billet, at least it will be a change from my billet in Barnet. Neither feminism nor theosophy shall vex me here; I shall be spared the Great

---

2 Major Morton, Master of the Whaddon, lived at the Abbey, Aston Abbots, near Aylesbury.

3 *Bucks Herald* (1 October 1943) reported the war experiences of the Whaddon's newly appointed Norman Brown, former whipper-in of the Warwickshire Hounds, who in 1918 had become huntsman of the Rome Hunt (founded in 1840 by the sixth Earl of Chesterfield). Brown and his family were fluent in Italian, and had cherished friendships in Italy despite enduring privations and threats before their repatriation in January 1943. The Rome kennels were expropriated as a German wireless station.

Pyramid and Raja Yoga; and the spirits of Pythagoras and Gerald Heard[4] shall be absent from El Biar. Thus consoled, I turned the key in the door, and went in.

In the centre of the room an elderly man was sitting at a table, surrounded by untidiness. He was dirty and decomposing, and smelt, as that sort of people does smell, especially in Algiers, of stale sweat and endives. He had a dirty brown skull-cap on his head, and wire-rimmed spectacles on his nose. His name was M de Bernardi.

We exchanged formalities, and then I began to move towards my bedroom; but he stopped me, and with a sudden, irrelevant look, asked me when I was born. Surprised, I told him, and then, after a moment's reflexion, he nodded approvingly. '*C'est bon*', he said; '*c'est exactement comme le général Giraud.*[5] *Ah, monsieur, vous avez de la bonne chance ... vous avez du courage – on ne peut pas vous faire peur*'. I smiled at the incredible wrongness of his diagnosis; but with a wave of his hand he disposed of any answer, and then, rising, he grasped me earnestly by the arm and placed his face close to mine. The smell was overpowering. A look of fanaticism was in his eye. With his disengaged hand he pointed, as evidence of his veracity, to the old books and papers that littered his room. The tone of his voice sank to a confidential but portentous whisper. '*Je suis astrologue*', he explained; '*je suis l'élève de plus grand astrologue de nos temps, – de Max Roehm*' (or some such name). And he added that he went but seldom to bed, choosing to work all night, every night, on a book that would reveal new secrets to the world. *Les Derniers Mystères*, it would be called, *les Astres et les Mains nous parlent*; and numerous yellow sheets of it, covered with writing in violent ink, lay prominently to hand. Then he went off into the minutiae of the horoscope, the conjunctions and ambiguities of Saturn and Sagittarius; and my limited vocabulary failing to keep pace with him, I found an opportunity to retire to bed. Next day I fled, and for the

---

4 Gerald Heard (1889–1971), author of *The Ascent of Humanity: an Essay on the Evolution of Civilisation from Group Consciousness through Individuals to Super-Consciousness* (1929) and *Pain, Sex & Time: A New Outlook on Evolution and the Future of Man* (1939). In 1938 Heard settled in California where he devoted himself to oriental mysticism and awed the locals with his suave, pretentious and empty rhetoric.

5 Henri Giraud (1879–1949) escaped from Schloss Königstein near Dresden after two years in German captivity in April 1942. He succeeded the assassinated Admiral Darlan as commander-in-chief of French troops in Algeria, Morocco and Tunisia in December 1942, and retained that post until 1944.

remainder of my stay in Algiers I slept in my battle-dress on the mess-room sofa.

———————

I looked down from the plane that was taking me to Egypt, and there, for hundreds of miles, saw the vain, purposeless Mediterranean sea throwing its waves wearily, eternally, upon the long, empty, desert shore. It was a symbol of futility, of that purposelessness that so perplexes and dismays me. Only its giant dimensions made it impressive, like the purposelessness of millions of solar systems spinning aimlessly in the meaningless void.

εἶδον Πυραμίδων μεγάλην θέσιν,[6] I have seen the Pyramids, and the ruins of the Roman world in Syria and North Africa; I have seen Vesuvius in full eruption, and Mount Etna capped with snow; the red desert of Libya and the white desert of Sinai; and, in Palestine, grave Arab patriarchs fustigating their sad brown donkeys through the scented Jewish citrus-groves. But I have no nostalgia for these things; casual acquaintance is for humanity, places require intimacy for their enjoyment; and anyway, the Mediterranean is a vulgar sea, there is no subtlety in it, its colours are crude, its trees are not deciduous, there is no mystery in its skies, its waves do not whisper, it has no twilights. In the great woods of Buckinghamshire is my spirit's home, and in Northumberland, in the valley of the Till.

———————

It isn't a mist, – for a mist is a delicious thing that creeps down English valleys in the night-time, leaving a cool trail of dew, – it's a stinking, pestiferous miasma that hangs over the city of Basra; and as I sat in its chromium-plated hotel, contemplating it, I recognised that whatever disgruntled travellers have reported of it is true. Like Bahrain, and perhaps other cities of the Persian Gulf, it smells of singed wet flannel; and the Euphrates seeps through it, generating dusty palm-trees and mosquitoes. Was it really here that our civilisation began? It seemed incredible; let us rather give the priority to Egypt, I said to myself,

———————

6 I saw the great site of the Pyramids. This is the opening of a hexameter, which Professor Michael Reeve suggests T-R composed. It resembles an epigram by Antipater of Thessalonica, *Anthologia Graeca* 9.58, extolling the temple of Artemis at Ephesus: verse 4 refers to μέγαν αἰπεινῶν πυραμίδων κάματον, 'the mighty labour of the soaring pyramids'.

and went in to dinner to escape these morbid reflexions. And at the same time they issued forth from the bar, the European colonists of Basra, mirthless men with paperish yellow faces. The damp heat had ironed out their souls, and like the lotus-eaters, having drunk the gin-and-bitters of Basra, they wished only to live on there, among the mud houses, and the festering waterways, and the Shatt-el-Arab Hotel, with its bed-bugs and its execrable local gin.

And yet how trivial are these outward things! For sitting on a stool at Basra, I learned from a casual fellow-passenger that he had once, in the west country, bred a pack of basset hounds; and at once the miasma parted, the heat and the smell vanished away, the gin tasted exquisite, the paper-faced colonists sparkled with wit and culture, and the glorious heaven shone down on Basra, cradle of our civilisation.

A fantastic growth, it seemed to me, every time I looked at the New Delhi of Sir Edwin Lutyens, a style without ancestry, without posterity, an archi-tectural sport; and I compared it, according to my varying mood, now with the Pyramids of Egypt, now with the great statues of Easter Island, now with the megaliths of Avebury or Stonehenge. All the same, as my eye sought to comprehend that great pink and white symmetry of palaces and pagodas, fountains and obelisks, ornamental ponds and regal statues, I couldn't help thinking of those Roman magnificos of whom Gibbon wrote, who 'were not afraid to show that they had the spirit to conceive, and the wealth to execute, the most grandiose designs'.

In the past six weeks I have spent 130 hours in the air; but I am not air-minded; to me flying is boredom punctuated with fear. The solid earth is my element, the green earth of England with its woods and streams and hills, its hedgerows flowering in the springtime, its haystacks and cornshocks in the autumn, and, in winter, a pack of hounds streaming over the grassland and the plough. What variety there is in an acre of English soil! but 4000 feet up, and there isn't even a field-mouse.

I set out, a passionate potamolator, to look upon the rivers of the East. I expected a Shannon, a Thames, a Tweed, or a parallel to the Rhône and the Danube. I visited the Euphrates – a dreary desert stream; the Ganges, a brown and wretched water; and marooned in Karachi, I made my host send me 70 miles to see the Indus, only to find a colourless channel fringed with scrub. Still, the Nile is a noble river, and James Robertson[7] speaks highly of the Congo; and I still have the Niger to visit, and the Limpopo, and the Irrawaddy, and the Brahmaputra, and the Yangtsekiang.

The Solution

May 1944

How dreary they all are, the utopias of the human mind! Angels eternally strumming their servile alleluias; paradisiacal gardens watered by appetising almond-eyed tarts; a Nirvana of conscious non-existence; endless spaniel-eyed contemplation of an abstract quality; a grey social equality for ever and ever. Even perpetual change becomes tedious and trifling for lack of underlying consistency. Even thought fails to satisfy when the matter for it has run out. Only in finite time can man find significance; for Eternity is a bottomless void.

The life of man is finite, thank God, short, thank God, or what would he do with it on this apple-shaped planet? He can only aim at making it a work of art before he dies, and so to cheat the blind malevolence of chance and time. Some can make a long life into a work of art; they can reckon on seventy years and work slowly, like Flaubert, who spent seventeen years on one slim work; they spread the purpose of their lives over many years, and reap the triumph of maturity. Gibbon achieved such a life, and Haydn, and Horace; and many must have aimed at it whom fate has prevented with a too early death. And others make a triumph of youth, as Keats and Shelley and Achilles and Richard Hillary; for of them it was that Euripides wrote, Whom the gods love, die young; they have concentrated the purpose and meaning of their lives into a brief spell, and have embalmed it in the preservative of immortal youth. But many of them Fate has mocked with a hateful longevity, as T.E. Lawrence, who might have been an Achilles, but lived uselessly and miserably for twenty years too long; and Tennyson, who might have been a Keats, but for the tragedy of survival.

---

7 Possibly (Sir) James Robertson (1899–1983), sub-governor of the White Nile 1937.

Yet even of these it can be said, *Penser c'est l'homme.* They aren't heedless flowers that blow and perish; they have thought their lives into shape, a shape worthy of survival. Dust and heat, blood and tears, thought and vigil created the art of Keats, as his letters show; and Achilles was an intellectual, the only intellectual among the heroes of Homer.

Having discovered this truth, how easy it all becomes! The vast chaos of the universe arrays itself at last in an orderly pattern; the great enigmata of the world resolve themselves like melting snow. I am no longer becalmed. I know what to do. To write a book that someone, one day, will mention in the same breath as Gibbon, – that is my fond ambition. And if I fail, at least I shall say, as it was said of Don Quixote, *Si no acabó grandes cosas, murió por acometerlas.*[8]

And the rest of life, the interstices of this grand design – well, it is enough, by the pleasures of society, and the taste of divine solitude, to keep melancholy at bay.

Marshal Pétain

The invasion of Europe was expected, and to the Germans even old Pétain seemed a danger, sitting in Vichy, far from their careful tutelage. So the château of Rambouillet was put at his disposal, and thither he was ordered to go; and he was ordered to go voluntarily. Old Pétain did as he was told; he summoned the papal nuncio, doyen of the *corps diplomatique*, and said what he had been told to say about his departure; and the nuncio told his colleagues, and the Vatican. 'The marshal at first seemed timid', he reported, 'but brightened afterwards, and in the course of our interview sang some religious canticles which he had learnt at school'.

What an old ninny!

---

8 Even if he did not achieve great things, he died in their pursuit (quoted to T-R by Pearsall Smith).

Thirty

Charles Stuart had heard some foolish opinion, he said, that a man couldn't change his mind after the age of thirty. But it's quite true, I protested; and we argued about it. Then I challenged him to produce an instance of anyone who had radically altered his view after thirty. He couldn't. But could I, he asked, substantiate my thesis by examples? Well, one can never conclusively demonstrate a negative proposition, but one can try; so I mustered an impressive list of converts, men who had shed one set of beliefs and assumed another, and at what age had they performed this trick? Had any of them been over thirty? There was Loyola, who was certainly younger; and Dante, who was thirty; and Wordsworth – well, we looked him up, and I think he was thirty or rather under it; and Milton, who, at 29, wrote *Lycidas*, and therein signalised his change from humanism to puritanism; and Tennyson, who wasn't actually a convert, but ceased to be a poet at 30; and John Donne, who stopped writing love-poems at 29, and when he began again, behold, he had become a theologian; and Newman, whose conversion dated from his Sicilian journey, or so I said, because that conveniently fitted my theory; and St Augustine; and I think Charles James Fox and Strafford come in quite handy too. Charles looked gloomier and gloomier, and I got more and more exhilarated, as I multiplied the sombre instances. Why, I said, it isn't only that one can't change after thirty; thirty is the end of life, the end of adventure in thought and spirit and experience; the rest is a static epilogue, the repetition of earlier discoveries. I wonder how old Shakespeare was when he wrote

> That time of life thou dost in me behold
> When yellow leaves, or few, or none, do hang
> Upon those boughs that shake against the cold,
> Bare ruined choirs, where late the sweet birds sang …[9]

A doddering old introvert, one thinks, drooling away a decrepit old age at Stratford-on-Avon. But how old actually was he? We consulted an edition of the *Sonnets*. Shakespeare was forty-five when they were published. That looked rather bad. But another glance encouraged me, for I read that the likeliest period of composition was 1592–8, and the likeliest date 1594–5; and in 1594 Shakespeare was 30.

---

9 T-R slightly misquotes sonnet 73.

Macaulay had a happy life, too, I couldn't help reflecting, as I put down that admirable work, his *Life and Letters*, by G.O. Trevelyan. He wrote a great work, which gave purpose to his life; he knew the relative value of public and private ambitions, and acted accordingly; he knew the delight of literature, which compensates for all the reverses of life; like Gibbon, he prized reading above all the wealth of India. And yet I cannot include him among my immortals; that complacency, that lack of subtlety, of sensitivity, of doubt repels me. He seems never to have known unhappiness, or made mistakes; when he appreciated Euripides and Thucydides, it was with the mind only, not with the experience. 'I don't care what authors say', says Logan, 'it's what they whisper that I like'; but Macaulay never whispers, he shouts; a sustained, brilliant, remorseless rhetorical shout. How he shouted down the poor Quakers who came to remonstrate with him about his treatment of William Penn! and they were quite right too. Throughout his work and his life, one comes across that infallible, that vulgar egotism:

- Everyone thought me right, as I certainly was.
- I dined yesterday at Holland House; all Lords except myself.
- Precious fellow! to think that a public functionary, to whom a little silver is a bribe, is fit society for an English gentleman!

No, he won't do. Though a man may be right in all his judgments; though he speak with the tongue of an angel; though he shine at Holland House; yes, though he makes cracks at the Puseyites and eat roast-goose on fast days, and have not subtlety, – it's no good; he won't do.

I dined at Christ Church, and the Dean[10] invited me to apply for a studentship there after the war. I said I would. Then there was a pause; and afterwards he edged gingerly towards a further point. What were my views on religion? Was I anticlerical, or did I merely 'dislike certain clergymen? For of course that was bound to weigh with some of the electors …'

I boggled. Is this the liberal, tolerant, intellectual Oxford I so like and admire? I asked myself. Have we relapsed into the days of religious tests? The dean looked uncomfortable; I knew that he was no heretic-burner; he was

----

10 John Lowe (1899–1960), Dean of Christ Church since 1939.

merely thinking of the old, embittered, repressed, obscurantist figures who must also have their say, and who must be answered. So I answered him.

Of course I made a mess of it. I was taken by surprise; the whole question bewildered me; and I was inhibited by the desire to be both veracious and polite. In the end I wasn't even lucid. When I was back at Barnet, I thought it over; I must get it clear, I told myself, and answer clearly next time I'm asked this complicated question. So I examined my position.

Firstly, its doctrine isn't true. It is based either on metaphysical premises, which for me have no validity; or on deductions from frail and maggoty texts which support nothing. The Creation, the Fall of Man, Original Sin, the Atonement, the Virgin Birth, the Divinity of Christ, the Immortality of the Soul, the Day of Judgment – these fundamental pillars of Christian doctrine are, intellectually, trash; and so is the doctrine of all other religions too. Admittedly there are some ingenious sophists who say that they are true in some other, non-intellectual way; but to me there is only one standard of truth, and by that they are false.

And yet, although the arguments on which it rests, and the conclusions which they entail, have been exploded again and again, by the scientists, and philosophers, and scholars of three centuries, it is clear that this hasn't involved the disappearance of religion; which must therefore repose on other than intellectual foundations. In fact, the ease with which, when all the apparent props have been demolished beneath it, the old Temple remains suspended in mid-air, while its priests run up alternative supports, of more modern material, suggests that these props, so far from being essential elements of the building, are mere external décor, added by the directors to appease the high-brows; like the architecture of suburban cinemas.

When, then, is the real basis of religion?

It seems to me to be psychological; and although the distinction is perhaps artificial, it is convenient to distinguish, for this purpose, individual and social psychology.

For the individual, religion fills an important void; it gathers up and harmonises his irrational impulses; it provides an outlet, or a substitute, for dark and sinister passions, which it formalises in a pattern of which anthropologists, by now, have fairly well established the elements; and insofar as it regulates these passions (as in restraining dionysiac manifestations), it has also a practical value. Sometimes, however, it excites them into fanaticism and persecution; and that is a different matter.

Socially, religion is the invisible cement of a social order, which (such is social psychology) is incomplete without it. In this sense, ideologies are not generically different from religions; and in this sense religions must be appropriate to the social forms which they envelope, as Catholicism is to a static, agricultural society, and may be to a static society of industrial feudalism, but is not to an expanding commercial society. If it is not appropriate, then either it is adjusted or it goes; for it is not intellectual discredit which kills religions, but social inappropriateness.

In both the above senses, religion is neither true nor false, but simply a psychological fact, like sex. However much the symbolism of sex may be discredited intellectually, it is part of man, and won't be disposed of. And equally, it's no good proving religions wrong. Repressed, it merely becomes fanatical. Some people may be able to do without it, as some people are sexless; but in society both are small minorities, whom the rules of society can afford to ignore.

These are the essential origins and conditions of religion. But religion also has a secondary character that has grown with time. It is like a stream which rising from a psychological source, runs through human life, both enriching and bedevilling it, and drawing to itself, as it progresses, a number of inessential tributaries; and these tributaries, rising elsewhere, enrich the main stream by their contributions; for they consist of various human values which, though in fact irrelevant to religion, and logically separable from it, often become mixed up in it, and find in it a channel which carries and preserves them. Thus the doctrine of the dignity of man is, in origin, not Christian but Greek; but Christianity has taken it over, in the form that every soul is worth saving; and the doctrine, now threatened, can perhaps best be defended as part of Christianity.

My practical attitude is therefore as follows:

1. Religion is a purely human institution, based on human psychology. Being human, not divine, it merits no special reverence, and its extravagant claims deserve ridicule; but being human, it is entitled to the respect (no more) that we owe to humanity. The differences in merit between one form of religion and another are differences not of intellectual truth, but of practical value, or harmlessness; like the differences between political constitutions.

2. Since religion is necessary to humanity, it is impractical, as well as irrelevant, to denounce it as untrue, and proper to find out, and

recommend (or avoid opposing) that form of it which is most commendable, or least objectionable.

3. Those forms are least objectionable which are socially most appropriate, and which incidentally preserve, or support, important secular values.

In fact, I support the poor old C of E, of which I am a member (like Garrod, I am an Anglican, not a Christian), because it does (except where perverted) support civil liberty; it has (if we except some high-church nonsense and some low-church vulgarity) a certain constitutional relation to common sense; and its sound relation to the civil power is some guarantee against extravagant pretensions.

Like Hume, I commend the Church of England for its very indifferency.

———————

June 1944

Gerald Heathcoat Amory has been killed, in Normandy, a few days after D-Day.[11] He is the last of my Oxford friends; for Kenneth Swann had been killed a few days earlier, and Tony Widdrington is missing in Italy since January.[12] I never thought I should be affected so little by this last loss. In fact I merely felt as if one of my own lives had ended, the happiest of all my lives, it is true, but still mine, not his; and about one's own death, even about one of one's own deaths, one is not sentimental.

For five years this life has been dying, slowly. The loss of each of my friends, who had shared it, and of whom it largely consisted, was a stage in its extinction. John Field's death was the first gasp, Gerald's the last. Now it is totally extinct, and a new life, consisting of new friends, must begin. How different it will be!

———————

11 Edgar FitzGerald ('Gerald') Heathcoat-Amory (1917–1944), Eton and Christ Church. His father Ludovic had been killed on the French battlefields in 1918; his eldest brother Patrick had been killed in Libya in 1942; his RAF brother Michael had been killed when his aircraft crashed in Lord Bingley's grounds at Bramham in 1936.

12 Anthony Widdrington (1914–1944), Major in Royal Inniskilling Dragoon Guards, whose father owned Newton Hall, near Shilbottle, Northumberland.

And yet how delightful that life was! or at least how romantic it seems, viewed selectively from a colder, darker epoch. How effortlessly we lived, in that golden period, in Oxford, in Northumberland, abroad; hunting foxes and hares, drinking and talking, reading new books and old books, walking hounds in the early summer mornings through Garsington and Cuddesdon and Coombe Wood, watching for the emergence of each new wildflower in those comfortable fields and hedgerows and water-meadows, making new intellectual discoveries in those hours of infinite, astronomical leisure. How delightful to sit in a beautiful Oxford room, south-facing through great bow-windows over the Christ Church Meadow, rook-racked, river-rounded, writing a book, after an early walk, amid pleasant interruptions …

I wonder if it was really as perfect as it seems.

June 1944

Gilbert said of Peter Shaw's anecdotes that they partook of the bolster, not the pillow. 'They kill, but not by penetration.'

Bywell   Sept 1944

I had travelled north by the night-train. It was early in September, that golden month, with April the most perfect of the year, and since this would be the only day of it I would enjoy (for in the afternoon I was to go into hospital for an operation), I resolved to exploit it. When I walked out of the station, the dawn was breaking; it was cool and fresh; never till then had I thought that Newcastle could be beautiful; but at that moment the city was silent, enveloped in a thin ground-mist, above which the exquisite hooped spire of St Nicholas seemed to rest in the pure air, poised gently on the golden haze. Overcome with happiness, I took a tram to Scotswood Bridge, and standing there, looked down the river at the roofs and chimneys of factories and warehouses that loomed between the floating mist and the clear pink sky. Below me, I could hear the water; if I looked hard, perhaps I could see a grey ripple, or an idly paddling seagull. At dawn, even an industrial city has a calm, dignified beauty.

I felt like Wordsworth on Westminster Bridge. And then a lorry passed, and I hailed it, and the genial driver took me to Prudhoe, and I walked along the Tyne in the fresh, clear morning till I came to Bywell with its stone bridge, and great park, and mansion, and two parish churches standing side by side, incongruous, like deserted monoliths, in that now unpeopled spot.

There are some experiences, some images, too perfect to be varied; they can only be repeated. When I reached the hospital in the afternoon, I found my operation postponed for a day, so I had another September day to spend. How should I spend it? I knew no alternative that would not be an anti-climax, a waste of this unexpected reprieve. I got up before dawn, walked down to St Nicholas, poised on the mist, took a tram to Scotswood Bridge to look down the Tyne, and a lorry to Stocksfield; and then walked to Bywell to linger again by the river and the bridge, the park, the mansion, and the two ancient, empty churches.

Burma   Oct 1944

To the modern soldier, the possibility of Eternal Damnation is replaced by the threat of Burma, and in Belgium the British Liberation Army, as it is called, ironically interprets its initials as 'Burma Looms Ahead'. But in my mind the deterrent features of Burma, its diseases, its poisonous insects, its treacherous people, its beastly jungle warfare, and the Japanese armies that infest it, though I try conscientiously to envisage them all, are all dimmed and eclipsed by the imagination of those great teak-forests, so dark and sepulchral (it is said) that Europeans go mad in their pitchy shade. When I look at the map, and see, symbolically enregistered there, the great Chin Hills, cleft by the deep longitudinal watercourses of the Salween[13] and the Sittang,[14] the Chindwin and the Irrawaddy,[15] then in spirit I feel carried away to those enchanted forests, full of darkness and mystery and malign influences.

---

13 The river Salween rises in Tibet, passes through the gorges of Yunnan, meanders through Burma and Thailand before disgorging into the Andaman Sea – a distance of 2,185 km.

14 The Sittang flows for a distance of 420 km between the Salween and the Irrawaddy.

15 The Chindwin is a tributary of Burma's longest river, the Irrawaddy (2,170 km).

My Religion   Oct 1944

If I had a religion (and I sometimes feel that I behave as if I was in search of one), I would be a pagan. For it is among meadows and hills, clear streams and woodland rides, that I find serenity of mind; in deep forests and dark caverns, among lonely crags and howling tempests that I feel the inadequacy of man; in the starry night and by the desolate seashore that the triviality of temporal existence oppresses or comforts me. If satyrs were one day to pop up and pipe to me among the Cheviot Hills; if a troop of nymphs were suddenly to rise with seductive gestures from a trout-pool in the Breamish; if dryads and hamadryads were to eye me furtively as I hunted the tangled thickets of Hell Copse or Waterperry Wood; I would not feel in the least surprised – I already half assume their presence there. But if God were to speak to me through the mouth of a clergyman, or to appear to me in any of the approved Christian attitudes, then indeed I would begin to ask questions.

A Trick of Memory   Oct 1944

I have a trick of memory that has perplexed me now for almost six years, since I first noticed it, in a meadow in Burgundy in the spring of 1939. There is a flower, a common flower, which I see regularly every year in the fields and hedgerows, *Asperula odorata* to the botanist, but to the ordinary countryman it is familiar under a more ordinary English name.[16] But what is this name? It is that which no amount of reference to Bentham & Hooker, no mnemonic tricks or studious repetition, will fix in my mind. I am as incapable of recalling it now as on any other occasion when I see it or think of it; all that I can recall is that it does not, as I had once desperately imagined, begin with the letter S. And I know now that it is useless to look it up; I have done that too often. In a few months it will be out again in the hedgerows, mocking me with its incurable anonymity.

The stuff of our dreams, like the images of our poetry, seems rather to be found in this unsorted garbage of our minds than in our real problems

----

16 *Asperula* is known as woodruff, but *Asperula odorata* has been reclassified as *Galium oderatum*, bedstraw.

and purposes which it clothes and disguises. Last night, I dreamt that I went to Tiverton, to Cherithorne Barton, the home of Gerald Heathcoat Amory's mother, whither I had often been invited by him in the old days, but had never gone; but now I was invited again, and on arrival I met the old lady (if she is old), and standing in a shaded courtyard beside the house she said that Gerald had often spoken of me, adding 'You know Gerald has been killed'. I knew, and made some sympathetic observation, adding that I had always expected to visit her with him, but now I had been brought by …

She paused, waiting for me to mention the name of that other son who had brought me, but whose name I had forgotten; not Pat, who, I knew, had been killed earlier, but another, whose name stuck in my mind so that I couldn't utter it.

I thought; she waited; the suspense became unbearable; I perspired with frustration; I began to know that I would never recover it now; why wouldn't she ease the situation by speaking it? But she was silent in the shaded court-yard. I rehearsed a few names to myself, like Charles and John, to see if they sounded plausible; but they were no good, they wouldn't do.

At last the tension was released; a feeling of relief began to overcome me; I knew that I was waking up; and as I woke, it all dawned upon me. There was no other son. It was Gerald of whom I was thinking, who had taken me thither; but having agreed that he was dead, I couldn't admit the logical absurdity. I had therefore invented a double for him; but when it came to naming the double, this logical absurdity caught me up again.

In our dreams we can experience logical absurdities; but it is less easy to utter them.

Gilbert said that genius consists not in giving a new answer to an old question, but in setting a new question.

Dream   Dec 1944

I dreamt I was in Bletchley Park, with a file under my arm, walking gravely from hut to hut, as were hundreds of other human termites in that vast and complicated laboratory; and behold, suddenly, across my path, in and out of the labyrinth of huts and buildings, there streamed a pack of hounds, crying merrily after a fox, and horsemen pounding after them, half a dozen of them at the most, for they had evidently run from far, shedding their superfluous followers. What pleasure illuminated my meaningless activities at that moment! The poor old Whaddon Chase! I exclaimed to myself, and I greeted the huntsman when they checked beside me; but though he returned my greeting with a formal salute, I couldn't help noticing that he wasn't the huntsman I was used to, but a pale, lanky, expressionless figure, with a long face, very like the late Duke of Northumberland to look at;[17] and his long pink coat seemed made of some thin, almost transparent material. So I turned to the Master, and greeted him, expressing surprise to see him out with his hounds, since there was foot-and-mouth disease here at Bletchley, which (it was said) had stopped the Whaddon altogether, and had driven the Bicester away to the outermost corners of their country. But even as I was in mid-speech, I realised that neither was this the master I knew, but a pale, long figure, with an axe-like face, almost transparent, and a bright but remote, inattentive eye. 'These are not the Whaddon Hounds', he replied to my observation, in a cool, toneless voice, 'these are the Corkery Hounds, and we pay no attention to foot-and-mouth disease, or anything like that'. And as he ended, a hound spoke, and at once the huntsman touched his horn, a faraway, silvery twang, and the entire pack broke immediately into full cry, and the whole irrelevant pageant galloped away into the distance, like a pack of ghosts chasing their fox back again out of the world into fairyland.

---

17 'He was slight and wiry, red-haired and red-moustached, with a curious lift to the outermost corner of his lower eyelids, which contrived to give him both a far-sighted and slightly aggressive expression' (Gavin Maxwell, *The House of Elrig* (1965), 114); with his 'pale face, aggressive nose and mouth, and fierce, intolerant eyes ... His Grace had ... the appearance and the ferocity of a large and articulate ferret' (J.G. Lockhart and Mary Lyttelton, *The Feet of the Young Men* (1928), 126, 131).

1945

The closing months of the war did not abate Trevor-Roper's exasperation with the permanent officials of SIS, who seemed to him pompous ninnies. In the interval between German capitulation in Europe and Japanese submission in Asia, Trevor-Roper had a restorative visit to Northumberland, devised new intellectual projects and re-defined the criteria of his working life. He tested literary London, and savoured the ironies of his excursions there. He also celebrated a new arbiter of prose style in the form of Charles Montagu Doughty, author of Travels in Arabia Deserta *(1888). The book was so reliable in its topography and helpful in its anthropology that it was consulted by British Intelligence during the Second World War, which may be how Trevor-Roper came upon it. Doughty was a private scholar of reticent manner, headstrong temperament and fearless candour who mixed with farmers and gamekeepers in England, and with Bedouins in the desert. He travelled rough, endangered himself and mopped up foreign languages. Everything about this shy, fierce man and his multi-lingual book attracted Trevor-Roper. During the summer and autumn of 1945 the latter went to war-devastated Germany, where after a bibulous conversation with Dick White and H.L.A. Hart he was deputed to investigate Hitler's death in his Berlin bunker. His interrogations and delving culminated in a press conference before the world's press, the writing of a best-selling historical masterpiece and a lifelong expertise in Nazi Germany. Returning to Oxford, he felt sharp misgivings about academic life.*

Literary Forms   Jan 1945

Nothing more surely demonstrates the infecundity of Roman poetry than its inability to discover new forms. The Greeks, whenever any of them perfected a form, declared it a classic, and relegated it steadfastly to the past, never to be used again. To write epic hexameters after Homer was considered poor taste, and even five hundred years afterwards, Apollonius was severely blamed for seeming to try. Who wrote personal lyrics after Sappho and Alcaeus, or triumphal odes after Pindar, or tragedy after Sophocles and Euripides, or old comedy after Aristophanes, or new comedy after Menander? As each form found its master, it was admired; and the admirers turned aside in search of a new; for there is no dead-end more final than perfection. When Quintus Smyrnaeus[1] and Nonnus[2] ultimately sought to revive old forms, then indeed Greek literature had run its course. But the Romans took up the Greek metres, and when the Augustans had perfected them, their successors just went on churning them out – Statius,[3] Lucan,[4] Valerius Flaccus,[5] Silius Italicus,[6] Ausonius,[7] Claudian,[8] successive generations of dreary hacks. From the death of Horace and Virgil to the end of the Roman Empire, is there any genuine poem – except perhaps the *Pervigilium Veneris*?[9]

We need a new form now, a prose form to replace the novel, for the novel is played out. What great artist has written a novel since the writers of the last century perfected and killed it, since Proust and Joyce elaborately and ceremonially embalmed and buried its corpse? Since then, we have witnessed the floundering and frustrations of artists, turning this way and that in their

---

1 Quintus Smyrnaeus (late fourth century AD), Greek epic poet feebly derivative of Homer.

2 Nonnus (end of fourth century AD), profuse, monotonous Greek epic poet using Homeric hexameters.

3 Publius Papinius Statius (*c.* AD 45–96), court poet to Emperor Domitian.

4 Marcus Annaeus Lucanus (AD 39–65), poet who plotted to kill Emperor Nero.

5 Valerius Flaccus (d. *c.* AD 90), author of epic poem *Argonautica* dedicated to Emperor Vespasian.

6 Silius Italicus (*c.* AD 25–101), consul and author of the epic Latin poem *Punica*.

7 Decimus Magnus Ausonius (*c.* 310–*c.* 393), a Gaul, a poetic trifler and dull, puerile prose-writer.

8 Claudius Claudianus (*c.* 370–*c.* 404), a Greek from Alexandria, wrote poetic panegyrics, epistles, epigrams.

9 A fourth century poem, apparently set in Sicily, describing the annual spring awakening of the natural world – an unprecedented subject matter, and marking a transition from Roman forms.

bewilderment, groping and fumbling in the dark for some new form which they cannot find, the ghost of the novel still haunting and obsessing their minds. Arthur Koestler's *Darkness at Noon* is, I think, a great work, but not of course a novel, in spite of its apparent form. And now Cyril Connolly has produced 'a word-cycle' as he calls it, *The Unquiet Grave*, which Logan and Raymond Mortimer enthusiastically hail as a masterpiece; but wrongly, for a masterpiece entails a form, and the Note-Book is a negation of form. The notebooks of Leonardo are of value as evidence for the study of Leonardo; but Leonardo is worth studying not for their sake but for the sake of the Mona Lisa and the Last Supper, which are of absolute value, and of which the notebooks do but catalogue the unhewn raw material, as the fragmentary, the fluctuant miscellanies of Coleridge are the unformed molten mass from which the magic wand of the artist (so rarely exercised) produced *The Rime of the Ancient Mariner*. Between the notebook and the masterpiece must intervene a great act, an act requiring labour and patience, the act of a demiurge: the imposition of artistic form. This transformation is an indispensable, an essential condition of art; St Augustine's *Confessions* is a masterpiece because, by toil and sweat, through lonely vigils and intellectual agony, he imposed a unity on his fierce, recalcitrant, tumultuary imaginings, and wrought a new vessel capable of holding them. That great and necessary effort, and therefore the making of a masterpiece, is incompatible with laziness, as the life of Coleridge too frequently demonstrates, as Cyril Connolly himself guiltily recognises:

'The more books we read, the sooner we perceive that the only function of a writer is to produce a masterpiece. No other task is of any consequence.' (p 1)

'A lazy person, whatever the talents with which he starts forth, will have condemned himself to second-hand thoughts, and to second-hand friends.' (p 44)

St Augustine, he always comes to the rescue. 'But your new form', Logan once said to me, when I spoke to him on this important topic, 'won't come from people like you or me; it'll come, as Greek tragedy came, and Roman satire, and the picaresque novel, and Shakespearean drama, from low-life, the life of the people. Why, all the cultivated Elizabethan critics and men-of-letters thought the new drama a very vulgar, plebeian affair, altogether beneath their notice …' But I wasn't altogether convinced; for the image of that intolerant old African, with his hot-house rhetoric, his chromatic imagination, his steaming repressions, seemed to arise before me out of a lurid, simmering volcano, and puff away these facile generalities.

The Ostrich

In 1941, when Maltby, that farting exhibitionist, was first spouting and blowing in the warm sea of undeserved favour, and Cowgill, that purblind, disastrous, megalomaniac policeman was fanatically, and systematically, and successfully obstructing the work of intelligence, Gilbert wrote a short poem, which incidentally had paradoxical consequences; for Maltby, hearing of it from some unknown and unauthorised source, immediately ascribed it to me, and thenceforth for a long time avoided my presence, preferring to seek consolation by burying his fat face in the supposedly less flinty bosom of Gilbert, the real author. The rhyme ran thus:

> The hunted Ostrich hides his head,
>> Exalting still his venal bottom;
> His hunter, not a whit misled,
>> No sooner sees than he has shot him.

> Even so, when S.I.S. is slain,
>> Two fated members shall have slain us:
> Cowgill, our sand-embedded brain,
>> And Maltby, our exalted anus.

Well, the situation has changed now. At last, at long last, after four years of total war (*tantae molis erat*), Cowgill has been sacked. But not Maltby. No, that more adaptable, more farcical, perhaps even more disreputable figure, has at this same moment swept off to India, cock-a-doodling in temporary red wattles, and leaving in his wake a nimbus of loud and flatulent boasting. Another verse was clearly required to complete the poem. Gilbert supplied it:

> The Ostrich now has lost his head,
>> Which does not vitally affect him;
> He eats and breathes and talks instead
>> *Via* his undiminished rectum.

I like poor old Malcolm Muggeridge.[10] Of course, having no interest in the

---

10 Malcolm Muggeridge (1903–1990), pre-war correspondent of the *Manchester Guardian* in Soviet Russia, wartime SIS agent in Lourenço Marques, post-war broadcaster and editor of *Punch*, Catholic convert after his meetings with Mother Theresa, was in old age an

truth, he is obstinately wrong in most of his opinions. If I have argued with him, while enjoying his hospitality in Algiers or in Sussex, that has never been with any expectation of persuasion, but solely in order to develop a thirst, which he will hospitably slake. For Malcolm rides hobby-horses. They aren't very nimble hobby-horses – in fact they are mostly nice old creatures which, after twenty years in a dray, have retired to a field of long grass, expecting no greater exertion than occasionally to have their noses scratched by friendly children. But such repose is not allowed them, for Malcolm selects one of them, the oldest and weariest of all, and vaulting into the saddle, rides it with whip and spur, and brings it home all in a paste and lather, with flanks heaving, nostrils dilated, eyes staring, and mouth all bloody and foaming; so that any admiration we may be disposed to feel for the virtuosity of his horsemanship is drowned by our pity for this poor, over-driven and belaboured quadruped.

One of Malcolm's hobby-horses is Samuel Butler, that now superseded god for whom I nevertheless still tend in my heart an unpretentious shrine. But Malcolm, having discovered, by patient research and the expenditure of a fiver here and there among aged tarts and servitors, that Samuel Butler shared his mistress with Festing Jones, and had a curious partiality to anaemic and spotty young men, has brilliantly deduced that *Erewhon* must be a very bad book, and Butler's theories quite untenable; and has written a remorseless, swingeing broadsheet to say so, which so shocked poor old Desmond McCarthy that he couldn't bear to speak to Malcolm again.[11] But, like Boswell, 'I have ever delighted in that intellectual chymistry which can separate good qualities from evil in the same person'; and so I shall continue, I hope, to enjoy his company, while leaving his books, of course, unread, and his arguments, of course, unheeded.

Accidie

March 1945

Fits of depression, dank, meaningless, infinite glooms, increasingly overcome me. Perhaps this is the medieval *accidie* so tiresome to the rudimentary

---

ostentatiously repentant debauchee. 'Intellectual double-agent, his only decisive posture is of pretentious indecision: he knows where he doesn't stand' (Frederic Raphael, 1978).

11 Muggeridge, in *The Earnest Atheist* (1936), smirked at Butler's affection for his future biographer Festing Jones and other men. McCarthy retaliated against the book in two articles in the *Sunday Times*.

psychologists of those times. I wonder what is the purpose of life; and though I have thought out, and know, the answer to this oppressive question, I yet find no satisfaction in answering it. I wish I were dead. Why can't I perish unobtrusively? Why do planes never crash when I am travelling in them, why do V-bombs always miss me? I vainly ask. But only my friends are killed, one after another, with sickening regularity, who have no wish to die; and my gloom is increased by this thought also. So I turn for relief to literature, and sometimes find my own condition there, elevated into a momentary sublimity by the magic art of Aeschylus, of Euripides, of Shakespeare, of Leopardi, of Housman, and of that brutal and lecherist old Psalmist-King. Purged somewhat, I feel better, and assure myself that I have yet something to do in the world; to go back to Oxford, and there to devote my leisure to the pursuit of that beckoning, irresistible *Fata Morgana*, Truth. So I go down to Oxford again, hitch-hiking along the familiar roads, through that often-hunted country, to look upon that medieval city, that island of culture where learning is still valued, and fostered, and free. But what I find there is very different from this fondly imagined ideal. I find a few thwarted old men conspiring furtively in alcoves, devising schemes to perpetuate their momentary, accidental and disastrous ascendancy. 'We must have less irreverence in future', I overhear them saying, 'less study; more religion perhaps, certainly more games. We have sinned in the past, and have paid for it dearly; we must elect more carefully in the future; thought is an unhealthy thing. The advance of culture is a mistake; it must be stopped; it is leaving us behind. It's intellect that does all the damage; what we want is a good third and a hockey-blue. Pass the port, Muggins! Crabbet, the port! Canon Mumpsimus, the buzz is yours!'

Of course it isn't really like this, I try to persuade myself. This is only *accidie*.

Agenda   March 1945

And what do I want to do? Well, first I want to examine fully and seriously the social and political significance of religious revivals, on which I think I have something to say which will be worth saying. I shall divide religious revivals into two categories: ideologies (like early Christianity, and Lutheranism, and Calvinism, and other phenomena of the Reformation), which are not really revivals but innovations, though the formal conservatism of men has represented them as revivals, nor exclusively religious, as that word is commonly understood, since they embrace also our modern ideologies of Marxism and Fascism; and real revivals, such as the Oxford Movement in England, and the parallel movements on the Continent, and the clerical reactions in France under Napoleon III and Marshals MacMahon and Pétain, and the officially bolstered orthodoxy of Russia; and doubtless there will be good instances from Ireland and Spain and Naples also. And I think that such a study will show that ideologies, though in part an intellectual retrocession, are an essential means of changing the basis of society, and can therefore be weapons of progress, but that revivals are always a phenomenon of social as well as intellectual reaction. And in defining the concepts and terminology necessary to my study, I shall incidentally show, firstly, that social progress consists exclusively in the raising of the standard of living of a society, and that those who attempt to attach to it a spiritual or any other kind of significance, are invariably fostering social reaction (as St Paul, and the Gnostics, and the Mystics, and Gandhi); and, secondly, that there is no direct relation between artistic and social values, – indeed that artists have often (like Theognis, and Alcaeus, and Aeschylus, Plato and Dante, and S. Juan de la Cruz, and the Romantics) been reactionary in their politics, and that high civilisation, in an artistic sense, is generally a social anachronism, occurring in societies in which the ruling class has become, through security, negligent of its proper function (which is of ruling), and only retains an economic supremacy (as the Renaissance popes, and the English Cavaliers, and the French aristocracy after the failure of the Fronde, and the English aristocracy of the Regency). On this subject it seems to me important to be clear; to let it be known that there is no such conception as 'progressive art'; that the form of society influences only the details of an artist's work and his relations with the public; and that the last word on the matter was said by Whistler: 'Art happens.' Or perhaps this was only the penultimate word; I shall say the last.

And if C.S. Lewis[12] should come badly out of my examination, – well, facts must be faced, however reluctantly!

---

12 Clive Staples Lewis (1898–1963), Fellow of Magdalen College, Oxford and English tutor there, was described by T-R in 1951 as 'a powerful mind warped by erudite philistinism, blackened by systematic bigotry, and directed by a positive detestation of such profane frivolities as art, literature and (of course) poetry'.

But of course I can't prudently publish this work just yet. What would the monks and mandarins of Oxford say?

As for scepticism, it is a fine flower, and blows on the cool mountain-top of Olympus, to be plucked and enjoyed by the free and happy dwellers on those delightful heights. But those who live below, in the sweat of their brows, among the thorns and thistles, under the shadow of bleak rocks, scorched at noon and shivering at night, they seem to need the comfort of some super-natural assurance.

Art is a flower that sometimes smells sweeter when its roots are in corruption. Scepticism butters no bread.

And then there is that subject which tempts and beckons me: *A History of the English Ruling Class*; although how to impose form on so vast a subject is a problem which at present baffles, and may ultimately frustrate me. Still, it would be an enjoyable task, to portray the rise and heyday and decline of that fascinating, adaptable yet consistent chamaeleon, the mercantile aristocracy of England. For 300 years they have governed here, carried gently, automatically upwards on a moving staircase; rat-faced squires and lawyers who bought abbeylands from Henry VIII and titles from James I, who squeezed bishops under Elizabeth, enclosed commons, and exploited mines, and adventured to America and the South Seas. Some move up faster than others, of course; some walked with the stairs, and some bounded up two steps at a time; but even those who stood still were carried upwards at an adequate rate. Of course there were casualties; some were elbowed off the stairs, and some fell off through inadvertency; and there were some thrusters and climbers who took a fall through their ambition, or got caught in the machinery and perished there. But as a class, they moved with the stairs, sitting pretty through the Civil Wars, beckoning discreetly to Dutch William; and when the years of crisis were safely over, how splendid, how secure, was their heyday! Their huge houses built by Vanbrugh and Hawksmoor, their gardens laid out by Repton and Capability Brown, haughty patrons of fashionable genius, their rents flowed in at an unexpendable rate, and they seemed to rule the world. It's true, the moving stairway came to a standstill early in the nineteenth century, which was inconvenient and perplexing to some of them; and then actually began to move backwards, which was worse; but the pace was slow, and the more intelligent members contrived, by well-regulated movement, to remain stationary. The pace has quickened now, and their movements are less digni-fied; only the nimbler members can adjust their position rapidly enough to ensure survival, and the rate of casualties is a good deal higher; and beside them (mortifying sight!), they see another moving stairway sliding steadily, effortlessly upwards, and carrying aloft a vulgar, jostling, indecorous crowd, their successors.

Gilbertiana

Gilbert said of old Bamford, of I.P.I., that he was 'the sort of thing quadrupeds leave behind them when they go through bristly hedges'; and Harrison, a dreary and portentous Cambridge schoolmaster who came to RSS, he described as 'like a haystack that has been mouthed but not eaten by cattle'.[13]

He spoke of his own 'casual but hygienic attitude towards the Verities'; and (perhaps in illustration of this) described a Deacon in the church as being one 'who can dispense the Word but not the Victuals'.

Perfection

When perfection has been reached, there's nothing to do but to break it up and start again.

Roman Catholic Historians   April 1945

How corrupt these RC historians are! I have read David Mathew's book on *Catholicism in England*, and a very fluent book it is, and very pleasant sketches it gives of this and that figure in English life who happened to be RC; but why they were RC, or why the RCs were regarded as a foreign element in England after the Reformation, or why more than a limited measure of relief was long denied them, or what 'Popery' and 'Vaticanism' meant or were taken to mean,

---

13 Percival Bamford (1886–1960) of Indian Political Intelligence.

or whether there was any foundation for the charges against them, or wherein their views of society or politics were peculiar, – these are questions which evidently seemed irrelevant to that gently tittering, blandly smiling, *tout pardonnant*, over-subtle convert. So far, indeed, this is not corrupt; it might be merely impercipient. But when we look for an explanation, or analysis, or vindication, or even an account of such well known facts as the Archpriest Controversy, the furious animosity between Milner[14] and the Old Catholics, the tortuous intrigues of Manning against Newman, – of all this, there is nothing said, nothing at all.

Of Milner, the good bishop says that 'a detailed description, even entering into trivial habits and traits, will be an aid in making the position quite clear'. A detailed description therefore follows. 'His appetite was hearty, and he was particularly fond of boiled corn beef. He had a developed taste for the more plebeian forms of fish, and a curious dislike for cheese.' 'Puns did not appeal to him, but in other respects he had a fund of homely humour, and had two songs which he was prepared to sing upon occasion. A rather insufficient knowledge of rubrics was offset by calmness in ceremonies, a loud but uncertain singing voice, and permanent self-possession.' 'Italian plasterwork appealed to him.' 'He liked white flowers for the altar, or alternatively decorations made from gold and silver paper.' 'His favourite prayer was the *Adore Te*.'

Well, all this is very attractive, I said to myself, as I read these personal details, but what did Milner *do*, and why was he considered so controversial a figure? And since David Mathew said nothing about Lingard,[15] who after all was quite a significant figure in the RC world of the time, I sent for Haile and Bonney's *Life of Lingard* and took it to Newcastle to read in the hospital there. And in it I found that there was indeed something more to be said, or at least denied, about Milner, than that he liked fried skate and Italian plasterwork and the *Adore Te*. I found that he was convicted of unscrupulous mendacity; that the Midland district petitioned the Pope against having him as vicar-general; that his name was excluded from the *terna* on the death of Bishop Stapleton, and his exclusion supported by Cardinal Borgia at Rome; that his

---

14 John Milner (1752–1826), Bishop of Castabala and Vicar Apostolic of the Midlands, Catholic emancipationist.

15 John Lingard (1771–1851), Catholic priest whose *History of England from the First Invasion of the Romans to the Accession of Henry VIII* was in eight volumes.

newspaper was suppressed at Rome; that he attacked Lingard savagely under one name in this paper, and then wrote under another name praising his own attack; that he pretended officially to represent persons who had openly disclaimed him; that he intrigued to get Lingard's *History* condemned, and Lingard disgraced; and a great deal more besides. All of which may indeed be explained, or justified, or even denied; but Mathew doesn't even mention it. His 'detailed description' stops short of such irrelevancies; it is more important to him that Milner had a curious dislike to cheese.

As for Newman and Manning, there is a whole chapter under that heading; but nothing is said of any opposition between them. A sympathetic account is given of each, and then Mathew winds up with an epitaph on Manning: 'It is only necessary to notice further that he suffered, and his reputation eventually survived, two posthumous misfortunes; the misuse of his correspondence with the naive Msg Talbot, and the mismanagement through which Purcell obtained the charge of his official biography. In the development of Catholicism in England, Cardinal Newman and Cardinal Manning were complementary.'

This was too much; so I wrote to Mathew, since he happens to be a personal friend, and asked him in what way Purcell 'misused' the correspondence other than by using it. Was Purcell dishonest? Did he tamper with the material? Did he invent, or omit? For it isn't Purcell's judgments that are so damaging to Manning – he never makes any – it's his quotations.

Mathew replied evasively. Possibly misuse was too strong a word, but in the circumstances of hostility between Purcell and Manning's executors he doubted whether Purcell could have been objective. And then he slid away under aesthetic generalisations. Perhaps he had lived too closely under the shadow of both, but he couldn't say he really found either Manning or Newman an 'appealing' character.[16]

---

16 Mathew's undated reply read, 'The "mismanagement" was this. Purcell apparently never obtained any real authority to write Manning's Life but persuaded the executors to let him have the Cardinal's private papers for this purpose. When he had taken away half the executors decided that they had made a bad mistake, and he was refused permission to examine the remainder. I think the term "mismanagement" is justified. "Misuse" is perhaps more questionable. In the state of feud that had developed between Purcell and Manning's executors and Cardinal Vaughan who supported the latter, I do not myself think that the correspondence was set out objectively. I admit, however, that that is a matter of opinion and if I am incorrect "misuse" is not the exact expression. I suppose I have lived with their memories too long, but I do not think that I really find either Manning or Newman finally very appealing.'

Perplexed, I then turned up the original reviews of Purcell in the hostile, ultramontane RC press. But I found that all the objections were to the publication, and none to the authenticity of the damaging documents. 'The sacred cause of truth', protested the *Dublin Review*, 'is only too likely to suffer from this attempt to tell everything without reserve or favour'; and the reviewer confessed to 'some misgivings' about the publication of the diaries, 'for we cannot be sure that this was Cardinal Manning's own desire'. As for the correspondence with Mgr Talbot, 'it contains many things which no discreet editor would have given to the public'. 'There are higher considerations than mere interest', protested the virtuous *Month*, 'to which a biographer should attend. In using his materials, he should be careful to respect privacy ... How then can the Cardinal's biographer be excused for publishing so many letters and documents which were clearly never intended for the public eye?' The only valid point made by any commentator is that the dispute with Newman was 'as Mr Purcell rightly allows, a question of principle and policy, and not a mere personal squabble'. But throughout David Mathew's book, there is no reference, not merely to the quarrels, but to the principles and policies on which differences of opinion might be entertained. 'In the development of Catholicism in England, Cardinal Newman and Cardinal Manning were complementary'; as good and evil are doubtless complementary in the best of possible worlds.

I should like to write something on the RC historians, blowing them all sky-high, and exposing their dishonesty; to show that since the end of the Middle Ages the RC church has never had a social policy, the Reformation being a frank exchange of social for purely political ideas (*cf* the English Church after 1660). The real continuators of the religious-social system were to be found among the (essentially reactionary) protestants, like Latimer and Laud; if the RC church had represented any programme of social justice, it would have appeared, with Diggers and Levellers etc, in the Interregnum; but it didn't. The English RCs claimed relief and emancipation in the 18th & 19th centuries precisely on the grounds that they entertained no social doctrines different from those of contemporary English protestants (This is reflected in the historical writings of e.g. Berington[17] and Lingard). The RC revival of

---

17 Joseph Berington (1746–1827), author of *The Faith of Catholics* and *The Literary History of the Middle Ages*.

Wiseman and Manning was based on foreign (Italian and Irish) support, and that of Newman on aesthetic, romantic reaction against industrialism; neither was in any way connected with social claims or ideals (did Carlyle or Marx ever associate themselves with Roman Catholic claims?). The Rome to which all these revivalists appealed was the socially irresponsible Rome of Gregory XVI and Pius IX, and the Baroque Rome of the 17th century (note their explicit hostility to the Gothic Rome of the Middle Ages). The equation of the policy of the Roman Church with opposition to capitalist abuses, the thesis of Belloc & co, corresponds with no facts and was never made till the end of the 19th century, when it was indirectly and dishonestly derived from Marxist discoveries.

Nevertheless, I have a weakness for what I regard as the less disreputable side in the age-long quarrel between ultramontane and cisalpine RCs. I like to think of the quiet rural existence of those families in the North, and in old Lancashire, and in folds of the Cotswold and Chiltern Hills, whom the Reformation passed by, and whose old faith has survived because their lives were simple and elemental, outside the developments of time. I liked visiting Ampleforth; and I enjoyed, recently, visiting Ushaw College in co. Durham, the Douai of the North. It was in April 1945, and Waldo Acomb,[18] the librarian of Durham University, a smooth and final convert – his father was an evangelical hot-gospeller, a disciple of Spurgeon, – gave me an introduction, and I went there to lunch, and found that great, heavy, classical mansion sitting squarely in its windy park; and the President, Msg Corbishley,[19] greeted me hospitably, a delightful man, of antique simplicity and quiet courtliness, who led me round those vast corridors, and showed me great chambers, chambers of horrors, some full of grotesque statuary, some of relics, some of stuffed birds and uteruses, equally grotesque, so that it was only by his devout genuflexions, or the omission of them, that I could distinguish the sacred from the profane. At lunch I met an old priest, who was introduced as Mr Bonney,[20] the author of the *Life of Lingard*; but he was very vague when I asked him about that subject. It was simply a passing phase, he explained, this interest in biography;

---

18 Henry Waldo Acomb (1891–1962), librarian of Durham University 1934–1945.
19 Thomas Corbishley (1903–1976), Jesuit priest, was D'Arcy's successor as Master of Campion Hall, 1945–1958.
20 Edwin Bonney (1873–1946), Professor of Sacred Eloquence at Ushaw, published *Life & Letters of Lingard* (1911).

he was stimulated to it by the presence of Lingard's papers at Ushaw. But that was forty years ago, and now he had other interests, – to be precise, he was knitting ecclesiastical nappies, in the old, medieval tradition; and he turned to accept a bowl of sliced beetroot from his neighbour, a grey, devout-looking layman who, sixty years ago, had been a pupil at the place, and had then disappeared to Austria, no-one knew why, and had now returned, no-one knew why either, to feed silently on the cold beef and beetroot of his old school in the windy pastures of county Durham. I asked about Martin Haile, Bonney's collaborator. She was a woman, he explained, and her real name was Marie Hallé,[21] but she wrote under a man's name so as to be taken more seriously. 'Poor lady, she wasn't interested in scholarship, but money: she wrote potboilers, Catholic potboilers, lives of Mary of Modena and I don't know who else; and I happened to find her working on Lingard when I was, so we combined. Poor lady! She came to an untimely end, flattened by a bus as she crossed the road to the Brompton Oratory for her regular devotions ...' So I shed a perfunctory tear, and stepping out of that great house, stopped a passing lorry and returned to Durham, and so home.

Oxford   May 1945

Odi et amo; I love Oxford, and I hate it. When I remember it I love it; for memory is a romantic organ, and perhaps I only remember my youthful illusions of the place – gay company, happy conversations, intellectual interests; walking hounds through the scented fields of Garsington and Cuddesdon early on summer mornings; days of study in the cool & spacious upper reading room of Bodley, or my own high and luminous room in Merton; evenings spent sociably over Stilton cheese and claret in the Christ Church buttery. But when I visit Oxford, now, in war-time, the sixth year of war, I hate it; its dreary company of old men, haters of learning and intellectual activity, envious of the absent, fearful of their return. They know they are despised; secretly

---

21 Marie Antoinette Hallé (1845–1925), daughter of the conductor Sir Charles Hallé, was killed by a motor-cycle rather than a bus. Under her masculine pseudonym she published *Queen Mary of Modena* (1905), *James, the Old Chevalier* (1907), *Reginald Pole* (1910), and *An Elizabethan Cardinal* (1914).

they despise themselves; but they dare not ask the cause or seek the remedy, for knowledge, to such as those, is as death.

'A class', says the excellent Kautsky[22] ('The renegade, philistine, petty-bourgeois Kautsky!' screams the miserable Lenin), 'a class or community which is in process of decline, or hopelessly trodden down by others, will always oppose itself to the knowledge of truth. It will not use its intelligence to define clearly that which is, but will try to discover arguments whereby to pacify, console, and deceive itself ...' It is a well-discernible tradition: the monks and peasantry of the 16th century; the high-priests and diggers of the 17th; the clericals of 1830; the mystical omphaloscopes of Russia and India; the British Israelites and Theosophists of Cheltenham and Droitwich; Marshal Pétain and his nursling-brood; and these flea-bitten bats who squeak *Peccavi* among the cob-webbed cloisters of Oxford.

Kent   May 1945

I had often read of my family, in course of my historical studies; an inconspicuous race, but representative of the class to which they belonged; Kentish squires who rose to wealth on the ruins of the monasteries, but remained Roman Catholic till it was positively inconvenient not to adjust themselves. When James I threw titles on to the market, they were the first buyers, paying £10,000 for their barony; they appeared before the Star Chamber as enclosers in the next reign; vexed Archbishop Laud by harbouring a nest of papists on their lands; changed their religion as convenience dictated after the Restoration; were borough-mongers in the eighteenth century; and when the tide of the aristocracy began at last to turn, obedient as ever, they turned with it, and left, as they ebbed, casual deposits in the West Country and in North Wales – at first in castles, then in villas, symbolical in their decline as in their ascent. Only once have they claimed to rise above parish history, and then only by chance, in the reign of Henry VIII, when one of the family married the daughter of Sir Thomas More, and wrote the earliest and best of

---

22 Karl Kautsky (1854–1938), Marxist theoretician who embraced social democracy and denounced Bolsheviks.

his biographies. It wasn't a very romantic match it seems. William Roper (says Aubrey) was offered his choice of the two More daughters, so he rode over to choose, and finding them both naked in bed, lying on their backs, he deftly tweaked the bedclothes away that he might study them at better advantage; whereupon they, being modest virgins, turned quickly over on their bellies; but he said they were too slow, he had seen what he wanted, and slapping Margaret on the bottom, chose her, as a practised epicure might select a capon from a poulterer's stall. Thus the Ropers obtained a saint in their family tree, which has not indeed improved their morals much, though it gets me a cordial welcome in many popish institutions which might otherwise be more fastidious. As the Italian nobleman, who also had a canonised ancestor, said to Samuel Butler, one is enough.

These and such observations occurring to me one May morning when I had no work to do, I reflected that I had never been to East Kent, where all this happened, and where some branches of the family are said to linger; unadventurous dynasties, who had cultivated their cornfields and cherry-orchards unobtrusively for six centuries or so. So I took a train to Chatham, and an obliging lorry-driver took me along the Watling Street to Teynham, where I alit, and walked through the orchards to Conyer, to begin my investigations. It was a cluster of houses settled in a warm, maritime swamp. The air was soft and sickly. I remembered Kentish agues and the local rhyme

> He who would not live long,
> Let him live at Teynham, Murston, or Tonge.

The Teynhams had all died young, till they abandoned their titular marshes. But in the inn at Conyer I learnt facts sufficient to guide me to Teynham Court and enquire for Mr Roper-Dixon.[23] The family were away, I was informed; they had gone to Cambridge, their other country-house, a few miles to the south; for like feudal landlords, they led a nomadic existence, grazing from manor to manor through the seasons. So I walked to Cambridge, and there found these far distant relatives, who, though our connexions were back in the reign of Henry VIII, seemed to know who I was, or must be, and pressed me hospitably to stay to lunch, and told me their history. It seemed to centre upon

---

23 Roper Dixon (1874–1948), of Cambridge and Teynham, married Maude Kellick in 1901: they had two surviving sons Stewart Roper Dixon (1906–1986) and Ronald Roper Dixon (1909–1996).

a famous pack of hounds which they had once owned, when they emerged, rich and splendid profiteers, from the Napoleonic wars; and of which they gave me an eloquent, well-documented account. It was an extravagant pack, apparently, eating up one of the Roper farms apparently every year; and after ten years, when they had eaten ten farms, they had to go, and were sold to the Empress of Austria. Then I asked about Lynsted, a great Elizabethan house, with pre-Elizabethan avenues, the home of another, less remote branch of the Roper family, which had parted from the main stream quite recently, in the reign of Queen Anne. Should I go there? Would the Roper-Lumley-Hollands give me tea?[24] But the Roper-Dixons were discouraging on this point. The Roper-Lumley-Hollands had fled, they explained, fled to Brazil, pursued by the just execrations of all classes among their neighbours. Word had indeed come from Rio de Janeiro recently that they were threatening to return; but if so, I was assured they would be resisted. 'We will fight on the beaches …' Meanwhile the army had taken over Lynsted. So I didn't go in there, but walked on through fields and lanes till I came to Hollingbourne on the Kentish Downs, and found a lorry-driver to take me back again to London and the present, out of the antiquated, feudal, genealogical Kentish past.

Classical and Romantic   June 1945

I have pretended, and still pretend, to a classical style and classical values; to a love of the 18th century in all its attitudes and expressions, – its firm, complete and polished world of knowledge, and thought, and prose, and poetry, and art, and architecture. But the pretence has never really been successful. Why not drop it, and admit it was a pose? That the baroque and the romantic are what I really love?

There are times in the history of man when the elements of civilisation are so adjusted that their relations form naturally and effortlessly a consistent pattern, and a perfect unity seems to enclose the whole; but these are short times,

----

24 Wilfred Roper-Lumley-Holland (1868–1947), of Lynsted Park, Kent, married in 1922 his kinswoman Mary Vivian Lumley-Holland (1877–1955), lady of the manors of Bedmangore, Lodge, Newnham and Teynham. The Elizabethan core of Lynsted survived inside a Georgian exterior.

of rare and distant occurrence, like the brief flowering of a centenarian aloe. The elements change, and their relations cannot be preserved. The Palladian front cracks, the plasterwork peels, and the wild foxglove and the rosebay seed in the interstices; the trim lawn is overgrown, the topiary yews thrust out shapeless limbs, the fluted sundial sinks awry on its pedestal, and where then are the classical world and the essential unities? For it is of the relations of elements, not of elements themselves, that intellectual worlds are constructed.

And yet a classical relationship is the final justification of a whole world, the brief moment of its perfection, when the moving elements (and if they live, they must move) stand to each other at last in perfect symmetry.

The pattern cannot be frozen; the elements must move on, and the symmetry is lost; but it may be regained with other elements. And perhaps our new world, the world of Marx and Freud and Einstein, that seems now so harsh and disorderly, will one day assume such a classical harmony before it too crumbles, against a pink sunset, into romantic ruins.

Dicksie Marshall June 1945

I took Dicksie Marshall out fishing on the Till, and as we passed Chillingham Park his memories were brightened by the familiar landmarks. 'At that point', he said, indicating a decayed portion of the park wall, 'my brother Antony and I dragged five deer over the wall. We had been poaching in the Park', he explained casually, 'and had shot five of them, and they were lying in the bracken, three in one heap and two in another, when his lordship heard the firing, and issued forth from the castle with blood in his eye. So we stowed our guns out of sight, and hid ourselves, separately, in clumps of bracken; and by and by old Tankerville came up to us, and I could hear him stumping about within twenty yards of my hiding-place, blaspheming; but he never found us, nor the dead deer either. So he stood there, waiting, thinking we would move; but we sat still, and very uncomfortable it was, crouching in the wet bracken, for he stayed a full half hour; and then he got bored with staying, and went back to the castle, and we came out and dragged the deer to the wall there, where we had a man waiting outside the park with a pony; and once over the wall we gutted the deer, and loaded them on to the pony, and took them home. But curiously enough, Lord Tankerville guessed who had done it, and next time we met, he accused me of poaching his deer. So I protested he was grossly insulting me, it was the last thing I would think of doing; but of course, if I shot a deer on my own land, and wounded it, and it got away into Chillingham, I would naturally follow it; mere common humanity required that I should put the poor beast out of its agony …

"'Common humanity indeed!" snorted his lordship; "you may call it common humanity, but I call it plain poaching."

"'You may call what you like," I said, "but nothing is going to stop me performing an act of charity to a poor wounded animal."'

'And what would you have done', I asked Dicksie when he had finished this tale, 'if he had found you crouching in the bracken, and the five dead deer?'

'Well, in that case', said Dicksie meditatively, 'there would have been nothing for it but to threaten to scrag him on the spot unless he promised to say and do nothing about it. We could scarcely have pretended we were following five wounded deer.'

Then he told me of other occasions, and how he made a practice of shooting Lord Tankerville's deer. They were never fed in the park, he explained, so they used to get out through the numerous gaps in the wall and feed on the farms thereabout, thus giving rise to an alliance between the outraged farmers and the Marshall brothers, who soon discovered that the deer had a favourite feeding ground in their preserves, in Oakey Wood in Amerside Law. So a man was posted regularly at one of the gaps in the Park wall, to close it after the deer had left, and prevent their return; and the Marshalls posted themselves conveniently; and as the deer issued from Oakey Wood on the way back to Chillingham, they were mowed down; and the friends and dependents of the Marshalls, the fellow poachers and conniving farmers, and auxiliaries of all kinds, fed on venison for many days afterwards.

He told me other stories, too; how, by the use of some gypsy preparation called Neverstray, which acted as a lure to pheasants, he had regularly lured all Lord Tankerville's pheasants out of the Park to Oakey Wood, there to be shot for his own purposes; how, posting himself securely in a hedgerow between Colonel Bridgeman's beaters and Colonel Bridgeman's guests at Harehope, he had decimated Colonel Bridgeman's pheasants with a silent .22 rifle before they ever reached the legitimate guns; and how the late Lord Tankerville, among other freaks, had sought to repair the fading splendours of Chillingham by breeding orchids, sending highly paid experts to Brazil, and covering acres of the park with costly greenhouses. 'That's what's going to put Chillingham on its feet again', he said proudly to old Marshall one day, showing him a large spotted bloom. 'That's what's going to put Chillingham a few feet still further under the sea', replied old Marshall bluntly. And correctly too; for when Tankerville, after laying out over £100,000 in orchidiculture, held the great show and sale which was to launch Chillingham on a new era of magnificence, the total proceeds of the venture were £700, not enough even to pay for the greenhouses.

There was indeed one unfortunate incident, on which Dicksie touched but lightly; when he had been poaching Lord Tankerville's water, and Lord Tankerville emerged from behind a willow-tree, and greeted him with a somewhat sinister implication.

'Very nice bit of water here', remarked Dicksie unconcernedly, spinning a deadly minnow.

'Yes', replied the sententious peer. 'It's my favourite spot. I call it the Sanctuary.'

'Indeed', said Dicksie, 'and why?'

'Because it's sacred, and I never give anyone permission to fish it.'

But these incidents are of rare occurrence. In general Dicksie has prayed the prayer of Samuel Butler. 'Vouchsafe O Lord to keep us this day without being found out.' And the Lord has heard him. He is very seldom found out.

When I try to envisage those old feudal landlords who were left behind by the capitalist revolution of the sixteenth century, – those northern and western squireens who supplied the leaders of reactionary feudal revolts and conspiracies, – the romantic cavaliers of the Civil Wars and the Northumbrian Jacobites of 1715 – I tend to see the image of Lord Tankerville in his decaying park, with his troublesome deer and wild cattle, and his desperate remedies for a failing estate; and of Dicksie Marshall with his predatory habits and reactionary charm. Certainly his politics fit the analogy; for when I told him that he ought to pay a country call on Beveridge, who has taken Tuggal,[25] and is therefore a near neighbour to Dicksie at Anstead, he was indignant at the thought of such recognition. 'If Beveridge comes to my house', he said firmly, extracting a fishing-fly from his wife's decayed hat which he always wears on

---

25 Sir William Beveridge leased Tuggal after his election as Liberal MP for Berwick-on-Tweed in 1944. T-R voted for him in the general election of 1945 – in which Beveridge was defeated. Tuggal was used as the territorial designation of Beveridge's barony gazetted in 1946.

these expeditions, 'he will be sent to the back door'. As for Laski[26] (for it was at the time when Winston was insulting the electorate by his campaign), 'he isn't even a white man'.

They are well portrayed, these types, by Macaulay, and by Fielding, *feras consumere nati*,[27] and by Sir Walter Scott: as Ellangowan, and Sir Hildebrand Osbaldistone, whom Scott must have based, I think, on Sir James Clavering, a 17th century Northumbrian, who (I find) boasted to the minister of his sabbatarian devotion, explaining that on Sundays he never went visiting, but stayed at home and read Dugdale's *Baronetage*; as Sir Hildebrand read Gwylim's *Heraldry*.

Arabia Deserta   June 1945

It is something to discover new enthusiasms at the advanced age of 30; and ever since I read Doughty's *Arabia Deserta* in hospital last year, I have realised that a new element has entered my experience, a new authority admitted to my canon of style. How can I lose myself – how during the past year I have lost myself – in those two divine great volumes! What a new world has been opened to my comprehension, a world of bleak rocks and waste ravines and terrible solitudes; a world of nature not benign and pastoral, not even luxuriant and fantastical, but hard and empty as the moon; a world of men intolerant and fanatical, governed and circumscribed by elementary convictions and narrow taboos. What a new world of style too; a style that has arisen, new and sudden, amid the drawing-room journalese of late Victorian England; a style without obvious ancestry, save in the remote ages of Chaucer and Spenser, springing up fresh and spontaneous after lapsed centuries, like the river Alpheus, far from its source; a style simple, with an ancient but not an archaical simplicity; a style like the style of Blake, or El Greco, that cannot be related to its age or native country, but is a true artefact, comprehending and concealing in itself alike its origins, its development, and its perfection. No wonder it appalled the publishers, and scared away the public of that

---

26 Harold Laski (1893–1950) held the chair in political science at the London School of Economics and was chairman of the Labour Party 1945–1946. He was a compulsive liar.

27 Born to consume the beast of the fields, as Fielding says of Squire Allworthy in *Tom Jones*.

illiterate age. One publishing-house would only consider it if 'the book is put into shape by some competent man who can amend the style in accordance with English idiom'; 'the manuscript', protested another, 'ought to be taken in hand, recast, and practically re-written, by a practised literary man'; but Robert Bridges, when he picked up the book, found that it 'stands out of the flatness of modern literature as Etna from Sicily'.

Like all great works it begins well. There is no preamble, no havering. We plunge at once into the centre of the subject:

> A new voice hailed me of an old friend when, first returned from the Peninsula, I paced again in that long street of Damascus which is called Straight; and suddenly taking me wondering by the hand, 'Tell me (said he), since thou art here again in peace and assurance of Ullah, and whilst we walk, as in the former years, towards the new blossoming orchards, full of the sweet spring as the garden of God, what moved thee, or how couldst thou take such journeys into the fanatic Arabia?'

Yet to this primal question there is no answer in the two volumes. Indeed, it is Doughty's charm that he never asks himself questions about himself; he is the least introspective of writers; unlike Lawrence, who, in all his travels, all his writings, was consciously fashioning and illuminating and adjusting his self-portrait, Doughty seems never to have considered the problem of his own motives. He went out to Arabia quite simply, in extension of his earlier European journeys, pursuing his study of the Earth, 'her manifold living creatures, the human generations, and her ancient rocks'. Nor did it seem to him a strange or unheard of thing, requiring explanation, that an English poet, an invalid, should travel, alone, unprotected, for two years, openly professing the hated Christian religion, through the unvisited and inhospitable wastes of fanatic Arabia. In the quiet simplicity of his character, the unquestioning, yet not unphilosophic, extraversion of his outlook, he is like one of those rare and admirable saints whose saintliness is the direct, clear expression of a complete and unitary nature, an uncompounded, elemental limpidity. How simple was his belief in the undogmatic religion of Christ, in the beneficent colonising power of England, his hatred of the slave-trade, of untruthfulness, of injustice. Beaten and scorned, thrust out of doors, robbed and dishonoured, made to travel on foot across the burning desert sands, threatened with violence, abandoned defenceless in the empty, inhospitable waste, how often could he have escaped this fanatical injustice by the utterance of a word, 'Khalîl, thou become a Moslem; it is a little word, and soon said', his Arab hosts protested, who could not comprehend this meaningless eccentricity. 'Only say, Khalîl, thou art a Moslem; it is but a word to appease them.' But that word he would never say; Mohammed was to him 'a dire imposter'; 'a little salt of science would dissolve all their religion'; 'it had cost me little or naught (he admits) to confess Konfuchu or Socrates to be apostles of Ullah, but I could not find it in my life to confess the barbaric prophet of Mecca, and enter, under the yoke, into their solemn fools' paradise'. And so the despairing Arabs washed their hands of his safety:

> 'Eigh Khalîl,' said he, in that demiss voice of the Arabs when the tide is turned against them, 'what can I do? I must ride after the Kâfily; look, I am left behind!' He mounted without more ado, and forsook his father's friend among murderers.

But why did he go? What gadfly impulse, what beckoning ideal, led him, the descendant of prosperous, home-loving Suffolk squires and parsons, on those incredible journeys? Certainly it was no romantic affectation. Never has anyone written so clearly, so coolly, or with such good reason, about the horrors of the Mohammedan east, the mental aridity of Islam, the fickle, uncharitable, intolerant, mercenary, mendacious, servile nature of the Arabs, their parasitic way of life, their threadbare, repetitious sophistry, their dreary prophet, their hateful religion. 'What had the world been', he exclaims, 'if the tongue had not wagged of this fatal Ishmaelite!' The Koran is 'a solemn farrago'. Why then, we despairingly ask, did he go? Or why, having gone, did he continue there, against his first intentions, nearly two years in those inhospitable deserts, losing by degrees his health, his few supplies of money and medicine, his books – all but two German scientific volumes, and the black-letter volume of Chaucer's *Canterbury Tales* which accompanied him throughout those desperate wanderings? For surely it is not enough to say, with Hogarth, that he did all this to live cheaply.

To every generalisation, there are saving clauses. If Doughty knew, and knowing, in general, despised the Arabs, there was yet one quality in Arabia which appealed to his simple comprehensive nature: its own ancient simplicity, against which the innumerable petty miseries of existence were but tiresome reminders of a difference between man's nature and man's ideal. It is this antique simplicity of the desert life, with its compact world, its elementary but sure conventions, – the rights of the coffee-booth, of the fellow-traveller, of hospitality: the bread and the salt, the brotherhood within, as the intolerance without, the religion – that struck a corresponding chord in Doughty. Such was the world of Homer, with its insistence, in a like harsh and perilous and hostile world, on the rights of the poor and the stranger, its few but humane conventions in the intervals of savage feuds, the intermissions of implacable nature; and surely Doughty was thinking of Homer when he wrote, for instance, of the cheerful Bedouin watch-fires 'glimpsing up and down in the dark, nigh the camp, in the wilderness'.

As in the Heroic Age, so in Arabia, the life of man is 'a weak accident', a short and precarious animation in the cracks and crannies of a hostile, impersonal world. How hostile, how impersonal, only the style of Doughty can adequately represent, that gigantic style, as ageless, and dateless, at first sight perhaps as forbidding, as the rocks themselves of Sinai or the volcanic harra which it has described:

> We look out from every height upon the Harra, over an iron desolation; what Uncouth blackness and lifeless cumber of volcanic matter! An hard-set face of nature without a smile for ever, a wilderness of burning and rusty horror of unformed matter. What lonely life would not feel constraint of heart to trespass here! The barren heaven, the nightmare soil! Where should he look for comfort?

And thus he describes the terrible heat of Arabia:

> The summer's night at end, the sun stands up as a crown of hostile flames from that huge covert of inhospitable sandstone bergs; the desert day dawns not little and little, but it is noontide in an hour. The sun, entering as a tyrant upon the waste landscape, darts upon us a torment of fiery beams, not to be remitted till the far-off evening. No matins here of birds; not a rock-partridge cock, calling with blithesome chuckle over the extreme waterless desolation. Grave is that giddy heat upon the crown of the head; the ears tingle with a flickering shrillness, a subtle crepitation it seems, in the glassiness of this sun-stricken nature: the hot sand-blink is in

the eyes, and there is little refreshment to find in the tent's shelter; the worsted booths leak to this fiery rain of sunny light. Mountains looming like dry bones through the thin air, stand far around about us: the savage flank of Ybba Moghrair, the high spire and ruinous stacks of al-Jebâl, Chebâd, the coast of Helwân! Herds of the weak nomad cattle waver dispersedly, seeking pasture in the midst of this hollow fainting country, where but lately the swarming locusts have fretted every green thing. This silent air burning about us, we endure breathless till the assr; when the dazing Arabs in the tents revive after their heavy hours. The lingering day draws down to the sun-setting; the herdsmen, weary with the sun, come again with the cattle, to taste in their menzils the first sweetness of mirth and repose. The day is done, and there rises the nightly freshness of this purest mountain air: and then to the cheerful song, and the cup at the common fire.

And yet, even here, even in Arabia, there is for Doughty 'that subtle harmony of Nature, which the profane cannot hear'. After the long, burning day, there comes the cool evening; a spring bubbles in a desert cistern; an acacia blows among the parched rocks; and when at last a bird does sing, a rock-thrush or a silver-voiced siskin, how sweetly it sings in that rocky solitude:

> Many a time the passenger hears at unawares her short descant ringing upon the waste moors, in perplex desert ways, in the awe and the Titanic ruins of desolate mountains, with a silver sweetness, as it were the voice to his soul of some benign spirit …

How can we square the evident sincerity and directness of Doughty's character with such a style as this, a recondite, alembicated style, of infinite subtlety, of elaborate and assorted wealth? It is like a net that has been dragged through the great sea of language, and brought up again full of the miscellaneous, exotic contents of that infinite deep ocean, whose surface is so smooth and same, whose depths are so strange and various. There are pearls and mother-o'-pearl, bright shells and strange starfish, silver fish and sea-flowers and marine monsters and detachable mundungus; there are words from Persia and Arabia, words from Chaucer and Spenser and the Bible, fantastic fossilised words from unknown quarries, words from dialects and dictionaries, learned and sophisticated words, new words newly made, old words with new, or ancient and exacter meanings; all of which Mr Walt Taylor has learnedly analysed and tabulated in his pamphlet on *Doughty's English*. And yet Doughty's character was simple, straightforward, perspicuous. But this simplicity lay in itself only, in the harmonious, effortless integration of his own character; he was indeed incurious about his own motives, his own nature, but his attitude to the outer world was adult and philosophic. He would analyse and dissect, though not over subtly, the characters he met in Arabia, giving to each a living personality before he passed on into the vast impersonal desert. And his art is similarly careful and complex and excogitated; for in it he was interested as never in himself; which (though it seem platitudinous) is the true criterion of an artist; and it was in search and study of language, as much as of stones and ruins and Nabataean inscriptions, that he made that memorable pilgrimage.

The result is a pure style; all the carefully sought diversities, the exotic words, the ancient constructions, are digested and integrated and harmonised by that simple personality of which it is the expression. Doughty is neither baroque (his personality was too complete) nor classical (his style is too elaborate); he is unique, a law unto himself in English literature. And yet, in the richness of that literature, is there no parallel? Doughty would perhaps have disclaimed it; for he recognised no master later than Spenser, the last poet of the age of gold. (In all his works and letters, says Hogarth, there is no mention, no recollection, of Milton or Shakespeare). Nevertheless, in that period of 'the decadence of the English language', there is one voice, the firm, self-possessed voice of Sir Thomas Browne, to whose richly brocaded periods the voice of Doughty seems often, no less firmly, no less richly, as it were a belated echo, to reply:

> Languor of hunger, the desert disease, was in all the tents. *Mâana lôn*, 'we have nothing left', said the people one to another. The days passed by days in this weakness of famine, in forgetfulness of the distant world, and the wasting life of the body. The summer night's delightful freshness in the mountains is our daily repast; and lying to rest amidst wild basalt-stones, under the clear stars, in the land of enemies, I have found more refreshment than upon beds and pillows in our close chambers. Hither lies no way from the city of the world, a thousand years pass as by daylight; we are in the world and not in the world, where Nature brought forth man, an enigma to himself, and an evil spirit sowed in him the seeds of

dissolution. And looking then upon that infinite spectacle, this life of the wasted flesh seemed to me ebbing, and the spirit to waver her eyas wings unto that divine obscurity. I thought I could number twenty and more flitting meteors in every hour. And Sâlih, because Khalîl was an European, looked to read in my simple sayings the enigmatology of Solomon.

The Solway Firth
June 1945

I was determined to look again, be it only a Pisgah glimpse, at the Solway Firth; so when my declining health advised me to go home for a week's leave, I resolved to use this opportunity; and getting out of the night-train at Newcastle, I took a tram to Scotswood Bridge, and there found a friendly lorry-driver bound with a load of Oxygen to Carlisle, and went with him to Greenhead. Thence I meant to walk along Hadrian's Wall to Housesteads, confident that from one of the crags there, from the Nine Nicks of Thirlwall or from Melkridge Height, I should see that distant, twinkling water, that enchanted tidal waste. So I climbed those deserted promontories, and standing there among the foxgloves and the cranesbill and the turf-covered relics of that gigantic rampart, I gazed westward through the noonday haze,

ἔκαμον δέ μοι ὄσσε
αἰεὶ παπταίνοντος ἐπ᾽ ἠεροειδέα πόντον,[28]

but to no end; the Solway Firth is plainly invisible from those modest heights; it must have been from some other spot that I remember long ago to have glimpsed it. So I walked away to the east, following the Wall, through those delightful pastoral solitudes, where only the bleating of sheep from dale after dale breaks the silence; rowans and birch-trees sprang from the rocky outcrop below me, wild thyme and rest-harrow from the smooth turf above, the June sun burnt me, and a soft breeze refreshed me; it was a delightful walk. But I had never seen the Solway. And then, resting on a rocky ledge above Crag

---

28 My eyes grew weary as I kept straining to see hazy land (Odysseus at Homer, *Odyssey*, 12.232–3). For παπταίνοντος ἐπ᾽ standard editions give παπταίνοντι πρός, which means the same.

Lough, I suddenly realized, what I had long concealed from myself, that I was ill; and descending to Wade's Road I stopped a car and rode to Newcastle, and so home, and spent a week in bed, and read *Guy Mannering* again.

But after I had been up two days (for I was determined to go), I was taken to Blindburn in the Cheviots, north-west of Alwinton, and after lunch I walked and walked, over the old Roman Dere Street, down the Cottonhope Burn to Byrness, over the fells by the Blackhope Nick to Kielder; and after a night spent at Bewshaugh Farm (the farmer, Mr Newton, a former shepherd, from Jedburgh),[29] on again next morning up the Lewisburn valley, and over to Bewcastle Fells, a killing struggle, over peat-hags and bogs and clefts, making every mile as two; and at last, from Sighty Crag, I saw it, a sheet of twinkling water and a long reach of desolate sand, the Solway Firth; and at the same time I heard the bubbling of a spring nearby among the moss, and slaked my thirst with its cool dark water; for my throat was parched with that long weary climb. After which I felt as I daresay the Israelites felt when, from a hilltop, they viewed the Promised Land, that it wasn't really very different from anywhere else; still, it was something to be out of the wilderness. I felt that too, and dropping lightly down the fells I met a shepherd, the first human face I had seen for eighteen miles, and so to Bewcastle, where I found, against all probability (for it is a lonely steading) another man, in the middle of a field, delivering lime from a lorry. So I asked him for a lift, and he took me to Brampton, whence I gradually found my way home. He drove a lime-lorry now, he said, but he had once lived far away in Northumberland, and had spent his childhood in the village of Powburn, where his uncle was the policeman. So I told him that I had been born in the parish of Powburn, in Glanton, and from that time we were intimate friends.

Image

'Doris never throws anything away', remarked Catriona as she tossed a carton of decomposing shrimps into the fire; and then she described the condition of

---

29 In 1981 Bewshaugh farmhouse was submerged under Kielder Water, the largest man-made British reservoir.

the larder in Moore Street under that conservative economy: jugs of sour milk, tins of blotched and dappled paste, decaying kippers, and jars of curdled gravy nourishing a thin grey mould, 'like that tall grey grass that waves sparsely over some dreary bog'.[30]

———————————

July 1945

Dining with Malcolm Muggeridge is like picknicking on a volcano. The climate, the elevation, the verdure, the scenery, the hock and the sandwiches are all perfect; but one can never be quite sure that there won't be an eruption. It was thus when I dined there the other night. He had a beautiful flat, in Buckingham Street, with a large and beautiful dining-room looking south over the first Duke of Buckingham's water-gate to the Thames; and it was a beautiful long light summer evening; and the music of the band from the Victoria Embankment drifted, rarefied and refined, up to our high upper window. The meal was excellent too, the party convivial, the conversation well shared. There were Malcolm and Kitty, Hugh Kingsmill,[31] myself, and a foreigner, whose name and nature I never learnt, but he might easily have been a Belgian, and he had worked for, or with, S.I.S. in Algiers. 'Only one thing I must remember', I kept saying to myself as I savoured this fragile felicity: 'on no account get involved in any serious topic on which you care.' For alas, it must be admitted, Malcolm has two fatal qualities: an appalling indifference to truth, and the dreary, sneering cynicism of the disillusioned radical. Once a young Cambridge revolutionary, – indeed a member of the Communist Party – he went to Russia and was repelled by it;[32] and now, a journalist on the staff of the *Daily Telegraph*, he is ready, if encouraged (and he is easily encouraged), to pour out that endless stream of sterile, mirthless ribaldry on any subject which has ever enlisted the interest of an intellectual.

Of course it was a failure; of course I yielded to Kingsmill's questions when

———————————

30 Moore Street is on the Cadogan estate in Chelsea, but neither Doris nor Catriona are identifiable.

31 Muggeridge's friend and mentor Hugh Kingsmill (1889–1949) was younger brother of Sir Arnold Lunn but used a *nom de plume* as journalist, biographer and anthologist.

32 Muggeridge was neither a Cambridge revolutionary nor a Communist party member.

Malcolm was busy brassing away on some other topic; of course Kingsmill then appealed to Malcolm for his opinion; and then, of course, the rest was inevitable. The air became suddenly dark and lurid, charged with ominous clouds, and down it rolled, that inexorable molten stream; and under the rain of burning ashes all life was gradually extinguished. 'Malcolm', said Kitty timidly, 'the landlord is outside, and I think he would like to be asked in for a drink'. 'Later, Kitty, later!', said Malcolm, impatient of the interruption, and swept on. Desperately, when a rare interstice opened, or seemed to open, in the flow of lava, I sought to change the subject; but I was overborne; or a titter from Kingsmill filled up those short and precious intervals while Malcolm drew breath. The Belgian looked both bored and shocked; I think his prejudices were outraged by the subject; but Malcolm didn't care. Ultimately it was over. The scene was one of desolation. The clouds of ash were still suspended in the air. Not a living tree, not a habitable cottage was left on the devastated mountain-slope; only a few scorched stumps, a few ruined walls, rising above the lava-flood, and an universal dry smell of dust and burning. The landlord had never come in. The guests took their leave shamefacedly, as if they had shared some guilty experience. Only Malcolm seemed confident and complacent; and he firmly announced that he would come to my club for lunch next week, as if conscious of a great social success.

General Elections July 1945

When I visited Logan in July 1945, I found him low, very low. He was down in the unfathomable realms of Proserpine, he said, and nothing could interest him, nothing excite him more. But he would emerge, in a month or two, into the alternative condition of euphoria, – for such is the nature of his cyclical depression; meanwhile he was underground.

I spoke of books and pictures; I gave him social gossip and political gossip; but he remained sunk in gloom. Then I spoke of the general election, and Winston's deplorable campaign. 'Ah', said Logan, 'you don't understand. English elections have never been serious affairs. They are Saturnalia; periods set apart for licensed buffoonery and the innocent discharge of repressed absurdity…' I asked him whether he remembered the Oxford election of 1880, which Sidney Owen had once described to me; when Sir William

Harcourt[33] was defeated; when Hall,[34] the Tory brewer, and Morrell,[35] the Liberal brewer, to prove the value of their political opinions, distributed free beer from morning till midnight; and the City was afterwards, in consequence of a parliamentary enquiry, disfranchised for five years for electoral corruption unparalleled even in that malodorous constituency. No, said Logan, he didn't remember that; that must have been before he came to England from his half-forgotten transatlantic home. But in 1906, – oh! that was the best, the most glorious, the most famous and beneficent election ever. 'The Tories', he exclaimed, sitting up in his chair, his ancient eyes suddenly gleaming, 'were *wiped out*! It was Heaven!' And then, the momentary illumination over, his eyes became gradually dull again, and he sank back into his chair, and returned to the dark realms of Proserpine from which, for an instant, he had been transported by that heavenly recollection; and I left.

Götterdämmerung

Now that the German war is over, and the surviving grandees of Nazi Germany are captured and talking, what poor, inflated vulgarians, what weak pretenders they all turn out to have been, how absurd and byzantine that fantastic court at Berlin and Berchtesgarden and in the peripatetic Führerhauptquartier! When Hermann Rauschning,[36] in 1939, published his conversations with Hitler, credulity was strained at the scenes he described, scenes of nihilistic bombast uttered among high Wagnerian mountains, against a more immediate background of spinsterish tea-parties, Bavarian rococo woodwork, cuckoo-clocks

33 Sir William Harcourt (1827–1904), Liberal MP for Oxford City, was obliged by parliamentary rules to offer himself for re-election in 1880 after his appointment as Home Secretary, and was defeated by 49 votes after a contest that was corrupt on both sides.

34 Alexander Hall (1838–1919), a popular Oxford brewer, was elected (with support from Oxford publicans) as Conservative MP for Oxford City in a by-election of 1874 but defeated in the general election of 1880. His victory over Harcourt in the 1880 by-election was challenged by temperance enthusiasts and declared void.

35 Herbert Morrell (1845–1906) was elected in 1891 as Tory (not Liberal) MP for the Woodstock division of Oxfordshire.

36 Hermann Rauschning (1887–1982), landowner near Danzig, joined the Nazi Party in 1926 but became a constitutionalist and fled abroad in 1936. The authenticity of his reported conversations in *Hitler Speaks* (1939) is contestable.

and cream-buns; and when Marcus came over to us in the summer of 1944, and described the German political situation, the plans and ambitions of Himmler and his satraps, we distrusted such fantastic, looking-glass accounts, not realising how absurdly and unreally uneducated men think and act who for ten years have alternately jostled and grovelled around the altar of Absolute Power, isolated from the free and civilised world. But events have proved that it was all true. I should like to see a complete study made of the last months of that exotic circus, from 20th July 1944 to the end, when the Thousand Year Reich was breaking up, when the Führerprinzip had no more validity, and that vast, vaunted pyramid of obedient discipline had become a contracting cage in which all were fighting against all; when grandiose plans were being declared, plans of Alpine Redoubts and Scorched Earth and Werewolves and Wagnerian Twilights, and no one had any time to consider them, for every man was busy with his own plans for negotiation or deception or denunciation, and escape, in the face of that inevitable defeat which, to the very last, none might even mention to the demented tyrant.

Meanwhile here are snippets:

SS Oberführer Eugen Dollmann[37] was Himmler's representative in Mussolini's Italy. He was Höchster SSuPf Italy, and SS Liaison Officer to C-in-C South West; and it was he who escorted Mussolini to see Hitler on the fatal 20th July 1944. Exactly one year later, he described the experience to SS Ostubaf Elling,[38]

---

37 Eugen Dollmann graduated from the University of Munich in 1926, and moved to Rome. A handsome, cultivated man-of-the-world, interested in archaeology and the arts, he joined the Nazi Party in 1934. During the war, from the German Embassy in Rome, he acted as the SS's wartime representative throughout Italy and as its liaison officer with Mussolini. He was also Hitler's Italian interpreter. During the final stages of the war he entered secret negotiations with the Americans (notably Allen Dulles) to obtain the early surrender of German forces in Northern Italy. After the war Dollmann was recruited as a paid informant of the US Office of Strategic Studies, and transferred to the American zone in Germany 1947. His cover as an anti-Communist agent was, however, compromised, and he returned to Italy working for CIC in 1948. By 1950 (strapped for money) he was supplying Italian intelligence with knowledge of secret SS arms caches and US intelligence. Moved to Lugano in 1951 but expelled from Switzerland in 1952 – supposedly on grounds of homosexuality. Went to Spain where he engaged in intelligence work. A CIA report of 1952 on Germans living in Spain characterised Dollmann as notorious for blackmail and double-dealing. He published his memoirs, and later opened the Hotel Dollmann Splendide in Munich.

38 Georg Elling, said to have been a renegade Catholic priest researching the life of St Francis of Assisi, spoke fluent English, French and Italian, and was installed in the German Embassy to the Vatican in 1943 to monitor the British envoy to the Vatican, Sir D'Arcy Godolphin Osborne (later 12th Duke of Leeds).

formerly economic adviser, and representative of RHSA Amt VI, in the German Embassy to the Vatican:

Dollmann: A year ago today exactly I escorted the Duce from Florence to Germany. The train was scheduled to leave at one o'clock on the 20th July. We were in the station, when suddenly an air-raid alarm was given and the whole train had to be blacked out.

Elling: But it was daylight surely?

Dollmann: Yes, it was broad daylight, and all the same the whole train had to be blacked out; all the windows were covered over, and we sat there in the dark. When we arrived at the station – we were going to the Führer's HQ – the Führer was there to meet us, white as a sheet, and his whole staff. Himmler, Göring, Keitel,[39] Ribbentrop, and so on, they were all there. I got out after the Duce, and heard Hitler saying to him, 'I've just had the greatest piece of luck I've ever had'; and then he went on to tell him about the attempt on his life. Afterwards the Führer and Mussolini and myself went to have a look at the place where it happened. It was a mass of debris.

At five o'clock there was a big tea-party; it was amazingly interesting. All of them were there, in the Führer's GHQ, and over tea they all began arguing and shouting at one another, and each one putting the blame on the other because the war had not yet been won! Ribbentrop raved against the generals, because they had betrayed us to England, Dönitz[40] raved against the generals, and the generals raved in their turn against Ribbentrop and Dönitz. The Führer kept pretty quiet the whole time, and Mussolini was very reserved too. Graziani[41] began telling him about his adventures in Africa, when all of a sudden someone happened to mention the 30th June 1934. The Führer leapt up, in a fit of frenzy, with foam on his lips, and yelled out that he would

---

39 Wilhelm Keitel (1882–1946), *Oberkommando der Wehrmacht* (commander-in-chief of military supreme command) 1939–1945, was Hitler's lackey; hanged.

40 Admiral Karl Dönitz (1891–1980), naval commander-in-chief 1943–1945, designated in Hitler's will as head of state and supreme commander, and ruled Germany for three weeks.

41 Rodolfo Graziani, Marchese di Neghelli (1882–1955), the most loyal to Mussolini of the Italian marshals, notorious for his butchery during and after the conquest of Abyssinia, appointed as Viceroy there in 1936 and Governor of Libya in 1940.

be revenged on all traitors, that Providence had just shown him once more that he had been chosen to make world history, and shouted about terrible punishments for women and children; all of them would have to be put inside concentration-camps! He shouted about an eye for an eye and a tooth for a tooth for everyone who dared to set himself against divine Providence. It was awful, and it went on for about half an hour! I thought to myself, this man must be mad. I don't know why I didn't go over to Allies there and then. Mussolini found it most unpleasant. Meanwhile more tea was served by the footmen in white, and Graziani started discussing with Keitel the question of AA troops that we wanted from the Italians.

Then a call came through from Berlin, to say that order had not yet been restored there. The Führer answered the call, and started yelling again, gave full powers for shooting anyone they liked, why wasn't Himmler there yet [presumably there meant Berlin], and so on. Then came the lovely bit: 'I'm beginning to doubt whether the German people is worthy of my great ideas.' At that of course there was a tremendous to-do; they all wanted to convince the Führer of their loyalty. Dönitz and Göring came out with all they had done, Dönitz told him about the blue-eyed boys in blue – damned rubbish – and Göring started having a row with Ribbentrop, and Ribbentrop shouted at him, 'I am still Foreign Minister, and my name is *von* Ribbentrop!' Göring made a pass at him with his field-marshal's baton. I'll never forget that scene! The Führer was in a very peculiar state at that time. It was the time when his right arm began to develop a tremor. He sat there almost the whole time, eating his coloured pastilles.

Elling: What sort of pastilles?

Dollmann: I don't know, some sort of medicine probably. He always had a tube of pastilles of all colours in front of him, and kept on eating them. He would be quite quiet for a time, and then suddenly he'd break out like a wild animal, and wanted to get at everyone, women and children too, into the concentration camp with the lot of them, he was the one Providence had chosen, and so on.

Elling: What sort of a man was Bormann?[42] Was he there too?

---

42 Martin Bormann (1900–1945) succeeded Rudolf Hess as the omnipotent party chancellor in 1941 and consolidated his power as Hitler's personal secretary from 1943.

Dollmann: A fine nonentity in world history! I've never heard the man say anything sensible. Of course Keitel had the luck to have the Führer fall straight into his arms when the bomb went off; that saved him for the German people for another year!

So it goes on, down to the last month, when the whole hierarchy was in dissolution, when conflicting orders were going out in all directions, and every man was thinking of himself alone. And at the centre, what a spectacle do these once powerful figures present? Like Roman Emperors, the creatures of concubines and catamites, of eunuchs and freed men, so, in their fools' limbo, we find them managed by random influences: Hitler by his doctor Morell,[43] and by Eva Braun,[44] and by her opportunist brother-in-law, Himmler's liaison officer, Fegelein;[45] Himmler by his doctor Gebhardt,[46] his astrologer Wulff[47] and his masseur Kersten.[48] Only Goebbels, the one intellectual of the Party, the prize-pupil of the Jesuits of Bonn, retained to the last his fanatical integrity,

---

43 Theodor Morell (1886–1948), Hitler's physician and companion 1936–1945 and owner of lucrative factories producing quack medicines. T-R described him during his internment by the Americans: 'a gross but deflated old man, of cringing manners, inarticulate speech and the hygienic habits of a pig.'

44 Eva Braun (1912–1945), for 12 years the mistress and for 38 hours the wife of Hitler.

45 Hermann Fegelein (1906–1945), former stable lad to Christian Weber, was an ignorant, illiterate horse-fancier who joined the Nazi Party in 1930, became Commander of the SS Riding School in 1937, Himmler's representative at the Fuehrer's headquarters, General in the Waffen SS and consolidated his position by marrying Margarete ('Gretl') Braun (1915–1987), Eva's sister. Executed outside the Bunker after trying to desert Hitler.

46 Karl Gebhardt (1897–1948), orthopaedic surgeon who joined the Nazi Party in 1933, was Himmler's physician from 1938 and soon his political confidant. Major General in Waffen SS, President of German Red Cross in 1945, performed surgical experiments on women inmates at Ravensbrück and Auschwitz; hanged.

47 Wilhelm Wulff (b. 1893), Himmler's astrologer, was a student of poisons and Sanskrit, who participated in the SS project to harness supernatural powers.

48 Felix Kersten (1898–1960), Esthonian by birth, fought in Finland's war of liberation from Russia and became a fashionable Berlin physician and masseur. After being recommended to Prince Hendrik, consort of Queen Wilhelmina of the Netherlands, he joined the Dutch royal household, but was visiting Berlin when the Germans invaded Holland in 1940. Trapped there, he became personal physician to Himmler. Kersten interceded with Himmler on behalf of prisoners in German camps, and was credited by the World Jewish Congress with rescuing 60,000 Jews. The Dutch government nominated him for the Nobel Peace Prize in 1952. T-R later befriended Kersten, whose story intrigued him.

still struggling for the crumbling relics of power, still preaching the fiery ideology of nihilism. Appropriately he chose a Roman death, coolly and rationally ordering his doctors to inject himself and his whole family with poison; a noiseless suicide, the logical conclusion of an intellectual process. Himmler's end was mean, Hitler's Wagnerian.

Himmler, that once terrifying figure, who had concentrated in his person all the power of the state, had now abandoned it to Bormann, or dissipated it among his centrifugal subordinates. Paralysed by cowardice and indecision, he wavered helplessly among his own illusions. 'If only I could see Field-Marshal Montgomery', he confided to his staff in those last days at Flensburg, 'I am confident I can arrange peace'; and at the same time he admitted his post-war ambition – to be Prime Minister of Germany under Dönitz! This was the man who told Count Bernadotte that he was the only sane man in Germany, while Hitler was making grandiose plans for rebuilding Buckingham Palace, and Göring, clad in a Roman toga, was painting his finger-nails blue; and then, to prove it, broke off his discussion of peace and war to digress for an hour on Runic inscriptions! Mean and sordid to the end, Himmler never even contemplated a heroic death. In vain Berger[49] tried to persuade him to go and die in Berlin:

> On Sunday morning I went to the Reichsführer at once. He said, 'Everyone is mad in Berlin; the Führer is raging, saying the Armed Forces have deceived him all along, and that now the SS is leaving him in the lurch. I still have my Escort Battalion here, 600 men, mostly wounded or convalescent. What am I to do?' I said, 'You go straight to Berlin, Herr Reichsführer, and your Escort Battalion, too, of course. You have no right to keep an Escort Battalion here when the Führer intends to remain in Berlin and defend the Reichschancellery …' The words failed me to voice my disgust; I was at the end of my tether. I said, 'I am going to Berlin and it is your duty to do so too'. He telephoned Fegelein. I said, 'What sort of a Reichsführer are you? Why don't you speak to the Führer in person? He did so. Hitler was very short with him. 'Yes, you can come to Berlin …'

---

49 Gottlob Berger (1896–1975) became a Nazi in 1922, one of Himmler's trusties, chief of staff of the SS and chief of its Berlin headquarters from 1940.

So Himmler and Berger went to Berlin. It was April 22nd, the day of Hitler's final breakdown; and they found him in the Reichschancellery, trembling with rage and Parkinson's disease, in a darkened cellar, surrounded by frightened toadies, while the Russian shells, sometimes nearer, sometimes farther, burst around them in the city. The military situation was hopeless. What was he to do? To go south, in the wake of the Army and Air staffs? Or to stay in doomed Berlin?

> The Reichsführer SS told him how senseless it was to remain, and spoke for a long time. I said no, that was out of the question; he couldn't betray the German people. Hitler remained silent. It was very easy, I went on, to put a bullet through one's head, or to take one of those pills or capsules that are issued, which work instantaneously. He couldn't desert the people, after they had held out so long and so loyally. He must share its [sic] fate …

'Long and loyally' … that wasn't Hitler's conception of the German people's attitude to its leader:

> 'Everyone has deceived me!' he shrieked. 'No one has told me the truth! The Wehrmacht has lied to me! Finally the SS has left me in the lurch!' He went on and on in this vein, at the top of his voice. Then his face went bluish-purple. I thought he was due for a stroke at any moment. I had the impression he had had a stroke already, on his left side – but of course they kept one in the dark. His arm, which a fortnight before used to jerk, was suddenly still, and he never put his left foot properly to the ground. He didn't rest his left hand, either, as he used to do; he only rested his right hand on the table.

When Berger left, Hitler stood up. He had to prop himself up. His head was shaking, his leg was shaking, 'and all he kept saying was, "Shoot them all!" or something like that'.

It must have been after Himmler and Berger had left that Hitler received the generals. It was the same day; but he had now made up his mind. The witness is Generalleutnant Koller.[50] When he entered, Hitler and Goebbels had already determined to commit suicide. The generals protested. It was cowardice, they said; hadn't Hitler said so himself when the Mayor of Leipzig committed suicide? But protests were vain. At last Hitler had given up hope of victory. He would stay and perish in Berlin. As for the future, he would give no orders; let them send for Göring.

> 'There wasn't a single soldier,' protested someone (I think it was Jodl), 'who would fight under the Reichsmarschall.' The Führer said, 'There's no question of fighting now. There's nothing left to fight with here, and if it's a question of negotiating, Göring can do that better than I.'

This, I think, is the last recorded utterance of the Führer. When Göring received the message from Koller, and breezily accepted the charge, he found he had the hateful Bormann to deal with. Perhaps Hitler was already dead; perhaps he was at last totally mad; perhaps, oblivious of his own orders, he did in fact order the arrest and execution of the presumptuous Reichsmarschall. 'Shoot them all! Shoot them all!'

But Himmler, though he had been pushed to Berlin to face his hysterical master, had no intention of staying there to share his fate in the ruins of the Chancellery. Sneaking back to Schleswig-Holstein, he spun out his misconceived negotiations. After the coup by the General Staff, he continued to hang about Flensburg, with his huge retinue, an embarrassment to his successors, a humiliation to his subordinates, impervious to hints, blind to realities, attending conferences to which he had not been invited, unable to realise that he was now a back-number, confiding, to his embarrassed lieutenants, his outrageous hopes and impossible ambitions; until he was ultimately sent away, only to be captured and end his life biting a capsule, naked, in a British ward-room.

At least, compared to this sordid ending, there is in Hitler's demented finale, in the mystery which envelopes its circumstances, something of a Götterdämmerung. [SAGG 1288. 1293. 1317. Statements of Göring & Kaltenbrunner].

---

50 Karl Koller (1898–1951), chief of Luftwaffe general staff 1944–1945, imprisoned near Oxford 1945–1947.

Imperial Legacies

We were sitting in the East India and Sports Club, Charles Stuart, Rory Cameron[51] and I, under the solemn but flamboyant portraits of those great 18th century Nabobs, pink-coated, white-wigged, pot-bellied, red-faced, imperious grandees, who look splendidly out from the staid white panelling of those stately rooms, and we spoke of India and its associations for us. I spoke of the contrasts between its tropical exuberance, its luxuriant sexual architecture and its exorbitancies of tyrant power, and the record of prim, firm government by disinterested but dull Victorian officials. Charles said tersely that no good had ever come out of India except the money his family had made there. But Rory supported my aesthetic view of the matter. The Indian connexion had given to England, he said, a redeeming touch of exoticism, and his hand pointed involuntarily to a full-blown, puce-faced, arbitrary nabob on the wall; it was the legacy of a great colonial empire. You saw it in Portugal, too, he said, but faded and dingy and decayed, now only an ancient memory of tropical splendour surviving inappropriately amid encroaching jungles and ant-heaps and beachcombers and venality …

And Spain? I asked; for this redeeming touch of the exotic somehow seemed lacking to my imagination of Spanish life. But then I recalled that after all there is an alternative to this arrogant insular imperialism; and looking again with the mind's eye at those panelled walls, I seemed to see, not a gallery of opulent, pursy, highly coloured 18th century magnificos, but a continuous series of identical, black-robed, ascetic, olive-complexioned, thin-nosed missionaries: the wandering Francis Xavier,[52] the devoted Las Casas,[53] the long succession of anonymous Jesuits in China and Paraguay.

All the same, I thought, when I had adequately considered this imaginary portrait-gallery, I prefer the Nabobs.

———————

51 Roderick ('Rory') Cameron (1914–1985), who had official war-work in London, created famous gardens at his homes, La Fiorentina at Saint-Jean-Cap-Ferrat and Les Quatres Sources near Ménerbes in Vaucluse.

52 St Francis Xavier (1506–1552), missionary from Navarre and co-founder of the Jesuits.

53 Bartolomé Las Casas (1484–1566), Dominican priest in Spain's Caribbean and American colonies.

There are two kinds of happiness says Pascal (I think): the happiness of those who don't know (which I take it is the complacent bliss of the Guards Officer), and the happiness of those who know (which I suppose is the satisfaction of the mystic, which some think desirable); and between these two there is the unhappiness of those whose knowledge is imperfect.

Well, I know the first kind of happiness; and I know the intermediary stage; and as for the final state, well I'm not sure I don't prefer the stupid bliss of the drunken earthstopper to the virtuous smugness of the self-chloroformed saint.

It is from the incompleteness, the discontent, of the middle category that all art, all literature, all discovery, all progress in the world has come; not from the gaping beatitude of the satisfied omphaloscope.

The first, elementary happiness I know every time I go into the country, as I know it now, staying at Rory Cameron's fishing house in the gentle valley of the Wye.[54] I come, bringing all manner of problems which I hope to solve in these quiet solitudes: personal problems, general problems, intellectual problems, which bother me like gnats and stinging flies on my working days. 'Only let me take a few days in the country', I say to myself, 'and by some cool stream, or in some flowering wood, I will consider and resolve them all'. But when I get to the woods and streams, what do I do? All day I walk among the woods and hills, never considering these urgent matters, and in the evenings, I fish, standing knee-deep in the gently swirling stream, till the wild-duck and the woodpigeons have gone home, and the water has become black around me, and its gurgling has grown loud against the stillness of the light; and then I put up my rod and walk back, too tired to think, and throwing off my clothes, am asleep. And the books which I take on these felicitous holidays are unread, and the notes unscribbled that I have intended to write; and the gnats, that have disappeared during this brief sunshine period, will yet emerge again to pester me on my return.

Content to the mind, says the great Halifax, is as moss to a tree; it binds up so as to stop its growth. And Hobbes complained of Chatsworth that though there was a good library there, which the Earl of Devonshire stocked by his instructions, nevertheless the want of learned conversation was a very great inconvenience. Upon which Aubrey comments sadly (recalling, no doubt, the

---

54 Pen-y-Lan, Glasbury-on-Wye, shared with his heroin-dependent mother Enid, Countess of Kenmare.

tedium of that long, drunken 'delitescency' at Glasely Hall, Salop), 'Methinks in the country, in long time, for want of good conversation, one's understanding (wit, invention) grows mouldy'.

Lanthony

Leaving Glasbury early, I walked one day over the fields to Tregoyn, and percolating up steep, winding lanes, and over the moors, and up Lord Hereford's knob,[55] found myself in the Black Mountains; and there a stream arose, and walking down the valley I came to Capel-y-ffin, and later to Lanthony.

It was a long walk to an unimportant place, and the Abbey is only fit for picnic parties, and, what was most disappointing of all, there was only half-a-pint of beer left in the inn, when I arrived there, weary with the distance; and the climb up the mountain-side afterwards, in the high heather and the hot sun (for I was misdirected by the postman) was a serious strain on the temper; but no part of it could be omitted, for it was a sacred journey, a pilgrimage; and I had determined to make it from the moment I saw the name Lanthony marked on the map. For it was through Lanthony that I discovered the Scudamore Papers; one of my small, but personal, contributions to the totality of learning.

It happened thus:

Although the worthy Bliss[56] had done his work very thoroughly and collected a vast number of Archbishop Laud's letters from various MS and printed sources, he had somehow failed to notice Laud's early correspondence with Lord Scudamore,[57] which must therefore have been, in 18.., more than ordinarily inaccessible. But in 1727, these and the rest of the family papers had been gathering pious cobwebs in Holme Lacy, the mansion of the Scudamores in Herefordshire, and had been examined there by the nonjuring parson of

---

55 One of the Black Mountains in the Welsh borders.

56 James Bliss edited seven volumes of Laud's writings in the mid-nineteenth century.

57 John, 1st Viscount Scudamore (1601–1671), Ambassador to France: 'the remarkably studious, pious and hospitable life he led, made him respected and esteemed by all good men, especially by Bishop Laud, who generally visited him in going to and from his diocese of St David's' (Sir Bernard Burke).

the place, Matthew Gibson,[58] who, in that year, published a meritorious guide to his parish, and actually quoted from them. What had happened to them in the interim?

Long researches into the history and antiquities of Herefordshire had led me nowhere. My head was full of the names of county families, of Scudamores and Baskervilles, Mynors and Crofts, their Tudor houses, their topiary gardens, their conscientious proliferation. I knew much about careful pomiculture and devotion to lost causes, and virtuous squires and snobbish parsons; but I was no nearer the papers. Then I thought of pedigrees. Could it be that, after all, there are some useful ends to which the otherwise derisory labours of heralds and genealogists ultimately tend?

To think of heraldry is of course to think of Michael Maclagan, himself like some tall, but rather bedraggled heraldic bird, as he strolls round the gardens of Trinity College, ruminating on G.E.C.'s *Complete Peerage*, and deploring the rude health and interminable longevity of Rougedragon Herald and Clarenceiux King of Arms.[59] I found him in his richly emblazoned rooms, piously fingering the *Almanac de Gotha*, in tooled morocco; and after drinking a glass of sherry, and hearing about a few lords, his relatives, I asked him to get me out a pedigree of the Scudamore family; which he did, a grand and pompous scroll, embellished with a good deal of technical fustian about chevrons gules and wyverns prurient or; and after I had scrutinised it at length, and learned that the direct line of the noble family of Scudamore had died out, *sine prole*,[60] in 1820, with the mad Duchess of Norfolk,[61] and that the possessions had gone to the Stanhopes,[62] and that Holme Lacy had been sold, in 1901, to an Australian brewer called Lucas-Tooth[63] (for all these facts were added as garnish to the Pedigree), I wrote to Lord Chesterfield,[64] and he

---

58 Matthew Gibson, rector of Door, and author of *View of the Churches of Door, Holme Lacy and Hempsted* (1727).

59 Correctly Rouge Dragon Pursuivant and Clarenceux King of Arms.

60 Without issue.

61 Frances (1749–1820), granddaughter of 2nd Viscount Scudamore and heiress of Holme Lacy, became a lunatic soon after marrying Charles, 11th Duke of Norfolk.

62 Holme Lacy was inherited by the Duchess of Norfolk's cousin Sir Edwyn Stanhope, whose son succeeded as 9th Earl of Chesterfield in 1883.

63 Sir Robert Lucas-Tooth (1844–1915) bought Holme Lacy, with 3,396 acres, for about £200,000 in 1909 – not 1901.

64 Edward Stanhope, 12th and last Earl of Chesterfield (1889–1952).

replied courteously, saying no, he had no such papers; but he had relatives, a great number of them, and to them he forwarded my question, and perhaps I would hear from them; which was very civil of him.

After that, some months elapsed; and then, out of Yorkshire, came a letter written in the spidery but dogmatic handwriting of an ancient English dowager, unaccustomed to doubt or contradiction. She was Enid, Countess of Chesterfield,[65] and she knew where the papers were. They were in Chancery, she said; and she knew it because her husband had said so, about forty years ago, parenthetically; and her husband was always right. Why he had said so, and à propos of what, she had forgotten; but she was sure he had said so; and if he had said so, it was true.

But at the Public Record Office they said no; and the evidence that I produced from Yorkshire didn't seem convincing to those *Esprits de l'Escalier* in Chancery Lane.

Ultimately of course the old lady was vindicated; for it turned out that there was a large collection of documents called the Duchess of Norfolk's Deeds, in Chancery; and though they were uncatalogued, yet someone had recorded that a Cartulary of Lanthony Priory was among them; and at the utterance of that word I knew I was on the right track. For Lanthony (my researches into local history had established) had gone, after the Dissolution, and after the usual phases of speculative ownership, to the family of Porter; and the Porters had ended with an heiress who (according to the Pedigree) had married the first Lord Scudamore. So if a Cartulary of Lanthony Priory had got into the papers of the Duchess of Norfolk, it could only be by way of the Porters, and the Scudamores, and the mad Duchess. This evidence seemed more plausible to the PRO; and before long I had an order from the Lords of H.M. Privy Council, entitling me to view these otherwise inaccessible documents. So I came up to London, my flanks heaving with anticipation, like the Bicester bitches in full cry in the heavy-scenting Monday country, and put up at a Hotel round the corner; and every day, at stroke of 9.30, I arrived at the PRO, and rootled among those dusty boxes; and every now and then, like a truffling pig, I would utter a proud excited grunt as I extracted, out of the mass of private and diplomatic correspondence, and accounts and newsletters

---

65 Enid, Dowager Countess of Chesterfield (1878–1957) was a race-horse owner, breeder of Labradors, ardent in the hunting-field and excellent shot. Her husband, who had sold Holme Lacey to Lucas-Tooth, was Master of the Horse under the coalition ministry of 1915–1922.

of the past, bundles of letters of Thomas Cromwell,[66] or of Elizabeth's Earl of Essex,[67] or of Sir Thomas Bodley.[68]

It wasn't till the second time over that I found the missing letters of Laud. They had been endorsed 'Letters of Mr Meneven', which was at first deceptive (Laud's signature as bishop of St David's was Guil. Meneven). I printed them as an appendix to my book. The letters of Sir Thomas Bodley I have just sent to Creswick[69] for the *Bodleian Record*. The other papers await a catalogue.

Michael Maclagan was somewhat chagrined that I didn't mention him in the preface to my book; for the sight of his name in print always comforts him. I cannot feel quite guiltless in this matter. I ought to have done it.

Art and Political Power   August 1945

There is a theory, sometimes explicitly, often implicitly advanced, that the greatness of nations is in some way measurable by their culture, or commensurate with it.

There is no truth in this theory; none at all.

To be sure, the golden age of Athenian art and literature was the 5th century BC, and Spanish literature flourished with Spanish power; but it takes more than two coincidences to prove a general connexion.

What of Homer?

What of Lesbos in the 7th century BC, a faction-ridden island in which (incidentally) the poets were on the side of the doomed aristocratic reaction?

What of Dante, that disgruntled Ghibelline in the crumbling courts of Italy; and Leopardi and Goethe? What national greatness did they represent?

All these poets died, 'leaving great verse unto a little clan'.

---

66 Thomas Cromwell (d. 1540), architect of the Reformation and minister to Henry VIII, by whom he was created Earl of Essex and summarily executed as a traitor three months later.

67 Robert Devereux, 2nd Earl of Essex (1565–1601) of the 1572 creation; soldier and courtier, also executed.

68 Sir Thomas Bodley (1545–1613), diplomat and benefactor of Oxford university library.

69 Harry Creswick (1902–1988), Bodley's Librarian and Student of Christ Church 1945–1947, Librarian of Cambridge University and Professorial Fellow of Jesus College, 1949–1967.

And conversely, was not Rome great under the Antonines, and England under Queen Victoria, and Germany under Bismarck, and is not America great now? But what artists have these golden ages of power produced? When artists were born in them, they were snuffed out, or corrupted, like Tennyson and Millais.

There is clearly no basis for such a theory.

That scientific knowledge is commensurate with political power is a proposition worth examining; but art is a law unto itself. It happens.

———————

August 1945

I walked along the Wye one afternoon, upstream from Glasbury. It is a noble river, flowing, broad and stately, among those gentle, pastoral Welsh hills. Yes, it shall have its cult in my religion of Potamolatry. The bank was clothed with a kind of touch-me-not, a pink variety which I had not seen before (I think it doesn't grow in the north). I was in a nostalgic mood, for it was my last day; and as I strolled along the river-side, exploding the pods with my stick, I reflected upon that delightful valley, and asking myself whether any civilised life had ever thriven in these Welsh solitudes. I thought of the days before the civil wars, the days of the Cavaliers; and thinking of them I was suddenly aware of a new truth, hitherto concealed from men, but which I shall perhaps reveal to them: that the culture of that exquisite generation was to a large extent Welsh, or at least flourished in the quiet borderlands of Wales.

Not only in Wales, of course; for it flourished in England also; but in feudal England, in the north and west, and a few pockets elsewhere inaccessible to the new capitalist agriculture and industry. There its patrons still kept an old, almost medieval form of society, an ancient, but fading splendour, an obsolescent, wasteful economy, an antique hospitality; and there the culture of the humanist Renascence, the culture that had blossomed most fully under James I, still survived, a belated flowering, in those sheltered corners. For culture is different from ideas; culture is a way of life, and ideas are the explosive forces that break up that way of life. Culture lives in traditional haunts, a delicate, coloured flower, a poppy in a sheltered garden, whose petals are easily blown away; while ideas are like saxifrage, growing close to the present, stubby, unbeautiful, but hardy and hopeful plants.

So I began to think of those feudal Maecenases in their overgrown palaces. There were the Cavendishes, for instance: the wealth of the Reformation had doubtless swollen their fortunes, but it had not changed their lives in the remote wilds of Derbyshire.[70] And in the north, there were the Percies, declining in their crumbling castle of Warkworth ('this worm-eaten hold of ragged stone'),[71] and the other Cavendishes (for the magnificent Earl of Newcastle was Lord Ogle of Bothal in his mother's right);[72] and on the Welsh borders were Scudamores, and the Marquis of Worcester,[73] who kept up an impossible state at Raglan Castle, and numerous less splendid magnates. All these were cavaliers, romantic and unfortunate subjects; and it was at their courts, not at those of the great Puritan lords, that the humanist culture still survived. The Cavendishes patronised Hobbes who hunted and hawked with them, and celebrated, in Latin verse, the wonders of the Peak. The Earl of Northumberland[74] was the aristocratic centre of Hariot and his circle.[75] In Wales, the Marquis of Worcester, while he ruined himself for an ungrateful King, himself studied mechanics and hydrostatics, inventing gadgets and waterworks; the Carberies patronised Jeremy Taylor and Henry Vaughan;[76] the Conways Henry More and Jean-Baptiste van Helmont;[77] the Countess of Derby protected the fugitive Crashaw;[78] and it was at Carnarvon Castle that the still humanist Milton produced *Comus*, the

---

70 The Cavendish family, seated at Chatsworth in the Peak District, were created Earls of Devonshire in 1618 and Dukes of Devonshire in 1694.

71 The Percy family received the earldom of Northumberland in 1377, a new creation of the earldom in 1557, a third creation in 1749 and a dukedom in 1766.

72 William Cavendish, 1st Duke of Newcastle (1593–1676), royalist commander and great horseman, corresponded with Hobbes on the subject of flying.

73 Edward Somerset, 2nd Marquess of Worcester (1602–1667), royalist.

74 Henry Percy, 9th Earl of Northumberland (1564–1632) was imprisoned in the Tower of London 1605–1621 after the Gunpowder plot; a patron of mathematicians; chess player and pioneer tobacco smoker who died of cancer.

75 Thomas Harriot (1560–1621), a pensioner of Northumberland's, introduced the notations < and > and contemporaneously with Galileo constructed telescopes to study sun-spots and comets.

76 Jeremy Taylor lived at Golden Grove, Carmarthenshire, the seat of the royalist general Richard Vaughan, 2nd Earl of Carbery (*c.* 1601–1686), to whom Taylor dedicated *Holy Living* and *Holy Dying*. His son the 3rd Earl was Dryden's patron.

77 Jean-Baptiste van Helmont (1580–1644), alchemist, physician and philosopher.

78 Charlotte Stanley, Countess of Derby (1599–1663), whose husband was beheaded in 1651, defended Lathom House when it was besieged by 2,000 Parliamentarians.

finest of his early works. And the Metaphysical Poets, now that I thought of it, were Welsh too, Vaughan and Herbert and Traherne. Even John Aubrey, that epitome of the decayed and charming cavalier, who, fifty years later, as he hid in Shropshire from bailiffs and creditors, gathered the gossip of that sympathetic age,[79] – he too was half-Welsh, a cousin of Vaughan the Silurist, and had once, before his misfortunes, been a squire in Brecknockshire.

To all such societies, cultured, epicurean, Phaeacian societies, their crisis must come, when they are forced to face the present, and live in the present, and either adjust themselves to it, or flee from it into an unreality of their memories or their imagination. The society of the 1930s was not, after all, a corrupt society. In it too there were many delightful islands, where a cultured life was led and appreciated. But Munich came, Munich that gave the shock to both the hosts and the guests at those eloquent banquets, reminding both that the world had changed out of doors.

In the seventeenth century the cultured cavalier aristocracy and their cultured humanist guests faced their Munich too. It came, like ours, in a peaceful decade, a seemingly prosperous decade, the 1630s, when from all the passions and wars that distracted the Continent England seemed happily exempt. In the midst of that false prosperity, that artificial political calm, one by one, the great magnates had to choose their sides in the impending struggle, and risk the property which they had too long taken for granted; and the humanists too, one by one, had to make their choice, and adventure themselves in that world of ideas in which they had for so long been happy sojourners at others' expense. It was between 1630 and 1640, it seems, that Hobbes underwent his belated conversion from humanism to logical realism, and shedding, in one great divestment, the tolerant culture of his early years, became the uncompromising theorist of naked power. It was in 1637 that Milton, setting his juvenilities finally behind him, proclaimed himself, in *Lycidas*, no longer the poet of Arcadia but the prophet of political puritanism. While those gentler spirits, those less formidable, less systematic thinkers, turned aside from the cold, raw touch of this new reality, and in those gentle Welsh valleys, those last sanctuaries of the defeated, imagined for themselves their warmer, private

---

79 [T-R's footnote]: NB Aubrey's sources: 'old father Symonds'; 'old Sir Robert Harvey of Brampton Bryan Castle'; 'old cosen Whitney'; 'old Tho Tyndal'; 'old Major Cosh'.

worlds of esoteric mysticism. For Munich leads not only to the Battle of Britain, but to California.[80]

Friendship

'Friendship in the middle-classes', says Logan, 'is founded on respect; in the world of fashion they simply adore men and women whom one would not dream of trusting round the corner'. The lower classes too, in my experience, have their own individual form of friendship: it consists in doing things for each other.

Freud

In Germany, Herbert Hart and I were discussing Freud, and I explained how I had come at last to disown that crackpot old genius who once seemed so important in our lives. My conversion began in Burgundy, in the spring of 1939, when I read, in the *Psychopathology of Everyday Life*, that when we meet people in the street, and, seeking to step aside, find ourselves still opposite to them, we are unconsciously concealing from ourselves, but not from the acute psychologist, our irrepressible erotic impulses. At the time, I solemnly noticed and remembered this new truth; but afterwards, when, in the streets of Oxford, or Alnwick, or London, I found myself in such a predicament, and my way barred not by bright-eyed girls or irresistible ganymedes, but by bottle-nosed old porters, and somnolent sandwich-men, and corpulent, perspiring mothers-of-eight, then I felt that reason and experience failed to support this never very conclusively demonstrated theorem. And then I read *Traumdeutung*,[81] and lit upon a dream which the old boy was interpreting with a great show of expertise, and which, thanks to his brilliant analysis, was

---

80 Aldous Huxley, Christopher Isherwood and Gerald Heard left England before the war, and became votaries of Hollywood mysticism.

81 *Die Traumdeutung* was published by Freud in 1899, and is known in English as *The Interpretation of Dreams*.

obediently proving what was required of it. All went well up to a point; but at that point the supply of evidence seemed to have run out, the logical implications to have been exhausted. For a moment I doubted whether he would pull it off. The argument was becalmed; how would he set it in motion again? The master was equal to the occasion. 'Now the hat', he boldly stated, as one enumerating a truism, 'represents the human penis'. From that moment it was plain sailing again. A gentle wind had blown from the right quarter, the sails were filled again, and the ship slid into its appointed harbour; but my faith in the Freudian system had gone for ever. Like the Marxist system, it could prove anything.

'But have you read *Moses and Monotheism?*' asked Herbert; and he reminded me how, in that work, in which the history of the ancient Hebrews and the growth of their religion are psychologically deduced from the hypothetical neuroses of Moses, the evidence, at one point, seems similarly to have stopped short of the conclusion. Is Freud disconcerted? Not at all. 'At this point', he interposes casually, as if it were the most natural and reasonable thing in the world, 'it becomes necessary to conjecture that at the age of fifteen Moses lost, for a time, all sensitivity in his penis …' Again the calm is overcome, the wind has blown, the sails bulge once more, and the argument glides effortlessly home to its desired conclusion.

E.S.P. Haynes

I had written something on Hobbes in the *New Statesman*,[82] and received a letter about it from E.S.P. Haynes,[83] whose *Lawyer's Notebook* I had once read with pleasure; so when he invited me to come for a walk and then to have lunch with him, I accepted his invitation, and made my way, one Sunday morning

---

82 This full-page article in *New Statesman* of 28 July 1945 is reprinted in *Historical Essays*, 233–8.

83 Edmund Sidney Pollock Haynes (1877–1949), scholar of Eton and Balliol, a convivial solicitor with chambers in Lincoln's Inn, a man of wide reading and fixed routines, divorce-law reformer and libertarian, had in 1932 published *A Lawyer's Notebook* – modelled on Samuel Butler's. Lived at 38 St John's Wood Park until 1946, when he moved to Marlborough Hill; elected to the Athenæum in 1911.

in early September to his address in St John's Wood Park. I found his house, a large, dilapidated, Victorian house, in a derelict and overgrown region. A land-mine had destroyed the five houses on the right of it, and another five on the left, and he remained in the middle of this now jungled waste, the Casabianca (as he explained) of St John's Wood Park, still holding out against the owners of the site, the Eyre Estate I think, who, but for his obstinate resistance, would be able to clear the whole area and build lucrative modern flats. Not that his house was intact; far from it. The windows were broken; the walls bulged and cracked; here and there the roof gaped open; and as for the garden, only a bold and well-equipped explorer could cut his way through that tentacle wilderness to the pear-trees that were said still to struggle in its midst. When I rang the bell (which rang with a distant, cracked voice in some far chamber), the door was opened, and after a preliminary attack by a couple of large, unkempt, and vociferous dogs, there appeared a man so shabby and so dirty that at first I wondered whether this might be the gardener; but no – for no servant would be allowed to enter the house in such a condition, and anyway there was clearly no gardener; it must be, as it were, the master of the house. He was wearing an open-necked shirt which, when clean (but that was a long time ago) had been white; grey trousers, frayed, disintegrating, and indescribably dirty; his filthy black jacket gaped open down the seam and revealed a dirty white lining; his shoes were burst; and his puffy, pasty face emphasised, by a certain blotchy pallor, the universal dirtiness of his person. He took me indoors while we waited for his taxi, and I had leisure to examine the interior of his house. There were books everywhere, and furniture and pictures, some good, some bad, and old bottles and decanters and promiscuous miscellanea, and all covered with a thick coating of dust and cobwebs. The ceiling was missing in patches, and there were other signs of structural decrepitude; but that was presumably due to the bombs. When the taxi came, we motored to Ken Wood on Hampstead Heath, and walked there, the two dogs cavorting obscenely ahead of us. One of them, he explained, was inconvenienced by anal secretions, irresistible to dogs of all ages and sexes, which a weekly squeez-ing of its glands failed to cure. Then he talked, and his stories were always good. He showed me Lord Mansfield's house, and described the ingenious manoeuvre whereby that great lawyer had diverted the incendiary mob dur-ing the Gordon Riots. He told me of the great crisis which had convulsed, and nearly overthrown, the Athenæum, about 1850, in consequence of the dim and unilluminated urinoir in that respectable club. There was a radical journalist, he explained, called Roebuck,[84] who, every week, denounced the oppression of England by an insolent aristocracy; and this Roebuck, who was a very short man, happened to be quietly and conscientiously using the club urinoir one evening, when Lord Inniskilling,[85] snatching a moment from his potations, bounded in for the same purpose. Not seeing, in the dimness, the anyway inconspicuous Roebuck, already in operation, he set to work, and owing to the difference in stature (for Lord Inniskilling was of gigantic build), directed a ferocious jet down the journalist's neck. Explanations were useless. To the injured Roebuck this was but another instance of deliberate aristocratic insolence; he demanded the expulsion of Lord Inniskilling from the club; his hebdomadal eloquence became fiercer than ever; the members of the club took sides according to their politics; and it was several months before a compromise was achieved, by the statesmanlike formula that the constitution of the club had not provided for such an incident. So he talked on, and I liked his conversation, and was beginning to like him for it, and then, suddenly, the wind would shift, or our own relation to it change, and that smell would impinge on my perhaps too sensitive nostrils, the smell that I associate with Algiers, the smell against which the fastidious cardinal Wolsey fortified himself with fragrant pomanders, but against which I was, alas, quite defenceless.

Our walk over, we stepped into the taxi and returned to his house; and entering it through the vast kitchen I there became aware of a new characteristic of this strange old man; for there we found two ancient but benevolent creatures actively preparing food and condiments, peeling garlic and blending sauces with old fashioned industry and Cockney observations and a mixture of savoury smells which quite drowned all more habitual malodours; and from their conversation, which was incessant, it became clear that the old man had the low-life of St John's Wood Park properly organised, and that such excellent Dickensian characters could always be relied on to drop in and perform occasional menialities for the sake of so popular an old gentleman. My opinion of him was going up again, when he said that he must go and wash, and invited me to accompany him to his bedroom and there continue

---

84 The radical MP John Roebuck (1802–1879) was never elected to the Athenæum.

85 William Cole, 3rd Earl of Enniskillen (1807–1886). In 1826, while an undergraduate at Christ Church, he determined to amass the finest collection of fish fossils in the world, and travelled extensively to fulfil this aim. He housed the fossils in a pavilion at Florence Court, county Fermanagh. This great palaeontologist was elected to the Athenæum in 1830.

our conversation while he went through this much-needed ceremony. So I observed him remove his insanitary clothes, hopeful of seeing a change; but after a scamped ablution, he put on the same disgusting clouts again, and we went down to lunch. On the way down we passed an open door, and through it I saw a bedroom, swept and tidy, spotlessly clean, an incredible exception in this house of dirt and decay. 'My wife's bedroom', he said casually; and I realised how narrow was the empire of Mrs Haynes in this great masculine mausoleum. The lunch was quite admirable; excellent roast beef, perfectly cooked, and quantities of everything; for the entire table was so loaded with side-dishes and sauces that there was barely room for the two of us to sit at one end of it; and we dashed off a bottle of sherry, and one of claret, and half a decanter of port. At the end of it, I felt thoroughly reconciled to the old man, and although I declined interest in the library of works on flagellation which he offered to show me, I found myself promising him a bottle of college port, and left him, snoring rather loudly in one of his disintegrating armchairs, on the best of possible terms. All the same, though I sent him the port, I find I have not yet resumed personal contact. I must first get a pomander.

The Death of Hitler

On November 1st 1945 I held a press-conference in the Hotel am 200 in Berlin, and told the assembled correspondents that they could abandon their feverish search for Hitler in gothic grottos in the Alps, and lonely Bavarian latifundia, or castle-crowned rocks, and mist-enshrouded islands in the Baltic sea. He was dead; dead, burnt, and dissipated on April 30th 1945; and then I expounded the newly established truths of that dark, and hitherto unexplored, period from April 22nd until the Russians captured the Chancellery in Berlin.

It was a fascinating piece of historical research – a fig for Archbishop Laud; he never led me, or could have led me, on those delightful journeys, motoring through the deciduous golden groves of Schleswig-Holstein, and coming, on an evening, when the sun had just set but the light had not yet gone, and the wild duck were out for their last flight over the darkening waters, to the great Danish castle of Ploen, gazing like a sentinel over those white autumnal lakes. Of the compotations and conviviality which were a necessary part of my researches it is not necessary to speak; all the same, I had deeper and more hilarious bouts over Hitler than ever I had over Laud.

The whole business, now that I think of it, began in a bottle; for it was when I was drinking hock with Dick White and Herbert Hart in Bad Oeynhausen that my researches were first instituted. I was interested in the subject, and from a variety of casual sources had picked up a good deal of unsystematic information, some right, some wrong; and over the third bottle of hock I was drawing on this reservoir of conversational raw-material, and was telling rather a good story, as I thought (though I have since discovered that it was thoroughly inaccurate) about the last highly charged days in Hitler's Bunker. 'But this is most important!' exclaimed Dick, his eyes popping, as they sometimes do, out of universal eagerness of spirit. 'No one has yet made any systematic study of the evidence, or even found any evidence, and we are going to have all kinds of difficulty unless something is done. Already the Germans are saying that the old boy's alive, and the journalists are encouraging them, and the Russians are accusing us of concealing Eva Braun.' So he asked me if I would accept the job, and of course I said yes, although I was already overwhelmed with commitments, having promised to polish off the entire German Intelligence Service in a month, as well as to make a full study of German economic espionage (which fortunately I already knew to have been negligible). So I simply sent a message to London to cancel my Class B release and reckoned on dealing later with the inevitable plaints of my numerous, but easily manageable superiors; and then I went straight to Frankfurt to interrogate Albert Speer,[86] and start, at last, the systematic process of first establishing who was present in the Bunker during those days, and, secondly, of finding and cross-examining those whose presence had been established. How easy all problems are, how infallibly the darkest mystery yields to the deadly force of pure reason! Admittedly the full details aren't yet available, since I missed Frau Christian,[87] Hitler's secretary, by eight days when I called at her mother-in-law's house at Ebernburg, among the rock-sheltered vineyards of the Palatinate;

---

86 Albert Speer (1905–1981), Reich Minister of Armament and War Production, whom T-R found a reliable informant.

87 Gerda Daranowski (1913–1997) was working as a secretary for Elizabeth Arden's cosmetics business when she was recruited to Hitler's staff in 1937. She married Eckhard Christian of the Luftwaffe in 1943. She and her fellow secretary Traudl Junge declined poison capsules before escaping the bunker. She was captured and raped by Russian soldiers.

and if the Americans hadn't obstinately forgotten how they had disposed of SS Hstup Helmuth Beerman,[88] of Hitler's SS Begleitkommando, whom they captured, I would not be deploring the loss of the most valuable witness of all. As for the Russians, they hold Hans Baur,[89] Hitler's pilot, and captured Johann Rattenhuber,[90] head of the Reichssicherheitsdienst, who gave orders for the burial of the bodies; but it is unlikely that any information, or civility, will be forthcoming from those incompetent and obstructive barbarians of the East; who incidentally left Hitler's diary unnoticed in his chair for five months, until a British officer picked it up.[91] Nevertheless, the main lines are certain; there is enough to convince any rational being; I have examined all alternative versions and found them pure myth; I believe that I have even silenced the journalists, those indefatigable mythologists; and I hope, in time, to complete the story as the evidence comes in. It's a pity Pontius Pilate didn't crack a bottle of Ksara wine with (say) Gallio[92] in the year 30 AD; a systematic cross-examination of the eleven apostles, the guards of the sepulchre, the soldiers, high-priests, and miscellaneous women, might have prevented a great deal of error. But then Pontius Pilate was far less intelligent than Dick White.

Gilbert

In my studies of character, I like to detect dominant motives: love of ease, or of power, or of money; the desire to please, the quest of security, the need of sexual gratification. These irrational but necessary impulses are, to me, the keys to character, the mainsprings of life, the directing force of reason, and when they cease to operate, life itself has no meaning, no motive power, and must cease. But I must confess that Gilbert baffles me, for he alone, of all

---

88 Helmut Beermann (b. 1911) of the Fuehrerbegleitkommando (Hitler's SS bodyguard).

89 T-R interviewed Hans Baur (1897–1993) in October 1955 after his return from Russian captivity.

90 T-R interviewed Johann Rattenhuber (1897–1957), who commanded Hitler's bodyguard, in October 1955 after his release by the Russians.

91 This refers to Hitler's appointments diary, a copy of which is preserved in the Dacre papers.

92 Junius Annaeus Gallio (d. AD 65), Seneca's brother.

the characters I know, seems totally without any such impulses. Of all the specimens in my album, he alone is an entire neuter. Religion, that great complex of human irrationalities, the dionysiac element of the mind, has never touched him. Brought up as an atheist, he has never deviated into belief or persisted into fanaticism. Even as an undergraduate, he maintained what he calls his 'casual but hygienic attitude towards the verities'. 'Religion', he once declared, 'is the protest of man against the non-existence of God'; and against such non-existence he, being a rational, negative man, feels no need to protest. Art to him is a racket, poetry a racket, even the moon has, at times, been pronounced a racket. Music is so many centuries of misdirected energy. Personal relations have no importance to him; he never corresponds; he has compared himself to a banyan tree, of whose many roots none is indispensable. He is quite imperturbable; through years of intimacy I have never known him ruffled. His mind is like a perfect sausage-machine: so long as the offal is put steadily in, the processes work, and the sausages come steadily out, – very good sausages too, well-formed, nutritious and highly flavoured. The machinery never breaks down, never even creaks. But no offal, no sausages; and he cannot supply the offal himself, it must be introduced from without. He is completely dependent on external direction; left to himself he has no resources but boredom and sleep. He will not even take a day off unless it is arranged for him; 'unorganised leisure is such a bore.' Take away his work, and give him no substitute for it, and he is becalmed; he does not know how to get through the day.

Reelkirchen

'It's a colonial life', said Dick, 'it has many pleasures, an easy, splendid life; but it would be fatal to take it for granted: it is artificial, and closes up the mind. Better to live in a two-roomed flat in foodless, servantless, overcrowded, undersupplied England, where there is at least some pressure on the mind. Life in Kenya is doubtless like this; but look at the people who come back from Kenya, and see what Kenya has done for them.'

We were sitting in his elegant *Schloss* at Reelkirchen in Lippe-Detmold, a fine 18th century country house, not too large, moated and walled about, at the foot of the Teutoburg Hills. He had expelled a tiresome German baron from it, Baron von Studnitz I think,[93] a pretentious globe-trotting superficial snobbish toadying friend of Ribbentrop, and had introduced a hotelier and his family, whose hotel in Rheydt had been destroyed, and who now, as his servants, had no ambition but genuinely to ensure that he and his guests wanted nothing. At that moment they were arranging copious *Vorspeise* on the table, and bringing in an adequacy of slender bottles, while we sat, after our walk, round a huge log-fire, and the golden September sunlight flowed in through the stately windows; then the whole family, bowing obsequiously like a cornfield in a breeze, with a rustle of *Bitte schön* and *Herr Brigadier*, announced the preliminaries of a five-course lunch.

All that Dick says is true; nevertheless, the days that I have spent at Reelkirchen are amongst the happiest in my recollection. On my first visit, Klop was there too, which added to the pleasure of it. Klop is Ustinov.[94] He is, or was, a Russian, a member of that most attractive, educated, civilised, cosmopolitan, but politically ineffective class which survives in the pages of Tolstoy and Turgeniev: the intellectual aristocracy of old Europe, the pre-revolutionary Russian upper-class, who now, like disembodied ghosts, wander homeless in western Europe, their palaces and country houses abandoned to the more practical rule of uncivilised, ruthless Red Millionaires.

Klop's father was very rich, and his mother brought into the family a monopoly of the most exquisite caviar in Russia. In 1914, when war was

---

93 Hans-Georg von Studnitz (1907–1993), an official in the press bureau of the German Foreign ministry 1939–1945, had married Marietti Freein von Mengersen. Reelkirchen (Lippe) belonged to August von Mengersen. The Studnitz family, including a daughter, retreated to Reelkirchen to escape the bombing of Berlin in the later stages of the war. A translation of his diaries of 1943–1945 was published under the title *While Berlin Burns* by George Weidenfeld in 1964.

94 Jonah Freiherr von Ustinov (1892–1962) detested his forename and was always known as 'Klop', the Russian for bedbug. Born in Jaffa; educated in Palestine, Dusseldorf, Yverdon, Grenoble, and Humboldt University in Berlin. Served as a German aviator in the First World War, and then worked in Amsterdam for Wolff's, the German news agency. Married in 1920 the painter Nadia Benois, whose mother was the product of an affair between a Swiss engineer and the daughter of Emperor Theodore II of Abyssinia; Sir Peter Ustinov the actor was their son. Klop was a long-serving press officer in the German Embassy in London until dismissal in 1935 on suspicion of Jewish ancestry. He was in 1935 recruited by MI5 for whom he apparently worked until 1957 (agent U35 in Guy Liddell's diaries). Peter Ramsbotham stated that Klop provided the list of British Nazi sympathisers which resulted in the arrests under Regulation 18B in 1940. Dick White called him the 'best and most ingenious operator I had the honour to work with'.

declared, Klop's father summoned his sons before him and told them the facts. 'War has broken out between Germany and Russia', he explained. 'I am a cosmopolitan. I do not believe in dynastic or national wars, and naturally I don't expect my sons to be prejudiced by irrational loyalties. If you wish to enlist, your choice will doubtless be guided by intellectual motives.' Thereupon this old Russian courtier made a brief but luminous survey of the financial position, explaining in scholarly detail the origins and contingencies of the fortune they had all hitherto taken for granted, and of which by far the greatest part, as was now clear, came from investments in Germany.

Fortified with this relevant knowledge, Klop took the decision taken by enlightened self-interest and fought in the first German war in the German air-force. He is now an Englishman, with a beautiful great country-house in England; and his psychological skill has been invaluable to our Intelligence throughout the war.

For Klop has a general theory, a theory which others may indeed hold, but which he alone can personally demonstrate. He believes that every man, even the most silent, the most desperate, the most costive, can always be persuaded to tell the truth. It is true that many resist, that many are inhibited, that some prefer silence, and some lies, so that interrogators often suppose the truth to be unobtainable from them. But that, says Klop, is a heresy; for in every man, whatever his superficial variations, there is, without any exception, a spring of veracity which, once found and tapped, will always play. If an interrogator says that a man has no such spring, he merely means that his own technique has failed to lead him thither; but the spring is there all the same, and Klop, by his inexplicable psychological water-divining, will soon discover it, and inserting the point of his spade, will cause the dry desert earth suddenly to open, and a fresh jet of limpid truth to bubble up.

Of course it is only for difficult and interesting cases that we use Klop; for common spies and thugs and criminals, Tin-Eye Stephens,[95] that harsh

---

95 During the war the monocled, xenophobic Robin ('Tin-Eye') Stephens (b. 1900) ran camp 020 at Latchmere House, Ham, where captured German agents were interrogated and broken. He had previously worked in the Judge Advocate's department in India and for the National Fitness Council. In an internal MI5 history, he declared that 'a first-class interrogator' must have 'an implacable hatred of the enemy'. After Germany's capitulation, he took charge of the interrogation centre in the lower Saxony spa of Bad Nenndorf, where conditions were so cruel that he was court-martialled in 1947. After his acquittal, which he partly owed to Dick White, he was recruited by MI5 and sent to Accra, 1948.

illiterate bruiser, is quite enough. One doesn't chop faggots with a razor. But for Zech-Nenntwich, for Schellenberg, even for the desperate Kaltenbrunner, Klop was our man; after a short and civilised preamble, in Klop's country house, or in a well-furnished London flat, the springs would break suddenly forth, and the buckets would be filled, and those astonishing tales of incomprehensible ideals and feverish conspiracy would be brought home to water our knowledge of life in Nazi Germany. When I met him at Reelkirchen, it was Hilger[96] whom Klop had come out to handle. Hilger had been German Minister in Moscow from about 1920 till 1941, when he had indiscreetly warned Ribbentrop of the dangers of war with Russia; whereupon he had been recalled and had disappeared into a concentration-camp. Now, in 1945, he had emerged blinking into the sunlight again to meet a small, sympathetic and totally spherical gentleman who asked him whether he did not remember an incident in Petrograd in 1917, when a little man was about to be shot, and Hilger had interceded for him with the sanguinary Bolsheviks, and he had been spared. No, said Hilger, still blinking, and not yet quite able to sort out the epochs in his complicated and changing career. Well, said Klop, I sha'n't forget it, for I was the little man; and thereupon the conversational preamble began; and at exactly the right moment Klop inserted the point of his spade where he saw a weakening of the soil, and the spring broke through and sent up a great jet into the air, and Klop caught it in a bucket as it fell, and now he had brought his shining bucket to Reelkirchen, and we listened, as we drank our Apfelsaft, to the details and the causes and the meaning of the Russo–German pact of 1939. Then we spoke of more general topics, and I realised, as often since, that Klop is after all a feminine character, and his

---

96 Gustav Hilger (1886–1965) was born in Moscow of German parents and trained as a construction engineer. He was interned in Russia as an enemy alien during the First World War; afterwards worked for the German Red Cross and Nansen relief agency repatriating German prisoners-of-war from Soviet Russia. Following the restoration of German–Russian diplomatic relations in 1923, he was appointed to the German Embassy in Moscow and remained there until the German invasion of 1941. He was Ribbentrop's interpreter in the negotiations with Molotov and Stalin which resulted in the Nazi–Soviet pact of 1939; afterwards Ribbentrop's adviser on Russian affairs. Captured at Salzburg on 19 May 1945, caged with other prisoners at Mannheim, he was transported to the US, and incarcerated for nine months at Fort Meade undergoing interrogation. At the time of the Nuremberg trials he was working in Germany on projects supervised by US Army Counter-Intelligence. He worked at CIA headquarters for several years until 1953 when he took up an official post in the German Foreign Office; sought as a war criminal by the Soviets, who took his wife and daughters as hostages.

wonderful skill in eliciting confidence has its intellectual counterpart in a too personal view of all matters, making his political judgment particularly quite negligible; for his political friends, one must admit, belong to that declining class to which he also, when he had a class, had belonged: the faded aristocratic demi-monde of continental Europe. Still, we laughed at his solution of the German problem, – 'I want the Germans to be not only a pastoral people', he explained, looking more ridiculous than ever as his hands opened like petals in the sunshine, 'but an opium-smoking people'. Then I asked him about Wilhelm Keppler,[97] a cracked economist, the leading spirit of the so-called *Freundeskreis des RfSS*, whom I had interrogated in a cell at Oberursel; and Klop, who knows everyone, knew Keppler too, and told me his story: how Keppler's mother had once heard a knock on her door, and opening it, had seen a wild man, with wild eyes in a bedraggled raincoat, who had walked in and stood by the fire, and, without removing his raincoat, had delivered a speech lasting 2½ hours; and Frau Keppler hearing it, had believed that here surely was a messenger from God, and whenever the wild man came to that town again, she had put him up and ministered to him; and how, when the wild man had become Führer of Germany, he had sent to Frau Keppler and asked what reward she would choose, and she had replied, 'Mein Führer, I have a son, Willi, who is not very intelligent, and whom I would fain see landed in a safe job'; so Wilhelm Keppler was made the Führer's economic advisor, and (as a parergon) expert on Eastern affairs in the German Foreign Office, and was sent to London to the World Economic Conference in 1933. There, inevitably, he met Klop, circulating among his cosmopolitan friends in the antechambers, and Klop asked him about this new leader who had arisen to control the destinies of Germany, what sort of a man was he? Whereupon a light from heaven had gleamed in Keppler's eyes, and he had replied, '*Der Führer hat eine Antenne direkt aus dem lieben Gott.*'[98]

My second visit to Reelkirchen was later in the same September, and Peter

---

97 Wilhelm Keppler (1882–1960) was a banker and manufacturer whom Himmler introduced to Hitler: there is no substantiation of Klop's story about his mother. Elected to the Reichstag in 1933, appointed Reich Commissioner for economic affairs and Reich Commissioner in Austria after the Anschluss. Assisted Göring in implementing the Four Year Plan (1936); Obergruppenführer of SS (1942), sentenced to ten years' imprisonment (1949), but released through US clemency.

98 The Fuhrer has an antenna direct from dear God; but in *Last Days of Hitler*, T-R quotes Keppler as saying *direkt zum* – an antenna direct up to dear God.

Ramsbotham[99] was there, one of the most sympathetic and companionable of my friends; and he and Dick and I walked all morning over the gently rolling Teutoburg Hills, talking of abstract propositions, such as Truth and Validity, and concrete propositions, such as the Canons of Christ Church, for ten unnoticed miles; and when we came back, already the *Vorspeise* were being laid on the table, and the slender bottles were being carried deferentially forward, like aristocratic infants being passed up to the font; and after lunch Peter and I withdrew to bed for our siestas, as a gentleman must, and while we slept, there came a captain to the *Schloss* and wished to requisition it, and addressed himself to Dick, who was sitting by the fire in his shirt-sleeves reading some of my papers on life in the *Führerbunker*. For half-an-hour, Dick told us afterwards over the cakes and cognac, they had discussed the matter, and Dick had turned this way and that to save the *Schloss*. Of course, he said, it wasn't full now, – it was after all the week-end; he only had two of his staff officers in the next two rooms (he didn't say they were both fast asleep). Finally he had prevailed. 'But do you mean to say', we asked, 'that you argued with the man? Don't you realise you're a brigadier? You should have ordered him away!' Dick opened his eyes in sudden realisation of the obvious. 'Good heavens!', he said, 'I had forgotten about that. I treated him as a rational being and discussed the case on its merits ...'

'A fig for Dick's melancholy theories', I thought to myself as I left that delightful spot; 'it's the company, not the setting, that makes life colonial or provincial, and with such company I would live happily in Uganda'; and since Dick held to his views, and left Germany for the life of a harassed official in uncomfortable old England again, I held to mine, and missing his company there, never went to Reelkirchen again on any of my later visits to Germany. For I did not wish to spoil such delightful recollections by a repetition in less perfect circumstances; remembrance of felicity is too rare and precious to be thus lightly jeopardised. Besides, there came a Bostonian American to the Schloss, of ossifying wealth and smug republican principles, who sinned against the basic principle of society by supposing that there are some subjects which may not be mentioned or discussed, – such as sex, or religion, or President Roosevelt, whose name (he observed with satisfaction) had never

---

99 (Sir) Peter Ramsbotham (1919–2010), T-R's lifelong friend. Lt Colonel in the Intelligence Corps 1943–1946, Allied Control Commission in Germany 1947–1950, Ambassador to Iran 1971–1974 and to USA 1974–1977; active in disaster relief.

been uttered in his family for fifteen years. Wretched young prig, how could he ever breathe the same air as Klop? Of course he didn't for long. One day Klop came thither when he was there, and seeing on one of the walls a pietistic picture in the style of Salvator Rosa of a rapturous, upward-looking virgin pressing the point of an arrow to her naked breast, remarked that it was clearly of phallic significance; whereupon a cold damp cloud of silent disapproval descended upon the place, stifling all breath and talk. And when Klop mentioned that his family, after the Revolution in Russia, in a fit of idealism, had renounced their caviar monopoly to the new glorious free republican Russia, the Bostonian (Klop afterwards said), hearing the sacred principles of private property thus dishonoured, looked at him with the outraged eyes of a bigot who has heard the sacrament blasphemed, in silent indignation.

———————

Having dealt with Hitler, I returned to England. I saw my friends, cracked several bottles with them, polished off a few items of work, had my mare clipped for the hunting, got up my car, collected some petrol, and motored to Oxford in the highest of spirits, looking forward, after a suburban life in Barnet, and an urban life in London, and a colonial life in Germany, to books and drink and intellectual society once more.

How delightful it seemed as I walked down the Broad again on a clear, cold November day, and allowed my eye to rest on a decaying nose of one of our Roman emperors who guard the Sheldonian theatre. How exhilarating is the intellectual life, how buoyant the air of a learned place, how beautiful its architecture and associations. I looked forwardly to a fresh taste of this, as it now seemed, half-forgotten flavour, and settled down with enthusiasm to a life in Christ Church.

The first night I sat next to Keith Feiling. He expounded his views on the cosmos. 'The outlook is very black', he said gloomily, filling a large glass brimful of port; 'there is no faith, no hope, no morals; and the political situation is worse, infinitely worse than in 1938'. 1938 of course means Neville Chamberlain, and since Feiling evidently thought Chamberlain a more inspiring topic, I enquired about his researches into the life of his hero. He brightened a little at first; his studies had convinced him, he said, that Chamberlain was an even greater man than he had supposed. He had now finished his book, and it was in the hands of the printer. Had he, I asked, heard of Gen. Halder's revelations, of which a summary had appeared in the Press, and which bore so vitally on the whole question of Munich? No, he replied, he knew nothing of that; and when I explained the significance of this new evidence – how a plot by the German General Staff might have overthrown Hitler's government in September 1938 but for Chamberlain's too eager compliance, he looked suddenly bored with the whole affair, so I turned tactfully to my other neighbour, Michael Foster.[100] He (I had already learnt) had just refreshed a meeting of the Governing Body with an inspiring speech on the subject of the proposed undergraduates' dance. We must understand, Foster had said, that we are now in a new era; that there is to be a new Heaven and a new Earth and a new Christ Church, for the former things have passed away; in future (he had emphasised with melancholy relish) there will be no drink and no dances and no gaudies and no pleasure of any kind at all; and as a supererogatory mortification he had suggested that the dons should in future have the same food as the undergraduates. Knowing of this recent utterance, I determined to avoid any contentious subject, and merely asked him about recent contributions to philosophy – for I had just obtained K.R. Popper's book, *The Open Society and its Enemies*, which seemed to me an important work.[101] Had Oxford, I asked, produced any contribution to Truth in this subject? Foster said he had not heard of Popper; but he considered that the most important constructive philosopher in England today was undoubtedly C.S. Lewis. I was struck dumb, and in the silence overheard a voice further down the table (it was the voice of Sir Max Page)[102] saying: 'Of course we can't *shoot* those people at Nuremberg; some formula will have to be found to get them off.' Next morning I turned up for breakfast in a chastened mood, and heard without astonishment Feiling's remark that Arthur Bryant was 'growing every year in stature', and the complacent announcement from someone else that an undergraduate who had refused to be confirmed at Eton was now supplicating for that important spiritual experience.

---

100 Michael Foster (1903–1959), D.Phil from University of Kiel, lecturer in philosophy at Aberdeen University until elected in 1930 as tutor in philosophy at Christ Church – later Censor. A puritanical Christian, cripplingly shy and defensive, he gassed himself in his college rooms.

101 (Sir) Karl Popper (1902–1994), philosopher, had published *The Open Society and its Enemies* in 1945. T-R reviewed it in *Polemic*, a journal of philosophy and aesthetics associated with Ayer.

102 Major General Sir Max Page (1882–1963), Consulting Surgeon to the Metropolitan Police and the Army.

What a set of old crashers! I said to myself; shall I ever stick it out? And my heart, that volatile organ, sank heavily down towards my stomach, which itself was feeling weak and hollow after a Christ Church breakfast; and I wondered why I had ever returned to this world of disconsolate reactionary gloom. But that night at last I knew there would be a change, for Hookie Hill[103] was coming to dine, whom for four years I had dismissed as dead, but who in fact had been a prisoner of the Japanese, working on the Death Railway in Malaya and Siam, where he had buried most of his companions, but himself had survived. From him at least I could expect a breath of the old world, – and yet, I reflected, could I really be sure? For suffering and captivity work hardly on a man's mind, which fact the clergy (so Robert Blake[104] assures me) ruthlessly exploit.

Hookie arrived, and though his skin was yellowed, and his hair grey, he seemed well, and I asked him about his experiences. I am a different man now, he said; and I trembled to hear the words. But having begun, I felt I must persevere, and know the worst, so I bade him speak freely of the spiritual experience to which he referred. 'In my prison-camp', he replied meditatively, 'I had leisure to consider many things which I hadn't thought of before'. I pressed him further. To what particular reorientation of his thought did he refer? 'Well', said Hookie, 'I have now decided that if I were condemned to drink only one wine for the rest of my life, I would choose Burgundy'. A great cloud rolled away from my spirit as I heard this sane answer, and I said, 'but come, Hookie, there are some excellent clarets'. 'I thought of that too', he answered, 'and I know my answer to that: there hasn't been a decent claret since 1892'.

After that my spirits rose, and when I learnt from J.C. Masterman that Hookie has applied as steward, I decided that if he came here, I could perhaps stay here after all.

---

103 Denys Vivian ('Hooky') Hill (1896–1971), captained Worcestershire at cricket 1928, lived in Christ Church 1934–1938 as adjutant of the Oxford University Officers Training Corps. In 1941 he commanded the mobile anti-aircraft defences in Malaya, was a Japanese prisoner-of-war working on the Death Railway 1942–1945, where he gave heroic aid to fellow prisoners; a cheerful, efficient Steward from 1945.

104 Robert Blake (1916–2003) was appointed (with tactical help from T-R) to succeed Frank Pakenham as lecturer in politics at Christ Church in 1946. As Student and tutor in politics at Christ Church 1947–1968 he became a staunch ally of T-R in university intrigues. A historian of the Conservative Party: appointed Provost of the Queen's College in 1968 and to a peerage in 1971.

1946

The first post-war year saw Trevor-Roper consolidate his reputation as an expert on the last days of Hitler. Logan Pearsall Smith died three months into 1946: 'to the last he was giving what he described as "hilarious death-bed cocktail parties, 6–7 daily, only sincere mourners and earnest-minded legacy-hunters invited",' as Trevor-Roper told Charles Stuart on 14 March.

Hitler's Will [1946]

I had been in Oxford about ten days only when the ghost of Hitler called me back again to Germany. I received a telephone-message: a document had been found which seemed to be Hitler's will; was it genuine? Now I knew that Hitler had written a will, for among Dönitz's papers found at Flensburg there was a telegram which referred to it, giving its date (29 April) and some of its contents, and Dönitz himself had spoken of a written document confirming his authority, which had been addressed to him but had been lost on its way from Berlin to Flensburg. So when I looked at a photostatic copy of this newly found document, and found it consistent with my knowledge, I was predisposed to believe it genuine, and stepping into an airplane I flew to Germany to learn the full tale of its discovery.

The bearer of the document was Heinz Lorenz, the representative of the DNB in Hitler's Bunker.[1] He had been questioned long since and had babbled

---

1 Heinz Lorenz (1913–1985) was press secretary in Hitler's bunker in April 1945.

inconsistently and incoherently about the last days, of which, he hinted, he had marketable knowledge. But since he claimed to be a Luxembourg journalist called George Thiers, and could give no reasons for the knowledge that he claimed, he was ignored until one day, his mendacity having come home to roost, he was arrested, and in the course of search the document was discovered, sewn in the lining of his coat. Interrogated, Lorenz told his whole story, how he had left the Bunker with two companions, each carrying a set of documents, Willi Johannmeier[2] and Wilhelm Zander,[3] whom he had last seen in Hanover in May. I had never heard speak of Zander, but the name of Johannmeier was familiar to me: he had been General Burgdorf's assistant in the Bunker.[4] I therefore believed that Lorenz was telling the truth and resolved to pursue the other witnesses of it.

Johannmeier was soon found. He was living quietly with his parents at Iserlohn. I had him detained and interrogated; but he denied everything. He had never been in the Bunker at all, he said. He had been in hospital at the end of the war, and the *Zusammenbruch* had caught him on his way to rejoin his unit. Dissatisfied, I went myself to Iserlohn, and at last, after long questioning, he admitted that he had been in the Bunker, and that his first story had been untrue. But of Hitler's will, he said, he knew nothing, nothing at all. He had been ordered to escort two men, Lorenz and Zander, through the Russian lines. He had understood them to be the bearers of documents to Dönitz and Schoerner,[5] but of what documents it was not his business to know. He was simply a soldier detailed, as one practised in such adventures, to be their escort. From this second version of his story it was quite impossible to move him. Even my last gambit, suddenly to pass him the document itself, had no effect. With mask-like features he turned the pages and looked curiously at the contents. No, he said, he had never seen it before; and he handed it back. Having seen the secret document, he now had to be kept apart from the other prisoners, and he disappeared into solitary confinement. After I had

---

2 Willi Johannmeier (1915–1970), an army adjutant in Hitler's bunker.

3 Wilhelm Zander (1911–1974), Bormann's adjutant.

4 Wilhelm Burgdorf (1895–1945), Hitler's chief adjutant, killed himself two or three days after his master.

5 Ferdinand Schoerner (1892–1973), responsible for Nazification of the German army, promoted to Field Marshal in 1945 and charged with defending Berlin from the Russian advance; a savage disciplinarian who was imprisoned by the Russians for war crimes and by the Germans for the manslaughter of four soldiers.

gone, Brunnarius, who was in charge of the camp at Iserlohn, interrogated him again; but he got no further, and reported to HQ that he was convinced that Johannmeier's second story was the truth.

Meanwhile at HQ another drama was being unfolded. The Major General Intelligence, Gen. Lethbridge,[6] had seen the document, and seeing it, like all brass-hats when faced with a document, he had quailed; and when asked whether it should be treated as secret or public, he had shrunk trembling from such a decision, and passed the question up to the Chief of Staff. And the Chief of Staff had also trembled, and had referred the question still further, back to London, to the JIC. When I had returned empty-handed from Iserlohn to Bad Oeynhausen, Peter Ramsbotham told me of these developments, and we agreed, over a bottle of hock, that this deplorable pusillanimity must be overcome by action: for on the JIC the irrelevant voice of old Menzies would be raised, timidly demanding suppression; 'and yet this', said Peter, 'is a historical document. Who are these brass-hats that they should feebly demand the suppression of historical documents?'

Hereupon I made a proposal. 'Give me a car', I said, 'for ten days, and I will go to the American Zone and look for Zander (for Zander's home was in Munich), and if I should find him and his documents I should of course have to hand the documents over to the American authorities; and if they should choose not to suppress but to publish them, that would be too bad, but it would be no business of ours: for the choice is theirs.' When I look back on it, I am astonished at this proposal, for all the evidence we had collected about Zander showed that he was missing. His wife and mother-in-law in Hanover had given us photographs and addresses and referees, but all led nowhither. Zander had set out from Hanover in May, and had never been heard of since; he had disappeared. I had absolutely no reason to suppose that I should find him.

Still, I said to myself, there is no reason to suppose that I sha'n't either. All problems are soluble, and in plain fact people don't disappear on dry land. The war was over when Zander left Hanover. He either reached Munich or he did not. If he did, I shall find him; if he did not, he was probably swept into a American internment-camp. So I went to Frankfurt and studied the records of

---

6 Major General John Lethbridge (1897–1961), chief of Intelligence of British Army on the Rhine 1945–1948.

the internment-camps; and not finding any trace of Zander there, I went to Munich, and hunted further.

I hunted in vain. I found his flat and ransacked his belongings, but plainly they had long been undisturbed. All evidence ran dry; it really seemed that Zander had disappeared. And since it was by now Xmas eve, and the Americans were all beginning to disappear for a week's holiday, I felt that I could not face a week of midwinter, frustrated and alone, among strange faces in a foreign town; and standing by a table in the HQ of the CIC in Munich, I began to gather up my papers, and prepared to go back to the British Zone and to tell Peter Ramsbotham that I had boasted too soon; for I had failed.

O weak reprehensible despair! It was while I was even thus shuffling my papers that a few chance words dropped by a casual stranger, like St Augustine's *Tolle lege*, changed my whole fortune. Two Americans walked past my table, and one of them, glancing at my papers, said to the other, in an undertone, 'Zander again!', and passed on.

At once I pounced on him. What did he mean? I asked. He assured me it was nothing. I protested that it was something. I had come, I said, all the way from the uttermost north only to look for Zander. Was he alive or dead? and if alive, where? The American replied that he had merely had a friend whose German girlfriend had once been the closest friend of Frau Zander. As in all German close friendships there had been a bitter and permanent quarrel. Now the girl would tell anything she knew to sweeten her revenge.

I decided to stay and exploit this situation, and after spending Xmas with the polite French at Seefeld, near Innsbruck, I set systematically to work on an entirely new set of evidence; for it was clear that all evidence which derived from Frau Zander was tainted at the source. With brilliant ingenuity, she had spread so universal a false trail that even Zander's mother genuinely believed him dead. Only to her best friend had she revealed, unwittingly, the truth. From this moment I have adopted the principle that if you wish to find out the worst about a German, you should consult his best friend.

The details of the enquiry are unimportant. Suffice it that two days after Xmas, having motored all day and all night in a jeep, through mud and sleet and snow, I stood, at 3.0 in the morning, in the village of Aidenbach, near the Austrian frontier; and posting a man with a revolver at each corner of the crucial house, since none answered our knocking, I sent a German police-man to climb through the window and open the door. Then I went in and broke into a bedroom; and from the bed saw emerging a long pursued symbol of hope, a giant nose: the unmistakeable nose of Bormann's assistant, SS Standartenführer Wilhelm Zander. His name, he said, was Wilhelm Paustin, and he was a merchant.

I made him dress and then drove him through the rest of the night to Deggendorf on the Danube, and locked him up in the prison there while I slept for an hour, and then all day to Munich; and there, exploiting his weariness (but he cannot have been wearier than I), interrogated him. He made no resistance. He answered everything. The documents, he said, were in the bottom of a trunk labelled Wilhelm Paustin, which he had deposited for safekeeping with Frau Unterholzner in the village of Tegernsee. They were. They consisted, as I knew from Lorenz that they would consist, of Hitler's two testaments, his marriage-certificate, and a covering-letter from Bormann to Dönitz, presaging the end. I went straight to the HQ of US Third Army at Bad Tölz and told them the facts. As soon as I had gone, General Truscott[7] sent for the journalists and told them everything, taking the credit to Third Army.

When I returned to Bad Oeynhausen, Peter Ramsbotham met me. 'The JIC has funked a decision', he said, 'and referred it to the Cabinet'. But all that seemed academic now, since banner headlines were announcing the fact in England, America and the world. We were only concerned to complete the story, and therefore the first thing I did was to send to Iserlohn for Johannmeier, in order to complete the victory by the reduction of that last obstinate garrison. He came down next morning in a truck, and all the morning I wrestled with him, but in vain: I could not move him. He was too tough to be bullied, too proud to be cajoled, and casuistry could not weaken those firm elementary loyalties. But have I not often maintained that reason will solve all problems? I resolved to try reason, and bringing him round to my side of the table, I led him through all the evidence which made his story incredible to me. 'And now', I asked, 'if you were in my place, could you possibly believe that story?' 'No', he replied, 'I could not; but it is nevertheless true'. In despair I left the room. It was New Year's Day and we were alone in the HQ. I could not have him on my hands all day and I had nowhere to put him. I decided I must telephone for a truck to take him away and admit failure.

---

7 Lucian Truscott (1895–1965), US major-general, formed and trained the Rangers, an American force modelled on the Commandos, and led assault troops into Italy. T-R considered that he behaved dishonestly in arrogating credit for the discovery of Hitler's will.

But while I was out of the room, trying to put a call through to Neundorf, Johannmeier had leisure to think, and thinking he caught up with my reasoning, and came to a decision; and so, when I had returned, and had begun again, rather to fill in the time than out of any hope of success, my mechanical questions, I became aware of a change in his attitude. Instead of blocking every assault, he was seeking guarantees in case of surrender; and when I responded to compliancy with compliancy, he said quietly, '*Ich habe die Papiere*'.[8] Where? I asked. 'At my house in Iserlohn', he replied, 'buried in a glass-jar in the back-garden'.

I put Johannmeier into a car and drove him to Iserlohn. On the way I asked him what had decided him to surrender. 'In your absence from the room', he replied, 'I went over the matter in my mind, and it seemed to me that if those other two, who were both Party members, and had done well out of the Party, had so easily betrayed the trust reposed in them, then it was quixotic in me, who was not a member of the Party but only a soldier, to defend the position they had abandoned.' At Iserlohn we left the car behind, for he wished to avoid publicity, and walked together to his house. It was now dark, and since the ground was frozen hard, he took an axe from the hall and we went out into the back garden. He found the spot, opened the ground with the axe, and dug up the glass-bottle. Then he broke the bottle with the head of the axe and drew out the documents: Hitler's private testament and a covering letter from Burgdorf to Schoerner describing the circumstances of its dictation 'under the shattering news of the treachery of the RfSS'.

Next morning I arrived early in Bad Oeynhausen and met Peter Ramsbotham. The storm had now broken, he said, in the calm, complacent tones of one who is not in the least alarmed by such cataclysms. We were both quite indifferent by now to the indignation of our superiors. I sat down and wrote an account for the Press. While I was writing, the telephone rang. It was some colonel who called himself assistant to Major-General Intelligence. He was in great perplexity. The Major-General was in England, he said, and the whole matter had recently been referred to the Cabinet. The Cabinet, after several days, had decided that all facts and documents concerning Hitler's will were to be kept a dead secret. The very next day the Press of the world had blazoned it abroad, and the Major-General must have read it on the front

---

8 I have the papers.

page of his *Daily Mirror*. Today the Major-General was returning to Germany and would want to know the reason why. What was he to say to the Major-General? I told him that we had merely followed up a routine intelligence matter which we could not delay until generals made up their minds. The revelation had been made by General Truscott who was entitled to make it with reference to documents found in his area. And I added, privately, that brass-hats could not expect the world to wait upon their portentous indecisions. The colonel added, privately, that he agreed. Then I stepped into an aeroplane and flew to England. Over the Channel I saw a Dakota flying on the opposite route, and pleased myself with the thought that it was carrying the Major-General back to Germany, with thunder in his eye.

At Aidenach, as I stumped round the deserted village streets looking for the house in which Zander was staying, fearful of every clatter lest I should cause an alarm, I suddenly saw that an upper room in a house was lit up. 'What can that mean?', I said to the local German policeman. 'What can anyone be doing at this hour of the morning?' But he was not disturbed. There were only two conceivable causes, in his world, for a light at 3.0 in the morning, and he answered, without surprise or hesitation, '*Sie spielen Karten, oder die Kuh ist crank*'.[9]

> Met we on hill, in dale, forest or mead,
> By paved fountain or by rushy brook,
> Or in the bleached margent of the sea ...[10]

Logan died on 2 March 1946, and a great section of my life seems to me to have ended with that death. No one else has had such an effect on my personal history. It is ineradicable.

I first knew him in 1940. Nichol Smith told me one day, when I was visiting Oxford, that a friend of his, Logan Pearsall Smith, had been struck by

---

9 They're playing cards, or the cow is sick.
10 *Midsummer Night's Dream*, act 2, scene 1.

my book on Laud, and had asked him about me, and thereafter had written to me, and had had no reply. The fact was, of course, that the letter had never reached me, or I would naturally have answered, for I had long been an admirer of *Trivia*; so I wrote to him explaining my omission, and he invited me to come and see him, and I went, and we became acquainted, and I saw him often, so long as I was near London, and he wrote to me regularly, for six years, until his death.

What did I learn from him? When I ask myself this question, I do not know how to answer it, for I learnt everything. My whole philosophy seems, now that I consider it retrospectively, to have come from him, and what I would have been without him I cannot envisage, cannot imagine.

From that day when, walking alone around the Christ Church Meadow, I had resolved to trifle no more among the twigs of matter, but to try to understand the root of it, I had, for two years, forsaken all literary and artistic interests. I neglected poetry and prose; cared nothing for music or pictures, read neither Gibbon nor Homer, but only studied, and studied only essential monographs and laborious theses; and in the book that I was myself writing, on Laud, I consciously ignored the temptation of style. I only sought to understand, and to this extent, though I understood imperfectly, it is at least an honest book. But neither humanity nor divinity reached it, and therefore it is also incomplete and a narrow book. I cannot now think why Logan thought so highly of it.

For it was Logan who afterwards re-interested me, in a time when the war had separated me from desperate academic study, in style and the world of sensation, and enabled me thus to fill in the hard structural pattern of thought which I had thus evolved; and how can I express adequate gratitude for such an experience? – who showed me that life is short, and three parts routine, and most of it comedy, and can only be saved from triviality and given significance by some ideal to which all else, or at least much else, and that much including many humane pleasures and meritorious aims, and especially power and success, must be sacrificed, as by the merchant who sold out to re-invest all in one pearl of great price; and that style is an ideal worthy of this sacrifice. This I learnt from him and believed, and I still believe it, and shall, I hope, continue, like Gibbon, to value reading above the wealth of India. For in his life and conversation, among the tinkle of coronets and the wild extravagant gossip, and the exquisite relish of high life and *la comédie humaine*, of which it was also witness, he illustrated this philosophy to me so vividly that although it has not become mine, at least mine can never be altogether emancipated from its influence.

'The indefatigable pursuit of an unattainable Perfection, even though it consist in nothing more than the pounding of an old piano, is what alone gives a meaning to our life on this unavailing star.'

'We should nourish our souls on the dew of Poesy, and manure them as well.'

September 1946

> Illi robur et aes triplex
> Circa pectus erat, qui fragilem truci
> Commisit pelago ratem
> Primus, nec timuit praecipitem Africum
> Decertantem Aquilonibus
> Nec tristis Hyadas nec rabiem Noti …[11]

Feelingly I read these words from my pocket Horace as I sat on the crumbling volcanic summit of the Esja, having gained Iceland at last after five days of tempestuous buffeting in the North Atlantic sea. What could have impelled me, I sometimes wondered in the height of the storm, to face that terrible voyage? Curiosity, incredible romanticism, and the tedium of Europe. I had resolved to go somewhither, but not to Europe again, that devastated continent I know too well, nor to America, which somehow I could not yet face; and then, looking at the map of the Temperate Zone to see what corners of the visitable earth remained when these rejected areas had been subtracted, I had seen that forgotten island, tucked away at the top of the page, in the northern ocean, hieroglyphically marked with eternal icecaps, and giant craters, and storm-broken creeks, and inhospitable wastes, and great fishful rivers with romantic unspeakable names. So I wrote to Thomas Cook's and said that I wanted to go to Iceland; and they replied that it was impossible to go to Iceland; and that determined me to go, and I went.

---

11 Horace, *Odes*, I, iii, 9–14: Oak and brass of triple fold/ Encompass'd sure that heart, which first made bold/ To the raging sea to trust/ A fragile bark, nor fear'd the Afric gust/ With its northern mates at strife/ Nor Hyads' frown, nor South-wind fury rife (Professor Conington's translation).

And now, how shall I forget it? A month I spent there, alone, and walked along the grey northern seashore, from Blönduós,[12] watching the Arctic terns, the last of the season, lingering before their winter migration to the south; and walked with my fishing-rod (for Lionel Fortescue[13] had made me free of his rivers, though a total stranger, on the mere indirect rumour of my going) up the river Fnjóská, now camping at the falls above the estuary, where it plunges through romantic gorges, now staying in remote earth-built farmsteads on the upper stream, fishing for trout and char. A noble river it is, as are all Iceland's rivers, broad and swift and clear, deep and unfordable, rolling loudly down from the inner hills over a bottom of round, clean, shining stones. Truly Iceland is a potamolator's paradise. And then there are those hills, those desolate identical ruined volcanic stacks that rise in forbidding series, one behind the other, all along the river valleys, till the eye loses itself in that crystalline translucent northern air: mountains now fresh and rose-coloured as the sunlight smiles on their bare tufta crests, now lurid and iridescent as broken shafts of light strike them variously at sunset or under gathered clouds, now – when the sun is blotted out – suddenly terrible, bloody or jet-black, like gaunt sacrificial monoliths. But most of all what I loved about Iceland was that quality which invested all these things, the inexpressible solitude. Solitude, to be enjoyed, must be absolute: there is no qualification of it, nor gradations in it: it is or it is not; and in Iceland a land for four-fifths of it literally and totally empty, it is. I walked over those mountains, breathing that thin, intoxicating air, and knew that I could, if I wished, walk for days and never apprehend the sight of man. Only the piping of golden-plover and dunlin broke that elemental silence; if there was life at all, it was only bird-life – ptarmigan and grey goose and whooper swan, and now and then a pair of ravens flapping majestically up and down that majestic river, which seemed, in that dead silent world, to be alone living and even divine, like a pagan river, Alpheus or Scamander or Eridanus. So I wandered across that enchanted country, and visited Mývátu[14] and

---

12 A coastal town in northwest Iceland bisected by the river Blanda, which is renowned for salmon fishing.

13 Lionel Fortescue (1892–1981), a retired Eton master, created a famous walled garden at Buckland Monachorum on the edge of Dartmoor.

14 Mývátu is a desolate area of lava flows dominated by a large, shallow lake, Mývátu – the lake of midges.

Thingvellir,[15] and my only human companions were in books – for I had Horace always with me, and Herodotus, and the letters of Charles Lamb – until one afternoon, sitting on a jut of *hraún*[16] of some long-frozen reach of obsolete lava-tide, I felt a thirst for a pint of beer, and all the romance of Icelandic solitude became suddenly dim, and reflecting I thought that the nearest pint of beer was probably in Cromarty or the Isle of Skye, or perhaps in Donegal, and between it and me there lay many miles of shadowy mountain and echoing sea. So I went to Akureyri and enquired there; but when I spoke of boats, they laughed at me, saying no, there were none, and none would be, at least till the spring. Then I went to Reykjavik, and had the same answer.

But as I walked along the street of Reykjavik I heard myself hailed, and behold, it was an old Faroese sea-captain with whom I had made friends on the way out; and hearing my predicament he sent me to his friend Geir Thorsteinsson,[17] an Icelandic trawler-owner, whom at last I found, not a moment too soon, for he was seeing his trawler the *Karlsefni* away on a journey to England to sell her catch of fish. So I leapt aboard, and after four days of sousing tempest, night and day, gladly I saw the rock of St Kilda, and dropped at last into the lea of the Hebrides, and glid in calm water down to Fleetwood, and took train to Northumberland, and was at home again.

---

15 Thingvellir (southwest Iceland) is a rift valley between the Eurasian and north Atlantic tectonic plates, where the North Atlantic ridge rises above sea-level; a place of outstanding beauty and the site of the earliest Icelandic parliament.

16 Lavafield.

17 In 1915, when the North Sea was closed to mercantile marine, Geir Thorsteinsson visited New York City to try to inaugurate Icelandic exports of dried herrings, wool and mutton to the USA.

1947

From Christ Church Trevor-Roper made a foray into Germany to interview survivors of the plots against Hitler. After writing character sketches of the men he met, he abandoned his journals notebook for which college duties, book reviewing and journalistic commissions allowed no time. With his wartime drudgery in government offices behind him, he had, indeed, no need of recreational writing, stylistic exercises or dialectical sparring to keep his prose and intellect in trim.

The Last Days of Hitler   1947

Having established the truth about Hitler's death, it seemed to me that I might as well record it, for only a short and businesslike summary of the facts had been submitted to the Cabinet and the Quadripartite Intelligence Committee; and Dick White, who had been the originator of my researches, thought so too, for it was after all a piece of history, and we knew well enough that there were journalists at work, eager to imagine and to falsify. So we discussed it together, and we agreed that the book would have to be authorised, and Dick said that the body which must authorise it was the J.I.C. But will they do it? I asked. 'No', said Dick; 'at least not if you submit it to them as a proposal. No government agency will ever sanction a proposal of which they cannot forsee the effect, and old Menzies, by habitual custom and sclerosis of the mind, is sure to say No, for that is the only word he can utter. But if you were to write it first, and take the risk of their decision, and then submit the text to them, then they would at least see the limits of what they were allowing; and although Menzies would still say No, Harold Caccia[1] and I could probably see it through.'

So I wrote the book. I wrote it in the spring and summer of 1946, in the evenings, during the term; and in the vacation Solly Zuckerman[2] lent me an airplane, and I flew to Germany, to the trial at Nuremberg, there to collect further evidence, to interrogate Berger and Gebhardt, and to resolve remaining doubts. And meanwhile Frau Christian had at last been run to earth, and Frau Junge,[3] Hitler's other secretary, and von Below[4] had been discovered, quietly studying law at the University of Bonn, who had carried Hitler's last valediction from the Bunker, and other answers to old queries were coming gradually and belatedly in, except of course from the Russians, who remained for ever obstinately mute. In due course my book was written, and I sent the text of it to Dick White for the J.I.C., and they considered it; but dark doubts and obscurantist fears disturbed the complacency of poor old Menzies, and sitting in Broadway Buildings he trembled, and sent Tim Milne[5] to the J.I.C. to speak for him, having (as it appears) previously instructed him to say neither Yes nor No, for safety's sake, but to mean No.

Unfortunately these instructions were rather difficult to carry out, because the committee was managed by the chairman and the secretary; and since the chairman was Harold Caccia and the secretary Dick White, who have clear and educated minds, Milne got very short shrift from them. 'Do you

---

1 (Sir) Harold Caccia (1905–1990), later Lord Caccia, Assistant Under Secretary at the Foreign Office 1946, Ambassador in Washington 1956–1961, Permanent Under Secretary at FO 1962–1965.

2 (Sir) Solly Zuckerman (1904–1993), later Lord Zuckerman, professor of anatomy at Birmingham University 1943–1968, wartime Scientific Adviser to Combined Operations HQ with the rank of RAF group-captain, chief scientific adviser to the Ministry of Defence and the British government during the 1960s.

3 Gertraud ('Traudl') Humps (1920–2002), daughter of a Munich brewer and widow of an SS officer named Junge, typed Hitler's will and left the bunker with Baur, Rattenhuber, Gerda Christian and others. She was captured and imprisoned by the Russians.

4 Nicolaus von Below (1907–1983), Hitler's air force adjutant 1937–1945, author of *At Hitler's Side* (2001).

5 Ian ('Tim') Milne (1912–2010) had been T-R's Christ Church contemporary, and proved an enduring friend. He succeeded Cowgill as head of Section V, MI6's counterespionage section handling Abwehr decrypts, and ran SIS in the Middle East in the mid-1960s.

mean yes or do you mean no?' Harold Caccia demanded; and Milne, whose instructions precluded from answering so clear and direct a question, sought lengthily to prevaricate. But since he could not answer it, he was ignored and left irrelevantly mumbling on one side, while the committee agreed that the book should be published.

They made only one condition: no 'M' material was to be used. Now unfortunately one of the best passages in the book – Dollmann's account of the interview between Hitler and Mussolini on 20 July 1944 – was 'M' material. So I told this to Dick and asked him to get it allowed if he possibly could; and in the end it was agreed that I might publish it, provided I wrote it in *oratio obliqua* and omitted the name of Dollmann; which I did. Shortly afterwards Macmillans sent me the proofs of Allen Welsh Dulles' book, *Germany's Underground*, to read for them.[6] There I found Dollmann's account, with Dollmann's name, in *oratio recta;* so perhaps we needn't have been so scrupulous after all.

Fosterity   1947

Michael Foster believes in austerity. He believes that the world is going to the dogs, and can be saved only by Jesus Christ and ceaseless mortification of the flesh. Secretly, I think he is rather glad that it is going to the dogs, and certainly he doesn't seem to want to save very much of it; nor does he seem to foresee with pleasure the period when the crisis will be over, and Christ and mortification can be dispensed with again. Against pleasure in general, and the pleasures of the table in particular, he has declared an irreconcilable war.

When four courses appear at high table, he firmly selects and refuses the most succulent, or dines at the BAs' table to be sure of worse food; and at Governing Body meetings he proposes the abandonment of the Gaudies, not because they are expensive but because they are Sin. This philosophy is known as Fosterity.

---

6 Allen Dulles (1893–1969), Director of the CIA 1953–61. As wartime station chief for US intelligence in Berne, and station chief in Berlin after the Nazi surrender, he had contacts with German anti-Nazi plotters, as described in *Germany's Underground* (1947).

I'm afraid I must, in some convivial moment, have told all this, or some of it, to Michael Beaumont;[7] for he came as my guest to the Gaudy in January 1947, which Michael Foster had sought in vain to cancel, and as the revels deepened he turned to me and said, Where is Foster? I looked round the room, and there, sure enough, he was. He was standing on top of the steps leading up to the high-table dais, and looking down upon the scene of pleasure with saddened, disapproving gaze; and his posture, his look, and his elevation at once caused an image to spring to my mind, – the image of Moses as he stood suddenly still, half-way down from his colloquy with God on Mount Sinai, and saw, with shocked eyes, the children of Israel naughtily frisking round the golden calf.

Adverbs
1947

Shortly before his death Logan told me that he had at last discovered the great enigmatical, elusive secret, the secret of Style. For eighty years he had sought that fugitive elixir, polishing and re-polishing his careful prose in the fond hope that instinctively or accidentally or unconsciously he might stumble upon it; and now, when he was too old to write another book, when its discovery was to him the discovery not of an instrument but of a mere intellectual fact, he had discovered it. What is it? I asked. *Adverbs*, he replied; and then, an Archimedean excitement enlightening his eyes, he dwelt enthusiastically upon that exquisite, magical, unexploited part of speech. He asked me about Greek adverbs and Latin adverbs, we talked about that great adverb in Horace *insolabiliter*, and Lucretius' *insatiabiliter*, and I alleged (wrongly, I am since told) that Sophocles used an adverb ἀσφαδαστώς. Then Logan set feverishly to work. If he was too old to compose, he was not too old to revise; and he worked, through *Trivia* 'realembicating and readverbalising' the last edition that he was personally to deliver. When it was complete, he sent me a copy, and looking through its pages I found such recondite new adverbs as

---

7 Michael Beaumont (1903–1958) bought Wotton, near Aylesbury, from Lord Temple of Stowe in 1929 – the year of his election as MP for Aylesbury. A rumbustious Master of the Bicester and Warden Hill Hounds 1945–1947, when he moved to Ireland to escape punitive taxation on his American investments.

abracadabracally (which isn't in the Oxford English Dictionary, but I think he had found it in Poole's *Parnassus*); and in one entry I found a significant change: 'I am sad only', he had written, 'at the thought that Words must perish, like all things mortal; that the most perfect Metaphors must be forgotten when the human race is dust'. But this passage had now been altered. 'I am sad only', it now read, 'that Adverbs must perish, like all things mortal ...'

When Logan was dead I did not forget his last literary discovery, and reading again Apuleius' *Metamorphoses*, that great baroque Latin work, I realised that he too had made that same discovery, in the Latin tongue. And therefore when I had to write the Bodleian Oration I took him for my model and Logan as my guide and pleased myself with the boast that in that short competition I had ingeniously contrived to include no less than 73 adverbs: *iuxtim, oppido, furtim, fartim, cursim, ubertim, affatim, angulatim, aggeratim, foliatim, fistulatim, seriatim, discretim, quadrifariam, examussim, ambifariam, forinsecus, pedetentim, saepicule, fastidienter, contraversim, pullatim ...*

Germans   1947

In March 1947 I revisited Germany, for I was interested in the German opposition, of which so much nonsense has been written, and wanted to see the few survivors of the little group that really planned the Plot of 20 July 1944 – Stauffenberg[8] and his friends – but which has either been ignored (because they were reactionary aristocrats) or buried among the virtuous ineffective democratic groups who have taken, or been given, the credit for it.[9] The *New York Times* made my journey possible and I went to Frankfurt and then to Heidelberg, and there I called on Professor Radbruch,[10] a jurist at the University, and asked him questions about contemporary thought and politics.

---

8 Graf Claus von Stauffenberg (1907–1944), German war hero and instigator of the July plot to kill Hitler.

9 This visit informed T-R's article 'The German Opposition', *Polemic*, No. 8 (1947), 2–14.

10 Gustav Radbruch (1878–1949), Minister of Justice during the Weimar Republic, had been dismissed as Professor of Law at Heidelberg by the Nazis, but was reinstated after the war.

I asked him about the university. It was full, he said, but the students were non-political: after their disappointments they knew not what to believe, – everything must be somebody's propaganda – they were quite aimless now. Were there any teachers to whom they particularly listened? I asked. Oh yes, he answered, Professor Jaspers, the existentialist.[11] Why are they interested in existentialism? I asked. Not in existentialism, he corrected me, but in Prof. Jaspers, because he is a great man. They would listen to him whatever kind of philosophy he taught. My heart sank, and I asked in what way Prof. Jaspers was great: what had he done? '*Er hat ein grosses philosophische System in mehreren Bänden aufgebaut*'[12] he answered. My heart sank still lower at this exhibition of the mentality of the *Gelehrte*[13] coming so soon on top of the uncritical *heroismus* of the preceding sentence, and looking round the well-appointed comfortable bourgeois room in search of some saving conversational straw at which to clutch, I saw the works of Stefan George[14] in the Bondi'sche edition; so I asked Professor Radbruch whether he was an admirer of George. Oh yes, he said, he had been a personal friend of George, – not one of the initiates, but a friend. I asked him about the *Kreis*:[15] was Graf Alexander von Stauffenberg[16] (to whom I had a letter of introduction from the Baroness von Wangemheim)[17] a member of the *Kreis*? The old man looked aghast. The perpetual trembling of his hand (for he had Parkinson's disease or some such ailment) made him look even more horror-struck than he may have been. Certainly not! he exclaimed. The *Kreis* had nothing to do with any such political group. 'But I am not talking of politicians', I said, 'but of Count *Alexander* von Stauffenberg'. 'But you mean', he protested indignantly,

---

11 Karl Jaspers (1883–1969) had been removed as Professor of Philosophy at Heidelberg by the Nazis in 1937 because his wife was Jewish but was restored to the post in 1945. He left Heidelburg in 1948, took a chair at Basel University, renounced German citizenship and became a Swiss.

12 He has constructed a great philosophical system in several volumes.

13 Academic.

14 Stefan George (1868–1933), poet, essayist, an aristocratic but non-Nazi reactionary.

15 Circle.

16 Graf Alexander von Stauffenberg (1905–1964), youngest brother of Claus and Professor of Ancient History at Munich University 1948–1964.

17 Probably Inge, wife of Gustav, Freiherr von Wangemheim (1895–1975), silent film-star who played the vampire-hunter in *Nosferatu*, joined Communist party 1921, and fled Nazi Germany for the Soviet Union, where he was a scriptwriter and film director who survived Stalinist purges by denouncing colleagues.

'the man who tried to *murder* Hitler?' – uttering the words with shocked emphasis as if describing some activity which a *Gelehrte* at Heidelberg should not be expected even to mention. No, I said: his brother. But the old man was unconvinced and unconverted. No, he said with sudden firmness, Stefan George's friends were very extensive and intellectual and never had anything to do with such people; and the finality and disapproval of his voice made it clear to me that I asked an improper question and must go.

So I went, and a few days later (on 4 April) I called on Count Alexander von Stauffenberg at Uberlingen am See, Bilderschreibstrasse 39. A man of about 40, with grey hair but a young expression, he came to greet me wearing an enviable fur jacket and welcomed me into the house, and for a while we talked generally, and when I thought of his personal history, how his two brothers had been murdered[18] and his wife killed and himself thrown into a concentration camp, and his house and library at Würzburg (for he had been a professor of ancient history there) destroyed by bombing, I felt almost ashamed of my curiosity, and wondered whether I could decently touch upon the topic of the 20th July which had brought so little good to his cause and so much of disaster to himself; but his courtesy persuaded me that I might, and I explained to him my interest and the extent of my knowledge, and why I thought that his brother had been of more political significance than those have pretended who have written on the subject. Yes, he answered, his brother was more than a selected instrument: he had had views of his own; the misfortune was that he had had to be both man of action and political thinker of the group. He should never have gone to Rastenburg on 20 July: his place was in the Bendlerstrasse ...

But what were his political ideas? I asked.

You must meet my friend Prof Fahrner, he replied, and led me into another room where an oldish man was sitting, with scarce, wild grey hairs struggling upwards from his head, and a benign look, and gleaming luminous eyes.[19] Prof Fahrner, it appeared, has helped Claus von Stauffenberg to give form to his documents, and now he was living with Alexander von Stauffenberg in this house of exile and poverty overlooking the bourgeois beauty of the Bodensee.

---

18 His twin brother Berthold had also been killed by the Nazis after the July plot.

19 Rudolf Fahrner (1903–1988) was a disciple of Stefan George who befriended the Stauffenberg brothers. As an anti-Nazi, resigned from his post at Heidelberg University in 1936, and worked at a German institute in Athens at the outbreak of war.

Prof Fahrner explained that the military orders and announcements, including the Valkyrie orders, had been drafted and amended by the third brother Berthold von Stauffenberg, then in the OKM, since executed, and his castle at Wilflingen taken over to be the HQ of the fugitive Marshal Pétain. He argued with me that the 'opposition' had been divided into various groups, and admitted that Stauffenberg and his friends held themselves apart from the other groups, considering Moltke[20] especially, with his pacifist views, to be a visionary. When Stauffenberg's cousin Peter Yorck von Wartenburg[21] had told Stauffenberg that he was in touch with Moltke, Stauffenberg had gently puffed away such irrelevant associations. Nevertheless, Stauffenberg had not been entirely out of sympathy with Moltke. Stauffenberg's policy, like Moltke's dreams, had been based on Christian principles, non-denominational, inclusive ... And what was the policy? I asked. Claus, replied the Professor, believed that the classes in Germany were too antipathetic – the landowners too selfish, the lower classes too jealous – and he wished to bridge the gap by a redistribution of property, a reduction of the great estates to such a size that the landowner might cultivate it all himself ...

And how large would that have been? I asked – 100 hectares? (for a hundred hectares is the maximum allowed by the Russian land reformers in Germany).

Perhaps more, said the Professor, say 150; but I could see that he really meant a good deal more than that. Then he went on to explain how the land was to be redistributed among the peasants.

And what of industry? I asked.

Industry would be dismantled, he replied, except of course for *Handwerke* ...[22]

And the population?

The industrial workers would go with their industries, he answered. For

---

20 Helmuth Graf von Moltke (1907–1945) was a devout Christian and anti-Nazi. A jurist who made several pre-war visits to Oxford, he was appointed in 1939 as the Abwehr's adviser on international laws of war and martial law; unavailingly advocated compliance with Geneva and Hague conventions governing prisoners-of-war; resisted genocide and concentration camps. From 1942 he was a leader of the Kreisau Circle, a non-violent anti-Nazi group containing both Jesuits and evangelical clergy; executed for treason.

21 Peter Graf Yorck von Wartenburg (1904–1944) was a conservative who opposed militarism, refused to join the Nazi Party and was executed after the July plot.

22 Manual labour, or handicrafts.

instance, if France demanded the Krupp works as reparations, the Krupp works would have gone to France, and the Krupp workers too.

Then he envisaged a reduced population sustained by agriculture and handicrafts only? How large a population would that have been? 30 million?

Perhaps 40 million, he said.

I was bewildered. It seemed hardly less visionary than the Utopia of Moltke, only a little more sensible than the Morgenthau Plan[23] with which, in fact, he explicitly compared it. I remembered that in fact Stauffenberg had once been considered a nazi visionary, like so many of the idealist followers of Stefan George – he had been known as *der Nazigraf*, a phenomenon among the aristocracy by the intensity and simplicity of his convictions; and with a dry, inner irony I recalled how Hitler, in *Mein Kampf*, had also demanded a ruralisation of Germany. A vast population was not to be supported by industry, crowded together like coolies, but by the land. He referred to new land, to be conquered. Now that policy had failed, and the *Nazi-graf*, true to the original doctrine, wished to ruralise the population of Germany on the old land, and the superfluous industrial workers, instead of converted into colonists in conquered territory, were to become emigrants to the land of the conquerors. Even the phrases were almost the same. Hitler had referred to the corrupting, de-humanising influence of *Kuli-Faktorien*;[24] Stauffenberg, according to Prof Fahrner, had maintained that the German workers were *entseelt*[25] by industrial life.

I suppose he must have noticed my disappointment, for he broke off and said: 'It is for you to judge these ideas, for you can consider them coolly and dispassionately: our emotions are engaged. Claus was a man of such charm and exercised such a spell over all of us who came near him.' As he spoke his bright eyes brightened and his grey straggling hairs seemed to straggle more eccentrically, and he looked like some moon-faced maenad bewitched by the mere recollection of that compulsive personality. And Alexander v

---

23 In 1944 Henry Morgenthau, US Secretary of the Treasury, convinced President Roosevelt to endorse his plan whereby post-war Germany would be partitioned into two pastoral states. Industrial regions were to be annexed by neighbouring nations, or put under international control; and heavy manufacturing plants were to be dismantled or destroyed. The Morgenthau Plan was abandoned after Roosevelt's death, but influenced conditions in post-war Germany.

24 Coolie factories, i.e. using slave labour.

25 Deadened.

Stauffenberg agreed, more quietly and gently, that this was so: his brother had spoken perhaps little of his plans – which was indeed necessary, for others had spoken too much of theirs – but his friends had followed him implicitly, for they trusted him. As for himself, 'Claus told me very little, for Berthold was already involved and he wished not to endanger me too'.

Then I asked, gently and tentatively, whether Stauffenberg had envisaged an eastern solution, but they said no; and fearing that perhaps they were conservative and did not wish to think him radical, or that they thought me conservative and did not wish to represent him as a radical, I tried to indicate that I had no prejudices in the matter but was merely interested in the facts; but it was difficult to indicate it effectively, and still they insisted that though some would have called Claus radical, and though it was probably true that he would have made Leber chancellor (for he was certainly very close with Leber),[26] nevertheless he was anti-Russian, an entire Westerner. Then could his policy not have been described, as Leber had described it, as 'National Bolshevism'? They repudiated the suggestion with spontaneous laughter, and though not necessarily convinced, I pressed it no further.

Then Alexander von Stauffenberg spoke of his life in the concentration-camp, but I did not press him on the subject, for Maurice Bowra had told me how his wife had been shot down by the guards and her body brought in and showed to him as a measure of intimidation.[27] He had been in Flossenbürg[28]

---

26 Julius Leber (1891–1945) was elected to the Reichstag as a Social Democrat in 1924 and survived an attempt on his life after Hitler gained power in 1933. He was incarcerated in Sachsenhausen camp 1933–1937. An active member of the anti-Nazi resistance, he was seized by the Gestapo on 5 July 1944 and executed after months of torture. The July plotters envisaged him as their Minister of the Interior.

27 Bowra was wrong. Alexander von Stauffenberg had married in 1937 Melitta Schiller (1903–1945), an aeronautical engineer and aviatrix who was descended from a family of Jewish furriers. She had been dismissed from the Luftwaffe in 1936 because of her ancestry, but was recalled in 1939 as she was considered invaluable in developing navigation systems and as an intrepid test pilot. For the same reason, she was released from the concentration camp in September 1944, and died of bullet wounds after her aircraft was strafed by an American fighter over Bavaria in April 1945.

28 Flossenbürg, near Bayreuth, was the fourth concentration camp opened by the Nazis (1938) after Dachau, Buchenwald and Sachsenhausen. Bonhoeffer and Canaris were both executed there.

with Schlabrendorff[29] and Schuschnigg[30] and the rest, and had been taken with them to Capri, and finally had spent some time in an American camp in Wiesbaden; 'and there', he said, 'we found Rundstedt with us, which was very disagreeable; and he was very offended with us, because we refused to recognise him or speak to him. But he has been President of the Military *Ehrengericht* which had cashiered all of our friends out of the army in order that they might be handed over to the *Volksgerichshof*, and condemned and hanged.'[31]

Two days later I was in Munich, and there I called on Heinrich von Kleist,[32] the son of Ewald von Kleist.[33] He was living at 7 Voitstrasse. He was a young man of 25, and he received me with aristocratic reserve and independence, and indeed some distrust, as if I had called unannounced at his now lost Pomeranian castle of Schmenzin. I liked him the more for this independence of material prosperity, indeed almost admired him for it, it was so different from the abject humility and compliance of so many Germans, who behave, when visited, like criminals caught in the act. I explained to him the purpose of my visit; I was interested in 20 July, and that Achim Oster[34] had given me his address. He appeared unmoved. Did I want an interview? he asked. I said I would be grateful if he should find it convenient to speak on the subject, but if not, I would

---

29 Fabian von Schlabrendorff (1907–1980) failed to kill Hitler with a time-bomb disguised as a cognac bottle in 1943, and was tortured after the July plot; a judge of Germany's constitutional court, 1967–1975.

30 Kurt Schuschnigg (1897–1977) became Chancellor of Austria after Dollfuss's murder in 1934 but was toppled after the Nazi Anschluss in 1938, and survived seven years of incarceration mainly in Dachau and Sachsenhausen; Professor of Political Science at St Louis, Missouri, 1948–1967.

31 Field Marshal Gerd von Rundstedt (1875–1953) had sat with Keitel and Guderian in a military Court of Honour (Ehrengericht) which in the aftermath of the July plot expelled hundreds of officers from the army, thus passing them to the civil jurisdiction of Roland Freisler's People's Court (Volksgerichtshof), where they were sentenced to execution.

32 Ewald-Heinrich von Kleist-Schmenzin (b. 1922), an infantry officer, had been persuaded by his father to kill Hitler with a hand grenade in an earlier failed attempt. He was imprisoned in Ravensbrück camp after the 20 July attempt, but exonerated; subsequently a publisher.

33 Ewald von Kleist-Schmenzin (1890–1945) was a monarchist, Christian and lifelong anti-Nazi who went as Admiral Canaris's secret emissary to London in 1938 to deflect the British from their policy of appeasement. Involved in several conspiracies against Hitler; hanged.

34 Hans Karl Joachim Oster (1914–1983), army officer and member of anti-Nazi underground.

296 • *Hugh Trevor-Roper*

understand ... for after all, I recalled that his father and his friends had been executed after 20 July, and that he himself had only escaped by chance, and how could I decently rake over these still glowing embers, – especially since he did not, as Stauffenberg had done, charm away my doubts by friendliness, but remained, though civil, cool and reserved. 'I once gave an interview', he said, 'and afterwards I regretted it'. But he did not forbid me to go on, so I went on and explained that I had read most of the available material, both documents and printed books, but was not altogether satisfied with it ...

'Have you read Gisevius' book?' he asked.[35]

Yes, I said; and with a deprecating gesture indicated that I thought but little of that exhibitionist version; and he smiled as if in agreement, and the first barrier fell down.

And Schlabrendorff? he asked.

I said that I thought Schlabrendorff quite another matter: he was a man whom I respected, and I respected his book.[36]

Again he agreed, and the conversation at last going a little more smoothly I explained that I had intended, being interested in it, to write a book on 20 July, but had decided not to do so yet, since Allen Welsh Dulles had already written an interim book and the time was not yet ripe for a final book. But I was anxious to find out the facts while memories were still fresh, and so far as my studies went I was not satisfied that the available sources supplied the truth. For instance, there was the position of Stauffenberg ... and I described my doubts and views on the position of Stauffenberg. 'It seems to me', I said, 'that if Stauffenberg had succeeded, he would not have allowed Gördeler[37] to be chancellor'.

---

35 Hans Bernd Gisevius (1904–1974) had published *Bis zum Bitteren Ende* in 1946. A member of the Abwehr, he had in 1943 been appointed to a consular post in Switzerland, where he had contacts with Allen Dulles and was investigated by the Gestapo. His account of his part in anti-Nazi resistance was despised by those who had been at its heart.

36 T-R praised Schlabrendorff's *Offiziere gegen Hitler* (Zürich 1946) as trustworthy, sincere, 'scholarly and self-critical', and was moved by his description of life in the extermination camps: 'Schlabrendorff's book is a work of art. In the clarity of his style, the absence of rhetoric or abstraction, the simplicity and objectivity of his presentation, and the artistic unity of the whole, it is such a book as one has long since ceased to expect from a German writer' ('The German Opposition', 7, 9, 13).

37 Carl Gördeler (1884–1945), Mayor of Leipzig 1930–37 and wartime Reich Commissioner of Price Control, was prominent in a naive, indiscreet anti-Nazi group of industrialists and ex-officials; hanged.

He smiled, still a reserved smile, and said quietly, 'I don't think so either'.

Encouraged, I said that I would like to ask him for his story some time. Would he consider recording the facts for me while he recalled them clearly?

Ich habe nichts dagegen,[38] he said lukewarmly; but I persevered, with ever new polite periphrases of ever contracting diameters, and I wondered whether they could ever be contracted to a point? Then he said, 'How long will you be in Munich?', and I said, 'till tomorrow', and he said, 'shall we meet tomorrow, and I will tell you everything I know?' As he spoke the charm seemed suddenly broken: I heard a snapping of invisible bonds; and conversation, long pent in an artificial channel, ran suddenly free.

'The fact is', he said, 'that very few people still live who really know what happened on 20 July, and in general it is not they who have written or spoken about it. Most of the people who have written about it have done so in order to make halos for themselves; but political events should not be converted into personal halos. Von Oppen[39] knows some of the facts, and I know some, and von Hammerstein,[40] and Gerstenmaier[41] of course, and Gisevius – for though we dislike him, he was there and does know something. My part was small: I was there only a short time, during the arrest of Fromm.'[42]

'Schlabrendorff has described that', I said, 'and I understand he got his story from Fromm in prison. Had he any other sources that you know of?'

'No', he said; 'as far as I know he had it from Fromm'.

'And it is correct?'

'No. As always, Fromm lied. What happened was this …' and in brief he summarised the whole story which he promised to tell me in full next day: in expectation of which I listened but perfunctorily, and then asked him about his own history. His family was from Courland, he said; his great-grandmother was Gräfin von Leinst of Loss in Courland, and his grandfather had moved

---

38 I have nothing against it.

39 Perhaps Georg-Sigismund von Oppen (1923–2008).

40 Ludwig von Hammerstein-Equord (1922–1996), son of the 'Red General' Kurt von Hammerstein, was one of two brothers implicated in the July plot; later a journalist.

41 Eugen Gerstenmaier (1906–1986), evangelical Christian and July plotter; elected to Bundestag 1949, and its president 1954–1969.

42 General Friedrich Fromm (1888–1945) employed Claus von Stauffenberg as his chief of staff and knew of the July plot, but only denounced the plotters the day after their failure. He had Stauffenberg and three others shot in the War Ministry courtyard, and forced Beck into a messy suicide; but was arrested on Himmler's orders, and executed by firing squad.

to Pomerania and settled there, and his family estate there was Schmenzin, a large estate of some 11,000 morgen, or some 3,000 hectares. No, he was not related to the writer Heinrich von Kleist;[43] and the nazi Field Marshal Ewald von Kleist[44] he unconvincingly disowned. He had not visited his estate since the end of the war, but he had spoken to some who had been in Pomerania, and he knew that it was split up and lost beyond recovery.

I asked him if his fellow landowners in the East accepted the finality of their loss, as he did. He said there were some who hoped to recover their lands; but that, he said, was unreal utopianism. Those estates have gone for ever.

And what of the Bavarian landowners? I asked. What do they think about their properties? The knell has sounded in the east; do its echoes ring ominously in the south?

They sit in their castles, he said, and see no further than their noses; and he spoke with contempt of the Bavarians, a people good only at drinking beer and voting for the Church and particularism. But what good is particularism now? Particularism is dead, as Winston Churchill said at the Hague; but that great voice is not heard in Munich.

Next day he came to lunch and spoke again about politics and Bavaria and Winston Churchill, who, it seemed, in the thirties, had been in touch with his father Ewald von Kleist through Ian Colvin.[45] He was an idealist, it became clear, a sentimental, somewhat naive idealist, his idealism alternating strangely with Prussian realism; but those who embarked on that desperate adventure of 20 July could not have done so without idealism, which their later adventures in concentration camps and before *Volksgerichte*,[46] in hiding and poverty, can only have confirmed. That Winston Churchill should have been one of the representatives of his ideal seemed to me odd, but we reached a compromise on that matter, and then, after lunch, I questioned him. For two hours I cross-examined him, and he answered every question, simply and ingenuously, and there was no question which he did not answer. On Stauffenberg's views he agreed substantially with Alexander von Stauffenberg.

---

43 Heinrich von Kleist (1777–1811), dramatist and novelist.

44 Paul-Ludwig-Ewald von Kleist (1881–1954) was extradited for war crimes to the Soviet Union in 1948, and died in captivity there.

45 Ian Colvin (1912–1975), Berlin correspondent of the *News Chronicle*, had secret contacts with German generals.

46 People's courts.

Stauffenberg, he said, had been 'socialistically inclined': he wished to reduce landed property. Von Kleist had discussed these views with Schulenburg, and himself, with his 11,000 *morgen* in Pomerania, had found them excessive, an unjustifiable interference with property. He would have preferred confiscation of nazi properties only, and voluntary renunciation only by other landlords. Stauffenberg maintained that the Nazis had *entmenscht*[47] Germany by the policy of concentration-camps, the totalitarianisation of youth, the corruption of law, the war against the Churches, and over-industrialisation. The result was *Entseelung*.[48] So, 'in internal politics' (an interesting reservation), he was anti-nazi. There was, he maintained, *ein menschlicher Chaos im deutscher Volk*.[49] What then should be done? The German people must be re-humanised by gradual de-industrialisation, and return to the land. I cross-examined von Kleist on the details and implications of such a policy, but he slid away. It was the policy, he said, of Stauffenberg, accepted by Schulenburg, Peter Yorck von Wartenburg, Moltke and perhaps von Kleist; 'but I was a very young man'.

At the end of the conversation, which I have described in my notes on 20 July, I asked him whether he thought that von Hammerstein would be willing to speak to me if I should find myself in Berlin.

'You could call on him', he said, 'but I think he might not speak. I think you should have a letter from me. You would find him very reserved and cautious.'

'Well, I found you pretty reserved and cautious at first', I said.

'I?', he said incredulously. 'I am like an open book.' And indeed he was once he had been opened; but he took a good deal of opening.

---

47 Bestialised.
48 Perversion.
49 A human chaos on the German people.

Index

Abercrombie, Lascelles, 29, 48

Abyssinia, Mark Pilkington in, 169

accidie, 215–16

Achilles, a type, 199–200

Acomb, Waldo, 223

adverbs, 288–9

Aeschylus: his lively symbolism, 114; knew of homosexuality, 142; sublimity of, 216; reactionary, 217

Aga Khan: his horses, 134; symbolises the champagne age, 152

Agnes, Empress, recondite curiosity of, 72

Agostino di Duccio, 159

Ainsley, William, huntsman of Bilsdale hounds, 176–7

air, the, a tedious element, 198

Aitken, Eve, 106

Alcaeus, 212; quoted, 97; a reactionary, 217

Alderney, 162–3

Aldhelm, Bishop of Sherborne, his weak appetites, 72

Algiers, 195–7, 215, 239, 261

All Souls, Oxford, 5, 20; a Cornish village, 143

allegorical dream, 44

Alpheus, a divine river, 231, 283

Alps: Arnold Lunn a bore on, 89–90; Hitler's gothic grotto in, 262

Amanullah, King of Afghanistan, 100

ambition, my fond, 200

Americans: invade Europe, 128–9; spoil Mexico, 175; take their Christmas holidays, 277

Ampleforth Abbey (Yorks.), 177–8, 223

androgynes and genius, 150

angels: fascinate me, 27; genial theological hangers-on, 63; important problems concerning, 167

Anselm, St, 88

Antipater, 197n

Antonines, Rome under the, a great but inartistic age, 255

Apex Corner, 121

Apollonius Rhodius: his imagery, 115; his insomniant Medea, 148; blamed for writing epic after Homer, 212

apparitions, 83–4

Apperley, C.J. (Nimrod), 186

Apuleius, Lucius: a baroque writer, 6, 119, 289; read by Rideout, 145; the recreator of the Latin tongue, 191; re-read, 289

Aquinas, St Thomas, obsolete as the mastodon, 62

Arabia, 197, 232–5

Arabian Nights, The, 123

Archbishop Laud, 6, 7, 21, 32, 33, 87, 126, 153, 163, 251–4, 262–3, 281

Architect stood in Hanslope Park, An, 98

Ariosto, Ludovico, 167

Aristophanes: should be restored to English literature, 97; my patron saint, 122; inimitable, 212

Armstrong, (Sir) Thomas, 30–31, 127

Arnold, Matthew, 108

art: and the Counter-Reformation, 82; Fr. D'Arcy's views on, 104–5; and health, 121–2; no equation between progress and, 217; or between power and, 254–5

art-gangsters: Hitler's and Göring's, 137–9; Roman, 139–40

Arthurian mythology, 148

Ashton, James ('Jim'), 148

Ashton, John, 148n

Ashton, Colonel Samuel, 123

asperula odorata, 208

Aston Abbots (Bucks.), 194–5

Astor dynasty, 152

Astor, Gavin, 2nd Baron Astor of Hever, 104, 105

astrology, 196, 245

Athenæum Club, 50; serious dissension in, 260–261

Aubrey, John, 150, 151, 226, 250–251, 257

Augustine, St: a baroque writer, 6, 62, 119; baffling theological system of, 41; fascinates me, 62, 88; wrong kind of saint, 67, 88; his images, 115; his *Confessions*, 132, 213; his crisis, 163, 201, 277; a stormy introvert, 181; recreator of the Latin tongue, 191

Ausonius, 131, 212

Austen, Jane, 192

Austin, J.L., 5

autobiographies, 72–3, 79

Avignon, my misadventure in, 162

Axmann, Artur, German youth leader, 179

Ayer, (Sir) Alfred Jules ('Freddie'): at Oxford, 4, 8; *Language, Truth and Logic*, 41; his lectures complimented, 171; his meeting with Fr. Beck, 172; his colloquy with Frank Pakenham, 192–3

Aylesbury, 101, 122n, 185, 186, 190, 195n, 288n

baboons, on Monkey Hill, Maltby compared with, 114

Bach, J.S., 54, 60–61, 120–21

Bacon, Francis, a stylist, 6, 82, 113, 151

Bagehot, Walter, 30

Bahrain, 197

ballads, art of, 97, 110–111

Balzac, Honoré de, 192

Bamburgh Castle, 180

Bamford, Percival, 219

Baring, (Sir) Maurice, 159

Baroque writers, 62, 78, 107, 115, 119, 289

Barrington-Ward, John: his hexameters indistinguishable (by him) from Virgil's, 54; no idealist, 69; and Rideout, 145

Baskerville, Geoffrey, 106–8

Basra, 4; oscillating, subjective view of, 197–8

Bassenge, Gen.-Major Gerd, on Göring, 167

basset hounds, 4, 21, 182n, 198

bats, heads of S.I.S. compared to, 63

Baur, Hans, Hitler's pilot, 264, 286n

Bayle, Pierre, 72

beagles, 21, 32, 35, 36, 43, 66, 104n, 112, 120–21, 130, 163, 187

Beal (Northumberland), 179, 180

Beaufort, Henry Somerset, 9th Duke of, 183

Beaumont, Michael, 288

Beaumont of Whitley, Timothy, Baron, 21

Beck, Fr. Leslie, S.J., metamorphoses of, 171–2

beechwoods, cry of hounds in, 120

Beerbohm, (Sir) Max, 17, 108

Beermann, Helmut, 264

Belford (Northumberland), 130

Bell, John, High Master of St Paul's, 97

Bell, Walter, 161

Belloc, Hilaire, 56–7, 223

bells, their lugubrious effect on me, 117

Bellshill (Northumberland), unfortunate shoot at, 174

Below, Nicolaus von, 286

Berenson, Bernard, 4, 14, 50n

Berenson, Mary (*earlier* Costelloe), 14, 50n

Berger, Gottlob, 246–7, 286

Berington, Joseph, R.C. historian, 222

Berlin, (Sir) Isaiah, 5, 161n

Bernadotte, Count Folke, 246

Bernard of Clairvaux, St, 67, 88

Bernardi, M. de, an Algerian astrologer, 196

Berwick, Edith Noel-Hill, Lady, 160

Betjeman, (Sir) John, 58, 59

Beveridge, Jessy, Lady (*earlier* Mair), 132

Beveridge, William, 1st Baron, 132, 192, 230–231

Bewcastle Fells, 238

Bicester hounds, 21, 64–5, 93, 101, 111–13, 120–21, 181, 185–6, 187, 210, 253, 288n

Big Woods, Claydon, 190

Bills, Allan Maynard ('Jock'), 32, 43

Bilsdale hounds, 176–7

Binsey, the Thames at, 96

Binyon, Laurence, a perfectionist, 156

Birch, Francis ('Frank'), 99

birch trees, beauty of: in May, 92; in April, 155; in June, 237

Birkenhead, Frederick Smith, 2nd Earl of, 193

Bishop, Euston, 22, 109–110, 112

Bismarck, Otto von, 255

Blake, Robert, Baron, 273

Blake, William, 62, 231

Bletchley Park: croaking of raven at, 98–100; dream of, 209–210

Bliss, James, editor of Laud's works, 251

Boase, Thomas, a diner at Campion Hall, 103

boasts, 55, 162, 168

Boddington, Will, huntsman of Whaddon Chase hounds, 183, 194

Bodleian Library, 166, 224; New Bodleian architecture, 90

Bodley, Sir Thomas, 254

Bonney, Edwin, 220, 223–4

Bonzen, German generals on, 134

books: like icebergs, 154; claustrophobic effect of, 165–6

Boothby, Robert, Baron, aphorism by, 57

Borgias, 167, 169, 220

Bormann, Martin, 179n, 244–5, 246, 248, 278

Bossuet, Jacques-Bénigne, 62

Boswell, James: his letters burnt, 152; on friendship, 215

Botticelli, Sandro, 144; *Nativity*, 36, 63; *Primavera*, 36; dream-picture by, 144

Bowen, Elizabeth, 3

Bowra, (Sir) Maurice, 25, 57, 132, 294

Brauchitsch, Field Marshal Walther, 136–7, 138–9

Braun, Eva, Hitler's mistress, 245, 263

breakfast-time, spiritual blitzes at, 172–3

Breamish, River (Northumberland), 208

Bridgeman, Colonel Henry, 174, 229

Bridges, Robert, on C.M. Doughty, 232

Bridgewater, John Egerton, 1st Earl of, 151

Bright, John, 188

Brooke-Popham, (Sir) Robert, Commander-in-Chief Malaya, 55

Brown, Norman, huntsman of the Rome, and Whaddon, hounds, 195

Browne, Sir Thomas, 2, 6, 62, 82, 113, 119, 163, 236

Bryant, (Sir) Arthur, 31, 272

Buckinghamshire, 19, 20–21, 190, 197

Budle Bay (Northumberland), 130

buggers, can't be choosers, 57

'Bullseye', S.I.S. agent in Yugoslavia, 164

Burgdorf, General Wilhelm, 275, 279

Burke, Edmund, 94

Burma, fascination of, 207

Burton, Rev. J.H.S., 36

bushmen, Australian, nearer to us than the great Victorians, 142

Butler, Samuel: his influence on me, 2, 11–12, 31–2, 37, 47; his notebooks, 2, 11–12, 132, 259n; his index of *Alps and Sanctuaries*, 3; on art, 54, 106; on music, 54; his crisis, 164; heresy of M. Muggeridge on, 215; on saints, 226; his prayer, 230

Byron, George, 6th Baron: quoted, 91; in a false position, 143; could only realise his aims in death, 164

Bywell (Northumberland), 206–7

Caccia, Harold, Baron, 286–287

California, and Munich, 258

Caligula, 46

Cameron, Roderick ('Rory'), 249, 250

Campion Hall, 26; symposia at, 102–5, 171

Cape of Good Hope, triangular stamp of, 118

Capella, Martianus, 167

Carbery, Richard Vaughan, 2nd Earl of, his social circle, 151, 256

Carlisle, Rosalind, Countess of, her violence to the family claret, 152

Carlyle, Thomas, 223; his correct view of Newman, 34

Carroll, Lewis, *Through the Looking Glass*, 118

Catacombs, Roman, foxhunting through, 195

Cavaliers, cultured life of, 217, 230, 255–6

Cavendish family, feudal Maecenases, 256

Chamberlain, Neville: his exhilarating fall, 91; a missionary, 187–9; sources for his biography, 189, 271–2

Channon, (Sir) Henry ('Chips'), 159

Chapman, George, quoted, 89

Charlemain, 95, 148, 189

Charndon Wood (Bicestershire): reflexions in, 105–6; hunts from, 112, 120; a bye-day at?, 186

Charterhouse, a prig-factory, 40, 47, 70, 90, 116

Chatsworth (Derbyshire), thinness of conversation at, 250–51

Chatton Moors (Northumberland), 175

Chaucer, Geoffrey, and Doughty, 231, 233, 235

Cherwell, Frederick Lindemann, 1st Viscount, 10, 126

Chesterfield, Earls of, 195n, 252–3

Chesterfield, Enid, Countess of, 253

Cheviot Hills, 66, 100, 155, 165, 208, 238

childhood, 116, 166

Chillingham (Northumberland): its wild cattle, 130; castle, 165; depredations of Dicksie Marshall in, 174, 228–230

Chilver, Guy, a fool, 41

Chinkwell Wood, Brill, 186

Chipping Norton, Archbishop Juxon's foxhunt in churchyard, 187

Chopgate (Yorks.), 176–7

chorus-girls, unfairly treated by professors, 40

Christ Church, Oxford: Ch. Ch. Meadow, memorably circumambulated, 37–8, 40–41, 62, 281; Ch. Ch. manner, 48; rags, 57n, 146, 148–9; Governing Body, 124, 287; buttery, 224; post-war conversations, 271–3

Christian, Gerda, Hitler's secretary, 263, 286

Christianity, must have angels, 63

Church, John and Nim, 100

Churchill, (Sir) Winston: *My Early Years*, 79; Gen. Crüwell on, 133; his felicity, 140; his deplorable election campaign 1945, 231, 240; influence on von Kleist, 298

Circe, a nun in Connemara, 81

Circus, Roman, S.I.S. likened to, 114

Clarendon, Edward Hyde, 1st Earl of, 140

classical and baroque, 119

classical and romantic, 227–8

classical scholarship, 35

classics, theory of, 54

Claudian, a dreary hack, 54, 212

claustrophobia, spiritual, 166

Clavering, (Sir) James, original of Scott's Sir H. Osbaldistone, 231

Claydon Brook (Bucks.), 93; the Claydons, 181; Claydon woods, 190

clubs: Leander, 13, 96, 97, 107; Savile, 13; Vincents, 24n; Athenæum, 50, 260–261; Junior Carlton, 55n; Oxford University Golf, 69n; musty smell, 74; Carlton, 85n; Alnwick Cricket, 92n; Bletchley Conservative, 113n; Gridiron, 148; Guards', 150; Knickerbocker, 158; Gargoyle, 192; East India & Sports, 249

Cobden, Richard, 188

Coldingham (Berwickshire), 100

Cole-Adams, Walter, and the Hanslope sewage system, 98

Coleridge, Samuel Taylor: quoted, 155; his miscellanies, 213

Collison-Morley, Lacy, *Italy After the Renaissance*, 167

Colvin, Ian, 298

Compton-Burnett, (Dame) Ivy, her domestic torture chambers, 4

confessions, conditions for writing, 79

Congo, River, 199

Connolly, Cyril, 13, 15, 21, 57n, 89n, 102, 154; *The Unquiet Grave*, 213

conversation, 5–6, 15, 34, 40, 53, 90, 100, 157, 168, 251

Conway, Lady, and her circle, 38–9, 151, 256

Copenhagening of the French Fleet, 91

Corbishley, Mgr. Thomas, President of Ushaw, 223

Corkery hounds, a dream pack, 210

cosmic enigmata, 200

Costelloe, Mary (*later* Berenson), 14, 50n

Counter-Reformation, and art, 82

Courtney, Freddie, a Bicester bounder, 186

Cowgill, J.F., S.I.S. twirp, 24, 126, 170, 214

Crassus, Marcus Linnius, 139–40

Crawhalls, a party for the, 92

Crecora (Co. Limerick), 73–4

Creswick, Harry, 254

cri de coeur: in Euripides, Shakespeare and Leopardi, 30; none in Handel, 61; of custodian of Oxford crematorium, 187

Cromwell, Thomas, 151, 254

Cross, Frank Leslie, *Life and Letters of Darwell Stone*, 167

Crowsley Park (near Henley), 106–8

Cruise, Sir Richard, 184

Crüwell, General Ludwig, 132–9

cry of hounds: in dreams, 43, 210; in
    Tittershall Wood, 101; dwindling,
    112; in Stokenchurch beechwoods,
    120; heard through the blackout,
    123–124; swimming the lake at
    Wotton, 186; in churchyards, 187
culture and ideas antithetical, 255
Curry, John ('Jack'), a victim of Gilbert's
    cracks, 128, 161
Cyclops, disillusioned over Odysseus,
    108

Dalmeny, Lord *see* Rosebery, Harry
    Primrose, 6th Earl of
Dante: read in Cornwall, 30, 93; a
    mental pilgrim, 62; quoted, 62,
    162; re-reading, 71; his minute
    observation of flowers and birds, 105;
    his crisis, 163, 201; reactionary, 217;
    a disgruntled Ghibelline, 254
D'Arcy, Fr. Martin, S.J., 26, 193, 223n;
    his Oxford fishing-parties, 102–5;
    and Fr. Beck, 171
Darío, Rubén, Spanish poet, 127
Darlan, Admiral Jean-François, 128
Darwin, Charles, 12, 142n; on
    shooting, 35
David, King, 56
Dawson, Bobbie, huntsman of Bilsdale
    hounds, 176–7
Dawson, Richard ('Dickie'), with me in
    Ireland, 58, 60, 74, 80–82, 84, 86–7
de Gaulle, General Charles, 128
de Geijer, William, a faded snob, 153
de Quincey, Thomas, 72–3, 79
de Valera, Eamon, 85, 86
Dee, the sands of, 111
Defoe, Daniel, 192
Delhi, Sir E. Lutyens' architecture in,
    198
Delphi (Connemara), 82
Denniston, Alexander ('Alastair'), 98n,
    99

Derby, Charlotte Stanley, Countess of,
    256
Desdemona, my link with, 162
diary, pages from my, 91–3, 148–9
Dickens, Charles, 192
dictators, their tastes, 46
didicoy, 190
Digby, (Sir) Kenelm: a good letter-
    writer, 38–9; his fantastical notions,
    151
Diggers, the, 222
Dillwyn, Colin, 4–5, 22; his scheme for
    murdering S.G. Owen, 125
disillusion, a common misfortune, 108
Disraeli, Benjamin (1st Earl of
    Beaconsfield): in false position, 143;
    Victorian mastodon, 169
Dixon, Roper, 226
Doddershall Wood (Bicestershire), 120
Dodds, E.R., 25
Doggett, Arthur, 145–7
Doggett's Coat and Badge, raced for by
    bargees, 145–6
Dolan, Fr. Placid, 177–8
Dollmann, Eugen (loquitur), 242–5,
    287
Dominic, St, wrong kind of saint, 67,
    88
Don Pakenham de la Mancha, 110
Don Quixote, 95, 123, 192, 200
Dönitz, Grossadmiral Karl, 243, 244,
    246, 274, 275, 278
Donne, John: a stylist, 6, 82; a baroque
    writer, 62, 119; a mental pilgrim, 62,
    201; his conversion, 89;
    his imagery, 113; a stormy
    introvert, 181
Dorsch, Theodore Siegfried ('Ted'), 32
Dostoievsky, Feodor, 192
Doughty, C.M., his *Arabia Deserta*,
    211, 231–7
Douglas, Norman, 150, 166
Douro, River, 131

dreams, 42–6, 83–4, 144, 208–9, 209–210, 258
Drunkard's Corner, 23, 120
Dublin Review, 222
Dulles, Allen, 287, 296
Dumas, Alexandre, 113n, 192
Dundas, Henry (1st Viscount Melville), 94
Dundas, R.H. ('Robin'), 124n; vulturine character of, 114
dung, 48, 56, *see also* elephant dung
Durham, 223–4

eavesdrops, 132–9, 242–5
ecclesiastical history, necessarily dull, 33, 108
Edward the Confessor, St, his nighty at Campion Hall, 103
ego, problematic vocative of, 167
Egypt, 197
Einstein, Albert, founder of our world, 228
El Greco, 56, 62, 82, 88, 231
Elagabalus, 46, 135
Eldon, John Scott, 1st Earl of, 94
elemental, an apparition, 83–4
elephant dung, a perplexing phenomena in rural England, 97
Eleusinian Mysteries, 120
Elijah, 56; and the Priests of Baal, 118
Elisha, 56
Elling, Georg, 242–5
Ellis, Mrs, of British Honduras and Blackpool, 93
Elton, Godfrey, 1st Baron, 25; a type of intellectual obliquity, 31
Enniskillen, William Cole, 3rd Earl of, misdirected urination of, 261
Eridanus, a divine river, 96, 283
esoteric societies, won't do, 120
Essex, Robert Devereux, 2nd Earl of, 254
Eton College, 24, 128, 169, 272
Etruscans, 157

Eugster, General Sir Basil ('Bertie'), 155, 161
eunuchs, Chinese palace, heads of S.I.S. likened to, 63
Euphrates, River, 197, 199
Euripides: *cri de coeur* in, 30; quoted, 92, 150, 199; a goblinist, 150; Macaulay and, 202; inimitable, 212; sublimity of, 216
Europe, still the foundry of ideas, 128
Eynsham, the Thames at, 96

Fahrner, Rudolf, 291–4
Fairfax family, of Gilling (Yorks.), 178–9
faith, my early loss of, 117–18
Falstaff, a type absent from the Old Testament, 56
Farnell, Lewis, embarrassed by homosexuality in Pindar, 141
Farquhar, Sir Peter, Master of Whaddon hounds, 194
Fascism, 217
Fegelein, Hermann, 245, 246
Feiling, (Sir) Keith: an uninspiring tutor, 4; his torturous style, 26; contempt for, 31, 189, 271–2
fewmits (deer's dung), 48
Field, John: his death and character, 22, 66–7, 205; his influence on me, 28, 205
Fielding, Henry, 192, 231
Finemere Hill, Claydon (Bicestershire), 121
Firth, Sir Charles, 107
fishing: in the Till, 20, 155, 156, 162, 165, 228; its pleasures, 32, 37, 162; in Colonel Bridgeman's lake, 174; in the Wye, 178, 250; in Iceland, 283
Fitzgerald, Edward, 15
Flaccus, Valerius, a dreary hack, 212
flagellation: divergent views on pleasure of, 33–4; library of works on, 262

flattery, getting drunk on, 50, 51

Flaubert, Gustave, 6, 69, 119, 122, 191, 192, 199

Fletcher, Sir Frank, headmaster of Charterhouse, 42

Fletcher, Tom, 176

flying, boredom punctuated with fear, 198

form, literary, 54, 191–2, 212–13

Fortescue, Lionel, 283

Foster, Michael, 8, 272, 287–8

Fox, Charles James: and literature, 94; his conversion, 201

foxes: coastal, 130; in dreams, 210

foxhunting: curative effect of, 21–2, 64–5; with the Whaddon, 21–2, 122, 181–5, 186, 194–5; criticism of my, 30–31; perfect felicity of, 32, 33, 50, 52, 53; intellectual nature of, 35; in Ireland, 59–60, 86; with the Bicester, 64–5, 111–13, 121, 185–6, 187; in Tittershall Wood, 64, 101, 120; getting to the meet, 101, 121, 185, 189–90; in woods, 101, 105, 112, 120–21, 122–3, 186, 190; Exmoor hounds, 104n, 186; reflexions out hunting, 105; with the S. Oxon, 112, 120, 189; in Bucks, 119, 163; strange encounter out, 122–3; in Northumberland, 130–31, 175–6; in Mexico, 175; in Yorkshire, 176–7; hounds from the Berkeley, 183; huntsman from the Vale of the White Horse Hunt, 183; and divinity, 186–7; in Rome, 195; in dreams, 209–210

Fraenkel, Eduard, 115

Francis of Assisi, St, 67

Francis Xavier, St, 67, 88, 249

Frederick the Great, Macaulay on alleged homosexuality of, 141

freemasonry, 120

French Fleet, exhilarating Copenhagening of, 91

Freud, Sigmund, 2, 158; a founder of our world, 228; an old crackpot, 258–9

friendship and the classes, 258

Fritsch, Werner, Freiherr von, 134, 136n

Fromm, General Friedrich, 297

fungus, giant, members of S.I.S. likened to, 114

Galaesus, River, 121

Gallio, Junius Annaeus, 264

Gallo-Roman nobility, epistolary elegance of, 131

Galway, George Monckton-Arundell, 7th Viscount, pacificator of the great Whaddon row, 184

Gambier-Parry, (Sir) Richard, a genial rogue, 113–14, 185

Gamp, Mrs, a type absent from the Old Testament, 56

Gandhi, Mahatma, reactionary, 217

Ganges, River, 27, 199

Garganus, creaking oakwoods of, 121

Garigliano, River (*formerly* Liris), 121

Garrod, H.W., 6–7, 108, 167, 168, 205

Garrowby (Yorks.), 153n, 166

Gasquet, Cardinal Francis, 108

Gathorne-Hardy, Robert, 14, 15

Gawcott (Bicestershire), 112

Gebhardt, Karl, Himmler's doctor, 245, 286

general elections: 1935, 85n; 1945, 230n, 231, 240; saturnalian character of, 240–41; 1906, 241

genius: demands privacy, 57n; Hampshire on, 68; Shakespeare's, 78; Rowse on, 141; and impotency, 149–50; the sole illumination of life, 156; Ryle on, 209

George, Stefan, 290–91, 293

Gerstenmaier, Eugen, 297

ghosts, my Bible of, 118

Gibbon, Edward: one of the stylists, 6, 32, 82, 122, 189; can't harm the brain, 32; his footnotes canonical, 32; and Newman, 34, 189; his *Autobiography*, 72, 79; disgusts F. Pakenham, 87; not a baroque, 119; a type of human felicity, 141, 164; unread by Rowse?, 143; but read by Rideout, 145; on the Roman magnificos, 198; his achievement, 199–200; on reading, 202, 281

Gibson, Alexander, 124–5, 165

Gibson, Matthew, 252

Gil Blas (Lesage), 95, 192

Gill, Ernest, 9–10, 12, 24

Gilling Castle (Yorks.), 178–9

Gingerbread House, The, 100

Giraud, General Henri, astrologically parallel with me, 196

Girdlestone, Gathorne, 109

Gisevius, Hans Bernd, 296, 297

Gladstone, William Ewart, 168, 169, 188

Glasbury on Wye, 250n, 251

Gnostics, reactionary, 217

goat, unusual spectacle in King's Cross Underground station, 106

goblinism, 149–50

God, dropped from my universe, 117–18

Goebbels, Josef: a pupil of the Jesuits, the only intellectual of the NSDAP, 34, 245–6; his suicide, 246, 248

Goethe, Johann Wolfgang von, 122, 254

Goldberg, canon of Bach, 120–21

Goldsmith, Oliver, a comic, 107

Gördeler, Carl, 296

Göring, Hermann: like Xerxes, 91; his tastes, 135–9, 167; like Elagabalus?, 135; like the Maharaja of Kapurthala, 136; like the Medici?, 139; like the Borgia, 167; at Hitler's byzantine court, 243, 244, 246; Hitler's last use for, 248

Gothic cathedrals, pleasure of hunting in, 121

Götterdämmerung, 241–8

Graziani, Marshal Rodolfo, Marchese di Neghelli, 243, 244

Greatrakes, Valentine, 39

Gregorovius, Ferdinand, 143

Gregory XVI, Pope, 223

Grendon Wood (Bicestershire), 120

Grey, Constance, 174

Guards Officers, 150; complacent bliss of, 250

Gubbin's Hole (Bicestershire), 23, 112

Guy Mannering (Scott), 238

Haig, George ('Dawyck'), 2nd Earl, 103–4

Haile, Martin *see* Hallé, Marie

Halder, General Franz, 134, 271–2

Halifax, George Savile, 1st Marquess of, 127, 250

Halifax, Edward Wood, 1st Earl of, 153

Hall, Alexander (the Tory brewer), his missionary generosity, 241

Hallé, Marie ('Martin Haile'), 220, 224

Ham Green (Bicestershire), 121, 185; Ham Wood, 120

Hammerstein-Equord, Ludwig von, 297, 299

Hammond, John, perhaps a great historian, 107, 143

Hampshire, (Sir) Stuart: wartime colleague, 4, 10, 11, 55; his 'Self-Revelation', 16, 67–9; on Handel, 61; on women, 71; on Gibbon, 72; on clubs, 74; on R.H. Dundas, 114; on Macaulay, 142; on S.I.S., 149; on Valentine Vivian, 157

Handel, G.F.: his characters, 36; his serenity, 37; and Bach, 54, 60–61; Samuel Butler on, 54; no *cri de coeur* in, 61

Hannibal, 133, 140

Hanslope Park (Bucks.), sewage at, 98

happiness: moments of undiluted, 64–6, 121, 206–7; enigma of, 140–41, 162–4; solved, 199–200; types of, 250

Harcourt, William, 2nd Viscount, 123

Harcourt, Sir William, 240–41

Hardy, Thomas, 192

Harriot, Thomas, 256

Harrod, (Sir) Roy, 5, 170n

Hart, H.L.A.: wartime colleague, 4, 11, 211; on Americans, 128; on S.I.S., 129; on Freud, 258–9; and Hitler's Bunker, 263

hawking, 42, 151, 256

Hawkins, David, 28, 104, 105

Haydn, Joseph, a type of happiness, 141, 199

Haymarket, melancholy reflection in the, 71

Haynes, E.S.P., 11–12, 259–62

Headlam, Arthur, Bishop of Gloucester, 26

health, and art, 121–2

Heard, Gerald, 196

Heathcoat-Amory, Edgar FitzGerald ('Gerald'), 22, 205, 209

Hebrews, the, 56

Heidelberg University, 289–90

Heine, Heinrich, quoted, 36–7

Hell Copse (Oxon), 120, 208

Helmont, Jean-Baptiste van, 256

Henderson, Sir Neville, a missionary, 188

Henley (Oxon), 13, 96, 97, 100, 103n, 107, 147

Herbert, George, 257

Hermes, a classical periodical, 125

hermits *see* monks and hermits

Herodotus: quoted, 140; knew of homosexuality, 142; read in Iceland, 284

Hesiod, 92

Hess, Rudolf, his Messiah-complex, 134–5

Heydrich, General Reinhard, 134

Hilger, Gustav, 268

Hill, Denys ('Hooky'), 273

Hillary, Richard: the Byron of our age, 164; his *The Last Enemy*, 180–81; an Achilles-type, 199

Hillesden (Bucks.), 112

Himmler, Heinrich, 242, 243, 244, 245; his last days, 246–8

historiography, 106–7

Hitler, Adolf: home life and tastes of, 46, 135; on Churchill, 133; carpet-biter, 135; his art-gangsters, 137; impotent of course, 149; hard to diddle, 188; last days of, 211, 245–8, 262–4, 274–5, 285–7; scenes at his byzantine court, 241–5; his antenna from God, 269; plots against, 272, 289, 291–2, 295–9; his Will, 274–80, 286n; ruralisation plans, 293

Hobbes, Thomas, 6, 82, 250, 256, 257, 259

Hogarth, D.G., on Doughty, 233, 236

Hohler, Sir Thomas, 96

Holland House, 202

Holland-Hibbert, Wilfrid ('Biffy'), 187

Holy Island (Northumberland), 130, 179–80

Homer: quoted, 27, 34, 75, 108, 237; Bagehot on, 30; can't harm the brain, 32; his great images, 36, 105; his *Odyssey*, 40, 81, 108, 200, 254; a revelation to me, 40; hexameters, 54, 212; re-reading, 71; magic lines in, 75, 78; and Doughty, 234

homosexuality, 15, 27, 57, 68, 141–2

Hope, Hugh, 44
Horace, 21, 71, 212, 284, 288; in
  Calabria, 121, 155; a type of felicity,
  141; quoted, 154, 282; his sweet
  otium, 164, 199
Hortensius, Quintus, 139–40
Housman, A.E., 56, 74, 125, 216
Hugo, Victor, 192
humanists, 255–8
Hume, David, on the Church of
  England, 205
Hutchinson, George, treasurer of Ch.
  Ch. Oxford, 124

Iceland, 282–4
ideas, like saxifrage, antithetical to
  culture, 255
If you study the infinite classes, 115
illness: value of, 30; misery of, 91–2,
  110
images: various, 56, 70, 106, 113–15,
  158, 207, 238–9; Homer's, 105
impotency, and genius, 149–50
India, 198; its effect on England, 249
Indus, River, 199
Industrial Revolution, aesthetic
  opinions warped by, 223
inebriation: three methods of, 50;
  morning after, 96; cause of poetic
  afflatus, 97
Ingham, Felix, 83
Inniskilling, Lord *see* Enniskillen,
  William Cole, 3rd Earl of
intersexuality and genius, 150
introspection, 67, 90, 158
Ireland, 55, 100, 162–3, 175; its
  mansions, 53, 59, 74, 189; my
  memories of, 57–60, 73–4;
  conversations in, 58, 81; mythical
  bogs of, 80–81; Frank Pakenham's
  custody of, 85–7; mythology and
  insolvency in, 85, 148; a poor, half-
  witted gypsy relative, 190–91; its

writers saved the English language,
  191
Irrawaddy, River, 199, 207
Irvine, Andrew, 70
Islam, 233
It nearly broke her father's heart, 129
Italicus, Silius, 212
ivory tower, essential furniture of, 63–4

James II, King, 107, 151
James, Henry, 14, 157, 159
Japanese: mythology of, 96; deer of,
  123; armies of, 207; prisoners of, 273
Jaspers, Karl, 290
Jesuits, 80, 171–2; my former
  correspondence with, 103, 105;
  Baskerville's troubles with, 108;
  Ropers gave wealth to, 168; educators
  of Dr. Goebbels, 245; in China and
  Paraguay, 249
jet-mines, a north Yorkshire squire-trap,
  177
Joachim, Ursula, 171, 172
Joad, C.E.M., 129
Jodl, General Alfred, 136, 248
Johannmeier, Willi, adjutant in Hitler's
  bunker, 275–6, 279
Johnson, Clarence, 185–6
Johnson, Samuel, 6, 119
Jorrocks, a type absent from the Old
  Testament, 56
Joyce, James, 79, 191, 212
Juan de la Cruz, St, a reactionary poet,
  217
Julius Caesar, 169
Junge, Gertraud ('Traudl'), Hitler's
  secretary, 263n, 286
Jury, Charles, 32
Justinian, 169
Juvenal, S.G. Owen's edition of, 125
Juventud, divino tesoro, 127
Juxon, William, Archbishop of
  Canterbury, 187

Kaltenbrunner, Ernst, 248, 268

Kapurthala, Sir Jagatjit Singh Bahadur, Maharaja of, 136

Karinhall, Göring's country house: scenes at, 135–9; surprised Sir Neville Henderson, 188

Kautsky, Karl, *Communism in Central Europe*, 225

Keats, John, 48, 75, 199–200

Keble College, Oxford, 27

Keitel, Field Marshal Wilhelm, 243, 244, 245

Kelmscott, the Thames at, 96

Kelvin, William Thomson, 1st Baron, 113

Kent, its ancestral connexion, 225–7

Kenya, 265

Keppler, Wilhelm, cracked economist, 269

Kersten, Felix, Himmler's masseur, 245

Kidd, Rev. Beresford, 27

Kimmer Loch, Eglingham (Northumberland), 130

King's Cross, troglodyte conductress at, 106

Kingsley, Charles, 169; his *Sands of Dee*, 111

Kingsmill, Hugh, 13, 239–40

Kleist, Heinrich von, 298

Kleist, Field Marshal Paul-Ludwig-Ewald von, 298

Kleist-Schmenzin, Ewald von, 295, 298–9

Kleist-Schmenzin, Ewald-Heinrich von, 295–9

Knox, Dilwyn ('Dilly'), 99

Koestler, Arthur, *Darkness at Noon*, 213

Koller, General Karl, 248

Kyloe (Northumberland), 130

Lamarque, Geoffrey, 31, 148–9

Lamb, Charles, 284

Lambton, William, 183

Lamorna Valley (Cornwall), 92–3

Landon, Philip, 24, 128, 153

Lanthony, 251–4

Las Casas, Bartolomé Bishop, 249

Laski, Harold, 231

Latimer, Hugh, Bishop, a reactionary, 222

Laud, William, Archbishop: a reactionary, 222; vexed by the Ropers, 225; his correspondence with Lord Scudamore, 251–4, *see also Archbishop Laud*

Laval, Pierre, 138

Lawrence, T.E.: an admirer of Geoffrey Baskerville, 107; his complex masochism, 110; lived too long, 199; fashions his self-portrait, 232

Lawson, Frederick ('Harry'), 26

Lear, Edward, 118

Leber, Julius, 294

Leeds, D'Arcy Osborne, 12th Duke of, 242n

Lees-Milne, James, 15

Lenin, Vladimir, 225

Leonardo da Vinci, 121, 213

Leopardi: an individual genius, 29, 30, 254; an invalid, 122; sublimity in, 216

Lesbos, its poetics and power politics, 254

Lethbridge, Major-General John, 276, 279–80

Levellers, the, 222

Levens, Robert, 26

Lewis, C.S., 217, 272

Liddell, Guy, 1, 11

Life Guards, 2, 83, 169

life, purpose of: an insoluble enigma, 140–41, 156, 163, 216; solved, 199–200

Limerick, 58–60

Lincoln College, Oxford, 27

Lindisfarne Castle, 180

Lines, Tom, 112
Lingard, John, R.C. historian, 220–21, 222, 223, 224
literary judgments, 70–71
literature: forms in, 54, 132, 212–13; value of, 94–5
Lloyd George, David, 1st Earl Lloyd-George of Dwyfor, 103n, 140
Long, Sir James, 151
Longford, Francis Pakenham, 7th Earl of *see* Pakenham, Francis
Lonsdale, Hugh Lowther, 5th Earl of, in decline, 152–3
Lorenz, Heinz, Hitler's press secretary, 274–5
Lowe, John, Dean of Christ Church, 202
Loyola, Ignatius: closes minds, 34; wrong kind of saint, 67, 88; a stormy introvert, 181; his crisis, 201
Loyola Hotel (Dublin), 58
Lucan, a dreary hack, 212
Lucretius, 71, 160, 288; magic lines in, 75; quoted, 100
Lucullus, Lucius Licinius, 139–40
Ludlow Castle, 151
Lunn, (Sir) Arnold, a bore, 89–90
Lutyens, Sir Edwin, 103, 198
Lyell, Antony, 2nd Baron, 22, 169–70
Lyell, Sir Charles, 142
Lynsted (Kent), 227

Maas, Paul, a refugee scholar, poetically described, 115
Macaulay, (Dame) Rose, 15–16, 18, 131, 160
Macaulay, Thomas Babington, 1st Baron: on homosexuality, 141–2; and the geologists, 142; his happiness, 202; on squires, 231
MacCarthy, Sir Desmond, 15, 17, 215
Macclesfield, George Parker, 7th Earl of, 108
McCorquodale, Norman, 183

Maclagan, Michael: a faded snob, 153; his heraldic labours, 252, 254
MacMahon, Marshal Patrice de, Duke of Magenta, 217
Madan, Marjorie, 165
magic lines, 74–9
malice, 53, 106; one of the intellectual pleasures, 186
Maltby, Edward ('Ted'), 157; eloquent metaphorical description of, 114; like Plautus' parasites, 129; a farting exhibitionist, 214
Mandeville, Sir John, a yarn-spinner, 113
Manning, Cardinal Henry, 189, 220–23
Mansfield, William, 1st Earl of, and the Gordon Riots, 260
Marcus, German deserter, codenamed Dictionary, 242
Marett, Robert, Rector of Exeter College, 27
Marlowe, Christopher, 53
Marsh Gibbon (Bucks.), 65; famous hunt from, 112, 186
Marshall, Richard ('Dicksie'), character of, 173–6, 228–31
Marx, Karl, 223; a founder of our world, 228
Marxism, 217, 223, 259
Masterman, (Sir) John, 4, 42n, 114n, 168, 273
Mathew, David, Bishop of Apamea *in partibus*, 177, 219–22
maxims, 49
Maze, Paul, painter and social climber, 103–4, 104–5, 115
Medici, 139
Mediterranean Sea, an emblem of futility, 197
Melville, Henry Dundas, 1st Viscount, 94
memory, a trick of the, 208–9
Menander, 212

mens sana in corpore sano, 121–2

Menzies, Sir Stewart, 126, 276, 285–6

Meredith, George, 192

mermaids, 27, 158; enchant the lines that mention them, 62

Merton College, Oxford: High Table conversations, 7, 168; electric lights, 9; dispute in Combination Room, 41; rent-audit at, 186; high luminous rooms, 224

Metaphysical Poets, 257

Mexico, Dicksie Marshall's life in, 175

Micklem, General, 119

Milburn, Sir John, his beagles, 66, 130–31

Millais, Sir John, 255

Miller, Sir Hubert, 50

Milman, Henry Hart, *History of Latin Christianity*, 143

Milne, Ian ('Tim'), 286

Milner, John, Bishop, 220–21

Milton, John, 71, 95, 113, 156n, 236; a baroque writer, 6, 119; *Elegia Tertia*, 13; his drum-roll majesty, 30; can't harm the brain, 32; revelation of his *Nativity Ode*, 40; quoted, 45; killed blank verse, 54; magic lines in, 75, 77–8; *Comus*, 77, 151, 256–7; his crisis, 201; *Lycidas*, 256–7

Milvain, Colonel Roland ('Roly'), his hounds, 130

Missionaries, the, 187–9

Mithraism, 120

Model, General Walther, 135

Mohammed, 169, 233

Moltke, Graf Helmuth von, 292, 293, 299

moments in my life, memorable, 40–41

Mommsen, Theodor: his *History of Rome*, 129; on Hannibal, 140; on the Etruscans, 157

money and salvation, 53, 168

monks and hermits: unsavoury ruminations of, 35; macabre observances of, 166; their hospitality, 178; their simperings and the Industrial Revolution, 223, 225

Montaigne, Michel de, 132

Montgomery, Bernard, 1st Viscount Montgomery of Alamein, 109, 246

Month, The (R.C. paper), 222

Moore, George: a stylist, 6, 32, 82, 191; autobiography, 79; and Rideout, 145; impotent?, 149

More, Henry, 256; quoted, 38–9, 141; floral odour of his urine, 39

More, Sir Thomas, 88; his alliance with the Ropers, 225–6

Morell, Theodor, 245

Morgenthau Plan, 293

Morning Star, image of, 119–20

Mornington Crescent, alleged mortuary for dead tube-trains, 95

Morrell, Herbert (the brewer), his missionary generosity, 241

Morris, Frank, huntsman of the Cleveland, 177

Mortimer, Raymond, 15, 154, 159, 213

Morton Evans, Kenneth, 34, 157; and De Quincey, 72–3

Morton, Major Harold, Master of Whaddon hounds, 185, 195n

Moselle, River, 131

Mosley, Sir Oswald, 85

Muggeridge, Katherine ('Kitty'), 239, 240

Muggeridge, Malcolm, 13, 155n, 214–15, 239–40

Muir, Thomas, 94

Mummius Achaicus, Lucius, 139–40

Munich Conference: sharpened all our thinking, 38, 41; a shock to Phaeacia, 257; leads to California, 258

Murray, John, Master of Wrest basset hounds, 182n
Mursley (Bucks.), 122–3
Mussolini, Benito: degenerate appetites of, 46; a bewildered spectator at Hitler's court, 242–4, 287
mysteries, esoteric, no good, 120
Mystics: dreary, 199; reactionary, 217
mythology: my, 62–3; modern, 95–6; Greek, 96, 147–8

Nabobs, Anglo-Indian, 249
Napoleon I: an intersexual genius?, 150; his gay, irresponsible aristocracy, 152
Napoleon III, 217
nature, the subtle harmony of, 235
Nebulones, otherwise Earth-bubbles, 169–70
Nehring, General Walter, 134, 140
Nell, Herbert, 183
Nero, 46
New College, Oxford, and Magadalen Beagles, 120
New Delhi, Sir E. Lutyens' architecture in, 198
New Guinea, web-footed tribes in, 113
Newcastle-upon-Tyne, can be beautiful, 206–7
Newcastle-upon-Tyne, William Cavendish, 1st Duke of, 256
Newman, Cardinal John Henry, 201; inadequate pleasures of, 33; his *Apologia* glows with a luminous corruption, 34; a study in morbid vivisection, 79; and Gibbon, 189; and Manning, 220–23
Nichol Smith, David, 168, 280–81
Nicolson, (Sir) Harold, 159
Nile, River, 27, 199
Nimrod (C.J. Apperley), 186
Noke, sinister irregularities among inhabitants of, 113
Nonnus, a desperate poet, 212

Norfolk, Frances, mad Duchess of, and her Deeds, 252–3
Normanby, Oswald Phipps, 4th Marquess of, his turd, 146
North, Roger, 17
Northumberland, 7, 13, 17, 19–20, 92, 130–31, 155, 162–3, 173–5, 197, 237–8
Northumberland, Alan Percy, 8th Duke of, 173, 210
Northumberland, Henry Percy, 9th Earl of, 256
nostalgia, 197
novel, the, a dead form, 132, 191–2
Nuneham Park (Oxon.), 123
nuns, in Connemara, 81
Nuremberg trials, 272, 286
nymphs, 27, 52, 62, 96, 152, 208

O Mary go and call the cattle home, 111
Oakey Wood (near Chatton, Northumberland), 229
Oakley Wood (Bicestershire), 120
Odyssey (Homer): observations on, 40, 81, 200, 254; quoted, 108, 237
O'Mara, Stephen, agreeable Limerick bacon-king, 58–9
Oola, penny-in-the-slot at, sure find for Black & Tan hounds, 65–6
Oppian, 102
Oriel College, Oxford, 25n, 166
Orkney, Edmond Fitz-Maurice, 7th Earl of, 184
Osbaldistone, Sir Hildebrand, original of, 231
Osmotherly (Yorks.), 176
Oster, Hans Karl Joachim, 295
Otmoor (Oxon), 100, 112, 113
Ouida (Marie-Louise de la Ramée), 192
Ouspensky, Peter, 173
Oving (Bucks.), 120
Owen, S.G., 7–8, 124–5, 240

Oxford: manners, 5–9; wasted
years at, 47; golden days at, 205;
wartime, 216, 224–5; the monks
and mandarins of, 218; ambivalent
attitude to, 224–5, 272–3
Oxford Election 1880, 240–41
Oxford Movement, 217

paganism, a possible religion, 208
Page, (Sir) Denys, 99, 115
Page, Major-General Sir Max, 272
Pakenham, Francis ('Frank'; *later*
7th Earl of Longford), 4, 13;
dining with Belloc, 56–7; a
wonderful character, 85–7; on my
book, 87; his dinner-party, 90;
his bedside-book, 92; the ballad of
Sir Pakenham, 110–111; touched
in the brain, 185; cocktails with
Beveridge, 192; dinner with
Ayer, 192–3
Palermo, macabre monastery at, 166
Palmer, Thomas, 94
Palmerston, Henry Temple, 3rd
Viscount, 188
parsons, sporting, 186
Pascal, Blaise, 132, 250
Pater, Walter, 108, 150, 156n
Paul, St: on psalm-singing, 72; wrong
kind of saint, 88; his crisis, 163;
a stormy introvert, 181; a
reactionary, 217
Paulus, an Elemental, 83
Peacock, Thomas Love, a stylist, 5, 6,
32
Peat-Hag hare, 66
Penn, William, Macaulay wrong on,
202
Percy family, 170n, 256
Percy Foxhounds, 130
perfection: a fatal distemper, 192;
must be dismantled, 219; pursuit of
unattainable, 282

Pervigilium Veneris, a genuine poem,
212
Pétain, Marshal Philippe, 138, 189,
200, 217, 225, 292
Peter Damiani, St, 72
Pharaoh, misreads omens, 180
Philby, Kim, 170
Phillips, John, 54
Piddington Cow Leys (Bicestershire),
112
Pigg, John, a type absent from the Old
Testament, 56
Pilate, Pontius, relative unintelligence
of, 264
Pilkington, Mark, 169
Pindar: drum-roll majesty of, 30;
re-reading, 71; his account of the
Argonauts, 111; dangerously intimate
with homosexuality, 141, 142; on
genius, 156; inimitable, 212
Pius IX, Pope, 223
Plato, 13, 132, 142, 217
Plautus, the parasites in his plays, 129
Plumptre, Rev. Edward, *The Life of
Bishop Ken*, 33
Plutarch, knew of homosexuality, 142
poetry, suggested reason for my dislike
of modern, 106
Polecat End, Shabbington Wood
(Oxon), 120
Pontine Marshes, foxhunting in, 195
Poodle Farm (Bicestershire), 112
Poole, Joshua, *English Parnassus*, 289
Pope-Hennessy, James, 15
Pope-Hennessy, (Sir) John, 15, 159–60
Popper, (Sir) Karl, 272
port families on the Douro, 131
Porter family of Lanthony, 253
Portugal: illusions about, 131; its
imperial legacy, 249
Potamolatry, 198–9, 255, 283
Poundon (Bucks.), a forlorn spot, 113
Powell, Anthony, 3

Powell, Frederick York, 22

power: absolute, its vertiginous effects, 242; political, in relation to art, 254–5

Preston, Stuart, a humbug, 15, 158–61

Priestley, Joseph, 94

Procopius, a mendacious historian, 113

Proust, Marcel, 40, 68, 122, 212

Public Record Office, 253

Purcell, E.S., *Life of Cardinal Manning*, 189, 221–2

Puseyites, their minute scruples, 167, 202

Quainton (Bucks.), a hunting village, 21, 22, 65, 120

Quakers, browbeaten by Macaulay, 202

Quickly, Mrs, a type absent from the Old Testament, 56

Quintus Smyrnaeus, a desperate poet, 212

Quixote, Don, 95, 123, 192, 200

Racine, Jean, 69

Radbruch, Gustav, 289–91

Radio Security Service (RSS), 9–13, 24, 55, 126

Raleigh, Sir Walter (1554?–1618), 151

Raleigh, Sir Walter (1861–1922), 51, 157

Ramsbotham, (Sir) Peter, 269–70, 276, 277, 278, 279

Raphael, 82

Raphael, Frederic, 215n

Rattenhuber, Johann, 264, 286n

Rauschning, Hermann, 241

Raven Croaked in Bletchley Park, A, 98–9

Ray, River (Oxon), 112

Reay, Aeneas Mackay, 13th Baron, 13, 155

redshanks, used to breed on Otmoor, 112

Reelkirchen, 265–71

Reformation, 216–17, 222, 256

Reilly, (Sir) Patrick, 170

religion: Gilbert Ryle on, 42, 127, 168, 265; and cash, 53, 168; legacy of, 80; and society, 202–5; my religion, 205, 208

religious revivals and society, 216–17

Rembrandt, picture of raw meat by, favourably compared to holy topic, 104–5

Rhine, River, 96; robber-barons and bishops of, 131

Ribbentrop, Joachim, 179, 243, 266; 'my name is *von* Ribbentrop', 244

Rice, Arthur, 149

Rideout, John: embodiment of the plutocratic spirit, 101; and Doggett, 144–7

Rievaulx (Yorks.), 177

Rimbaud, Arthur, 69

rivers, 27, 34, 96–7, 121, 131, 198–9

Roberts, Mr & Mrs Harry, 123

Robertson, James, 199

Rochefoucauld, François de La, quoted, 179

Roebuck, John, 261

Roehm, Max, an astrologer, 196

Roman Catholics, and their historians, 219–24

Roman literature, no good, 212

Romantics, reactionary, 217

Rome: foxhunting in, 195; under the Antonines, 255

Rommel, Field Marshal Erwin, 134, 140

Roosevelt, Franklin D., 133, 270–71

Roper family, 225–7

Roper, Margaret, daughter of Sir Thomas More, 225

Roper, Sir William: his fragrant death, 88; his courtship, 226

Roper-Dixon family, 226–7

Roper-Lumley-Holland family, 227

Rosebery, Harry Primrose, 6th Earl of (*earlier* Lord Dalmeny), 182–5

Ross, Sir David and Lady, 25

Rossetti, Dante Gabriel: his *Blessed Damozel*, 114; in a false position, 143

Rot, Mirko, a Yugoslav Jew from Novisad, 131

Rothschild staghounds, 182–3

Rothschild, Victor, 3rd Baron, teased, 10–11

Rowse, A.L.: poor old, becoming a bore, 90, 107; his deplorable autobiography, 101, 121–2, 141, 154; once influenced me, 106–7, 153–4; on health and art, 121–2; on genius, 141; and Logan Pearsall Smith, 142–3, 154; a talented shit, 154; touched in the brain, 185

RSS *see* Radio Security Service

Rubberneck (my mare), 21–2, 126, 186; like me, 48; up a tree, 65

Ruling Class, history of the English, 38n, 150–53, 218–19

Runciman, Walter, 1st Viscount Runciman of Doxford, a missionary, 188

Rundstedt, Field Marshal Gerd von, 295

Ruskin, John, impotent, 149

Russell, Alys, 14, 15, 17–18

Russell, Bertrand, 3rd Earl, 14, 32, 50

Russell, John ('Jack'), parson, 186

Russia, a distant impregnable Amazon, 190–91

Rye, River (Yorks.), 177

Ryle, Gilbert: in Oxford, 4, 6, 7–9, 18; at Arkley, 10–11, 18; at Henley, 13, 96, 97–8, 100, 107–8; his quest for verbal precision, 16–17, 18; incites my Self-Revelation, 16, 50; a keen pedestrian, 19; on religion, 42, 127, 168, 265; on my diplomacy, 55; on New Bodleian architecture, 90; on Mornington Crescent, 95; on John Bell, 97; on conversation, 100, 157; ballads explained to, 110–111; on Irish nomads, 119–20; shares my dislike of S.G. Owen, 125; on faith and intellect, 127; on Jack Curry, 128, 161; on Philip Landon, 128; on Socrates, 129; and literary form, 132; on A.L. Rowse, 143; on Frank Taylor, 147; on mythologies, 148; on the Guards' Club, 150; on the next morning, 155; on Kenneth Morton Evans, 157; on Valentine Vivian, 157, 161; on duty, 161; on Dick White, 163; drunk, 164; and uninhibited character, 164; on a monastery at Palermo, 166; on Fr. Beck, 172; on Peter Shaw, 206; on genius, 209; S.I.S. ostrich, 214; on persons, 219; baffling character of, 264–5

St John's Wood Park, 260, 261

saints, 67, 88–9, 226, 250

Salden Wood (Bucks.), 20, 122–3

salvation and wealth, 53, 168

Santayana, George: an Etruscan, 157; admired by Stuart Preston, 159, 160

Sappho, 212

Sardanapalus, 46

Sassoon dynasty, 152

Saul, King, 56

Scamander, a divine river, 96, 283

scepticism, a high alpine flower, 218

Schellenberg, Walter, 268

Schlabrendorff, Fabian von, 295, 296

Schoerner, Field Marshal Ferdinand, 275, 279

Schulenburg, Graf Fritz-Dietlof von der, 299

Schuschnigg, Kurt, 295

Scott, Sir George Gilbert, 178

Scott, John (1st Earl of Eldon), 94

Scott, Sir Walter: readable by me, 191,

192; good on decaying squires, 231; *Guy Mannering*, 238

Scott's Emulsion, at Stancliffe Hall, dosage of, 117

Scudamore family and papers, 251–4, 256

sea lion, performing, Maltby compared to, 114

Secret Service: liberal choice of metaphors for, 63, 113–14, 214; disgust with, 73, 129; types in, 87, 129; am I a bore on?, 90; as bad as other esoteric societies, 120; eavesdrops, 132–40; Stuart Hampshire on, 149; Pat Reilly on, 170, *see also* Bletchley Park; Radio Security Service

Selby-Lowndes, William, 182–5

self-appreciation: by Stuart Hampshire, 16, 67–9; by Sir Hubert Miller, 50; by me, 50–53

self-mortification, 61

Semiramis, 46

sex, of angels, dubious, 167

Shabbington Wood (Oxon), 120

Shakespeare, William, 61, 64, 69, 156, 163, 170, 213, 216, 236, 280; *cri de coeur* in, 30; has no successor, 54; Sonnets, 68, 201; re-reading, 71; magic lines in, 75–7, 78–9; his character, 114–15; his imagery, 114, 121; at thirty, 201

Shaw, George Bernard, one of the deathless bores of our age, 90

Shaw, Peter, 206

Shelley, Percy Bysshe, 48, 150, 199

shop window, Catholic doctrine of the, 103

Sinbad the Sailor, 113

Singh Bahadur, Sir Jagatjit, Maharaja of Kapurthala, 136

S.I.S. *see* Secret Service

Skittywakky Ghost, 118

Smith, Logan Pearsall: influence of, 2–3, 6, 13–15, 18, 24, 29, 38, 280–82; his *Trivia*, 2–3, 13, 18, 22, 32, 281, 288–9; singing for his supper, 5; a stylist, 6, 32; among his Chelsea coterie, 13–18; and Stuart Preston, 15, 159–61; on flagellation, 33–4; on saints, 88; on the Japanese, 96; on clerical fishing, 102; his experience with Matthew Arnold, 108; on Jeremy Taylor's images, 115; on workers and drones, 141; and A.L. Rowse, 142–3, 154; on goblinism, 149–50; among the Etruscans, 157; his boasts, 162; on the purpose of life, 163; on whispering authors, 202; on Cyril Connolly, 213; on low-life, 213; on elections, 240–41; on friendship, 258; death-bed cocktail parties, 274; on adverbs, 288–9

Smollett, Tobias, 95n, 192

Socrates, 233; rather a Joad, 129

Solway Firth, 237–8

Sophocles, 212, 288

soul and intellect, 127

South Oxfordshire hounds, 112, 123–4, 187

South Oxfordshire woods, 120–21

Spain: imperial legacy of, 249; literature and power in, 254

spaniels, Shakespeare's and my dislike of, 115

Speer, Albert, Reichsminister, 263

Spencer, Herbert, 169

Spender, (Sir) Stephen, 13, 89–90

Spenser, Edmund, 95; and Doughty, 231, 235, 236

Spurgeon, Caroline, on Shakespeare's imagery, 114–15

spy, arrest of me as: in Dublin, 4, 87; in Cornwall, 92–3

Stancliffe Hall, near Matlock, 116–18

Stanhope, Sir Edwyn, 252

Stapleton, Gregory, Bishop, 220

Statius, 54; a dreary hack, 212

Stauffenberg, Graf Alexander von, 290–91, 293–5, 298–9

Stauffenberg, Graf Berthold von, 292, 294

Stauffenberg, Graf Claus von, 289, 291–2, 293–4, 296–7, 298–9

Stendhal, approved as a stylist, 6, 32, 191, 192

Stephens, Robin ('Tin-Eye'), 267–8

Sterndale Bennett, (Sir) John, 116

Sterne, Laurence, 192

Stewart-Liberty, Arthur, 28, 66, 148

Stokenchurch, memorable hunt in beechwoods at, 120–21

Stone, Rev. Darwell, 167

Strachey, Lytton, *Elizabeth and Essex*, 154

Strafford, Thomas Wentworth, 1st Earl of, 201

streams, gilding of pale, 121

Stuart, Charles, 10, 26n, 55, 61, 129, 142, 193, 201, 249, 274

Stuart, W.W.Y. ('Bill'), 164

Studley Wood (Oxon), 120

Studnitz, Hans-Georg von, 266

style: canon of, 6, 32–3, 54, 82; needs imagery, 18–19; the true elixir of life, 62; classical and baroque, 119; Doughty's, 231, 234–7; adverbs the secret of, 288–9

Sudley, Paul Gore, Viscount (*later* 7th Earl of Arran), 15

Surtees, R.S., 122, 191, 192

Swann, Kenneth, 64, 148, 205

Swift, Jonathan, 6, 119

Swinton, Gen. Sir Ernest, at Campion Hall, 103

Swinton, Philip Cunliffe-Lister, 1st Earl of, 55n

Synge, J.M., 191

Syria, 197

Tacitus, 193

Tahiti, 123

Talbot de Malahide, Isabel, Lady, 152

Talbot, Mgr. George, 221, 222

Tankerville, Charles Bennet, 8th Earl of, 174, 228–30

Tasso, Torquato, 95, 167

Tawney, R.H., a great historian, 107, 143

Taylor, Elizabeth, *The Sleeping Beauty*, 20–21

Taylor, Frank, Gilbert Ryle on, 147

Taylor, Jeremy, 115, 256

Taylor, Walt, *Doughty's English*, 236

Tennyson, Alfred, 1st Baron: a great poet, 47–48, 169; might have been a Keats, 48, 199; re-reading, 71; his conversion, 201; corrupted by Queen Victoria, 255

Tertullian, 89

Teynham (Kent), 226

Teynham, Lords (Roper), 226–7

Thackeray, William Makepeace, 192

Thames, River: at Henley, 96, 147; and elsewhere, 96–7, 131, 146, 239

Theocritus, 142; quoted, 92

Theognis, 27, 142, 217; quoted, 28

things: that fascinate me, 27, 52, 56, 62; that repel me, 71, 90–91

thirty, a climacteric age, 163–4, 194, 201

Thoma, Wilhelm, Ritter von, 132–9, 167

Thorsteinsson, Geir, 284

thought, necessary to art, 200

Thucydides, 71; and Macaulay, 202

Till, River (Northumberland): nostalgia for, 19, 165, 197; beagling through, 20, 131; fishing in, 20, 155, 156, 162, 165, 228

Tittershall Wood (Bicestershire), 64, 101, 120

Tod, Marcus, 25

Tolstoy, Leo, 191, 192, 266

Toynbee, Philip, 13, 90, 152n

Traherne, Thomas, 257

Trapassi, Pietro, 95

Travis, Commander (Sir) Edward, 98, 99, 100

Trevelyan, Sir George: *The Early Years of C.J.Fox*, 95; *Life and Letters of Lord Macaulay*, 202

Trevelyan, G.M., 17, 19, 20

Trevelyan, R.C., 15, 17–18

Trevor-Roper, Patrick, 15, 44, 88n

Trevor-Roper, Richard, 88

Trevor-Roper, Sheila, 44

Trewinnard (Cornwall), 93

Trollope, Anthony, 191, 192

Troy, 147–8

Truscott, Major-General Lucian, 278, 280

truth: and justice, 33; a *Fata Morgana*, 216

Turgeniev, Ivan, 192, 266

Tweed, River, 96–7

Twinn, Peter, 99

Tyne, River, 206, 207

upas tree, S.I.S. compared to, 114

urine, Henry More's, herbaceous smell of, 39

Ushaw College (Co. Durham), 223–4

Ustinov, Jonah, Freiherr von ('Klop'), 266–9, 271

utopias, dreariness of, 199

Vanbrugh, Sir John, 178, 218

Vaughan, Henry, the Silurist, 256, 257

Verres, Caius, 139–40

Victoria, Queen, 169, 255

Victorians: gloom, 48, 143, 152, 168; more remote from us than the Australian Bushmen, 141–2; than the Pharaohs, 168–9; drawing-room journalese, 231; golden age of power, 255

Virgil: Barrington-Ward and, 54; lack of magic lines in, 75, 78; insomniants in, 148; quoted, 180; genuine poet, 212

Virginia, 123

Vivian, Colonel Valentine, 24, 114, 126, 129, 157, 161, 170

vocabulary: my additions to, 16–17, 61, 289; improved by religion, 80

Volga, River, 96

Voltaire, quoted, 181

Wackenroder, Wilhelm, 122

Wakefield, Gilbert, 94

Wales, life in 17th century, 255–8

Walpole, Horace (4th Earl of Orford), 131

Walton, Izaak, quoted, 101

Wangemheim, Baroness von, 290

Ward, George ('Geordie'), 1st Viscount Ward of Witley, on Hillary, 180

Warnock, (Sir) Geoffrey, 8–9

waterclosets: at Hanslope Park, 98; in Bosnia, 100

Waterperry Wood (Oxon), 23, 120, 208

Watford by-pass, 185

Waugh, Evelyn, 3, 158n; needed in S.I.S., 172

Webb, Beatrice, 14

Weber, Christian, Gauleiter of Bavaria, 134, 245n

Wellesley, Lady Dorothy (*later* Duchess of Wellington), 159–160

Wells, H.G., one of the deathless bores of our age, 90

Whaddon Chase hounds, 21, 93, 122; the great Whaddon row, 181–5; their wartime decline, 194–5, 210

Wheeler, G., of Whitchurch, 181–2, 183–4

Wheeler-Bennett, (Sir) John, 12

Whistler, James McNeill, on art, 217

Whitchurch (Bucks.), 119, 181, 184

White, (Sir) Dick, 114, 129, 162–3, 211, 267n; and Hitler's last days, 263, 265–6, 270, 285–7; more intelligent than Pontius Pilate, 264

White, Rev. Henry, Dean of Christ Church, 170

Whitehead, Grace, 123

Widdrington, Anthony, 205

Wilkins, John, Bishop of Worcester, 187

Wilkinson, Colonel Cyril, 168

William III, King: Macaulay on his alleged homosexuality, 141; impotent?, 149; letters of English aristocracy to, 151, 218

Wilson, Sir Horace, a missionary, 188

Winslow, a Laodicean village in Bucks., 183

Wiseman, Cardinal Nicholas, 223

Wodehouse, (Sir) Pelham Grenville, 152

Wolsey, Cardinal Thomas, fastidium of, 261

women, 71

Wood, Peter, 104, 105, 110, 112, 149, 166

Woodeaton (Oxon), 112, 187

Woodlock, Fr. Francis, S.J., a visitor at Campion Hall, 103

woods, 105–6, 120–21, 197, 206

Wootton Underwood (Bucks.), 186

Worcester, Edward Somerset, 2nd Marquess of, 256

Wordsworth, William, 6, 156n, 207; on childhood, 116; why he became a bore, 164; his crisis, 201

Worlledge, Col. J.P.G., 59, 98n, 114n

Wotton (Bucks.), 21, 186, 288n

Wotton, Sir Henry, 142, 143

Wulff, Wilhelm, Himmler's astrologer, 245

Wye, River, 178, 250, 255

Xerxes, 91

Yeats, W.B., 191

Yorck von Wartenberg, Graf Peter von, 292, 299

Young, Arthur, 187

Zander, Wilhelm, Bormann's adjutant, 275, 276–8, 280

Zech-Nenntwich, Hans Walter, 268

Zuckerman, Solly, Baron, 286